Concentration Ca
Germany

The notorious concentration camp system was a central pillar of the Third Reich, supporting the Nazi war against political, racial and social outsiders whilst also intimidating the population at large. The camps were established during the first months of the Nazi dictatorship in 1933, and by the end of the Second World War several million men, women and children of many nationalities had been incarcerated in them. Some two million lost their lives.

This volume offers the first overview of the recent scholarship that has changed the way the camps are studied over the last two decades. Written by an international team of experts, the book covers such topics as: social life, work and personnel in the camps; the public face of the camps; issues of gender and commemoration; and the relationship between concentration camps and the 'Final Solution'. The book provides a detailed introduction to the current historiography of the camps, highlighting the key conclusions that have been made, commenting on continuing areas of debate, and suggesting possible directions for future research.

Jane Caplan is a fellow of St Antony's College, Oxford and a professor of modern European history. She has published extensively on the history of National Socialism, and is currently working on a study of registration, identification and recognition in Nazi Germany.

Nikolaus Wachsmann is reader in modern European history at Birkbeck College, London, where he directs a major research project on the history of the Nazi concentration camps. He has written widely on terror and repression in the Third Reich, including *Hitler's Prisons* (2004).

Concentration Camps in Nazi Germany

The New Histories

**Edited by Jane Caplan
and Nikolaus Wachsmann**

Routledge
Taylor & Francis Group

LONDON AND NEW YORK

First published 2010 by Routledge
2 Park Square, Milton Park, Abingdon, Oxon OX14 4RN

Simultaneously published in the USA and Canada
by Routledge
711 Third Ave, New York, NY 10017

Routledge is an imprint of the Taylor & Francis Group, an informa business

Typeset in Baskerville by
HWA Text and Data Management, London

British Library Cataloguing in Publication Data
A catalogue record for this book is available from the British Library

Library of Congress Cataloging in Publication Data
Concentration camps in Nazi Germany : the new histories / edited
  by Jane Caplan and Nikolaus Wachsmann.
      p. cm.
  "Simultaneously published in the USA and Canada" – T.p. verso.
  Includes bibliographical references.
  1. World War, 1939–1945 – Concentration camps – Germany.
  2. World War, 1939–1945 – Prisoners and prisons, German.
  3. Concentration camps – Germany – History – 20th century.
  4. Concentration camp inmates – Germany – History –20th century.
  I. Caplan, Jane. II. Wachsmann, Nikolaus.
  D805.G3C5918 2009
  940.53'185–dc22   2009021162

ISBN10: 0-415-42650-2 (hbk)
ISBN10: 0-415-42651-0 (pbk)
ISBN10: 0-203-86520-0 (ebk)

ISBN13: 978-0-415-42650-3 (hbk)
ISBN13: 978-0-415-42651-0 (pbk)
ISBN13: 978-0-203-86520-0 (ebk)

Contents

Contributors

Daniel Blatman is a professor at the Hebrew University of Jerusalem. He is the author and editor of numerous publications about the Second World War and the Nazi camps, most recently *Les marches de la mort. La dernière étape du génocide nazi, été 1944–printemps 1945* (2009, forthcoming in English, German and Italian).

Jane Caplan is a fellow of St Antony's College, Oxford. She has published widely on the history of National Socialism, including most recently an edition of Gabriele Herz, *The Women's Camp in Moringen: A Memoir of Imprisonment in Germany 1936–1937* (2006) and *Nazi Germany* (2008).

Karola Fings is the deputy director of the Cologne Document Centre on Nazi History and a lecturer at the University of Cologne. She has written widely about the Third Reich and Nazi terror, including the monograph *Krieg, Gesellschaft und KZ* (2005). She is currently working on a research project on the Łódź ghetto.

Harold Marcuse is associate professor of history at the University of California, Santa Barbara. In addition to a monograph about the history of the Dachau camp and memorial site, *Legacies of Dachau* (2001), he has published numerous articles about the reception history of Nazism throughout Europe.

Karin Orth is head administrator of the International Graduate Academy at Freiburg University. She has published widely on the history of National Socialism and on the history of science and humanities, including two monographs on the Nazi concentration camps, *Das System der nationalsozialistischen Konzentrationslager* (1999) and *Die Konzentrationslager-SS* (2000).

Falk Pingel is the deputy director of the Georg Eckert Institute in Braunschweig and has also taught at the University of Bielefeld. Since the publication of his pioneering study *Häftlinge unter SS-Herrschaft* (1978), he has continued to research and publish widely on modern German and European history, particularly the Nazi era.

Dieter Pohl is senior researcher at the Institute for Contemporary History in Munich and also teaches at Munich University. He has written extensively on the Nazi occupation and crimes in Eastern Europe as well as on the history of Poland and Ukraine in the twentieth century. His most recent publication is *Die Herrschaft der Wehrmacht* (2008).

Nikolaus Wachsmann is a reader in modern European history at Birkbeck College (University of London), where he directs a major research project on the history of the concentration camps in Nazi Germany. He has published widely on terror and repression in the Third Reich, including the monograph *Hitler's Prisons* (2004).

Jens-Christian Wagner is the director of the Dora-Mittelbau Concentration Camp Memorial. He has written extensively on the history of the Nazi dictatorship, especially on forced labour and the concentration camp system, including the monograph *Produktion des Todes* (2001). He also works on the cultures of memory after the Second World War.

Abbreviations

APMAB	Archive of the State Museum (Archwium Państwowego Muzeum) Auschwitz-Birkenau
BAB	Federal Archive (Bundesarchiv) Berlin
DAW	German Armaments Works (Deutsche Ausrüstungswerke GmbH)
DESt	German Earth and Stone Works (Deutsche Erd- und Steinwerke GmbH)
DP	Displaced Person
GBA	General Plenipotentiary for Labour Deployment (Generalbevollmächtigter für den Arbeitseinsatz)
GDR	German Democratic Republic (Deutsche Demokratische Republik)
Gestapo	Secret State Police (Geheime Staatspolizei)
HSSPF	Higher SS and Police Leader (Höherer SS- und Polizeiführer)
IfZ	Institute für Zeitgeschichte (Institute for Contemporary History), Munich
IKL	Inspection of the Concentration Camps (Inspektion der Konzentrationslager)
IMT	International Military Tribunal (Nuremberg)
NARA	National Archives and Records Administration, Washington DC
ND	Nuremberg Document
NKVD	People's Commissariat for Internal Affairs (USSR)
NSB	National-Socialist Movement of the Netherlands
POW	Prisoner of War
RM	Reichsmark
RSHA	Reich Security Main Office (Reichssicherheitshauptamt)
SA	Storm Troop (Sturmabteilung)
SD	Security Service (Sicherheitsdienst)
SED	(East) German Socialist Unity Party (Sozialistische Einheitspartei Deutschlands)
SHAEF	Supreme Headquarters Allied Expeditionary Force
SS	Protection Squad (Schutzstaffel)
StN	State Archive (Staatsarchiv) Nürnberg
TNA	The National Archives, Kew
UN	United Nations
UNRRA	United Nations Relief and Rehabilitation Agency
USHMM	United States Holocaust Memorial Museum, Washington DC
WVHA	(SS) Business and Administration Main Office (Wirtschafts-Verwaltungshauptamt)
VVN	Association of the Persecutees of the Nazi Regime (Vereinigung der Verfolgten des Naziregimes)
YVA	Yad Vashem Archives, Jerusalem

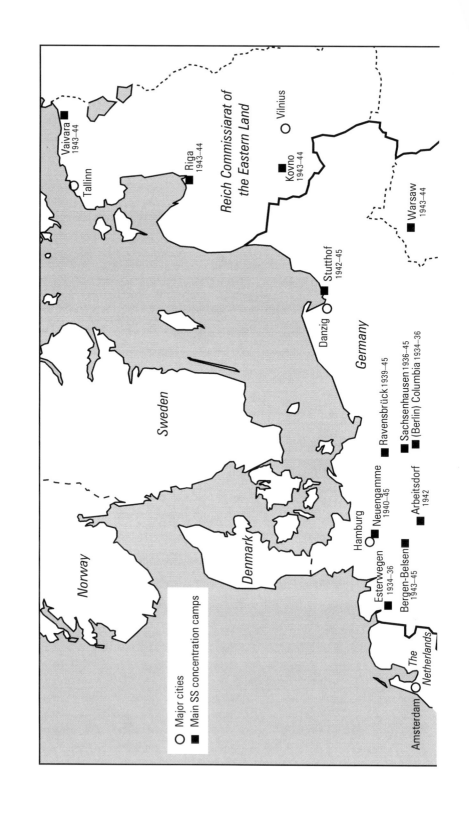

Norway

Sweden

Denmark

Hamburg

The Netherlands

Amsterdam

Germany

Danzig

Stutthof
1942–45

Tallinn

Riga
1943–44

Vaivara
1943–44

Vilnius

Kovno
1943–44

Warsaw
1943–44

*Reich Commissiarat of
the Eastern Land*

Esterwegen
1934–36

Bergen-Belsen
1943–45

Neuengamme
1940–45

Arbeitsdorf
1942

Ravensbrück 1939–45

Sachsenhausen 1936–45

(Berlin) Columbia 1934–36

○ Major cities
■ Main SS concentration camps

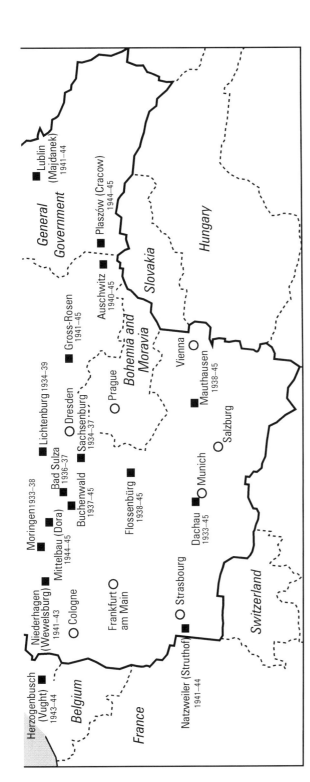

Map of the SS main concentration camps in Nazi Germany

This map shows the main camps under the Inspection of Concentration Camps (1934–42) and the SS Business and Administration Main Office (1942–45). The borders on the map depict Europe c.1942. The map also indicates the period during which each of the main camps was operational (some had already operated earlier as satellite or early camps). Dachau was already run by the SS in 1933. Moringen has been included as the first national camp for women, even though it did not come directly under the Inspection.

Introduction

Jane Caplan and Nikolaus Wachsmann

This collection of essays offers the first overview in English of recent scholarly research – the 'new histories' – on the Nazi concentration camps. Written by experts in the field from Germany, England, Israel and the USA, it provides a guide to the current state of knowledge and historiography on the subject for an English-speaking readership. Although each contributor is a specialist in his or her topic, the volume does not aim to present detailed archival research into selective aspects of camp history; nor is it a general or comprehensive survey of the camps as a whole. The collection is, rather, guided by the editors' belief that the remarkable scope and findings of the new histories now deserve to be made accessible to readers who are not specialists in the field. Each essay therefore approaches the Nazi camps from one of the key perspectives prominent in recent research, analysing and evaluating the scholarship on the topic and including extensive references to the secondary literature. The essays integrate a critical analysis of these historiographies, highlighting some of their main conclusions, commenting on continuing areas of debate and suggesting possible directions for future research.

The Third Reich was dominated by camps. Camps were everywhere, in cities and the countryside, inside Germany and in newly-conquered territory. The Nazi leadership was irresistibly drawn to the camp as an instrument of discipline and control – and not just for opponents of the regime. There were numerous camps for 'national comrades' (Volksgenossen), i.e. the majority of German men and women deemed worthy of membership in the mythical 'national community' (Volksgemeinschaft) that was the core of the Nazi vision of a rejuvenated Germany. Most prominent among these 'respectable' camps were those of the labour service, the Hitler Youth and the military, but there were many others run by party, state and private organizations; even aspiring lawyers and civil servants had their own camps. These camps may have had different remits, but they were all supposed to foster the positive ideals of the Nazi state, elevating the communal order over individualism and inculcating German citizens with the new ideology. The negative counterparts to these camps were, of course, the thousands of camps where real or imaged foes of the Nazi state were held in segregation from the national community. Here too, there were many types of camps – ranging from camps for political prisoners and convicts to those for deviant youths and refractory workers. They differed greatly in size, conditions and function, but were united by a common aim to terrorize their inmates and intimidate the wider population.[1] The extent of these camps is almost unfathomable: in the German state of Hessen alone, at least 606 camps have been counted; in the territory of occupied Poland, no fewer than 5,877.[2]

The most infamous site of Nazi terror was the concentration camp. Already in 1933, during the Nazi 'seizure of power', camps like Dachau and Oranienburg gained notoriety, not just in Germany but also abroad. Soon, a permanent system of concentration camps had been established under SS leader Heinrich Himmler – Hitler's trusted lieutenant – and his Inspection of the Concentration Camps (IKL). It was the camps under this supervision that were the 'concentration camps' in the strict sense of the term (as opposed to later 'death camps' such as Treblinka). As Himmler insisted in 1939: 'Concentration camps can only be set up with my authority.'[3] The concentration camp system became a central pillar of the Third Reich, supporting the Nazi war against political, racial and social outsiders. Inmate numbers fluctuated dramatically, as did the character and number of camps, which spread over parts of Nazi-occupied Europe during the Second World War. By the end of the war, several million men, women and children of many nationalities had been incarcerated in the camps. Some two million lost their lives in them.[4]

The SS concentration camps have long become symbols of the horrors of Nazi rule and modern violence more generally, the most extreme manifestation of terror in the 'Age of Extremes' (Eric Hobsbawm). Names like Bergen-Belsen, Buchenwald and above all Auschwitz – the largest camp of all, where around 1 million Jews were murdered – have become synonymous with institutionalized inhumanity and boundless brutality. The scale of the crimes was such that many leading minds have reflected on them. For the philosopher Hannah Arendt, for example, the camp was the 'true central institution' of a politics of 'total domination'.[5] Psychologists and sociologists, too, have written about the horrors of the camps – about violence, prisoner responses and SS perpetrators – adding to the vast number of articles and books by survivors and historians.[6] The importance of the concentration camps is incontestable.

History and historiography

First reports about the Nazi concentration camps were written as soon as they were established. Already in the early years of Nazi rule, accounts of abuse were published in exile by prisoners who had been released or escaped.[7] Relatives of murdered inmates also spoke out – in relative safety from abroad – about the crimes in the camps.[8] Further material was published by exiled Social Democrats and Communists, who collected eyewitness testimony to build up a comprehensive picture of brutality inside the camps.[9] Several of these accounts found an echo in the foreign press. At times, this became so loud that the Nazi authorities felt compelled to issue public denials, dismissing the reports as 'lies and horror stories'.[10] After the outbreak of the Second World War, the number of foreign publications inevitably declined, as did Nazi concern about foreign opinion. Still, eyewitness reports continued to emerge outside German-controlled territory, including the first systematic analyses of camp life.[11] Meanwhile, prisoners inside the camps risked their lives to keep secret diaries, determined to record what they saw for the future; others buried notes for later generations, or smuggled messages outside. Escaped prisoners also spread the truth about the camps: it was through daring escapes that the Western Allies learned details about the mass gassing of Jews at Auschwitz.[12]

After the end of the Second World War, the history of the Nazi concentration camps continued to be written, for many years, by survivors. With Hitler's Thousand-Year Reich in ruins and the remaining camps liberated, survivors lost no time to put their experience to paper. There was no collective silence or repression of memory in 1945. Quite the opposite: many survivors felt compelled to tell their story. Some inmates were still inside the liberated camps when they started to write, sometimes encouraged by Allied officers collecting material about Nazi crimes.[13] Former inmates also played a decisive role in immediate post-war trials of hundreds of SS leaders and guards. Prisoner testimonies were indispensable as most crimes had left no clear paper trail, and many official documents had been destroyed by the perpetrators towards the end of the war.

But survivors were driven by more than the desire to bring the guilty to justice. They also wanted bear witness to the atrocities and commemorate the 'drowned' (Primo Levi) who had perished without trace.[14] The immediate post-war years saw a wave of prisoner memoirs, in many different languages. Some have since become world-famous – including Primo Levi's own *If This is a Man*, first published in 1947 and rediscovered in the late 1950s and 1960s[15] – yet most others were soon forgotten and left to gather dust in libraries and attics for many years. In all, thousands of survivors recorded their memories of Nazi terror in the first years after the war. Many more have since followed suit, with the wave of recollections – written and oral – continuing until the present day and often adding important new perspectives on the camps.

Most survivor accounts tell individual stories of suffering and survival. But some also moved beyond the personal to capture something of the wider historical meaning of the camps. Fictional representations of the camps, for example, were already being published by prisoners in the immediate aftermath of the war.[16] At the same time, other survivors undertook a general analysis of the concentration camp system, describing its development, internal structure, living conditions, perpetrators and prisoner groups. Some of these studies left a profound imprint on public memory. Eugen Kogon's book on the camp system, drawing on testimonies by fellow survivors and some original documents, saw some 135,000 copies printed in Germany by 1947, just one year after its publication, and it is still widely cited today.[17] Former prisoners – trained historians among them – have also turned into faithful chroniclers of the camps they survived, writing important monographs and playing an influential role in research: Wacław Długoborski, for example, who had been imprisoned in Auschwitz between 1943 and 1945, later became curator of research at the State Museum in Auschwitz-Birkenau.[18] Another Auschwitz survivor, Stanisław Kłodziński, helped to found the *Auschwitz Journal* (*Przegląd Lekarski-Oświęcim*) in 1961, the first regular publication on a former SS camp.

The historical profession as a whole was slow to catch up. For many years, concentration camps – like the Holocaust – were not prominent on the agenda of academic historians. Influential studies were not published until the 1960s and 1970s, and even then they remained rare. The first general history, now widely forgotten, was published in 1960 by the East German historian Heinz Kühnrich, drawing largely on previously published material rather than archival sources.[19] The book was typical of orthodox Communist scholarship in the GDR, with its depiction of Hitler as a puppet of monopoly capitalism. And yet, with all its faults, Kühnrich still provided a first rough sketch of the camps' overall development and conditions. Just how rough a sketch it was become obvious only a few years later, in 1965, when the West German historian Martin Broszat published an organizational history of the camp system, which served as the gold standard of camp studies for several decades. Drafted as an expert report for the first Frankfurt Auschwitz trial (1963–1965), the study was based on thorough archival research and clearly demonstrated the changing functions of the camp system (Broszat himself saw his study as part of a wider project, but he soon had to abandon plans to edit a comprehensive history of all SS concentration camps, due to lack of resources).[20] Several years later, in 1978, another milestone study appeared, on prisoners' lives in the camps, written by a young West German historian, Falk Pingel, who is one of the contributors to this volume. A tour de force of scholarship, based on a wealth of prisoner accounts, official SS documents and statistics, Pingel's study went beyond the organization of the camp system to explore, in more detail than anyone before him, life and death inside the camps, focusing in particular on the experiences of political prisoners.[21] But ambitious empirical studies like those of Broszat and Pingel remained exceptions; few German historians showed any serious interest in the history of the Nazi concentration camps; and little of what existed was translated into English.

Outside Germany, too, academic research was only slowly edging forward in the 1960s and 1970s. Apart from Poland, the biggest strides were made in France, where several major studies appeared. The first was published in 1967 by Joseph Billig, a researcher at the Centre de la documentation juive contemporaine. Drawing on previously published material, Billig placed the development of the camp system into the wider context of Nazi ideology and Himmler's rise. Billig later followed this up with a more original study of the SS economy and camp labour.[22] Meanwhile, in 1968, another French historian, Olga Wormser-Migot, completed a weighty compendium to the concentration camps. The strength of her book was not so much its overall analysis as the wealth of empirical detail packed into its 650 pages. An expert on Nazi terror who had worked on Alan Resnais' seminal film *Nuit et Brouillard* (1955), Wormser-Migot consulted a range of archives in Western and Eastern Europe, as well as the Soviet Union, and was one of the first historians to make extensive use of the archives of the Tracing

Service of the Red Cross (recently reopened to scholars).[23] However, her book never received wide interest outside France and, like the studies of Billig, it has largely been forgotten, even by many historians of the camps.

By the end of the 1970s, then, only a few serious scholarly books on the concentration camps had appeared, though there was a common misconception – based, perhaps, on the large number of published memoirs – that the history of the camps had already been explored in great depth: 'It might now seem impossible to say anything new about the concentration camps', Alan Milward wrote back in 1976.[24] In fact, academic research was still its infancy, more than 30 years after the liberation of the camps. This only started to change from the 1980s onwards.

Since the mid-1980s, the Nazi concentration camps have become the subject of sustained research. The number of publications has increased exponentially, with scholars approaching the camps from many new directions – using a variety of sources, from major oral history projects to previously inaccessible files in the former Soviet bloc – to offer fresh perspectives on established topics and to open up new lines of inquiry. Important initiatives came from local historians, history workshops and museums within Germany. Meanwhile, the growing number of memorial sites at former camps turned into important hubs for scholarship, with regular publications, workshops and ever-expanding archives. Research at universities finally took off, too. Several important dissertations on the camps were published in the 1980s, based on painstaking research, and since then, the number of scholarly works has grown at great speed. The history of the Nazi camps has developed into a major and distinct field in the historiography of the Third Reich.[25]

Almost all recent scholarship has focused on specific aspects of the Nazi concentration camps, such as particular groups of inmates and perpetrators, or the development of individual camps and satellite camps. But some authors have tackled more general themes, such as forced labour and extermination policy, or the emergence and consolidation of the Nazi concentration camp system before the Second World War. Moreover, there are now several general histories of the Nazi camps. From a sociological perspective, Wolfgang Sofsky has provided an analysis of the camps as a system of 'absolute power', which offers original insights into the formation and operation of the camp society.[26] Sofsky's typological study has had a considerable impact on recent historical research, as several references to his work in the essays below attest. Karin Orth, one of the most influential of a new generation of German historians of the camps and another contributor to the present volume, has produced a remarkably clear and coherent organizational history. This has now replaced the earlier study by Martin Broszat as the standard work, but unlike Broszat's and Sofsky's work it has not been translated into English.[27] Meanwhile, the historians Wolfgang Benz and Barbara Distel have overseen the publication of the first comprehensive survey of the individual concentration camps, with a projected nine volumes, featuring articles on all camps and satellite camps; only now, after decades of extensive research, has it become possible to bring such an ambitious project to a successful conclusion.[28] Finally, the Center for Advanced Holocaust Studies at the United States Holocaust Memorial Museum has recently published the first volume in its projected vast seven-volume encyclopedia of Nazi camps and ghettos, covering the concentration camps and satellite camps.[29]

Approaches

No longer is the Nazi concentration camp unknown territory. On the contrary: more books have been published on the Nazi camps than any other site of detention and terror in history; the memoirs and academic studies written over the last two decades alone would fill an entire library. So why add yet another volume? For a start, the new histories of the Nazi camps have been far more encyclopaedic than analytic, far more empirical than critical. As a result, scholarship has become highly fragmented: for all the mass of details, it has become increasingly difficult to discern broader themes, developments and debates. Moreover, the majority of the new histories have been written by German-speaking historians: the recent boom of research has centred on Germany and Austria (there is also much new work coming out of Poland), with major conferences, research projects, databases, publication series and doctoral dissertations. Almost none of this research has been translated into English, not even recent standard works. So the implications of the new research remain widely unknown to English readers, who are likely to be much more familiar with the history of the Holocaust than the longer history of the concentration camps as such. As a result, ignorance, myths and misunderstandings about the Nazi concentration camps continue to persist, even among some experts in the field.

The present volume is intended to redress the lack of English-language publications on the history of the camps and to provide an authoritative account of the new research. The topics of the individual essays reflect questions that have been most conspicuous in current research – some of them, indeed, hardly even asked until very recently. How did the camps change between 1933 and 1945 (Wachsmann)? By whom and how were they administered and guarded, and with what purposes (Orth)? What governed the daily lives of different groups of inmates; is it possible to speak of camp 'society', or is that a misnomer (Pingel)? To what extent is recent work on the history of women and gender relevant to the history of the camps (Caplan)? What did 'ordinary Germans' know about the camps scattered across their own territory and parts of occupied Europe (Fings)? In a system designed ostensibly to re-educate recalcitrants by hard labour, what was the actual function of work in the camps (Wagner)? As racial exclusion became the dominant principle of Nazi terror, what was the relationship between economic and ideological rationales, between exploitation and extermination, concentration camps and the Holocaust (Pohl)? How are we to understand the last phase of the camps, when mass evacuations launched tens of thousands of men and women onto the infamous death marches (Blatman)? And what was the fate of these thousands of sites that scarred the face of Europe in 1945: to what extent has their history been forgotten or commemorated in the decades since the end of the war (Marcuse)? In the course of answering these questions, the essays also address a number of common issues that are prominent in the historiography of the camps. Three will be highlighted here: the relationship between typological studies of 'the camp' and empirical histories of the Nazi concentration camps; the periodization of this history; and new subjects of research and interpretive approaches.

The differences between typologies and empirical histories of the concentration camp are of considerable significance for our understanding of the phenomenon, as the essays by Nikolaus Wachsmann, Falk Pingel, Jane Caplan and Karola Fings demonstrate in particular. The contrast between them is a familiar landmark in the terrain of intellectual practice. Structural and typological approaches generate categories, models and ideal types that are intended to isolate the essential features of the object being studied, often for the purposes of comparison or as part of building or demonstrating a theory. Typologies tend to the synchronic: they compress points in time in the interests of identifying regularities and building the structure or model. History (in terms of the contrast being drawn here) is diachronic, concerned with particularities and with the messier process of change over time. At the same time, historians are well aware of the conceptual and methodological premises of social theory; structural explanations of the kind discussed in the essays by Pingel or Wagner, for example, have played a prominent role in the historiography of National Socialism, as we shall see further below.

Historians of the concentration camps can draw on a number of valuable typological studies, for example, Terrence des Pres' account of 'the survivor' and more recently the influential study by Wolfgang Sofsky, mentioned above, which is directly invoked in several of the essays.[30] However, the principal objective and achievement of the new histories has been the detailed empirical reconstruction of particular camp histories or aspects of camp organization and life, with close attention to differences among the camps and to changes over time. As Falk Pingel observes in his essay on inmates' lives, structural and institutional histories of the camps privilege their organizational and collective dimensions, to the detriment of reconstructing and explaining the variety and complexities of inmates' experiences and understanding their possible responses and chances of survival. Similarly, Karola Fings's essay on the public face of the camps, based on research into the interactions between camps and their neighbouring communities, contests Sofsky's stark model of the concentration camp as a 'closed universe', an isolated site of 'absolute power'. Fings shows how Sofsky's model ignores the economic and social networks that in practice embedded camps in their local milieux. The camps were 'community enterprises' that were far from invisible or unknown to the surrounding population, who often *created* a boundary between the camp and themselves by an active, intentional process of 'looking away'. In a different way, Caplan's essay notes the inadequacy of typological approaches that do not consider gender as a variable, and shows how this concept is needed for a full understanding of the camps' operations and effects.

Reconstructing the history of the camps at this level of empirical detail does not mean, however, that the system of the camps as a whole has been ignored:

far from it, since it is through acknowledging the very vastness and complexity of this system that the need for close empirical studies emerges. But plurality and dynamism characterize the contemporary image of the Nazi camp system to a far greater extent than in the past, when a few examples or periods stood in for the whole and effaced the hydra-headed character of this 'system'.

Periodization

This leads on to a second and closely related issue: the identification of the most salient changes in the camp system and individual camps over time. Periodization is one of the historian's most useful analytic and critical tools for intervening in the meaningless flow of time and imposing interpretative and explanatory clarity. How are we to identify and describe the significant moments of transition in the history of the camps, between their foundation within weeks of the Nazis' coming to power in January 1933 and their disappearance as the regime crumbled in 1945? Although the short life of the Nazi regime might suggest that periodization is of marginal value for understanding the camps, brevity was no guarantee of stability. On the contrary, the camps, like the regime itself, went through processes of rapid and radical change which need to be identified in order to understand how the first provisional camps established in 1933 mutated into the concentration camp universe of 1945.

The changing character of the camps is a theme that suffuses all the essays in this volume. Nikolaus Wachsmann's general overview of the history of the camps from 1933 to 1945, which is intended to provide a context for the volume as a whole, is organized according to the six different phases he identifies. Each of these phases – three before 1939 and three during the war – was by definition very short, but each had momentous effects on the nature of the camps and inmates' lives. Their sequence corresponded to major shifts in the character and aims of the Nazi regime, to changing constellations of power (notably Himmler's capture of the police and security apparatus) and to the different size, functions and character of the camp complex in peace and war. Explicitly or implicitly, the other essays adopt comparable periodizations, though they are not always identical to Wachsmann's since they are inflected by the specific aspect of the camps' history under consideration (and Marcuse's essay on the aftermath of the camps applies a chronology specific to the post-1945 period). Also, the periodization of the system as a whole does not, of course, necessarily correspond exactly to the phases in the history of any individual camp, which may have been of the utmost significance for the fate of its inmates; these can be identified only by close study of the camp in question.

In Karin Orth's essay on camp personnel, we see the impact of changes in the conditions and functions of the camps on both individuals and structures. SS guards were inducted into ever higher levels of brutality and murder by specific moments in the history of the camps, including the first murders of Jews in Dachau in April 1933 – 'a watershed of terror and group identity formation' – when SS men translated their antisemitic ideology into murderous practice, and the influx of tens of thousands of Jews in autumn 1938, which further ratcheted up the SS's norms of murderous violence. The socialization of SS men was reinforced by successive steps after 1939, as the war against Germany's 'enemies' became systemic and built up to full-scale genocide. After 1942, the camps were increasingly led by SS commandants already saturated in the culture of violence within the camps or at the Russian front, but incapable of administering the new regime of inmate labour exploitation. This set the scene for the 'catastrophic decline in living standards and ... soaring mortality rate' of the later wartime camps.

The economic exploitation of inmate labour in the camps and its relationship with mass murder form the focus of Jens-Christian Wagner's essay. In this perspective, the principal phases of the camps' history were marked by the changing functions of work. In the economically depressed conditions of 1933, forced labour by male prisoners was treated as a penal and terroristic 'educative' instrument, and competition with the fragile external economy was restrained. From 1938, however, the growing demand for workers – as rearmament boosted the economy – resulted in an increasing mobilization of camp labour. New camps for male prisoners like Mauthausen and Flossenbürg were established near stone quarries to allow SS enterprises to take advantage of the regime's new construction projects, while the new women's camp of Ravensbrück housed leather and textile production facilities that were intended to exploit female labour. Nevertheless, the camps remained places of murderous terror. Death rates in the quarries were atrociously high, for example, and Wagner argues that it was not until 1943 that the increasing demands of the war for manpower forced a transition towards the deployment of male and female camp labour into the war economy. The main camps gradually became more like transit stations, processing constant arrivals of new labour en route to the expanding network of satellite camps, and receiving return shipments of sick and exhausted workers who were to be left to die or be killed in the main camps. Because all these workers were ultimately viewed as expendable, Wagner goes on to question the utility of a sharp distinction between 'exploitation' and 'extermination', as we shall see below.

From the point of view of the inmates, Falk Pingel emphasizes how the circumstances of their lives were radically affected by successive changes in the type and size of the inmate population after 1933 and the relations among different inmate groups. First, political prisoners were superseded by 'asocials' as the 'typical' camp inmate; then came the first steps in the 'internationalization' of the camp population, with the annexation of Austria and partial occupation of Czechoslovakia in 1938; as the camps became more lethal, another gap – between 'veterans' and 'newcomers' – took on ever greater significance for the lives of inmates; and in a final phase, the camps became overwhelmed by the mass influx of prisoners during the war. Pingel shows how each of these periods created different conditions for the inmate population, notably increasing pressures on inmate solidarity.

Caplan's chapter views these developments from another perspective to show how the treatment of women inmates lagged behind that of men in terms of brutality and exploitation. The explosion of SS violence against male prisoners in Dachau in 1933, described by Karin Orth, had no counterpart in the case of women prisoners. The first women's camp comparable to those for men was established only in 1937, and it was not until well into the war that women inmates began to suffer the full horrors to which men had been already long been subjected.

Perhaps the most important turning-point in the history of the concentration camps was the date at which they became places of systematic mass murder, an issue discussed in particular by Wachsmann, Wagner and Pohl. Both Wachsmann and Pohl emphasize the significance of two mass murder programmes initiated by the SS in 1941 – codenamed '14f13' and '14f14' by the SS – that targeted prisoners before the systematic extermination of European Jews reached the camps. The first killed off sick and exhausted inmates, the second targeted Russian POWs transported to concentration camps for execution, including through the first experimental gassings in Auschwitz. Between them, these two programmes claimed over 40,000 victims, many of them Jews. Wachsmann points out that they represented a watershed in the history of the concentration camps, turning them for the first time into sites of mass extermination. Pohl's account of the relationship between the camps and the Holocaust also describes the intricate inflection of systematic murder and exploitation of Jews in the camps from 1942 onwards. During the war, more Jews were held in ghettos and forced labour camps than in the SS concentration camps. The massive exception was Auschwitz, the largest of the concentration camps, which had a majority of Jewish inmates from 1943.

Pohl's account of the final phase of the camps in 1944/5 dovetails with Daniel Blatman's essay on the death marches in the same period, i.e. the evacuation of the camps ahead of the Allied armies. The question of periodization is of the greatest significance for Blatman's interpretation of this murderous process. His analysis depends upon seeing the death marches as a distinct phase in the history of both the concentration camps and the 'Final Solution', rather than as the result of bad planning, logistical problems or the general chaos towards the end of the war. He argues that the marches were 'the last period of Nazi genocide, woven into the history of the concentration camps', and now directed not only against Jews but against all those seen as the existential enemies of a German society in collapse. The death marches constituted a phase of 'decentralized' extermination that was carried out by 'triggermen', whether from the SS or civilian militias (Volkssturm), who accompanied the marching columns of prisoners. Their discretionary power to decide the fate of their prisoners contrasted with the bureaucratic and hierarchical procedures of the earlier phases of genocide, but was ultimately guided by similar calculations of 'utility' and 'efficiency' under radically new conditions.

The final essay by Harold Marcuse on the fate of the camps after 1945 operates within a different chronology altogether, explaining how the postwar history of the camp sites can be divided into several phases, which corresponded in part to the different uses to which the camps were put after the war in Poland, Austria and Germany. Immediately after the liberation of the camps, the Allies opened up some non-evacuated sites to visits by the foreign press and to local German residents, as evidence of the atrocities perpetrated by the Nazi regime and as a kind of 'punitive pedagogy' for the Germans. This 'media blitz' of May 1945 was followed by intermittent publicity about the camps in 1945 and 1946, designed to justify the occupation regimes and the Nuremberg trials, after which their public visibility declined. Meanwhile, some camps had been put to other temporary uses: as collection points for displaced persons (DPs) pending repatriation, emigration or dispersal to other facilities; as detention centres for suspected German war criminals and political subversives; or as military facilities for the occupation forces.

Marcuse shows how some initiatives to memorialize the campsites and the suffering they had housed began simultaneously, notably the Polish state's immediate projects at Majdanek and Auschwitz; but elsewhere many camps were soon dismantled or abandoned as a result of local resistance to pressures for commemoration. Thereafter, the precise phases in the development and uses of camp memorials varied according to country and according to the groups of inmates recognized. Broadly speaking, Jewish inmates and political prisoners were the first groups to be publicly honoured and commemorated, the latter especially in the GDR where the camps were integrated in a broad culture of anti-fascist public education. But it was only from the late 1980s and 1990s that greater recognition began to be extended anywhere to some of the other prisoner groups, notably homosexuals and Roma/Sinti.

Scope

The changes in the commemoration of the camps are mirrored in the final point for discussion here: the movement of recent research to consider previously ignored or marginal groups and topics of investigation, and the emergence of new interpretations of the historical status and meaning of the concentration camps. It is the findings of this work that collectively constitute the 'new histories' presented in all of the essays. Nikolaus Wachsmann's introductory survey depends on this extensive new research for its emphasis on the great range and diversity of the concentration camp system and its perpetual, dramatic mutations. Karin Orth's groundbreaking research on the SS camp personnel, summarized in her essay here, has displaced the old image of most SS officers as individually abnormal sadists and monsters with a perhaps more disquieting sense of them as 'normal' men trained to operate in abnormal circumstances, a move also discussed for the specific case of women warders by Jane Caplan. The 'normality' of the SS officers was in a perverse way modern: Orth describes the SS camp leadership as a close network of 'terror experts', schooled in 'collective violence' and 'shared criminality' by their experiences in the Nazi movement before 1933 and then their training and rapid promotion within the camps. No such culture of solidarity was available to the inmate population as a whole. Falk Pingel's essay on the inmate population surveys the new research into the experience of different groups; these include not only the categories of inmates defined by the Nazi regime as enemies or outsiders – such as Jews, Jehovah's Witnesses, homosexuals, 'asocials' or Sinti and Roma – but also groups that exceeded these political or biopolitical definitions: women, children and young people. In assessing the contours and challenges of the camps' 'unsocial society', Pingel also considers such aspects as the character of communication in the camps – the dwindling of language into a brutal dialect of command and compliance – and inmates' attempts at cultural resistance to the general collapse of civilization and ethics. Pingel also assesses the virtually impossible ethical challenges posed by camp life: the political solidarities that preserved one group at the expense of others; the dilemmas and temptations of prisoner functionaries who wielded direct power over the inmates, including the power of life and death; and the unimaginable situation of the Sonderkommandos, the squads of male inmates of the Auschwitz concentration camp who were seconded to administer the extermination of Jews in the gas chambers.

New approaches to three of the most murderous processes in which the concentration camps were implicated – forced labour, the Holocaust and the death marches – are incorporated in the essays by Jens-Christian Wagner, Dieter Pohl and Daniel Blatman. All these authors repudiate an older separation of the history of the concentration camps from the history of the Holocaust, instead exploring the ways in which the concentration camps were intricately involved in the Nazis' project to exterminate the Jews. At the very end of this history, the death marches had attracted virtually no research until recently, and it was not until the 1980s that historians began to consider them as a something more than one aspect of the generally chaotic collapse of the Third Reich. But Blatman, as we have seen, interprets the death marches as the final phase of a parallel history of the concentration camps and genocide; and he develops a detailed interpretation of the motivations, character and objectives of this lethal process. Surveying the history of the camps from the beginning, Pohl aims to demonstrate another less researched aspect: the extent to which Jewish inmates figured among the larger concentration camp population. The proportion of Jews among camp inmates varied considerably and for different reasons at different times. At the point when the genocide reached its peak between 1942 and 1944, so great were the numbers that, even though most Jews were killed on arrival, those who initially survived – most of them adult men capable of work – pushed up the proportion of Jewish inmates in the camp system from no more than 10 per cent before the war to about one-third towards the end of 1944. Those who were inducted as prisoners lived and worked under the worst conditions and had the lowest rates of survival of any group. Yet Pohl observes that the camps were also, paradoxically, places where many Jews were to be found alive in 1945, for this was 'the only "legal" way left for them to live under German rule'.

The contradictory role of forced labour in the survival and death of Jews has been a matter of much debate in recent research and is discussed by both Pohl and Wagner. As is clear from both essays, this was not a straightforward matter of 'annihilation through labour', plausible as that concept might initially appear. Their capacity to work was the reason why some Jews were able to survive the first selections on arrival in Auschwitz (as well as in ghettos and labour camps), as well as the means by which they then perished rapidly and in large numbers. This complex issue involves the even larger and more contentious question of why, as Wagner puts it, 'some prisoners in the concentration camp system were exploited as forced labourers in order to meet economic targets, while at the same time many others were murdered for ideological reasons, even though their labour was actually urgently needed'. Often expressed as a contradiction between the rationality of economic calculation and the irrationality of racist ideology, this kind of statement also derives from longstanding disputes among historians about the systemic relationship between ideology and economics in Nazi Germany, and the difference between 'intentionalist' and 'functionalist' or structural explanations of the regime and its policies.

German historiography was convulsed by these important debates in the 1970s and 1980s: they turned partly on Marxist interpretations of fascist regimes and partly on the extent to which Hitler could be said to have directed the Nazi regime's policies according to his own antisemitic ideological priorities.[31] Since then, as Wagner points out, structural interpretations have rather faded into the background as research has moved away from objective interpretations of the regime as a whole to a new focus on the subjective motivations and experiences of those involved in it (as perpetrators, victims or bystanders). This latter approach figures prominently in the new historiographies discussed in most of the essays in this volume. Wagner himself suggests that a structuralist approach remains useful for understanding the economic rationale of forced labour in the camps and the fate of the workers themselves. He repudiates the implied identification of 'work' with 'economics' and 'extermination' with (antisemitic) 'ideology'. Instead, he argues that all concentration camp workers were regarded as expendable, and he proposes a structuralist logic in which 'self-made crisis situations [in the war economy] and the constraints alleged to arise from them … combined with a foundation of racism to produce the impetus for [the] radicalization' of the workers' exploitation.

Comparable to Wagner's essay in combining new empirical research with structural or theoretical perspectives is the essay by Jane Caplan on gender in the camps. Here too new empirical research, motivated by wider changes in the historiographical landscape, has substantially expanded what we know about several groups defined by gender – women, homosexual men and lesbians. The situation and experiences of these groups in the camps were often specific to their gender status – for example, their treatment by guards, their social relations and their chances of survival. The organization and staffing of women's camps were also very different from the standards that prevailed in the men's camps. But Caplan also discusses the deficiencies of a concept of gender that encompasses only those groups which deviate from the male norm, without questioning the status of 'men' themselves. Her essay reviews research that has deployed gender as an analytic category in order to examine the fate of men and masculinity in the camps, and to explore the intimate entanglement of gender ideology with the operations of power in the camps.

Finally, the essays by Karola Fings and Harold Marcuse take up the public status of the camps during the regime and in the decades since its collapse, both relatively new topics of research. These are obviously two very different aspects of the camps' history, but these two essays reveal a degree of convergence or even continuity between Germans' contemporary and postwar attitudes to the camps. As Fings points out, for a long time after 1945 Germans repudiated any knowledge of the camps in their midst, on the ostensible grounds that they were hidden and secret and that knowledge of them was dangerous. It has taken a good deal of work with relatively scanty sources to counter this self-serving claim of ignorance and to reveal how the camps were entangled in their local communities. Fings's essay is parallelled by Marcuse's account of the postwar reluctance, in West Germany and Austria especially, to see the camps live on as places of commemoration. Here too new research is uncovering the reasons for the considerable variations in the pace and scope of commemorative projects in different camps.

The research recounted in this volume has served to press the camps and their history into greater public prominence, while at the same time much of it has derived from initiatives within camp memorial sites to reconstruct, preserve and interpret this history for future generations. The writing of this history is far from finished. Contributors to this volume identify some of the gaps in each of their fields as well as the obstacles that stand in the way of its development. To some extent, this is a question of extending existing types of research across the whole breadth of camp history, including the early years of the war (Wagner) or the fate of the innumerable satellite camp sites after the war (Marcuse); expanding empirical information about the differential effects of forced labour through micro-studies of survival and mortality rates (Wagner); or developing historically founded comparisons of camps operated by different political regimes (Pingel). Several contributors also point to the difficulty of finding adequate sources or methods for researching complex questions like the motivations of perpetrators (Orth) or the full extent of contemporaries' knowledge of the camps (Fings). Similarly, some other topics absent from this volume indicate where further research is still needed – such as resistance or the liberation, to name but two.

Scholarship on the Nazi camps has too often been narrow and inward-looking, written with insufficient reference to wider debates about Nazi terror and the nature of the Third Reich and directed only at academic readers already familiar with the details of the history. We hope that this volume will help to redress some of these deficiencies, by mapping out major lines of interpretation and contention in scholarship about the Nazi concentration camps, and stimulating more systematic research in the future.

Notes

1 For an overview of Nazi terror in camps, see G. Schwarz, *Die nationalsozialistischen Lager*, Frankfurt: Fischer, 1996. More generally, see K. K. Patel, '"Auslese" und "Ausmerze".

Das Janusgesicht der nationalsozialistischen Lager', *Zeitschrift für Geschichtswissenschaft* 54, 2006, pp. 339–65.

2 Schwarz, *Die nationalsozialistischen Lager*, p. 85.

3 Bundesarchiv Berlin, NS 19/1919, Bl. 4–5: Himmler to Hildebrandt, 15.12.1939.

4 For the total number of dead, see K. Orth, *Das System der nationalsozialistischen Konzentrationslager*, Hamburg: Hamburger Edition, 1999, p. 346.

5 H. Arendt, *The Origins of Totalitarianism*, San Diego: Harcourt, 1976, p. 438.

6 Examples include V. Frankl, *Man's Search for Meaning*, New York: Washington Square Press, 1984; A. Pawelczynska, *Values and Violence in Auschwitz: A Sociological Analysis*, Berkeley, CA: UCP, 1979; R. J. Lifton, *The Nazi Doctors*, New York: Basic Books, 1986; M. Mann, *The Dark Side of Democracy*, Cambridge: CUP, 2005.

7 For example H. Beimler, *Four Weeks in the Hands of Hitler's Hell-Hounds. The Nazi Murder Camp of Dachau*, London: Modern Books, 1933; G. Seger, *Oranienburg. Erster authentischer Bericht eines aus dem Konzentrationslager Geflüchteten*, Karlsbad: Graphia, 1934; W. Langhoff, *Rubber Truncheon: Being an Account of Thirteen Months Spent in a Concentration Camp*, London: Constable, 1935.

8 K. Mühsam, *Der Leidensweg Erich Mühsams*, Zurich: Mopr, 1935; I. Litten, *A Mother Fights Hitler*, London: Allen & Unwin, 1940.

9 Union für Recht und Freiheit (ed.), *Der Strafvollzug im III. Reich: Denkschrift und Materialsammlung*, Prague: Melantrich, 1936.

10 Quote in M. Favre, '"Wir können vielleicht die Schlafräume besichtigen": Originalton einer Reportage aus dem KZ Oranienburg (1933)', *Rundfunk und Geschichte* 24, 1998, pp. 164–70.

11 Most famously, see B. Bettelheim, 'Behaviour in Extreme Situations', *Journal of Abnormal and Social Psychology* 38, 1943, pp. 417–52.

12 See M. Gilbert, *Auschwitz and the Allies*, London: Pimlico, 2001, pp. 231–9.

13 See D. A. Hackett (ed.), *The Buchenwald Report*, Boulder: Westview Press, 1995.

14 P. Levi, *The Drowned and the Saved*, London: Michael Joseph, 1988.

15 P. Levi, *Se questo è un uomo*, Turin: De Silva, 1947. English translation: *If This is a Man*, London: Orion, Deutsch, 1960.

16 See for example T. Borowski, *This Way for the Gas, Ladies and Gentlemen*, London: Cape, 1967; individual stories first published 1946–1948.

17 E. Kogon, *Der SS-Staat*, Munich: Alber, 1946. For Kogon and his reception, see N. Wachsmann, 'Introduction', in E. Kogon, *The Theory and Practice of Hell*, New York: Farrar, Straus and Giroux, 2006, pp. xi–xxi. For another early study of the systematic terror inside the camps, see B. Kautsky, *Teufel und Verdammte*, Zürich: Gutenberg, 1946.

18 See W. Długoborski and F. Piper (eds), *Auschwitz 1940–1945*, 5 vols., Oświęcim: Auschwitz-Birkenau State Museum, 2000, here vol. 5, p. 282. Monographs by survivors include S. Zámečník, *Das war Dachau*, Luxemburg: Comité International de Dachau, 2002; H. Maršálek, *Die Geschichte des Konzentrationslagers Mauthausen*, Vienna: Lagergemeinschaft Mauthausen, 1995, 3rd. edn; G. Tillion, *Ravensbrück*, Paris: Seuil, 1988.

19 H. Kühnrich, *Der KZ-Staat 1933–1945*, Berlin: Dietz, 1960.

20 M. Broszat, 'Nationalsozialistische Konzentrationslager 1933–45', in H. Buchheim *et al.* (eds), *Anatomie des SS-Staates*, Olten: Walter, 1965; English edn. 'The Concentration Camps 1933–45', in H. Krausnick *et al.* (eds), *Anatomy of the SS State*, New York: Walker, 1995, pp. 141–249. See also M. Broszat, 'Einleitung', in his *Studien zur Geschichte der Konzentrationslager*, Stuttgart: DVA, 1970.

21 F. Pingel, *Häftlinge unter SS-Herrschaft. Widerstand, Selbstbehauptung und Vernichtung im Konzentrationslager*, Hamburg: Hoffmann und Campe, 1978.

22 J. Billig, *L'Hitlérisme et le système concentrationnaire*, Paris: Presses Universitaires de France, 1967; J. Billig, *Les camps de concentration dans l'économie du Reich hitlérien*, Paris: Presses Universitaires de France, 1973.

23   Olga Wormser-Migot, *Le système concentrationnaire (1933–45)*, Paris: Presses Universitaires de France, 1968, and her briefer survey, *L'ère des camps*, Paris: Union Générale d'Éditions, 1973, pp. 29–250.

24   A. Milward, review of Billig, *Les Camps*, in *The Journal of Modern History* 48, 1976, pp. 567–8.

25   For an extensive survey of some of the recent literature, see N. Wachsmann, 'Looking into the Abyss: Historians and the Nazi Concentration Camps', *European History Quarterly* 36, 2006, pp. 247–78.

26   W. Sofsky, *The Order of Terror: The Concentration Camp*, Princeton, NJ: PUP, 1997.

27   Orth, *System der nationalsozialistischen Konzentrationslager*.

28   W. Benz, B. Distel (eds), *Der Ort des Terrors. Geschichte der nationalsozialistischen Konzentrationslager*, Munich: Beck, 2005–2009.

29   G. P. Megargee (ed.), *The United States Holocaust Memorial Museum Encyclopedia of Camps and Ghettos*, vol. 1: Early Camps, Youth Camps, and Concentration Camps and Sub-Camps under the SS-Business Administration Main Office (WVHA), Bloomington, IN /Washington DC: Indiana University Press and USHMM, 2009.

30   T. des Pres, *The Survivor: An Anatomy of Life in the Death Camps*, Oxford: OUP, 1976; Sofsky, *Order of Terror*.

31   See I. Kershaw, *The Nazi Dictatorship. Problems and Perspectives of Interpretation*, London: Arnold, 4th edn. 2000.

1 The dynamics of destruction

The development of the concentration camps, 1933–1945

Nikolaus Wachsmann

There was no typical concentration camp in the Third Reich. To be sure, the literature on Nazi terror is full of references to 'the' concentration camp. But we need to be clear that the camp depicted in such works (written largely by sociologists and philosophers) is an artificial and ahistorical construct, meant to illustrate broader questions and conclusions about the human condition; it does not fully reflect the complex history of the camps.[1]

For a start, the SS concentration camps were extremely diverse: they varied greatly in size, layout and conditions. No two camps were the same. 'How different everything was here, compared to Dachau', the German prisoner Edgar Kupfer-Koberwitz observed after his arrival in Neuengamme in early 1941.[2] And inside each camp, there was a gulf between individual inmates, whose fate was shaped by age, gender, nationality, ethnicity, religion, political views, social background, health, appearance, as well as pure luck. In 1943, Auschwitz meant something very different for Jews than for the few privileged German prisoners: the former were (with only some exceptions) gassed or worked to death; the latter were rewarded (at least temporarily) with proper beds, warm clothes, food and visits to the camp brothel. The contrast to the army of doomed, emaciated *Muselmänner* could hardly be greater.

What is most striking about the camp system, looking at the Third Reich as a whole, are its frequent mutations. The camp system never stood still; it was not static, but constantly evolved. In little more than 12 years, the concentration camps changed dramatically, not just once, but several times. A prisoner released from Dachau in the early months of the Third Reich in 1933 would barely have recognized the camp six years later, never mind in 1945. Of course it was not just the appearance of camps like Dachau that changed; their function within the Nazi web of terror was transformed, too, and with it the inmate population and its treatment.

Historians have long tried to capture the camps' dynamic history by dividing it into separate periods, building on pioneering work by Martin Broszat and Falk Pingel.[3] Today, there is considerable agreement on the major milestones in the camps' development, though questions about the weighting of different phases remain. For example, did the camps change so decisively in the last year of the

Second World War that one can speak of an entirely new stage? Or was this final year of terror still part of a broader development that had begun in 1941/2?[4]

This chapter provides a general outline of the complex history of the Nazi concentration camp system, highlighting major trends and turning points, as well as changes in function and conditions. It will focus on six distinct periods: the early camps, 1933–1934; formation and coordination, 1934–1937; expansion, 1937–1939; war and mass killing, 1939–1941; economics and extermination, 1942–1944; climax and collapse, 1944–1945. Of course, these periods were not fully self-contained. Some developments bridge different periods and there were always continuities from one stage to the next. Still, such a periodization offers the only way of capturing the dynamics of terror and destruction that shaped the Nazi concentration camps during the Third Reich.

The early camps, 1933–1934

In recent years, historians have gradually pushed Nazi terror against the mass of the German population into the background. As racism has moved to the centre of interpretations of the Third Reich, the scholarly focus shifted from the repression of 'ordinary Germans' to the Nazi war against 'racial aliens'. In turn, some historians have placed much greater emphasis on the consensual elements of Nazi rule inside Germany, culminating in the picture of a wildly popular 'Feel Good Dictatorship'.[5] But we cannot write domestic political repression out of the history of the Third Reich, least of all during the capture of power in 1933. For the 'Nazi revolution' was also a revolution of violence. It was a massive campaign of political terror that helped to turn Germany into a totalitarian dictatorship; only then could it become a racial state.

For Nazi leaders, 1933 was about securing power. Victory was no foregone conclusion: Hitler's appointment as Chancellor had only opened the door; the full conquest of the country still lay ahead. Propaganda and popular support played an important role here. But so did terror, indispensable during the rapid coordination of state and society. After all, most Germans had not backed Hitler; indeed, in the last free elections in November 1932, fewer Germans had voted for the Nazis than the two parties of the left, the Social Democrats and the Communists, whose paramilitary activists had long fought street battles with their Nazi rivals (especially the SA). For the Nazis, there could be no victory without the destruction of the organized working class.

As a result, the establishment of the Nazi dictatorship was accompanied by a storm of political violence against the left: houses were trashed, opponents beaten, party and union offices destroyed. By the end of 1933, hundreds of thousands of opponents had been abused, humiliated and injured, with many hundreds, if not thousands, killed. As for the number of those temporarily detained in 1933, figures probably reached 150,000 or even 200,000.[6]

In 1933, political detention was often chaotic. On the one hand, the rule of law – though already perverted – still applied: tens of thousands of opponents were arrested by the police as law-breakers, handed to the courts and put in jails and prisons run by the legal authorities. On the other hand, there was mass detention *without* such legal process, the hallmark of all revolutions. Many opponents were simply abducted by SA or SS men, who took their cue from Nazi leaders. Even more suspects – around 100,000 – were taken into indefinite 'protective custody' (*Schutzhaft*). Based on the Reichstag Fire Decree of 28 February 1933 (which abolished basic rights), protective custody was not yet fully regulated and various authorities – central and regional government, police and party – laid claim to it. The result was a free-for-all and in practice, protective custody was nothing more than kidnapping with a bureaucratic veneer. As one uncommonly upright SA Group Leader complained in July 1933: 'Everyone is arresting everyone else … everyone is threatening everyone else with protective custody, everyone is threatening everyone else with Dachau.'[7]

The prisoners detained without charge were held in hundreds of 'early camps'.[8] Again, there was much improvisation, as Nazi leaders had made no real preparations. Contrary to suggestions of some historians, the scattered references by Nazi leaders before 1933 to camps did not amount to much of a plan; when they came to power, the Nazi concentration camp still had to be invented.

To lock up the prisoners, the authorities often put existing places of confinement – such as police jails, workhouses and regular prisons – to dual use. By late May 1933, for example, all but one of the 14 large prisons in the Hamm judicial district held both regular state prisoners and inmates in protective custody.[9] In addition, many new places of detention were set up, largely during spring and early summer 1933. Local SS and SA men were particularly active, though they did not dominate (as some observers suggested). As historians have shown, state authorities, too, were involved in extra-legal detention from the start, collaborating with SA or SS camps and even founding their own.[10] Of course, one cannot really draw a clear line between party and state during the seizure of power; after all, SA thugs now often carried badges as auxiliary police men and senior Nazi activists had become leading officials in regional or state government.

There was no prototype of an early Nazi camp. In size, the new camps ranged from SA torture cellars, with a handful of prisoners, to the Prussian state camps in the Emsland moor with 3,000 inmates (September 1933).[11] As for the camps' appearance, there were no firm rules either. The authorities grabbed whatever space they could, including hotels and pubs, disused factories, sports fields, town halls, dilapidated castles, ships and abandoned army barracks. The watchword was improvisation, also with regard to the treatment of prisoners. Murder remained the exception, as the early camps were more about intimidation than killing. But beyond this, there were no agreed regulations: from camp to camp, there were great variations in terms of forced labour, food, discipline and everyday violence.

Despite their stark differences, the early camps shared the same overall mission: to crush the opposition (political opponents, mostly Communists, made up the vast majority of prisoners). This was no secret. Many early camps were established in the middle of towns and cities, and guards were often unable or unwilling to hide abuses. More generally, the Nazi press was full of glowing reports about the camps, sharply contradicted by scores of former prisoners – releases were frequent, with most inmates discharged after a few days, weeks or months – who talked to family and friends. Before long, all Germans had heard of the camps, though their understanding of what went on inside varied greatly.

Efforts to streamline the confusing system of detention began early and gathered pace from mid-1933. By then, many early camps had already closed down again. After all, most had only ever been intended as temporary sites. And as the regime gradually secured its position – symbolized by Hitler's call on 6 July 1933 to guide the revolution 'into the secure bed of evolution' – the early camps were starting to become expendable, or so it seemed.[12] Those camps still left behind included several large sites run by the individual German states: by September 1933, for example, the Prussian Ministry of Interior (under Hermann Göring) was in charge of six camps, holding at least 8,000 prisoners. Across Germany as a whole, prisoner figures initially remained high – in late October 1933, the Nazi daily *Völkischer Beobachter* spoke of 22,000 protective custody prisoners – but numbers did decline during autumn and winter, especially due to a Christmas amnesty, announced with much fanfare. By the end of the year, no more than a few dozen early camps were left.[13]

The early camps were born as political weapons. Set up during the seizure of power, they played a vital role in the Nazi assault on the opposition. Without the camps, the new regime would never have been able to establish itself so swiftly. Some early camps were prototypes of the later SS camps; at times, they were even called 'concentration camps'. But this term was still used loosely and it was not yet clear what it meant. For the camps did not emerge fully-formed: there were often more differences than similarities among them. Even at the end of 1933, camps still varied widely and there was no nationwide system: individual German states pursued rival visions, and even within states, matters were not always settled. And so the future of the Nazi camps was still unwritten: there was no agreement on what camps should look like, who should run them and how prisoners should be treated. It was not even clear whether the camps would survive at all.

Formation and coordination, 1934–1937

The Nazi concentration camp system was forged between 1934 and 1937. The question of who would run it was settled first. The SS Reich Leader Heinrich Himmler had his eyes on the camps for some time, certainly since late 1933, and soon succeeded. An important first step was taken in late May 1934, when SS men reorganized the Lichtenburg camp, which had hitherto been run, at least on paper, by Prussian civil servants. But this was just the beginning: Himmler was already making plans to take over further camps in Prussia and Saxony. The SS seizure of the camps had begun and before long, Heinrich Himmler was the undisputed master of the camps.[14]

This would have been impossible without Himmler's strengthening grip over the German police. His police career had begun modestly in March 1933 as acting Munich police president; but barely one year later, Himmler already controlled the political police (or Gestapo) in all German states. This gave him leverage over the early camps, not least because the Reich Ministry of Interior (in April 1934) passed the first nationwide rules for protective custody: it confirmed the Gestapo's key role in imposing detention and the centrality of concentration camps as places of confinement. Police protective custody became the cornerstone of the camp system.[15] The SS seizure of the camps was stepped up during and after the 'Night of the Long Knives' on 30 June 1934, when SS and police units eliminated the SA as a major political force. Within days, SS troops had formally taken control of three camps previously staffed with SA guards, with another camp following in mid-August 1934.[16]

This coordination process was managed by Theodor Eicke. If Himmler set the general direction of the SS camp system, Eicke was its motor. An overbearing, fanatical and querulous old Nazi fighter, utterly devoted to Himmler, Eicke carried the title 'Inspector of the Concentration Camps' since late May 1934 (officially from July 1934), and moved from camp to camp to 'establish order', as he put it. Initially, Eicke relied on little more than Himmler's support and his senior rank as SS Group Leader (he had been promoted as a reward for murdering SA leader Ernst Röhm). His position was strengthened in December 1934, when Himmler established the Inspection of the Concentration Camps (IKL) in Berlin; only camps under the control of this office were officially designated as 'concentration camps' in the Third Reich. Formally, the Camp Inspection was part of the state police apparatus, but Eicke also reported to Himmler as SS leader. Over the coming years, Eicke made the most of the camps' dual character as institutions of state and party.[17]

Eicke's model was the SS camp outside Dachau, which he had run himself between summer 1933 and summer 1934. Established by Himmler on 22 March 1933 on the site of a former munitions factory near Munich, Dachau was staffed by SS troops from April 1933 and quickly became the central Bavarian camp for police protective custody. It was the approach pioneered here – with both the political police (in charge of arrests) and the SS (in charge of the camp) united in Himmler's hands – which was soon extended to the whole Reich. This was also true for other core features of Dachau: the organizational structure with separate administrative departments; the formal division of SS men into those stationed around the camp's perimeter and those inside; draconian camp regulations and punishments such as whippings; and the creation of a professional corps of SS jailers. Commandant Eicke urged his men to be merciless ('tolerance means weakness') and it was no coincidence that Dachau was the most deadly of all the early camps, with 22 known fatalities in 1933.[18]

While Himmler and Eicke were busy establishing the SS camp system, its long-term future remained uncertain. The number of camps and inmates was still declining fast in 1934. Within a year, the official figure of Prussian protective custody prisoners had fallen from nearly 15,000 (31 July 1933) to just 1,243 (8 August 1934).[19] The emerging SS system was a small-scale operation with doubtful prospects. By summer 1935, there were just five concentration camps, holding no more than 4,000 prisoners; only 13 officials worked in the Berlin headquarters of the Camp Inspection.[20] At this early stage, the role of the SS concentration camps in German society was largely symbolic. As actual places of detention, they were dwarfed by hundreds of regular prisons, which held well over 100,000 inmates (including almost 23,000 political offenders). Given the much greater size of the established prison system – only in 1943 did inmate numbers in concentration camps outstrip those in regular prisons – it seemed as if extra-legal detention in camps might no longer be necessary, a view shared by some senior Nazi officials.[21]

Himmler had different ideas. He later called the mass releases from early camps 'one of the most serious political mistakes the National Socialist state could have committed'. Himmler's case rested on an apocalyptic view of the future. While some Nazi officials felt that the fight to secure the regime was already over, for Himmler it had only just begun: Germany was in grave danger from enemies who threatened everything, from the nation's political foundations and moral fibre to its racial health. The all-out battle against what he called 'organized elements of sub-humanity' – Communists, Socialists, Jews, Freemasons, criminals and others – might last for centuries and could not be won with traditional weapons; it called for a new approach free from legal constraints, combining SS, police and camps, just as Himmler had done in Bavaria. Eventually, Himmler's concept won the day, thanks to firm backing from Hitler, who appointed Himmler on 17 June 1936 as Chief of German Police.[22]

Hitler's involvement was vital. While he publicly kept some distance, never setting foot inside a concentration camp, he not only supported the establishment of the police-SS apparatus but also made several vital interventions in 1935. Hitler agreed, for example, with Himmler's refusal to release more protective custody prisoners in Bavaria. He also backed brutal violence inside the camps, pardoning several guards convicted of prisoner abuse. Finally, Hitler secured the financial future of the camps, which had long been a source of uncertainty, by agreeing that they would be fully financed from the Reich budget.[23]

Once it was clear that concentration camps would become a permanent feature of the Nazi state, SS coordination stepped up a gear. In 1936, several early camps not yet under the control of the Camp Inspection were closed down (or re-designated), with one of these camps (Bad Sulza) briefly added to the SS portfolio.[24] Theodor Eicke also started to shut most camps recently taken over by the SS. There were six official SS concentration camps in early summer 1936; by the end of 1937, just two of them were still operational (Dachau and Lichtenburg); the other four had all closed down.[25] In their place, Eicke had established two brand new SS concentration camps, seen as the future: Sachsenhausen (near Berlin) opened in September 1936 and Buchenwald (near Weimar) in July 1937.

These new concentration camps were different from almost all earlier camps: they were not found but purpose-built, planned as small cities of terror, with rows of barracks and roads, command posts and guard towers, sewers and electricity, workshops and SS quarters. The new model, Himmler enthused in February 1937, was a 'concentration camp for the modern age, which can be extended at any time …' This vision left a firm imprint on the entire camp system. Dachau, for example, was completely rebuilt in 1937/38 (with the Reich footing the bill) to resemble the new 'modern' camps; SS policy had changed so quickly that its first model camp had already become dated.[26]

By 1937, the foundations of the SS concentration camp system were in place. Instead of hundreds of early camps run by different authorities, the SS Inspection controlled all three large concentration camps for men (Buchenwald, Dachau and Sachsenhausen). In addition, the Camp Inspection established Lichtenburg as the first women's camp under direct SS control. The pre-war camps were overwhelmingly male spaces, both in terms of prisoners and personnel. Far fewer women were imprisoned and, for several years, they were not held in SS camps but in the Moringen workhouse, under a civilian governor. It was only in December 1937, with the re-designation of Lichtenburg, that female prisoners were fully integrated into the SS camp system.

The newly-built concentration camps, isolated and largely cut off from sight, were the domain of the SS; even the jurisdiction of the legal authorities now effectively ended in front of the barbed wire. Inside, discipline and terror had become more systematic: prisoners – now held much longer than before – did not wear their own clothes but a standard uniform, with the markings for different groups standardized from 1937/38.[27] And the camps for male prisoners were no longer staffed by a ragtag army of random recruits but with hardened young SS men – Eicke's self-styled elite of political soldiers, ominously called Death's Head SS. To be sure, prisoner numbers were still small. But the camps were already growing: numbers increased from 4,761 (1 November 1936) to around 7,750 (end of 1937).[28] The stage was set for a rapid expansion.

Expansion, 1937–1939

Heinrich Himmler had great plans for his concentration camps. On 8 November 1937 he told SS Group Leaders that he expected the camps to hold some 20,000 prisoners, and even more in the case of war.[29] Himmler's target figure was quickly reached and exceeded. Numbers shot up in the first half of 1938, in particular from spring onwards. By the end of June 1938, there were around 24,000 prisoners in all SS concentration camps: a three-fold increase in just six months.[30]

More prisoners meant more camps, and in the space of one year, the SS Camp Inspection (which moved its office right next to Sachsenhausen in summer 1938) opened three new sites: Flossenbürg (May 1938) near the Czechoslovakian border, Mauthausen (August 1938) in upper Austria, and Ravensbrück (May 1939) north of Berlin, the first purpose-built SS concentration camp for women (replacing Lichtenburg). By the time the Second World War broke out on 1 September 1939, the SS held 21,400 inmates in six concentration camps; all of these camps, with the sole exception of Dachau, had been established since 1936.[31]

The rise in prisoner numbers was linked to a major police assault on social outsiders. Himmler's initial focus was on alleged criminality. In March 1937, following orders to arrest 'professional and habitual criminals', the criminal police sent around 2,000 individuals (including many men with criminal records for theft and burglary) to concentration camps. In the following year, police raids were extended to 'asocials' (a catch-all term for all those deemed deviant). In late April 1938, the Gestapo arrested nearly 2,000 men – many of whom had been denounced as irregular workers by labour exchanges – and transported them to Buchenwald. These arrests were followed by an even bigger raid ('Action Workshy Reich') in June 1938, when the criminal police took more than 10,000 men – largely vagrants, beggars, pimps and itinerant casual workers – to concentration camps. As a result, the prisoner population changed decisively. Political prisoners were soon in a minority: at the end of 1938 the Sachsenhausen authorities classified some 57 per cent of all prisoners as 'asocial'.[32]

Crucially, the raids on social outsiders could build on existing practice, contrary to the impression sometimes given in the historical literature. For attacks on non-normative behaviour had been part of the Nazi policy of exclusion right from the start. While political prisoners had dominated the early camps, it is quite wrong to assume that they had been the only inmates.[33] As early as summer 1933, some local authorities had forced prostitutes and homeless men into camps. And from autumn 1933, such actions had become more extensive and coordinated, with many hundreds of beggars and alleged criminals taken to the camps.[34] Over the following years, police terror hit other outsiders, too (such as homosexuals), so that by the mid-1930s, more than one in five concentration camp prisoners were officially held as social outcasts.[35] In short, the late 1930s did not see a new approach to deviance, but rather the centralization and escalation of existing practice.[36]

What was behind this attack on German social outsiders in the late 1930s? There are different interpretations, along the main fault lines of Nazi historiography, emphasizing either functional or ideological forces. Clearly, the convictions of Himmler and his associates were important, driven as they were by their chilling vision of the police as a doctor removing all that was 'sick' from the German 'racial body': social discipline was fused with biopolitics, as deviance and degeneracy were seen as one. The determination to wipe out deviance, widely shared among regional and local police officers, found practical expression in the December 1937 decree threatening 'professional and habitual criminals' and others guilty of 'asocial behaviour' with preventive police detention (*Polizeiliche Vorbeugungshaft*) in a concentration camp, the basis for police raids in 1938.[37]

But economic factors now also came into play. Following the rapid recovery from the depression, Germany soon faced serious labour shortages, accompanied by concerns about labour discipline.[38] Himmler argued that selective arrests of 'workshy elements' would keep other suspects in line.[39] But in addition to enforcing labour discipline on the *outside*, Himmler became increasingly interested in economic exploitation *inside* the camps. While the punitive reality of camp labour remained unchanged, the SS began to pursue a more ambitious economic policy from 1938. The catalyst was the decision to exploit prisoners for Hitler's megalomaniac vision of rebuilding Berlin and other German cities. Financially supported by Hitler's architect Albert Speer, who was in charge of the construction programme, the SS in April 1938 set up a new company, the German Earth and Stone Works (Deutsche Erd- und Steinwerke GmbH), to supply building materials. Its main capital was prison labour: the new camps in Flossenbürg and Mauthausen were set up near quarries, and brick works were established near Buchenwald and Sachsenhausen. More forced workers were needed at these sites and the mass arrest of 'asocials' in summer 1938 was supposed to fill the ranks.[40]

So there was no single cause for the attack on social outsiders in the late 1930s. Its potency lay in the convergence of different objectives: it served as a general warning to all workers; it advanced the police agenda of 'racial general prevention'; it provided forced labour for the camps; and it strengthened the SS Empire (Himmler was always keen to extend his power and reach). Ideology, opportunism and expediency went hand-in-hand. Of course, for Himmler there was no difference between the national interest and his own: they were identical.

The camps of the late 1930s were not just about social outsiders, however. The police continued to target political opponents: since the mid-1930s, the circle was drawn wider, including émigrés (many of them Jewish) who returned to Germany and Jehovah's Witnesses. And following the expansion of the Third Reich in 1938/39, foreign prisoners started to arrive in larger numbers, for the first time, with thousands of Austrian political prisoners and hundreds of Czechs dragged to camps.[41] War was on the horizon, and Himmler asked the police to prepare the arrests of many thousands more opponents, from Germany and elsewhere – yet another justification for the expansion of the SS camp system.

Nazi racial policy also changed the face of the camps. The first German Jews had been taken to camps back in 1933. For the most part, they had been arrested as political opponents, not as Jews, but once inside, they had been singled out for special humiliation. Still, though they were more likely to be detained than non-Jews, overall prisoner numbers remained small.[42] This changed during 1938, the 'year of fate' for Jews in Germany. In early summer 1938, following the Anschluß, the Gestapo deported some 2,000 Viennese Jews to the camp system; shortly thereafter, the criminal police arrested well over 1,000 male Jewish ex-convicts (including many sentenced for offences against antisemitic laws) as part of 'Action Workshy Reich', fusing racism and 'asociality'. Most Jewish prisoners ended up in Buchenwald: on 4 October 1938, 3,124 of the 10,488 prisoners there (30 per cent) were Jews.[43]

Soon these figures were to rise even higher. On the evening of 9 November 1938, the Nazi leadership unleashed a nationwide pogrom against the Jewish population: Nazi activists destroyed thousands of homes, businesses and synagogues; hundreds of Jewish men and women lost their lives. During the night, Hitler personally ordered mass arrests and over the following days, around 26,000 Jewish men were dragged to the concentration camps in Buchenwald, Dachau and Sachsenhausen. All at once, Jewish prisoners made up the majority of inmates in the camps, which briefly swelled to around 50,000.[44] While the violence across Germany was quickly called off by Nazi leaders, inside the camps the pogrom effectively continued for several more weeks. The abuse of Jewish prisoners was unprecedented: deprivation, torture, suicide and murder reached new heights, as did corruption (SS men systematically stole money and valuables). Hundreds of

Jews died inside the concentration camps in late 1938 – possibly more than during the pogrom outside.[45]

The terror against Jewish prisoners was a glimpse into the future of the camps, foreshadowing the dire conditions during the war. It was an exceptional moment in the history of pre-war SS camps: never before had Jews made up the majority of inmates; never had there been more prisoners inside the SS camps; and never had the camps been more deadly: in the four months after the pogrom, more prisoners died in Dachau than in the entire preceding five years.[46] But the pogrom was no turning point in the camps' history. In November 1938, the ultimate goal of Nazi leaders was not the mass imprisonment of Jews or their murder; it was to terrorize Jews into emigration. This was why the vast majority of Jewish prisoners were quickly released again, scarred for life. Already by early 1939, Jews once more made up only a rather small group inside the SS camp system.[47]

In the final years before the war, the concentration camps became larger and more deadly. Just as the Third Reich became more radical – more belligerent abroad and more ruthless at home – so did the concentration camps; they were, after all, instruments of the Nazi leadership. The preparation for war also left its mark on the Camp SS. Himmler had military ambitions and as war loomed closer, Hitler agreed that the SS Death's Head units could also see action outside the barbed wire. In June 1938, Hitler promoted them to the status of standing armed troops; in the event of war, he later made clear, they would be given military duties at the front. This was accompanied by the rapid extension of SS Death's Head units, in terms of weaponry and personnel. The troops had already grown during the mid-1930s, but the real push came now, from 4,833 (end of 1937) to 22,033 men (summer 1939). It was the beginning of a development which saw SS troops emerge as rivals to the regular armed forces.[48]

War and mass killing, 1939–1941

'War came', the former Auschwitz commandant Rudolf Höß wrote in a Kraków prison cell in 1947, 'and with it the great change in the life of the concentration camps'.[49] And change the camps did, profoundly, already in the first period of the war (1939–1941). The camp system grew sharply, as Nazi terror hit much of Europe, and it was increasingly geared towards forced labour and mass death. But these changes did not occur overnight. There were major structural and administrative continuities with the pre-war period, and there were important personal continuities, too. True, Camp Inspector Eicke departed from his post to lead the new Death's Head division (part of the Armed SS) in battle, taking many guards with him (later, thousands of SS soldiers would return from the front to the camps). But many key positions in the concentration camp universe continued to be filled by veterans of the Camp SS – men like Eicke's former Chief of Staff Richard Glücks, who officially succeeded him as Inspector on 15 November 1939.[50] Most importantly, Heinrich Himmler continued to determine the overall direction of the camp system.

Himmler increasingly dominated the administration of Nazi terror inside Germany and abroad, largely through the Reich Security Main Office (RSHA), founded on 27 September 1939. From autumn 1939, more Germans were arrested and taken to the camps, including political suspects, social outsiders and Jews. Much more decisive, in the long run, was the further extension of Himmler's terror apparatus to foreigners (mostly detained as political suspects). Among those arrested early on in Germany and Nazi-controlled Europe were thousands of Czechs and veterans from the Spanish Civil War. But by far the largest group was made up of Polish prisoners. In Dachau alone, some 13,337 Poles arrived in just ten months in 1940.[51] The result was a major rise in prisoner numbers. By the end of 1940, inmate figures in the concentration camps had reached an estimated 53,000, rising further during the following year.[52]

Existing camps were already overcrowded by late 1939 and the Camp Inspection quickly expanded its portfolio. By summer 1941, it had added five new main camps (as well as several sub-camps). The first, Neuengamme close to Hamburg, was turned into a main camp from early 1940. Next was Auschwitz (Oświęcim) near Kraków, which officially operated as a concentration camp from June 1940. Now synonymous with the Holocaust, Auschwitz was not conceived as an extermination camp: until 1942, its main focus was on crushing the opposition in Poland. Two more camps, considerably smaller, followed in May 1941 at opposite ends of the growing Nazi Empire: Groß-Rosen in the east (Lower Silesia) and Natzweiler (Struthof) in the west (Alsace).[53]

The concentration camp system mirrored the wider reach of Nazi terror. But its growth also continued to be driven by SS economic ambitions. Hitler's visions of rebuilding German cities became ever more outlandish, requiring even more bricks and stone. SS managers promised to provide the goods and their eyes were on the camp system, with its supply of virtually free forced labour: Groß-Rosen and Natzweiler were originally picked as sites for concentration camps because of the local granite reserves, while Neuengamme was earmarked for new brick works.[54]

The next push for the expansion of the camps came after the invasion of the USSR on 22 June 1941, which further radicalized the Nazi regime. The dream of living space in the East seemed about to come true, resulting in terrifying plans for the deportation or murder of millions of local inhabitants as well as the influx of German settlers. Victory in the East would herald a new chapter in the history of the camps, Himmler believed: vast armies of prisoners – not tens but hundreds of thousands – would be enslaved for German settlement policy. In particular, he targeted Soviet Prisoners of War, vast numbers of whom had fallen into German hands. The SS quickly designed two huge concentration camps in Eastern Europe for Soviet POWs: in October 1941, construction began of a massive new camp in Lublin (today known as Majdanek) and of a new Auschwitz sub-camp in the hamlet of Birkenau. A few months later, a third new concentration camp was established in Nazi-occupied Poland, this time further north, in Stutthof, near Danzig.[55] By early 1942, as the SS expansion continued, there were 13 main concentration camps across the Nazi Empire.

But Himmler's plan to exploit Soviet POWs was overtaken by the deadly realities of Nazi rule. For a start, only around 27,000 Soviet prisoners arrived at the concentration camps in October 1941, far fewer than the well over 100,000 POWs the SS had hoped for. This was due, in part, to the murderous conditions inside the army's POW camps, which claimed countless lives. Life in the concentration camps also proved deadly. Held in makeshift compounds inside various concentration camps in occupied Poland and the Reich, Soviet POWs faced neglect and abuse on a massive scale. When the compounds were closed down again in spring 1942, only a few thousand prisoners were still alive. Far from turning the concentration camps into giant forced labour hubs for Nazi settlements, they became graveyards for Soviet POWs.[56]

Many other prisoners met the same deadly fate. In the early war years, forced labour became more torturous than ever. Day-to-day violence became much more lethal, too, and general conditions deteriorated, as overcrowding, hunger and epidemics spread, and the exhausting work on the construction and extension of camps claimed more lives. Of course, not all prisoners were hit equally. Only few Jewish men, for example, appear to have survived the early war years in concentration camps; for Jews, the camps were the most lethal of all places of discrimination and detention. By contrast, almost all women survived Ravensbrück in this period; due to the gender-determined delay in the use of SS terror against women – obvious already before the war – the attack on female prisoners continued to lag behind that of men.[57] Still, the overall death rate across the camp system increased sharply. This was also the result of systematic mass murder. Extra-legal executions – of individual men condemned to death by Himmler or Hitler – had started in autumn 1939, and before long, the authorities graduated to mass executions, with the camp officials as professional executioners: according to its own statistics, the Camp SS executed, on average, more than 250 individuals each month in summer 1942.[58] By this time, the Camp SS had also participated in two secret programmes of mass extermination, both of which commenced in 1941.

The first programme – codenamed 14f13 – primarily targeted ill and exhausted prisoners. Their number had grown quickly since the war started, and local SS men had taken increasingly radical steps to get rid of them, including murder. In early 1941, Himmler decided to get involved, not least to reassert the authority of central SS powers (officially, local SS men were not allowed to murder prisoners on their own initiative). Himmler's solution was to extend the Nazi 'euthanasia' programme – the murder of the disabled – to concentration camps. Working together, local Camp SS officials and roaming 'euthanasia' doctors selected prisoners 'who are no longer able to work', as the Camp Inspection put it. The victims were transported from the camps to one of the 'euthanasia' killing centres, where they were gassed. Between spring 1941 and spring 1942 (when 14f13 was scaled down), we can estimate that at least 6,000 men and women were murdered in this way. Among them were a significant number of Jews, as the murderous selections were also influenced by racial obsessions.[59]

The second programme of mass extermination – codenamed 14f14 – claimed even more lives. Once again, the orders came from the top of the SS-police apparatus; and this time, the killings took place inside the concentration camps themselves. The victims were Soviet soldiers selected for execution in POW camps in Germany, part of the Nazi policy of murdering suspected 'commissars'. The doomed POWs started to arrive in selected concentration camps from late August 1941 and were usually killed within days. By summer 1942, when the transports slowed down, at least 38,000 'commissars' had been murdered in the camps.[60] The Camp SS experimented with different killing methods. The most fateful trials took place in Auschwitz in early September 1941: inspired by the 'euthanasia' killings, the local SS began to use gas – prussic acid, known under the trade name Zyklon B – to kill hundreds of these Soviet 'commissars'.[61]

The significance of these two mass murder programmes has often been overlooked by historians.[62] This was a watershed in the history of the concentration camps: for the first time, they operated as large extermination centres. And it is impossible to fully understand the Holocaust in the camps without considering the earlier programmes of mass murder. For many structural elements of the Holocaust, which was to transform the camp system from 1942, preceded it: the mass deportations to elaborate killing facilities; the use of poison gas; the intricate camouflage of killings; regular selections to kill weak prisoners; ripping gold teeth out of the mouths of corpses – all of these elements of mass extermination in the concentration camps predated the Holocaust.

Economics and extermination, 1942–1944

By the end of 1941, the SS camps had already gone through a number of incarnations, from early sites of political terror to places of mass killing. But the camps were still changing, and it is the system that emerged in the final years of Nazi rule, from 1942 onwards, which has dominated the picture of the SS camps since the end of the war. It was only now that the goals of mass extermination and forced labour for armaments production – often regarded as the twin evils of the SS camp system – fully dominated. In the end, just one of these goals was reached: the camps were much better at mass killing than production.

From 1942, the focus of forced labour in the camps shifted from the future to the present, from building German cities and settlements to the war effort. This shift reflected a general turn in German policy. Following the failure of the Blitzkrieg against the Soviet Union and the US entry into the war, the regime faced a lengthy war on many fronts. To overcome labour shortages and to increase armaments production, it took further steps to rationalize and mobilize the war economy.

In March 1942, Himmler set out the future direction of the camp system, ordering its integration into the new Business and Administration Main Office (WVHA), the organizational hub of the SS empire under Oswald Pohl. In part, this was the conclusion of a long-term process. Since the late 1930s, the influence of Pohl's offices had grown further and further, so that his formal takeover of the camps presented no major upheaval. And in practice, Pohl continued to stick to his core interests. Closely involved in economic matters, he apparently left much of the other decisions to Glücks and his Inspection, which now operated under a new name as office (Amtsgruppe) D of the WVHA.[63]

By 1943, up to two-thirds of concentration camp prisoners were deployed in the war economy. But where did they work? Initially, Himmler had wanted to move production to the concentration camps. His goal, it seems, was the creation of an SS armaments complex. But this proved elusive. SS-owned enterprises made little headway and the growing cooperation with industry (building on earlier, isolated joint ventures) did not go to plan, either, as the SS failed to gain control over the few larger armaments factories established at main camps. The future lay elsewhere: instead of moving production *into* existing camps, prisoners were moved *outside* to existing or new production sites. In September 1942, Albert Speer, recently appointed as Minister for Armaments and War Production, secured Hitler's agreement that prisoners could be sent to established armaments works. This model soon dominated: the SS delivered prisoners to new satellite camps near state or industry-run factories and construction sites, effectively renting out its inmates, and profiting only indirectly (contrary to claims by some historians).[64]

As economic considerations became more pressing, the SS demanded higher output from the camps. In summer 1942, Pohl removed one-third of all camp commandants, replacing them with SS men regarded as more capable managers. More importantly, Himmler relentlessly increased his army of slave workers: more men and women were dragged to the camps than ever. In Buchenwald, three times as many prisoners arrived in 1943 than in 1942; they came from all over, especially from Eastern Europe, with Soviet men and women (largely civilians) established as the largest prisoner group in camp.[65]

SS leaders also made some empty gestures to improve conditions. In 1942, the number of deaths among regular prisoners had sky-rocketed: something like half of the approximately 180,000 prisoners registered in concentration camps between July and November had died during this period.[66] In response, the WVHA ordered camps to use 'any means available' to reduce deaths, as Glücks put it. But such instructions were barely worth the paper they were written on. In the past, historians argued that relative prisoner mortality declined significantly in 1943.[67] More recently, scholars have sounded a more cautious note. In several camps, conditions actually deteriorated; and improvements elsewhere were largely restricted to privileged prisoners and skilled workers. For the most part, the sharp fall in prisoner deaths occurred only in SS statistics, falsified to impress superiors.[68] Most glaringly, the SS figures remained silent about the Jews murdered during the Holocaust in the concentration camps.

Between summer 1941 and summer 1942, the Holocaust – the systematic extermination of European Jewry – emerged as German state policy.[69] And murder increasingly moved from mass shootings on the outside to gas chambers inside new death camps in occupied Poland: Chełmno (from December 1941), and the three 'Action Reinhardt' camps Bełžec (March 1942), Sobibór (May 1942), Treblinka (July 1942). These camps were run separately from the concentration camp system. However, two existing SS concentration camps also came to function as death camps: Auschwitz and Majdanek.[70]

Auschwitz was transformed most radically by the Holocaust. The first mass deportations of Jews arrived in March 1942 and over the coming months murder became extensive and systematic. Overall, nearly 200,000 Jews were deported to Auschwitz in 1942; it is likely that more than 180,000 of them died that year. Auschwitz was not yet the most lethal of all Nazi death camps, but it was by far the most deadly concentration camp, situated just inside the German border – not, as has often been claimed, far away in the 'nebulous East'.[71]

Jews deported to Auschwitz were destined to die. Most were murdered on arrival and were never even registered as inmates; following SS selections, they were taken straight to the ever-extending gas chambers. The rest, selected for murderous forced labour, joined other registered prisoners in the camp. From late spring 1942, Jews of various nationalities were by far the largest group among the regular prisoners in Auschwitz, even though they rarely survived more than a few months, making up the great majority of the around 69,000 registered dead in 1942.[72] Of course, there were many other prisoner groups in Auschwitz, too, and some of them also faced near-certain death. Starting in early 1943, more than 20,000 Sinti and Roma were deported to the camp, the culmination of years of brutal Nazi persecution. Most were held in the deadly special compound in Birkenau; any survivors were murdered in summer 1944 on Himmler's orders.[73]

Auschwitz became the capital of the wartime concentration camp system, just as Dachau had dominated the early period of Nazi rule. It is not that Auschwitz was completely different from the other camps: elsewhere, too, there was hunger and abuse, gruesome medical experiments and mass murder (in some cases using gas). But everything was more extreme in Auschwitz: nowhere else did so many prisoners die; and no other camp held more prisoners. Already one of the biggest concentration camps in early 1942, the mass deportations of Jews put it into a league of its own. By early September 1942, the number of registered prisoners had shot up to nearly 39,000 – more than one-third of all the around 110,000 prisoners in the entire concentration camp system at the time. And Auschwitz continued to grow, just like the whole camp system: by August 1943, there were 224,000 registered prisoners in all SS concentration camps, of whom 74,000 were held in Auschwitz.[74]

Previously, concentration camps had resembled small towns; Auschwitz turned into a metropolis. It grew so big that the WVHA divided it in November 1943 into three separate camps: the old main camp, the extermination camp in Birkenau (with its gas chambers), and the forced labour camp in Monowitz. This last camp had opened in late October 1942, right next to the building-site of a massive IG Farben factory, greatly extending the existing cooperation between the Auschwitz SS and the chemicals giant. Monowitz was the first large camp initiated by big business and built next to an industrial complex; it would become a model for the future relationship between industry and SS. For many prisoners, this was a deadly collaboration: Jews made up the majority of inmates in Monowitz, and almost all of the perhaps 25,000 dead.[75]

The Holocaust also led to the establishment of new concentration camps, almost all of them labour or transit camps. As the remaining Jews in Eastern Europe were pressed into forced labour, the WVHA in 1943 took over three work camps and ghettos – Riga in Latvia, Kovno in Lithuania and Vaivara in Estonia – as concentration camps. In January 1944, Cracow-Plaszów was added. These new camps, still the least-known elements of the SS concentration camp system, operated quite unlike the established camps: administrative structures were different, for example, and almost all the prisoners were Jews. Another new camp set up in connection with the Holocaust was Herzogenbusch (s' Hertogenbosch) in the Netherlands. Officially opened in January 1943, it functioned in part as a transit camp for Jewish men, women and children to the death camps.[76]

From 1942, the Nazi regime in general, and the concentration camps in particular, were driven by two imperatives: economics and extermination. Historians have often described this as a paradox: if the regime was so desperate for forced labour, why murder the Jews? But for Nazi hardliners, there was no such contradiction: economics and extermination were two sides of the same coin. Both were needed for victory: winning the war required the ruthless destruction of all perceived threats (with Jews seen as the greatest danger) *and* the mobilization of other resources for the war effort. In the case of Jews regarded as capable of work, the authorities brought both goals together in the idea of 'annihilation through labour', practised in Monowitz and elsewhere. For some Jews, forced labour therefore meant temporary survival; but none were supposed to live for any length of time.[77]

Auschwitz reached its murderous peak in the summer of 1944. Following the German invasion of Hungary in March, the Nazi authorities rapidly arranged mass deportations of local Jews. More transports than ever reached Auschwitz, with up to 10,000 men, women and children lined up for selections every day. In just three months, between May and July 1944, around 470,000 Jews (overwhelmingly from Hungary) were deported to the camp – just as many as had arrived during all of 1942 and 1943; the great majority were sent straight to the gas chambers.[78] It was at around this time, when Auschwitz realised its full genocidal potential, that the concentration camp system as a whole entered the last destructive stage in its development.

Climax and collapse, 1944–1945

The final chapter of the camps was written during the twilight of the Nazi regime from 1944. In early histories of the camp system, this phase was sometimes brushed over.[79] But this neglect has long been replaced by detailed studies, with recent accounts describing the terrifying last torrent of destruction.[80] Indeed, in many concentration camps, it was the final months which were the darkest of all.

The concentration camps did not fade away as the Nazi regime headed for total defeat. On the contrary: the closer the camp system came to collapse, the bigger it became. Within a year, daily prisoner numbers almost doubled, from 224,000 (August 1943) to 524,286 (August 1944). And numbers shot up further

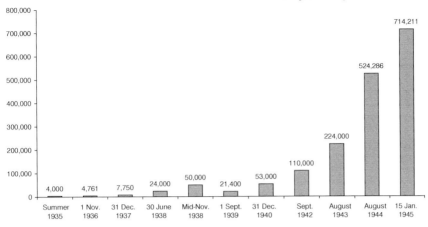

Figure 1 Daily inmate numbers in SS concentration camps, 1935–1945

still: by 15 January 1945, the SS counted some 714,211 registered prisoners in its concentration camps (see Figure 1).[81]

The growth of the camps was closely related to the regime's frantic hunt for forced labour. Arrests were stepped up across Europe, leading (after autumn 1943) to an expansion of prisoners forced into armaments production. Much of the impetus now came from outside the SS-police apparatus. Private industry became more proactive in its pursuit of concentration camp labour. And top Nazi officials, too, demanded more and more workers, with Albert Speer (in October 1944) taking charge of the deployment of concentration camp prisoners, a major blow for SS ambitions.[82]

The massive growth of the camp system was particularly pronounced inside the old German borders. Within a year, the number of registered prisoners in Buchenwald shot up from 19,641 (end of August 1943) to 82,391 (end of August 1944).[83] All across the German heartland prisoner numbers were rising sharply. In August 1943, the six concentration camps which had already existed before the Second World War, held a total of 104,500 inmates. By the end of 1944, they held 373,646 inmates. And numbers were still rising.[84] After the geographic balance of the camp system had tilted eastwards from 1942, it now decisively moved back again.

This shift was linked to the progress of the Allied armies. One concentration camp after another was shut down, with inmates moved away from the frontline. The first wave occurred between spring and autumn 1944: in Eastern Europe, the SS authorities ordered the closure of Majdanek, Warsaw, Cracow-Plaszów, and the Baltic camps (on the western front, Herzogenbusch and Natzweiler were abandoned). The second wave came in early 1945, with well over 100,000 prisoners from Auschwitz, Groß-Rosen and Stutthof forced towards camps further west, on foot, in trucks and open freight trains. The third and last wave came right at the end, in spring 1945, as the last remaining camps inside the old German borders were largely abandoned, too, with prisoners marched either north or south, towards the last unoccupied pockets. For inmates, the 'evacuations' in 1945 were death marches. Roads and tracks were littered with corpses: shot, frozen, starved to death. Whole treks perished: just 280 of some 3,000 prisoners who had set off from Birkenau on 18 January 1945 reached their final destination, some 500 kilometres away, two months later.[85]

Among the prisoners who arrived – often more dead than alive – in the remaining camps were many Jews. It was only now, in the last stage of war, that Jewish men and women became a major presence across the whole concentration camp system. Earlier in the war, only few Jews had been locked in camps inside the German heartland. In early 1942, the six SS concentration camps established before the war had held no more than around 2,700 Jewish inmates. This figure had fallen further, to around 350, by the end of 1942, following Himmler's order in autumn 1942 to 'make all concentration camps inside the Reich free of Jews' (part of the Nazi policy of deporting German Jews).[86] But in spring 1944, the regime reversed its policy. In the face of desperate labour shortages Hitler ordered that Jews should be exploited as forced workers *inside* the old German borders. Over the coming months, the SS selected more than 100,000 Hungarian Jews (largely women) arriving in Auschwitz for forced labour. Most of them were sent to camps deep inside Germany, soon followed by thousands of other Jewish prisoners. By late 1944, Jews made up the largest inmate group in many of the remaining camps.[87]

The camp system was changing fast, for one last time. Established rules and customs were quickly thrown overboard. Prisoner hierarchies, too, became less rigid, as practical considerations sometimes trumped ideological convictions.[88] The most obvious change was the proliferation of satellite camps. This course had been set back in 1942. But it was only now – during the final scramble for forced labour and the 'evacuations' – that the camp system was transformed. The desperate desire to press prisoners into the service of the SS, army, state and private industry – often without any sense of planning or logic – acted as a centrifugal force: a vast number of new satellite camps sprang up, rapidly spreading away from the main camps, until the whole of Germany was covered. In 1944, some 588 new satellite camps were set up; more new camps were established at the height of this boom, between July and November 1944, then during the entire seven years between 1937 and 1943. As a result, by the end of 1944 more prisoners were held satellite camps than in main camps, which came to resemble transit hubs: after registration, most new inmates were quickly shunted on to a satellite camp.[89] Prisoners were constantly on the move; the whole camp system was in flux.

Among the largest new camps were those aimed at moving war production – from petrol to fighter planes – underground, to shelter it from air raids. The SS played a major role in these deranged plans, through its powerful construction supremo Hans Kammler; at last, the SS leadership thought, it was gaining a proper foothold in armaments production. The first of these camps was Dora (near Nordheim), established in August 1943 as a satellite camp of Buchenwald. Initially selected for the production of so-called V2 rockets, plans soon grew more outlandish, turning Dora into a vast building site, with more than 30,000 prisoners

(September 1944) and its own satellite camps. In autumn 1944 it was promoted to the status of main camp (called Mittelbau), the last one founded by the SS. But in the end, Dora came nowhere close to realizing the dreams of SS and industry: its main result was not weapons, but the death of its prisoners (indeed, more people died making V2 rockets than were hit by them). For in camps like Dora, which focused primarily on building and construction, forced labour often proved lethal.[90]

Death dominated the entire concentration camp system in the final months of war. In most of the remaining camps, this was the deadliest period; in Mauthausen, for example, the monthly mortality rate between January and April 1945 reached an unprecedented 12.5 per cent.[91] Every day, prisoners faced a struggle for survival (the few privileged inmates being the only exception). Already gravely weakened – by death marches, slave labour and hunger – inmates faced the worst conditions ever. The camps were now hopelessly overcrowded, with new arrivals herded into already packed barracks and tents, or left to die in the open air. Illness and epidemics spread rapidly, with many ailing prisoners isolated in special areas, such as sick bays. Whole camps were set aside for the dying. The largest one was Bergen-Belsen (near Celle). Operating as a concentration camp since 1943, it was now used by the SS authorities as a dumping ground for sick prisoners. Death through epidemics and starvation soared in early 1945, following mass transports of men, women and children from abandoned camps: in March 1945 alone, some 18,000 prisoners died in Bergen-Belsen. Of course, murderous neglect was not the only cause of death in the concentration camps. Officials continued to use weapons and deadly injections, too, as well as the smaller gas chambers in camps like Mauthausen and Ravensbrück. Among the victims were prominent political prisoners and sick inmates. The camps liberated by Allied troops in spring 1945 were giant graves: most of those prisoners left behind by the retreating SS were either dead or dying.

We will never know exactly how many camp inmates died during the last convulsions of Nazi terror, but it is likely that between one-third and half of the over 700,000 prisoners still alive in early 1945 perished before the end of the war. This was a large share of all the dead in the concentration camps: between 1933 and 1945, an estimated two million or more men, women and children – including more than one million Jews – perished in these camps. Around half of them died in Auschwitz, the dark heart of the Nazi camp system.[93]

Looking at the overall development of the concentration camp system between 1933 and 1945, it is striking how often and how profoundly it changed, in little more than a decade. Change was built into the system, and the ability to adapt and reinvent itself was perhaps the most terrifying strength of the SS camp system. Born as a weapon against political opponents, the camps later became instruments of social, economic and racial policy, multiple functions which often overlapped. The prisoner population was transformed, too. Before the war, the vast majority of inmates had been German men. By 1945, German nationals had become a small minority as prisoners now came from all across Europe. And many of them were women: by January 1945, some 28 per cent of prisoners were female (there were also thousands of children).[94] Late in the war, hundreds of thousands of prisoners were held in hundreds of camps – a far cry from the early days of the coordinated camp system, with a handful of SS camps and a few thousand prisoners. As for life inside, the contrasts were equally stark. The relentless military order of the camp in the late 1930s had been replaced by dirt, disease and death by 1945. Most importantly, the vast majority of inmates before the war had survived; during the war, death – from abuse, neglect, forced labour and systematic mass extermination – swept through the camps.

And yet, there were also important continuities – in terms of structure, administration and personnel – across different periods in the camps' history. The move from one stage to the next was never a clean break but a transition. Social outsiders, for example, had already been targeted well before they briefly became the primary focus of the camps in the late 1930s; and systematic mass extermination had been pioneered in 1941, before the advent of the Holocaust inside the concentration camps.

There were also some remarkable parallels between the early camps of 1933 and the concentration camps of 1945. Just like the early camps, the new satellite camps were often established in makeshift locations, frequently in towns and cities, making SS terror much more visible. More generally, the Nazi camps were characterized, at both ends of the Third Reich, by chaos and improvisation. In 1933, the camp system had not yet formed; in 1945, it was collapsing, with camp personnel increasingly left to their own devices. Central SS control was weaker than it had been at any time since 1933/34, with outside agencies – such as Speer's office and private industry – more powerful than ever. As for the guards, recruitment was often haphazard, just as in 1933; by early 1945, the young, ruthless and committed German SS men were in a small minority. They were outnumbered by older men including foreigners, female guards (who were not allowed to join the Camp SS), and above all by veterans from the German armed forces.[95] The fact that several camps were at their most deadly during a time of declining SS domination remains one of the most striking aspects in the abysmal history of the concentration camps.

Notes

1   Important works include H. Arendt, *The Origins of Totalitarianism*, San Diego: Harcourt, 1968; W. Sofsky, *The Order of Terror: The Concentration Camp*, Princeton, NJ: Princeton UP, 1999; T. Todorov, *Facing the Extreme*, London: Phoenix, 1999. I would like to thank Jane Caplan, Christian Goeschel, Julia Hörath and Kim Wünschmann for their comments on an earlier draft of this chapter.

2   E. Kupfer-Koberwitz, *Als Häftling in Dachau*, Bonn: Bundeszentrale für Heimatdienst, 1956, p. 259.

3   Martin Broszat identified five separate phases; M. Broszat, 'The Concentration Camps 1933–45', in H. Krausnick *et al.* (eds), *Anatomy of the SS State*, Reading: Granada, 1982, pp. 141–249. Falk Pingel identified three phases, with several subdivisions; F. Pingel, *Häftlinge unter SS-Herrschaft. Widerstand, Selbstbehauptung und Vernichtung im Konzentrationslager*, Hamburg: Hoffmann und Campe, 1978, esp. pp. 13–15.

4 For the latter view, see U. Herbert, K. Orth and C. Dieckmann, 'Die nationalsozialistischen Konzentrationslager. Geschichte, Erinnerung, Forschung', in U. Herbert, K. Orth and C. Dieckmann (eds), *Die Nationalsozialistischen Konzentrationslager. Entwicklung und Struktur*, Göttingen: Wallstein, 1998, 2 vols, here vol. 1, pp. 17–40. For the former view, see K. Orth, *Das System der nationalsozialistischen Konzentrationslager*, Hamburg: Hamburger Edition, 1999. Orth's book offers the most systematic overview of the development of the camp system.

5 G. Aly, 'Die Wohlfühl-Diktatur', *Der Spiegel* 10, 2005, pp. 56–62. For a critique of this recent trend in the literature, see R. J. Evans, 'Coercion and Consent in Nazi Germany', *Proceedings of the British Academy* 151, 2007, pp. 53–81.

6 Using official figures, we can estimate that around 100,000 prisoners were taken into protective custody in 1933 (see J. Tuchel and R. Schattenfroh, *Zentrale des Terrors*, Frankfurt: Büchergilde, 1987, p. 114. See also J. Tuchel, *Konzentrationslager. Organisationsgeschichte und Funktion der 'Inspektion der Konzentrationslager' 1934–1938*, Boppard am Rhein: Boldt, 1991, pp. 100–107, 155; K. Drobisch and G. Wieland, *System der NS-Konzentrationslager 1933–1939*, Berlin: Akademie, 1993, pp. 104–105, 133–4). However, these official figures are incomplete, as the authorities apparently failed to record many prisoners who spent only a brief period in concentration camps (Bundesarchiv Berlin (BAB), R 43 II/398, Bl. 140–4: Wagner to Epp, 13 April 1934). In addition, there were many thousands of regular state prisoners, charged or convicted of political offences (N. Wachsmann, *Hitler's Prisons: Legal terror in Nazi Germany*, New Haven, CT: Yale UP, 2004, esp. pp. 115–16). Finally, an unknown number of opponents – perhaps tens of thousands – were kidnapped by SA, SS or other party activists, and dragged to torture cellars. Overall estimates are further complicated by the fact that many prisoners went through several places of detention.

7 Quote in P. Diehl-Thiele, *Partei und Staat im Dritten Reich. Untersuchungen zum Verhältnis von NSDAP und allgemeiner innerer Staatsverwaltung 1933–1945*, Munich: Beck, 1971, p. 95. In the past, extra-legal detention had occasionally been used in Germany during times of national emergency, but only in a restricted way. In Nazi Germany, there were no such limits. See J. Caplan, 'Political Detention and the Origin of the Concentration Camps in Nazi Germany, 1933–1935/6', in N. Gregor (ed.), *Nazism, War and Genocide*, Exeter: Exeter UP, 2005, pp. 22–41, here 27–8.

8 The term 'early camps', coined by Karin Orth (*System*, pp. 23–6), is applied here to *all* places of extra-legal detention, including SA torture chambers and protective custody wings in prisons. The term is more appropriate than 'early concentration camp', used by several other historians, as the latter suggested too much continuity with the SS camp system. As for the number of camps, a recent survey counts around 100, as well as an untold number of SA bunkers (W. Benz and B. Distel (eds), *Der Ort des Terrors. Geschichte der nationalsozialistischen Konzentrationslager*, 8 vols, Munich: C. H. Beck, 2005–2008, vol. 2, p. 9). In Berlin alone, more than 170 SA and SS places of torture were in operation in 1933 (I. Mayer-von Götz, *Terror im Zentrum der Macht*, Berlin: Metropol, 2008, p. 19).

9 For the figures, see Reichsjustizministerium (ed.), *Das Gefängniswesen in Deutschland*, Berlin: 1935, p. 39; J. Wisskirchen, 'Schutzhaft in der Rheinprovinz', in W. Benz and B. Distel (eds), *Herrschaft und Gewalt. Frühe Konzentrationslager 1933–1939*, Berlin: Metropol, 2002, pp. 129–56, here 154, Table 2.

10 See Tuchel, *Konzentrationslager*, pp. 38–45.

11 For the figure, see Drobisch and Wieland, *System*, p. 66.

12 Quote in J. Noakes and G. Pridham (eds), *Nazism. 1919–1945*, vol. 1, Exeter: Exeter UP, 1998, p. 171.

13 Drobisch and Wieland, *System*, p. 140, list some 21 camps. In addition, there were at least seven more early camps (Columbia-Haus, Dachau, Hohnstein, Fuhlsbüttel, Kuhberg, Vechta and Osthofen). For the October figures, see ibid., p. 136. For the closures, see ibid., pp. 42, 135. For the Prussian camps, see Tuchel, *Konzentrationslager*,

pp. 76, 103. The Prussian camps were Börgermoor, Esterwegen, Neusustrum, Sonnenburg, Brandenburg and Lichtenburg.

14   See S. Endlich, 'Die Lichtenburg 1933–1939. Haftort politischer Prominenz und Frauen-KZ', in Benz and Distel (eds), *Herrschaft*, pp. 11–64, here 35–7. See also Tuchel, *Konzentrationslager*, p. 319; J. Tuchel (ed.), *Die Inspektion der Konzentrationslager, 1938–1945*, Berlin: Edition Hentrich, 1994, pp. 28–9.

15   P. Longerich, *Heinrich Himmler*, Munich: Siedler, 2008, pp. 158–79; Broszat, 'Concentration Camps', pp. 160–4.

16   The three camps were Hohenstein, Oranienburg as well as Esterwegen (which Himmler had already placed under his authority in mid-June 1934), followed soon after by Sachsenburg. See Drobisch, Wieland, *System*, pp. 189–91; E. Suhr, *Die Emslandlager*, Bremen: Donant und Temmen, 1985, p. 38.

17   Quote in BAB, ehem. BDC, SSO, Eicke, Theodor, 17.10.1892, Eicke to Himmler, 10.8.1936; see also ibid., Dienstlaufbahn. More generally, see Tuchel, *Konzentrationslager*, pp. 162, 180–1, 209–10, 220–9.

18   On the early years in Dachau, see H. G. Richardi, *Schule der Gewalt. Das Konzentrationslager Dachau*, Munich: Piper, 1995; S. Zámečník, *Das war Dachau*, Luxemburg: Comité International de Dachau, 2004, pp. 19–61. On Eicke's regime, see K. Orth, *Die Konzentrationslager-SS*, Munich: dtv, 2004, pp. 127–32. For the quote, see United States Holocaust Memorial Museum, RG-11.001 M. 20, Reel 91, 1367-2-19: KL Esterwegen, Disziplinar- und Strafordnung, 1 August 1934.

19   For the figures, see Drobisch and Wieland, *System*, pp. 134, 203. Among the camps closed in summer 1934 were two (Hohenstein and Oranienburg) only recently taken over by the SS.

20   The five SS camps were Columbia-Haus, Dachau, Esterwegen, Lichtenburg and Sachsenburg. For the figures, see Tuchel, *Konzentrationslager*, pp. 203, 219; K. Schilde, 'Vom Tempelhofer Feld-Gefängnis zum Schutzhaftlager: Das "Columbia-Haus" in Berlin', in Benz and Distel (eds), *Herrschaft*, pp. 65–82, here 77.

21   Wachsmann, *Prisons*, pp. 113, 185, 393.

22   Quotes in BAB, NS 19/4003, Bl. 3–52: Himmler Rede vor den Staatsräten, 5 March 1936, here Bl. 10–11 (the first phrase cited here was deleted from Himmler's manuscript, presumably because he decided against voicing his criticism too openly). More generally, see M. Wildt, *Generation des Unbedingten. Das Führungskorps des Reichssicherheitshauptamtes*, Hamburg: Hamburger Edition, 2003, pp. 218–39; U. Herbert, 'Von der Gegnerbekämpfung zur "rassischen Generalprävention". "Schutzhaft" und Konzentrationslager in der Konzeption der Gestapo-Führung 1933–1939', in Herbert, Orth and Dieckmann (eds), *Konzentrationslager*, vol. 1, pp. 60–86.

23   See Broszat, 'Concentration Camps', pp. 167–8; Tuchel, *Konzentrationslager*, pp. 307–15, 324–5.

24   U. Wohlfeld, 'Im Hotel "Zum Großherzog": Das Konzentrationslager Bad Sulza, 1933–1937', in W. Benz and B. Distel (eds), *Instrumentarium der Macht. Frühe Konzentrationslager 1933–1937*, Berlin: Metropol, 2003, pp. 263–75.

25   The SS concentration camps in early summer 1936 were Bad Sulza, Columbia-Haus, Dachau, Esterwegen, Lichtenburg and Sachsenburg.

26   See G. Morsch, 'Formation and Construction of the Sachsenhausen Concentration Camp', in G. Morsch (ed.), *From Sachsenburg to Sachsenhausen*, Berlin: Metropol, 2007, pp. 87–194, quote on p. 89. For the rebuilding of Dachau, see BAB, R 2/28350, Chronik der gesamten SS-Lageranlage in Dachau, 1 March 1938.

27   For prisoner markings, see A. Eberle, 'Häftlingskategorien und Kennzeichnungen', in Benz and Distel (eds), *Ort*, vol. 1, pp. 91–109, here 92. For the camps and the law, see L. Gruchmann, *Justiz im Dritten Reich*, Munich: Oldenbourg, 1990, pp. 632–57.

28 For the 1936 figure, see Staatsarchiv Nürnberg (StN), Auswärtiges Amt to Missionen und Berufskonsulate, 8 December 1936, ND: NG-4048. For the 1937 figures, see Mahn- und Gedenkstätte Buchenwald (ed.), *Buchenwald. Mahnung und Verpflichtung*, Berlin, VEB, 1983, p. 698; Drobisch and Wieland, *System*, pp. 266, 271; Endlich, 'Lichtenburg', p. 23.

29 BAB Berlin, NS 19/4004, Bl. 278–351: Himmler Rede auf der SS-Gruppenführer Besprechung, 8 November 1937, here Bl. 293.

30 For the individual figures, see Gedenkstätte Buchenwald (ed.), *Buchenwald*, p. 698; S. Zámečník, 'Dachau – Stammlager', in Benz and Distel (eds), *Ort*, vol. 2, pp. 233–74, here 248; J. Skriebeleit, 'Flossenbürg – Stammlager', in Benz and Distel (eds), *Ort*, vol. 4, pp. 17–66, here 22; Endlich, 'Lichtenburg', p. 23; H. Kaienburg, 'Sachsenhausen – Stammlager', in Benz and Distel (eds), *Ort*, vol. 3, pp. 17–72, here 31.

31 For the inmate figure, see Pohl to Himmler, 30 April 1942, ND: 129-R, in *The Trial of the Major War Criminals before the International Military Tribunal*, 42 vols, Nuremberg: 1947–1949, vol. 38, pp. 363–5.

32 See P. Wagner, *Volksgemeinschaft ohne Verbrecher. Konzeptionen und Praxis der Kriminalpolizei in der Zeit der Weimarer Republik und des Nationalsozialismus*, Hamburg: Christians, 1996, pp. 254–8, 279–92; K. L. Terhorst, *Polizeiliche planmäßige Überwachung und polizeiliche Vorbeugungshaft im Dritten Reich*, Heidelberg: Müller, 1985, pp. 109–14; S. Langhammer, 'Die reichsweite Verhaftungsaktion vom 9. März 1937', in *Hallische Beiträge zur Zeitgeschichte* 1, 2007, pp. 55–77, here 62; W. Ayaß, *'Asoziale' im Nationalsozialismus*, Stuttgart: Klett-Cotta, 1995, pp. 140–65. For the Sachsenhausen figures, see Drobisch and Wieland, *System*, p. 288 (such statistics have to be used with caution, as SS labels were often misleading).

33 For this assumption, see for example W. Wippermann, *Konzentrationslager. Geschichte, Nachgeschichte, Gedenken*, Berlin: Elefanten Press, 1999, p. 44. For an overview of Nazi terror before the war, see N. Wachsmann, 'The Policy of Exclusion: Repression in the Nazi State, 1933–1939', in J. Caplan (ed.), *Short Oxford History of Germany: The Third Reich*, Oxford: Oxford UP, 2008, pp. 122–45.

34 See C. Schulz, 'Weibliche Häftlinge aus Ravensbrück in Bordellen der Männerkonzentrationslager', in C. Füllberg-Stolberg *et al.* (eds), *Frauen in Konzentrationslagern*, Bremen: Temmen, 1994, pp. 135–46, here 137; R. Otto, 'Rache an politischen Gegnern und Privatinteressen. Das Konzentrationslager Leschwitz bei Görlitz', in Benz and Distel (eds), *Herrschaft*, pp. 237–44, here 238; Ayaß, *'Asoziale'*, pp. 19–41; BAB Berlin, R 3001/alt R 22/1469, Bl. 6–9: Erlaß des Preußischen Ministers des Inneren, 13 November 1933.

35 See StN, Auswärtiges Amt to Missionen und Berufskonsulate, 8 December 1936, ND: NG-4048.

36 For a different view, putting much greater emphasis on changes in policing after 1936, see Herbert, 'Gegnerbekämpfung', p. 78. Until now, historians have often overlooked the widespread detention in camps of social outsiders in the early Nazi years; for a detailed account, see the forthcoming PhD dissertation by Julia Hörath (Birkbeck, University of London).

37 Quotes in Grunderlaß Vorbeugende Verbrechensbekämpfung, 14 December 1937, reprinted in W. Ayaß (ed.), *'Gemeinschaftsfremde'. Quellen zur Verfolgung von 'Asozialen'*, Koblenz: Bundesarchiv, 1998, pp. 94–8; U. Herbert, *Best. Biographische Studien über Radikalismus, Weltanschauung und Vernunft*, Bonn: Dietz, 1996, 164–5. More generally, see ibid., pp. 163–77; Ayaß (ed.), *'Gemeinschaftsfremde'*, pp. 124–6; Wagner, *Volksgemeinschaft*, pp. 262–79, 290.

38 See A. Tooze, *The Wages of Destruction*, London: Allen Lane, 2006, esp. pp. 260–8; M. Schneider, *Unterm Hakenkreuz. Arbeiter und Arbeiterbewegung 1933 bis 1939*, Bonn: Dietz, 1999, pp. 738–46.

39 See BAB, R 3001/alt R 22/1437, Bl. 60–1: Vermerk, 15 February 1937.

40 For the SS economy, see H. Kaienburg, *Die Wirtschaft der SS*, Berlin: Metropol, 2003, esp. pp. 455–61, 603–28.

41 Drobisch and Wieland, *System*, pp. 252–3, 280–1; Tuchel and Schattenfroh, *Zentrale des Terrors*, pp. 126–9; Zámečník, *Dachau*, pp. 95–8.

42 Among the early camps with the highest proportion of Jewish inmates (some 16 per cent) was Osthofen; K. Wünschmann, 'Jüdische Häftlinge im KZ Osthofen', in Landeszentrale für politische Bildung Rheinland-Pfalz (ed.), *Vor 75 Jahren. 'Am Anfang stand die Gewalt …'*, Mainz: LPB, 2008, pp. 18–33, here 20.

43 P. Longerich, *Politik der Vernichtung*, Munich: Piper, 1998, p. 164; Ayaß (ed.), *'Gemeinschaftsfremde'*, pp. 134–5; H. Naujocks, *Mein Leben in Sachsenhausen 1936–1942*, Berlin: Dietz, 1989, p. 77; H. Stein, *Juden in Buchenwald 1937–1942*, Weimar: Gedenkstätte Buchenwald, 1992, p. 33. See also A. Barkai, '"Schicksalsjahr 1938": Kontinuität und Verschärfung der wirtschaftlichen Ausplünderung der deutschen Juden', in U. Büttner (ed.), *Das Unrechtsregime*, Hamburg: Christians, 1986, pp. 45–68.

44 For Hitler's orders, see E. Fröhlich (ed.), *Die Tagebücher von Joseph Goebbels*, I/6, Munich: Saur, 1998, p. 181. Just before the pogrom, there were around 24,000 prisoners in the camps (Tuchel, *Konzentrationslager*, p. 217). Jews arrested after the pogrom were distributed as follows: Buchenwald: 9,828; Dachau: 10,911; Sachsenhausen: 5,000–6,000. See Stein, *Juden*, p. 41; B. Distel, '"Die letzte Warnung vor der Vernichtung". Zur Verschleppung der "Aktionsjuden" in die Konzentrationslager nach dem 9. November 1938', *Zeitschrift für Geschichtswissenschaft* 46, 1998, pp. 985–90, here 986; H. Kaienburg, *Der Militär- und Wirtschaftskomplex der SS im KZ-Standort Sachsenhausen-Oranienburg*, Berlin: Metropol, 2006, p. 119, fn. 6.

45 For the general conditions faced by Jewish prisoners, see Pingel, *Häftlinge*, pp. 91–6. In Buchenwald alone, at least 233 Jews died in the special camp set up in November 1938; Stein, *Juden*, p. 50.

46 Zámečník, *Dachau*, p. 102.

47 Only in Buchenwald did the number of Jewish inmates remain unusually high, making up almost 25 per cent of all prisoners in mid-April 1939; Stein, *Juden*, p. 70.

48 B. Wegner, *The Waffen SS: Organization, Ideology and Function*, Oxford: Basil Blackwell, 1990, pp. 106–19; C. Sydnor, *Soldiers of Destruction: The SS Death's Head Division, 1933–1945*, London: Guild, 1989, pp. 30–5; Drobisch and Wieland, *System*, pp. 257, 337.

49 Quote in M. Broszat (ed.), *Kommandant in Auschwitz*, Munich: dtv, 1994, p. 104.

50 For the development of the Camp SS during the war, see the chapter by Karin Orth in this volume.

51 B. Kosmala, 'Polnische Häftlinge im Konzentrationslager Dachau 1939–1945', *Dachauer Hefte* 21, 2005, pp. 94–113, here 96 (figures for March to December 1940).

52 Estimate based on figures in Zámečník, *Dachau*, p. 122; Kaienburg, 'Sachsenhausen', pp. 28–9; Gedenkstätte Buchenwald (ed.), *Buchenwald*, p. 699; Skriebeleit, 'Flossenbürg', p. 29; H. Maršálek, *Die Geschichte des Konzentrationslagers Mauthausen*, Vienna: Lagergemeinschaft Mauthausen, 1995, 3rd. edn, p. 125; B. Strebel, *Das KZ Ravensbrück. Geschichte eines Lagerkomplexes*, Paderborn: Schöningh, 2003, p. 180; F. Piper, *Die Zahl der Opfer von Auschwitz*, Oświęcim: Staatliches Museum, 1993, p. 45; H. Kaienburg, *'Vernichtung durch Arbeit'. Der Fall Neuengamme*, Bonn: Dietz, 1990, p. 155.

53 See Kaienburg, *'Vernichtung'*, pp. 152–6; S. Steinbacher, *Auschwitz. Geschichte und Nachgeschichte*, Munich: Beck, 2004, pp. 25–6; I. Sprenger, *Groß-Rosen. Ein Konzentrationslager in Schlesien*, Cologne: Böhlau, 1996, pp. 88–9; R. Steegmann, *Struthof. Le KL-Natzweiler et ses kommandos*, Strasbourg: La Nuée Bleue, 2005, p. 323. The fifth main camp was Niederhagen (close to Paderborn), which always remained a small local camp and closed down less than two years after its establishment on 1 September 1941; see K. John-Stucke, 'Konzentrationslager Niederhagen/Wewelsburg', in J. E. Schulte (ed.), *Konzentrationslager im Rheinland und in Westfalen, 1933–1945*, Paderborn: Schöningh, 2005, pp. 97–111. The SS Special Camp Hinzert was also placed under the control of the SS Camp Inspection (in July 1940), but never fully operated as a

concentration camp; see U. Bader and W. Welter, 'Das SS-Sonderlager/KZ-Hinzert', in Benz and Distel (eds), *Ort des Terrors*, vol. 5, pp. 17–42.

54 Kaienburg, *Wirtschaft, passim*. Neuengamme had first been established as a satellite camp of Sachsenhausen in late 1938, with labour on the first brickworks beginning in the following year.

55 J. E. Schulte, *Zwangsarbeit und Vernichtung. Das Wirtschaftsimperium der SS*, Paderborn: Schöningh, 2001, pp. 263, 332–41. Himmler had first chosen Lublin as the site of a massive labour camp – holding between 25,000 and 50,000 prisoners – during a visit on 20 July 1941.

56 For the figures, see R. Otto, *Wehrmacht, Gestapo und sowjetische Kriegsgefangene im deutschen Reichsgebiet 1941/42*, Munich: Oldenbourg, 1998, p. 189; E. White, 'Majdanek: Cornerstone of Himmler's SS Empire in the East', *Simon Wiesenthal Centre Annual 7*, 1990, pp. 3–21. More generally, see R. Keller and R. Otto, 'Sowjetische Kriegsgefangene in Konzentrationslagern der SS', in J. Ibel (ed.), *Einvernehmliche Zusammenarbeit? Wehrmacht, Gestapo, SS und sowjetische Kriegsgefangene*, Berlin: Metropol, 2008, pp. 15–44.

57 For mortality in Ravensbrück, see Strebel, *Ravensbrück*, pp. 180, 293, 506, 509. More generally, see the contribution by Jane Caplan in this volume.

58 See Glücks to Lagerärzte, 28 December 1942, reprinted in Gedenkstätte Buchenwald (ed.), *Buchenwald*, pp. 257–8.

59 For the quote, see StN, WVHA to Lagerkommandanten, 26 March 1942, ND: 1151-P-PS. For Himmler's involvement and other aspects of 14f13, see Landgericht Frankfurt, sentence of 27 May 1970, reprinted in C. F. Rüter and D. W. Mildt (eds), *Justiz und NS-Verbrechen*, vol. 34, Amsterdam, 2005, pp. 188–290.

60 Otto, *Wehrmacht, passim*. For individual camps, see Ibel (ed.), *Zusammenarbeit?*

61 S. Kłodziński, 'Die ersten Vergasungen von Häftlingen und Kriegsgefangenen im Konzentrationslager Auschwitz', in Hamburger Institut für Sozialforschung (ed.), *Die Auschwitz-Hefte*, 2 vols, Hamburg: Rogner & Bernhard, 1994, vol. 1, pp. 261–75. Among the first men gassed in Auschwitz were also some 250 prisoners, selected by SS doctors in the camp hospital.

62 For example Broszat, 'Concentration Camps', pp. 204–5. Only one monograph (in German) has been published on the murder of Soviet 'commissars' (Otto, *Wehrmacht*). Even more surprisingly, there is no satisfactory monograph on the 'euthanasia' murders in the camps; for the best brief survey in English, see H. Friedlander, *The Origins of Nazi Genocide*, Chapel Hill, NC: North Carolina UP, 1995, pp. 142–50.

63 See Kaienburg, *Wirtschaft*, pp. 403–12.

64 Ibid., pp. 28–30, 498-500, 1077-8; Schulte, *Zwangsarbeit*, pp. 213–35, 386–9. Among the early collaborations between SS and private industry was the small Arbeitsdorf concentration camp in Fallersleben, where prisoners briefly worked on a Volkswagen project between spring and autumn 1942; see H. Mommsen and W. Grieger, *Das Volkswagenwerk und seine Arbeiter im Dritten Reich*, Düsseldorf: Econ, 1997.

65 For the camp commandants, see Orth, *Konzentrationslager-SS*, pp. 205–6; 250–4. For Buchenwald, see Gedenkstätte Buchenwald (ed.), *Buchenwald*, p. 701; H. Stein, 'Funktionswandel des Konzentrationslagers Buchenwald im Spiegel der Lagerstatistiken', in Herbert, Orth and Dieckmann (eds), *Konzentrationslager*, vol. 1, p. 167–92, here pp. 179, 182, 187.

66 For the inmate figures, see StN, Pohl to Himmler, 30 September 1943, ND: PS-1469; Glücks to Lagerärzte, 28 December 1942, reprinted in Gedenkstätte Buchenwald (ed.), *Buchenwald*, pp. 257–8. Glücks lists more then 75,000 dead between July and November 1942. However, these figures were not complete: it is likely that many thousands of registered prisoners were omitted from internal WVHA statistics, including inmates who had been killed by injection or gas; see Piper, *Zahl*, p. 158; Zámečník, *Dachau*, p. 245.

67 For example Pingel, *Häftlinge*, p. 182; Broszat, 'Concentration Camps', p. 243. For the quote, see BAB, NS 3/426, Bl. 14: Glücks to Lagerkommandanten, 20 January 1943.

68 See M. Kárný, "'Vernichtung durch Arbeit'. Sterblichkeit in den NS-Konzentrationslagern', in G. Aly and S. Heim (eds), *Sozialpolitik und Judenvernichtung. Beiträge zur nationalsozialistischen Gesundheits- und Sozialpolitik*, Berlin: Rotbuch, 1987, pp. 133–58; Orth, *System*, pp. 192–8.

69 For the most detailed recent account, see C. R. Browning, *The Origins of the Final Solution*, London: Heinemann, 2004.

70 Majdanek apparently developed direct links to 'Action Reinhardt'; see P. Witte and S. Tyas, 'A new document on the deportation and murder of Jews during "Einsatz Reinhardt" 1942', *Holocaust and Genocide Studies* 15, 2001, pp. 468–86.

71 In late October 1939, Auschwitz (and the rest of east Upper Silesia) officially became part of the German Reich; see Steinbacher, *Auschwitz*, p. 18 (quote ibid.). More generally, see ibid., p. 84. For the figures of Jews in Auschwitz, see the statistics in J. E. Schulte, 'London war informiert. KZ-Expansion und Judenverfolgung', in R. Hachtmann and W. Süß (eds), *Hitlers Kommissare. Sondergewalten in der nationalsozialistischen Diktatur*, Göttingen: Wallstein, 2006, pp. 207–27, here 222–3; Piper, *Zahl*, Table D. In Belžec death camp, some 434,508 Jews were murdered in 1942; National Archives London, HW 16/23, GPDD 355a, no date (January 1943).

72 Piper, *Zahl*, p. 158. See also T. Iwaszko, 'Reasons for Confinement in the Camp and Categories of Prisoners', in W. Długoborski and F. Piper (eds), *Auschwitz 1940–1945*, 5 vols, Oświęcim, 2000, vol. 2, pp. 11–44, Table 1.

73 Steinbacher, *Auschwitz*, pp. 87–8.

74 For the figures, see StN, Pohl to Himmler, 30 September 1943, ND: PS-1469; Schulte, 'London', p. 223.

75 See B. C. Wagner, *IG Auschwitz. Zwangsarbeit und Vernichtung von Häftlingen des Lagers Monowitz 1941–1945*, Munich: Saur, 2000. For IG Farben, see also P. Hayes, *Industry and Ideology: IG Farben in the Nazi Era*, Cambridge: Cambridge UP, 2001.

76 For the new camps, see Orth, *System*, pp. 213–6; G. Schwarz, *Die nationalsozialistischen Lager*, Frankfurt: Fischer, 1996, pp. 200–204, 221–3, 232–4; W. Gruner, *Jewish Forced Labour Under the Nazis*, Cambridge: Cambridge UP, 2006, pp. 267–75. In July 1943, another concentration camp was set up, on the ruins of the Warsaw ghetto; prisoners were forced to cover up what was left of the ghetto following the murderous suppression of the uprising.

77 For the debate about ideology vs. economics, see the contribution by Jens-Christian Wagner in this volume. For the use of the term 'annihilation through labour' in Nazi Germany, see N. Wachsmann, "'Annihilation Through Labour'': The Killing of State Prisoners in the Third Reich', *Journal of Modern History* 71, 1999, pp. 624–59.

78 Steinbacher, *Auschwitz*, p. 87; Piper, *Zahl*, Table D.

79 See Broszat, 'Concentration Camps', pp. 247–9; Pingel, *Häftlinge*, pp. 220–8. See also J. Billig, *L'Hitlérisme et le système concentrationnaire*, Paris: Presses Universitaires de France, 1967, pp. 300–1.

80 The most important survey is Orth, *System*, pp. 222–336.

81 For the figures, see StN, Pohl to Himmler, 30 September 1943, ND: PS-1469; ibid., WVHA to Amtsgruppe B, 15 August 1944, ND: NO-399; Institute for Contemporary History, Munich (IfZ), Fa 183, Bl. 6–7. The 1943 figure refers to the average daily number of inmates in August; the 1944 figure refers specifically to 1 August.

82 Schulte, *Zwangsarbeit*, pp. 397–403 (for a different interpretation of Speer's new role, see M. T. Allen, *The Business of Genocide*, Chapel Hill, NC: North Carolina UP, 2002, pp. 263–4). More generally, see also M. Spoerer, 'Profitierten Unternehmen von KZ-Arbeit? Eine kritische Analyse der Literatur', *Historische Zeitschrift* 268, 1999, pp. 61–95, esp. 82–7.

83 Gedenkstätte Buchenwald (ed.), *Buchenwald*, p. 700.

84 See figures in StN, Pohl to Himmler, 30 September 1943, ND: PS-1469; IfZ, Fa 183, Bl. 6–7. Prisoner numbers in the six older camps would have been higher still at the end of 1944, had the Buchenwald subcamp Dora not been turned into a main camp.

85 Orth, *System*, pp. 216, 271–87, 305–36; Schwarz, *Lager*, pp. 204, 234; D. Blatman, 'Die Todesmärsche. Entscheidungsträger, Mörder und Opfer', in Herbert, Orth and Dieckmann (eds), *Konzentrationslager*, vol. 2, pp. 1063–92, here esp. 1077–8. On the death marches, see also the contribution by Daniel Blatman in this volume.
86 For the figures, see BAB, NS 19/1570, Bl. 12–28: Inspekteur für Statistik, Die Endlösung der europäischen Judenfrage, no date [1943], here Bl. 24; Schulte, 'London', pp. 220–7; L. Apel, *Jüdische Häftlinge im Konzentrationslager Ravensbrück*, Berlin: Metropol, 2003, pp. 303, 315; K. Külow, 'Jüdische Häftlinge im KZ Sachsenhausen 1939 bis 1942', in G. Morsch and S. zur Nieden (eds), *Jüdische Häftlinge im Konzentrationslager Sachsenhausen 1936 bis 1945*, Berlin: Edition Hentrich, 2004, pp. 180–99, here 198. For the quote, see StN, WVHA to Lagerkommandanten, 5 October 1942, ND: 3677-PS.
87 Orth, *System*, pp. 222–48. See also Stein, 'Funktionswandel', p. 187.
88 See the contribution by Jens-Christian Wagner in this volume.
89 See M. Buggeln, 'Building to Death: Prisoner Forced Labour in the German War Economy – The Neuengamme Subcamps, 1942–1945', in *European History Quarterly* (forthcoming). For the figures, see C. Glauning, *Entgrenzung und KZ-System*, Berlin: Metropol, 2006, pp. 121–3.
90 For Dora, see J. C. Wagner, *Produktion des Todes*, Göttingen: Wallstein, 2001. See also M. J. Neufeld, *The Rocket and the Reich*, Cambridge, MA: Harvard UP, 1996, p. 264. For Kammler, see R. Fröbe, 'Hans Kammler. Technokrat der Vernichtung', in R. Smelser and E. Syring (eds), *Die SS. Elite unter dem Totenkopf*, Paderborn: Schöningh, 2000, pp. 305–19. On production and construction in satellite camps, see also F. Freund, 'Mauthausen. Zu Strukturen von Haupt- und Außenlagern', *Dachauer Hefte* 15, 1999, 254–72.
91 M. Fabréguet, *Mauthausen. Camp de concentration national-socialiste en Autriche rattachée*, Paris: Honoré Champion Éditeur, 1999, pp. 166, 182–7.
92 Orth, *System*, pp. 260–69; 287–301. For Bergen-Belsen, see also A. E. Wenck, *Zwischen Menschenhandel und 'Endlösung'. Das Konzentrationslager Bergen-Belsen*, Paderborn: Schöningh, 2000. On gassings, see E. Kogon *et al.* (eds), *Nationalsozialistische Massentötungen durch Giftgas*, Frankfurt: Fischer, 1983, pp. 245–80.
93 For the estimate, see Orth, *System*, pp. 345–46; Sofsky, *Order*, p. 43 (both with missing and incorrect figures). For Auschwitz, see Długoborski and Piper (eds), *Auschwitz, 1940–1945*, vol. 3, pp. 230–1.
94 For this figure, see IfZ, Fa 183, Bl. 6–7.
95 For a recent survey, see J. Tuchel, 'Die Wachmannschaften der Konzentrationslager 1939 bis 1945. Ergebnisse und offene Fragen der Forschung', in A. Gottwaldt *et al.* (eds), *NS-Gewaltherrschaft. Beiträge zur historischen Forschung und juristischen Aufarbeitung*, Berlin: Edition Hentrich, 2005, pp. 135–51.

2 The concentration camp personnel

Karin Orth

For many years there was little research on National Socialism's perpetrators. Concentration camp guards were therefore also overlooked, with no studies of the SS in individual camps or in the overall system. Public perceptions of the camp SS were determined instead by survivors' accounts and sensationalist reports of concentration camp trials. In these, SS men and female guards appeared as monsters, pathological sadists remote from the mainstream of German society. Their conduct seemed inexplicable or at most explicable only in psychopathological terms,[1] and as such for many years it was not deemed a topic for historical inquiry.

One exception was the Israeli historian Tom Segev's dissertation on concentration camp commandants, completed in 1977.[2] In succinct sections, Segev reconstructed the deployments of 36 SS leaders who for varying lengths of time served as camp commandants. For this alone Segev's work was of pioneering value. The key findings of his study, which emerged under the auspices of a psycho-historical research project, were the ideological commitment of the commandants and their incremental 'process of inner hardening'.[3] However, as Segev investigated neither the commandant group in its entirety – there were 46 in all – nor the evolution of the concentration camp system and SS personnel policy, he was unable to shed light on what personnel were typical for each phase of the camp system. Similarly unclear were the events leading to this 'process of inner hardening', neither did he explore the social practice of terror.

Symptomatic of the monographs on individual camps is the fact that while the basic organisational structure of the camp SS is captured, the individuals comprising this apparatus are in most cases banished with a biographical note to the footnotes or appendix, and not conceived as independent actors. With only a little exaggeration, we might say that these historical subjects are assigned the status of extras to a ruling structure or idea, with the latter differing according to the perspective of the historian: from 'monopoly capitalism' to Wolfgang Sofsky's 'absolute power'.[4] However, as recent studies have shown, the members of the camp SS were far from being mere reflexive tools of a structure.

Empirical research into National Socialism and so-called 'perpetrator research' in particular underwent an explosion in the 1990s. Especially influential were the pioneering studies of Christopher Browning and Ulrich Herbert. Historians working in this field now offered not only descriptions of their subjects' actions and analyses of their social situation but also explanatory models of their motivation. To take just a few, Ulrich Herbert and, in his wake, Michael Wildt emphasised the ideological and generational 'charging' of leading figures in the Reich Security Main Office (RSHA), Christopher Browning the anti-Semitism, but above all the group dynamics of a military unit in his study of Reserve Police Battalion 101, and Daniel Jonah Goldhagen the 'eliminationist anti-Semitism' he saw as particular to almost all Germans.[5]

No approach, however, provided an all-encompassing explanatory model. In all probability, the different groups of perpetrators are too distinct for such an endeavour. Indeed, dissimilarities are striking even when the focus is restricted to the various perpetrators in the concentration camp system. These were very heterogeneous; there were men and women, elderly soldiers and very young men, Germans and non-Germans, SS men and prisoner functionaries, rank-and-file sentries and highly-decorated SS leaders, Protestants, Catholics and other religious believers, ideologues and Army conscripts, some who served only a few weeks and others who served the full twelve years of National Socialism, sadistic killers and others who treated inmates comparatively humanely. We know a great deal about some of these perpetrator groups, next to nothing about others. This reflects not least the density and quality of the available source material.

We still do not know exactly how many people served in the concentration camps between 1933 and 1945. But some indicators permit an approximate calculation: on 15 January 1945, when the prisoner population reached its peak, 37,674 men and 3,508 women were guarding the camps. The overall figure was certainly therefore many tens of thousands.[6] The entire guard personnel came under the auspices of the Inspection of the Concentration Camps (IKL) and later the SS Business and Administration Main Office (WVHA). It was organised into distinct guard and commandant staff personnel on the basis of a uniform principle dating from the early phase of the camp system. This separation of the 'inner' and 'outer' guarding of the camp – between the personnel of the detail that guarded the prisoners and the men guarding the protective custody camp itself – was one of the key characteristics of the National Socialist concentration camps.[7] The commandant staff, the true power and administrative headquarters of the camp, was itself subdivided into several departments. The guard detail, which guarded the camp perimeter and work details, was also divided into several companies depending on the size of the camp. These two key groups of camp perpetrators – the guard personnel and the SS officers of the commandant staff – will be analysed in more detail in this essay, with organisation, structure, social profile and outlook brought into focus.[8]

The guard personnel

The early camps, subordinate to the IKL, were each guarded by one SS unit. Up to the mid-1930s, there were five SS Death's Head Battalions (Totenkopfsturmbanne): Oberbayern (stationed in Dachau), Ostfriesland (Esterwegen), Elbe (Lichtenburg), Sachsen (Sachsenburg) and Brandenburg (Columbia-Haus).[9] The development of the concentration camp system from 1936 was accompanied by the expansion of the guard personnel. The SS leadership now consolidated the Death's Head Battalions into three units, which as of 1 April 1937 were assigned respectively to Dachau (First SS Death's Head Regiment, Totenkopfstandarte), Sachsenhausen (Second) and Buchenwald (Third). In the autumn of 1938, a fourth Death's Head Regiment was created for the new Mauthausen concentration camp. The primary function of the Death's Head Regiments was to guard the camp inmates and serve as perimeter sentries on work details outside the protective custody camp. According to the 'Discipline and Punishment Order for the Prisoner Camp' in force for every camp, the guard troops were forbidden to enter the prisoner camp proper without authorisation. Invoking these guidelines, members of the guard detail who appeared before Allied or German courts at the end of the war unanimously claimed that they had never entered the protective custody camp and so had had no contact with the inmates. The reality, of course, was quite different. In fact, the separation between the 'inner' and 'outer' zones barely existed in the prescribed strict form. The guard personnel, whose barracks were located right next to the camp, knew a good deal of the protective custody camp for the simple reason that their daily function was the surveillance of the inmates. Furthermore, that the guard personnel beat, tortured and killed inmates is confirmed in countless survivor reports.

Towards the end of the 1930s, the SS-Death's Head Regiments gradually lost their function as pure guard personnel. Ever since the 'Röhm-Affair' in the summer of 1934, Himmler had been expanding the SS organisation. This included both a numerical strengthening of the armed SS units and their reorganisation into a military formation in readiness for deployment in war.[10] To enable the deployment of replacement troops for the so-called SS-Verfügungstruppe (combat divisions of the SS, trained according to the regulations of the German Wehrmacht) in the event of war, Himmler ordered the expansion and militarisation of the SS-Death's Head units. Hitler supported and specifically authorised this development: his decree of 17 August 1938 redefined the duties of the SS and police and the delineation of their responsibilities from the Army. Through this decree and a complementary order dated 18 May 1938, the armed SS, particularly the SS-Verfügungstruppe, were able to become the 'nation's second bearer of arms'.[11] The militarisation of the SS- Death's Head units took place not least due to the Army's successful opposition to an augmentation of the Verfügungstruppe. By mid-1939, the head count of the SS- Death's Head units had reached 22,033.[12] If this figure is accurate, it was actually slightly higher than the number of concentration camp inmates at this time.

Yet the function of the SS-Death's Head Regiments was never intended to be the military instruction of the SS camp personnel and general training of SS recruits alone. The expansion of the SS-Death's Head units was decided not solely on military grounds, but also with the expectation on the part of the SS that the outbreak of war would lead to a surge in 'hostile elements' within Germany and in the occupied territories. These were to be 'fought' in the concentration camps. Therefore, alongside the military schooling of the SS-Death's Head units, reservists were drafted into the concentration camp guard personnel.[13] This so-called 'reinforcement' of the SS-Death's Head units (also referred to as 'police reinforcement') comprised in the main older men from the general SS (Allgemeine-SS).[14]

At the beginning of the war, Himmler assigned the military command of the SS Death's Head Regiments to Theodor Eicke – hitherto 'Inspector of the Concentration Camps and Leader of the SS-Death's Head Units'. Previously stationed in the camps, these units were now deployed to the 'outer front'. A few days after the outbreak of war, they marched into Poland and operated alongside the newly-formed SS task forces (Einsatzgruppen) behind the lines of the German army. The available source material suggests that the main target of their terror operations were the Jews of Poland. Shortly after the invasion, Hitler authorised the consolidation of the SS units into full divisions. In October 1939, Himmler ordered Eicke to withdraw the SS Death's Head Regiments from Poland and merge them into the independent SS Death's Head Division. This division participated in the Western campaign in 1940 and formed part of the occupation force in south-west France after the French capitulation. It was also among the first German divisions in the invasion of the Soviet Union in the summer of 1941. The history, and the self-perception, of the SS Death's Head Division on the Eastern Front was characterised by failure. Between the autumn 1941 and October 1942 it was almost completely wiped out in the Demjansk area to the south of Leningrad. It is unclear how many Soviet soldiers were killed in the Demjansk pocket: what *is* clear is that the rare victories of the SS Death's Head Division ended in the massacre of captured Soviet soldiers.[15]

In mid-November 1939, Himmler appointed Richard Glücks, Eicke's long-serving deputy and chief of staff of the IKL, to succeed him as Inspector of the Concentration Camps.[16] Initially still subordinate to the SS Main Office (SS Hauptamt), in August 1940 the IKL was transferred to the newly-created SS Leadership Main Office (Führungshauptamt).[17] The function of this office was to organise and co-ordinate the command of the so-called Armed SS (Waffen-SS); with the IKL now subordinate to it, camp personnel were deemed members of the Armed SS.[18] This formal bureaucratic restructuring, however, had little broader impact: as before, the IKL reported directly to Himmler. Responsibility for decisions over internment and release from the concentration camps too had changed only formally. It now lay with the RSHA, created in 1939 through the consolidation of the security police (Sicherheitspolizei, i.e. criminal police and Gestapo) and the SS security service (Sicherheitsdienst or SD). The RSHA, under Heydrich, was the heart of the SS leadership's intended 'State Protection Corps' (*Staatsschutzkorps*), formed by merging the members of the police and the SS.[19]

During the war there were major changes to the camp guard units. First of all, older men of the general SS took over, as planned, the posts of the SS Death's Head Regiments sent to the front line. Second, a not inconsiderable exchange of personnel with the front-line units developed as the SS leadership transferred wounded or otherwise unfit SS soldiers to guard roles in concentration camps, either permanently or pending their recovery for active service.[20] Third, with the dramatic increase in inmates, the SS needed more guard personnel. This led to notable structural changes, with the camps now being increasingly guarded by men – including ethnic Germans (*Volksdeutsche*) – drafted into the Armed SS over the course of the war. Countless conflicts developed between these men and the established pre-war personnel. The SS leadership even resorted to employing groups who did not belong to the SS; female guards, for example, although never more than 10 per cent of the guard personnel, were recruited partly from the workforce of companies and factories that requested female camps inmates for labour.[21] Increasingly, in the second half and particularly the final year of the war, Army and Air Force personnel too were assigned to the SS for concentration camp guard duties. By mid-January 1945, as many as 52 per cent of male camp guard personnel were former soldiers, and some were even responsible for the supervision of satellite camps.[22] The overall shortage of guard personnel was to some extent made good by the use of guard dogs and the delegation of some guard duties to prisoners.[23] In several camps a camp police made up of inmates, known as a *Lagerschutz*, emerged. Existing prisoner functionaries also had the opportunity to expand their roles. However, overall, the changing profile of the guard personnel did not improve the prisoners' prospects of surviving the camps, particularly in the final stage of the war.

Beyond this, little can be said about the concentration camp guard personnel. The sparse archival material does not permit a socio-statistical analysis.[24] What the investigations do reveal is that the guard personnel were not a homogeneous or static group. Both overall and at individual camp level, they were highly heterogeneous in terms of virtually every conceivable social-structural parameter – age, gender, nationality, membership of a National Socialist organisation.

Questions beyond pure statistics, involving qualitative methodological approaches, can be investigated still less and certainly not adequately answered.[25] The abysmal shortage of source material precludes a group biography or analysis of motivation. This loss, though, may not be as great as it seems. The importance of the guard personnel in the exercise of National Socialist terror in the concentration camps lies in structure rather than individuals. But matters are entirely different in the case of the second group of perpetrators to be considered in this essay. This group, the SS leadership in the camps' staff offices, were not simply of structural importance. Each had considerable latitude for action, depending on their own initiative. We can ask valid questions about the origin and socialisation of these men, their motivations and their behaviour. They can also be answered, at least partially, even if an all-encompassing analysis embracing every member of the commandant staff office is likely to be difficult or impossible on the basis of surviving evidence.

The SS commandant staff

The commandant staff office employed that select group of individuals who can be held primarily responsible for the crimes committed in the concentration camps. It was the central organisational and administrative unit of the concentration camp and the core troop of terror – the National Socialist functional elite. The members of the commandant office, especially those who were SS officers, bore a general responsibility and also fulfilled specialised functional roles. In contrast to the guard personnel, who experienced a high turnover, the men of the commandant staff were mainly stationed permanently in the camps, usually from the mid-1930s until the end of the war.

From the mid-1930s, the commandant staffs of all concentration camps were uniformly structured in the following departments:

1   Commandant/Adjutant
2   Political Department
3   Protective Custody Camp,
4   Administration
5   Camp Doctor
6   Guard Command[26]

In essence, this subdivision within the commandant staff remained operative in all main concentration camps until the collapse of the Third Reich.[27] Each department contained an internal hierarchy. At its head stood the department head, beneath him one or more SS *Führer*, and then in turn several SS *Unterführer* and men of lower ranks. Only a minority of the men deployed to the commandant staff held SS officer rank: in 1936, of a total of 269 men in commandants' staffs, just six held a leadership rank. By 1938 the number had increased to 577 men, of whom 90 per cent similarly held a low rank. Less than 2 per cent (11) were SS *Führer*, and around 7 per cent *Unterführer*.[28]

At the peak of the camp hierarchy, the group of commandants and department heads was extremely small in number. From 1933 to 1945, in all camps subordinate to the IKL and Office D (Amtsgruppe D) of the WVHA, the total is around 320 men. These leading figures, from now on referred to as the 'concentration camp SS', will be analysed in detail in what follows.[29] The conclusions on them could also be transferred with a degree of plausibility to other members of the commandant staffs.[30]

A large proportion of the members of the concentration camp SS belonged to the so-called 'war youth generation'. This generation had not experienced the First World War itself, but grew up with its myth, which, for a section of male youth, endowed them with identity. Predominantly, they grew up in middle-class families. They had mostly left school after completing *Volksschule* (eight years) or *Mittelschule* (ten years), and a high proportion learnt a technical or commercial trade. The men under investigation, therefore, did not come from the maladjusted extremes, but rather the very centre of Weimar society. We are dealing with members of those social strata hit hardest by the political and social crises of the Weimar Republic, those who saw themselves as most threatened by social decline. Indeed, the impact of the economic crisis to some extent affected both the commandants and the departmental heads, a proportion of whom lost their jobs temporarily or permanently in the 1930s.

On the whole, the future concentration camp SS established contact with right-wing radical *völkisch* circles in their youth or as young adults. Their presence here led them to the NSDAP, SA or SS at a relatively early stage. They joined the National Socialist movement in significant numbers before the 'seizure of power', on average already having joined by September 1931. However, this early date is perhaps less noteworthy – as we know, the middle classes were among the earliest supporters of the NSDAP – than their young age at joining. Half had joined the NSDAP or SS by the time they were in their mid-twenties. Shortly after the seizure of power, the SS offered them a full-time position – and with it the opportunity to escape an often precarious employment situation. At the same time, it gave these men the opportunity to professionalise their commitment to the movement they had supported since their youth. They seized the opportunity to combine their political activity with stability of employment and the aura of soldierliness. Their employment with the SS, which has been seen by historians as biographical accident,[31] turns out to be not so much coincidental as highly plausible in view of their early presence in right-wing milieux.

The members of the concentration camp SS generally entered the camps in the mid-1930s, serving initially for the most part in the guard personnel. Given that in 1935, 2,500 SS men were thus employed,[32] their presence is less remarkable than their swift promotion to leading positions in the commandant staff at a young age, in their early to mid-thirties. They had proved themselves more qualified and/ or committed than their peers and also established early contact with the men in control of promotion. These included the commandants, members of the IKL head office, and the camp 'guard leaders' who held a prominent position in the early camps, comparable to the rank of commandant. With the emergence of the camp system, Dachau, Buchenwald and especially Sachsenhausen became both centres of terror and meeting places for the concentration camp SS.[33] So too did the IKL, which from 2 August 1938 was based at Oranienburg near Sachsenhausen. Most of the concentration camp SS had by then advanced to the rank of departmental head. In the SS leadership of these camps, an intricate web of personal and professional relationships developed. Especially among the Oranienburg leadership, comprising the leaders of Sachsenhausen and the IKL, the system of relationships and patronage was decisive for camp staffing policy in the later years.

Personal relationships were integral to the social network of the concentration camp SS, whose social context was the notion of 'SS kinship' and a distinctive linguistic code. The emergent 'camp vocabulary' could be deciphered without difficulty by SS men and inmates alike, but not by those outside the concentration camp world. At its core, however, the network was held together by shared criminality, through a common socialisation in duty and forms of collective violence. The perpetrators were bound as a group by a shared division of labour. All members of the concentration camp SS had to undergo a type of initiation rite which inured them to their own feelings – as well as to the agony of the victims – and was designed to integrate them into the group. Their understanding of how to run a concentration camp was based on practical experience rather than the evening classes which were occasionally provided. Under National Socialism the concentration camp SS emerged as a group of terror experts, whose 'expertise' lay in their ability and readiness to put the regime's policies of annihilation into practice.

Whilst certainly not free of personal conflicts and quarrels, the 'comradely' relationships among SS leaders extended beyond the workplace. Social and cultural events like the 'camaraderie evening' (*Kameradschaftsabend*) and communal trips to the theatre were important aspects of the SS community. These also connected the SS men in complex ways to the towns and cities around the camps. They patronised local restaurants, cinemas and swimming pools, and appeared at parades and dances. Contacts and friendships were formed, marriages proposed and accepted. The camp's register office often conducted the marriage ceremony and the groom's SS comrades acted as best men and 'warrantors of the bride' on the obligatory questionnaire issued by the SS Race and Settlement Office.

The wives of SS leaders usually lived at their husband's place of work.[34] They and their children held an important role in the SS community. Leaders' families usually had their own houses, or at least flats, within SS residential areas located not far from the protective custody camp itself, and in many cases engaged inmates as servants, gardeners or labourers. This familial and social environment promoted close friendships, and was possibly deliberately intended by the higher leadership to do so. But its primary function lay in the suggestion of normality and stability. For the members of the concentration camp SS, their families symbolised the continuation of the German *Volk*, whose welfare they claimed to have been working for after the end of the war.

It was this shared functional socialisation that defined the concentration camp SS. Nevertheless, the forms of violence and terror they developed were not, as the sociologist Wolfgang Sofsky averred, anonymous and abstract.[35] They were structurally integrated and empirically diverse. Their victims, too, were chosen systematically rather than arbitrarily. The first murder in each of the early camps proved a collective watershed of applied terror and group identity formation. In Dachau the first violent excesses took place on 11 and 12 April; they were aimed principally, if not exclusively, at Jewish prisoners and culminated that night in the murder of four of them. Of the 21 prisoners murdered by the SS in Dachau in 1933, a highly disproportionate two-thirds were Jewish. On one hand, these murders showed that the SS had not yet devised a routine of killing. The first dead inmates were victims of violent excess, an orgy of flogging in which drunken SS men spurred one another on to murderous effect. On the other hand, they show how ready the SS was to translate its antisemitic ideology – before the seizure of power mainly a matter of words – into deadly practice. It is impossible to explain the exceptional degree to which Jewish prisoners were victims of their murderous terror without reference to ideology.

Another shared experience that helped to shape group identity dated from the second half of 1938. Since 1936 the Political Police had operated a prophylactic principle of preventive detention, which Ulrich Herbert has termed 'general racial prevention'; this now became official practice for the concentration camp

SS too. These were the victims of the so-called 'asocial' campaigns of spring and summer 1938, in which over 10,000 people ended up in the hands of the SS in Buchenwald, Sachsenhausen and, after its construction in August 1938, the Flossenbürg concentration camp. Immediately after the November 1938 pogrom, an estimated 30,000 male Jews were also taken to concentration camps. These two fresh measures of persecution dramatically altered the camps' inmate profile. The notable surge in violence and death rates in the second half of 1938 had little effect on the political prisoners. The Jewish prisoners, on the other hand, suffered a cruelty and brutality hitherto unknown in the history of the camps. Once again, the selection of Jewish victims reflected SS antisemitism. Of all the groups of camp inmates it was the Jewish, and not the political prisoners whom the SS felt entitled to torture and kill. National Socialist ideology functioned as a kind of grid, enabling these men to locate and home in on a victim.

The SS leadership's conviction at the beginning of the war that there was a need for a state protection force to combat 'inner' and 'outer' enemies was reflected in the concentration camps. Several members of the concentration camp SS, including seven men who were to be promoted to the position of camp commandant in the second half of the war, now moved to the 'outer' front by joining the leadership corps of the so-called SS-Totenkopf (Death's Head) Division. The majority of the concentration camp SS remained in the camps where Himmler needed them to mind the 'inner front' and for the planned expansion of the camp system. In them, commandants and departmental heads (some of whom now gained promotion to commandant) began to implement the regime's policies of annihilation towards certain inmate groups. For the first time, the camp system became the site of planned and systematic mass murder: of sick and weak prisoners from spring 1941 (the so-called 'special treatment 14f13') and from autumn of that year of Soviet prisoners of war classified as 'political commissars' and handed over to the SS leadership by the Army. With this programme of mass murder, the concentration camp SS reached a new level of terror.

Against the background of these two programmes of murder, the camp SS also turned its attention to its own experiments in killing. In Mauthausen-Gusen several thousand inmates were murdered in the baths during the so-called 'bath actions' (*Totbadeaktionen*) between October 1941 and spring, while in Auschwitz-Birkenau the SS experimented with gas chambers for the first time.[36] Thus on the 'outer' as well as 'inner' front the SS terror had reached a new pitch, quantitatively and qualitatively far surpassing the pre-war period.

The concentration camps and total war

The twin demands of genocide and forced labour – which had been looming since 1941 – characterised and brought functional changes to the concentration camp system in the second half of the war. There were no longer any restraints; the brutalised concentration camp SS let prisoners work themselves to death or starve in their hundreds of thousands and carried out the genocide of the European Jews. The deployment of non-Jewish prisoners for the war economy, preserving the powerful SS empire, saw the IKL integrated as Department D into the recently-established WVHA on 16 March 1942. The economic exploitation of non-Jewish prisoners was now accorded top priority. Simultaneously, however, the murder of European Jews in the IKL's two extermination camps (Auschwitz and Majdanek) became systematic; SS doctors and members of the commandant staff selected around 80 per cent Jews arriving at Auschwitz for immediate death. Those deemed fit to work toiled in Auschwitz or its many satellite camps until exhausted. Only in late autumn 1944 did the SS leadership halt the extermination programme, by which time at least 1.2 million people – including around 1 million Jews – had been murdered.[37]

Meanwhile, Oswald Pohl, head of the WVHA, saw no way to enforce the exploitation of inmates for the armaments industry with the current SS personnel in charge. In summer 1942 he therefore carried out a reshuffle of commandants in which a third of the incumbents were replaced. The new appointees came either from the concentration camp SS or the SS Death's Head Division. With this, the 'inner' and 'outer' front separation in force at the beginning of the war was collapsed; a majority of the SS leaders from the Death's Head Division had taken part in the war (almost all had been wounded in the 'Demjansk pocket') and now returned to concentration camp duty in the summer of 1942. Seven men from the leadership corps of the SS Death's Head Division became commandants in the second half of the war, at times comprising a third of incumbent commandants. The social network of the concentration camp SS, developed in the mid-1930s, had not sundered despite the despatching of its members to the 'outer front'. Contrary to the later protestations of some commandants, this return to the 'inner front' was in no sense fortuitous, but reflected their interpersonal and patronage network of the previous decade.[38]

The history of the concentration camps in the second half of the war shows clearly that the reshuffled commandant group was unable to enforce the new axiom of economic exploitation of inmates. The attempt to turn the camps into a well-organised and functional reservoir of labour for the armaments industry failed. It led instead to an enormous expansion of the camp system, with hundreds of satellite camps for assorted private and state-owned enterprises, accompanied by a catastrophic decline in living standards and a soaring mortality rate. But, as a result of their long service in the camps, the concentration camp SS (including Pohl's new commandants) seemed neither willing nor able to enforce the new line. Maltreatment and chicanery, violence and death: these were still the defining features of incarceration. Nor did corruption and personal enrichment wane, but remained a key symptom of the system and even increased. Pohl's commandants and the SS proved wholly incapable of effectively organising vast armament complexes of 10,000 and more workers.

The question of the motivation of Nazi perpetrators is, as the Goldhagen debate showed, just as fiercely discussed as it is inconclusive among historians and the public. Theoretically-driven explanatory models prove one-dimensional and are seldom supported by empirical studies. Essential to assessing motivation on a plausible empirical basis is the survival of significant subjective material for the actors. This is sparse indeed for the concentration camp SS. Contemporary documents with subjective content are rare and the explanations volunteered in court by the subjects are wanting in both quality and quantity, especially as regards their careers and the motivation behind their actions.[39] Insofar as motives can be distilled, they must come inferentially from the mosaic of witness testimony and the men's statements in post-war proceedings, together with the findings of historical research, information about the reality of camp life, and hence the concrete behaviour of the concentration camp SS.

Undoubtedly decisive for their behaviour was the dense social network of the concentration camp SS, to which they owed their rise. Relatively early in the 1930s, the SS leadership of camps Dachau, Buchenwald and Sachsenhausen formed a network of professional/specialist and personal relationships which came to dominate staffing policy in later years, and acted as a point of reference and orientation. Over time, the members of the concentration camp SS grew into a faction that, although divided by cliques, nevertheless became ever more thickly entangled. It was held together by criminality, through ongoing duty in the concentration camps, through jointly-devised and applied methods of torture and death, and through shared complicity in the murder of hundreds of thousands of people.

Further components of the network were corruption and enrichment, quarrels and intrigues, animosity and malice, bigotry and stupidity. The whole set-up was cushioned by approving superiors, who rewarded their men with promotions and decorations, and by the men's wives and children, who lived at the scene of their crimes and whose presence created stability and suggested 'normality'.

Through their shared duties and professional socialisation, conceptions of how to run and camp and treat its prisoners took shape. Ultimately, the men we are studying turned a group consensus into murderous reality: to name but the most important principles, that 'criminals' and 'asocials' were to be 'kept safe' in the concentration camps, that ill and debilitated prisoners were a 'burden' to be disposed of, that 'Russian commissars' – alleged to have killed Germans in barbarous ways – were to be 'executed', that Jews were to be 'eradicated'.

The members of the concentration camp SS primarily drew their motivation and rationale not from books, ideological schooling or intellectual analysis. Decisive instead was 'healthy common sense' (*gesunder Menschenverstand*). 'Healthy common sense' or 'everyday common sense' captures the reliance of (historical) agents on principles deemed 'normal' in their community, the validity of which was unquestioned and which could be reflexively applied. An alternative explanation that resorts to a theoretical maxim of norms anchored outside the group appears as unnecessary as it is dubious. Under National Socialism a dreadful meaning was applied to 'healthy common sense', as monitored in countless personnel files where it was typically registered with the phrase 'present'. It should be understood as a code for the racist and antisemitic consensus of the concentration camp SS, reflexively governing the actions of its members. This connection is an important key to understanding them.

Desiderata for further research would include studies of all those groups of perpetrators about whom our knowledge remains marginal, but this is likely to be precluded by the available source material. Worthwhile – and achievable on the basis of trial records – would be detailed analyses of the network of power relationships within the protective custody area of individual camps, between the SS men and prisoner functionaries. After all, this relationship partly governed the prisoners' prospects of survival. Finally, significant for the notion of a gender-specific development of violence would be a comparison between female camp guards and SS men. But independent of the precise research hypothesis, it seems axiomatic that the empirical findings of historians should be allied to the theoretical approaches of the social sciences, because this alone allows the construction of plausible – and possibly group-specific – explanations for the behaviour of the SS in the concentration camps.

Translated by Christopher Dillon

Notes

1 For older approaches to the psycho-historical research see G. M. Gilbert, *The Psychology of Dictatorship: Based on an Examination of the Leaders of Nazi Germany*, New York: Ronald, 1950; E. A. Cohen, *Human Behaviour in the Concentration Camp*, London: Free Association Books, 1954, pp. 211–76; H. V. Dicks, *Licensed Mass Murder: A Sociopsychological Study of Some SS Killers*, New York: Basic Books, 1972.

2 T. Segev, *Soldiers of Evil: The Commandants of the Nazi Concentration Camps*, New York: McGraw Hill, 1988.

3 Ibid. p. 316.

4 W. Sofsky, *The Order of Terror: The Concentration Camp*, Princeton, NJ: Princeton University Press, 1997.

5 C. R. Browning, *Ordinary Men. Reserve Police Battalion 101 and the Final Solution in Poland*, New York: Harper Collins, 1992; U. Herbert, *Best. Biographische Studien über Radikalismus, Weltanschauung und Vernunft 1903–1989*, Bonn: Dietz, 1996; M. Wildt, *Generation des Unbedingten. Das Führungskorps des Reichssicherheitshauptamtes*, Hamburg: Hamburger Edition, 2002; D. J. Goldhagen, *Hitler's Willing Executioners: Ordinary Germans and the Holocaust*, New York: Alfred A. Knopf, 1996.

6 Bundesarchiv Berlin (BAB), Slg, Schumacher/329, Liste der Konzentrationslager und ihrer Belegung vom 1. und 15.1.1945. The figures take into account the commandant staff as well as the guard personnel.

7 In concentration camp Ravensbrück this division only existed from 1941 onwards. See B. Strebel, *Das KZ Ravensbrück. Geschichte eines Lagerkomplexes*, Paderborn: Schöningh, 2003, p. 50, pp. 88–91.

8 Two perpetrator groups are excluded here; the camp medical staff and female guards.

9 Additionally there was a guard troop for the periodically-planned but never-realised camp Hamburg-Fühlsbüttel (Hansa). M. Broszat, 'The Concentration Camps 1933–45', in H. Krausnick and M. Broszat, *Anatomy of the SS State*, Reading: Granada, 1982, pp. 141–249, here p.186.

10 Compare in more detail B. Wegner, *The Waffen-SS: Organisation, Ideology and Function*, Oxford: Basil Blackwell, 1990.

11 For detail see ibid, pp. 106–7.

12 C. W. Sydnor, *Soldiers of Destruction: The SS Death's Head Division 1933–1945*, Princeton, NJ: Princeton University Press, 1990, p. 34. The headcount of the SS-

Totenkopfverbände in the 1939 budget was 15,496: K. Drobisch and and G. Wieland, *System der NZ-Konzentrationslager 1933–1939*, Berlin: Akademie Verlag, 1993, p. 338.

13 Compare Wegner, *Waffen-SS*, pp. 106–19.

14 The basis of their conscription was the 'Emergency Service Order' of 15 October 1938; Reichsgesetzblatt 1938, Teil I, S. 1441.

15 See Sydnor, *Soldiers of Destruction*.

16 Glücks was appointed retroactively on 18.11.1939. BAB/BDC, Pa. Glücks, SSO, Ernennungsurkunde. In the interim, head of the SS Main Officer August Heißmeyer directed the IKL; Broszat, 'Concentration Camps', p.205.

17 H. Buchheim, 'The SS – Instrument of Domination', in H. Buchheim *et al.*, *Anatomy of the SS State*, London: Collins, 1982, here esp. p. 270; Broszat, 'Concentration Camps', p. 205.

18 The term 'Waffen-SS' emerged in the winter of 1939/40 and replaced the older terms for armed SS-units (thus '*Verfügungstruppe*' and '*Totenkopfverbaende*'). Wegner, *Waffen-SS*, pp. 127–9.

19 Compare in more detail Buchheim, 'The SS', pp. 172–87.

20 See for example M. Kárný, 'Waffen-SS und Konzentrationslager', *Jahrbuch für Geschichte 33*, 1986, 231–61.

21 The female concentration camp wardens have hitherto been analysed primarily on structural-historical *Fragestellungen*. See for example G. Schwarz, 'SS Aufseherinnen in nationalsozialistischen Konzentrationslagern (1933–1945)', *Dachauer Hefte* 10, 1994, 32–49.

22 B. Perz, 'Wehrmacht und KZ-Bewachung', *Mittelweg* 36,1995, no. 4, 69–82, here 80.

23 B. Perz, '"… müssen zu reißenden Bestien erzogen werden. Der Einsatz von Hunden zur Bewachung in den Konzentrationslagern"', *Dachauer Hefte* 12,1996, 39–58.

24 Studies about single camp complexes also reach this dispiriting conclusion again and again. Compare most recently Strebel, *Das KZ*, p. 89.

25 The Polish historian Aleksander Lasik has attempted a historical-demographic analysis of the SS-*Wachsturmbann* for Auschwitz, but it is not methodologically convincing and is lacking a *Fragestellung* beyond the statistics. For a brief summary, see A. Lasik, 'Historical-Social Profile of the Auschwitz SS', in Y. Gutmann and M. Berenbaum (eds), *Anatomy of the Auschwitz Death Camp*, Bloomington, IN: Indiana University Press, 1994, pp. 271–87.

26 Eicke introduced this classification to concentration camp Dachau in 1934; see J. Tuchel, *Konzentrationslager. Organisationsgeschichte und Funktion der 'Inspektion der Konzentrationslager' 1934–38*, Boppard: Harald Boldt Verlag, 1991, pp. 148, 151–2; Broszat, 'Concentration Camps', pp. 181–4. For the role of these different departments, see G. Morsch, 'Organisations- und Verwaltungsstruktur der Konzentrationslager', in W. Benz and B. Distel (eds), *Der Ort des Terrors*, Band 1, Munich: C. H. Beck, 2005, pp. 58–75.

27 Those camps, which the WVHA took over as state-owned concentration camps in 1943 were an exception. In the concentration camps in the Baltic States and in the concentration camp Kraków-Plaszów, the enforcement of the inner camp structure only happened very slowly. For the internal structure of the numerous *Außenlager*, see K. Orth, *Die Konzentrationslager-SS*, Munich: dtv, 2004, pp. 53–4.

28 Figures according to Drobisch and Wieland, *System*, p. 275.

29 For the following discussion, see Orth, *Konzentrationslager-SS*, pp. 93–305. The discussion is based on the biographical analysis of the background and career of some 288 concentration camp commandants and heads of department (excluding camp doctors); see ibid., pp. 59–60, p. 87.

30 See H. Kaienburg, '*Vernichtung durch Arbeit*'. *Der Fall Neuengamme*, Bonn: Dietz, 1990, pp. 156–7, 343–5; I. Sprenger, *Groß-Rosen. Ein Konzentrationslager in Schlesien*, Cologne: Boehlau, 1996, pp. 98–100; Strebel, *Das KZ*, pp. 64–6; A. E. Wenck,

Zwischen Menschenhandel und 'Endlösung'. Das Konzentrationslager Bergen-Belsen, Paderborn: Schoeningh, 2000, pp. 106, pp. 115–17, 137.

31 See for example Segev, *Soldiers*, p. 267, 291.
32 Figures according to Drobisch and Wieland, *System*, p. 195, 257.
33 The concentration camp Ravensbrück seems to have had a similar function for the higher female guards (*Oberaufseherinnen*) and groups of female wardens.
34 See also G. Schwarz, *Eine Frau an seiner Seite. Ehefrauen in der 'SS-Sippengemeinschaft'*, Hamburg: Hamburger Edition, 1997.
35 Sofsky, *Order of Terror*.
36 Compare in more detail K. Orth, *Das System der nationalsozialistischen Konzentrationslager*, Hamburg: Hamburger Edition, 1999, pp. 131–41.
37 For numbers of victims and the discussion of the figures, compare F. Piper, *Die Zahl der Opfer von Auschwitz*, Oświęcim: Verlag Staatliches Museum in Oświęcim, 1993. See also M. Broszat (Ed.): *Rudolf Höß, Kommandant in Auschwitz* (Munich, 1992), pp. 163–4, note 1.
38 See for example Bundesarchiv Außenstelle Ludwigsburg, 405 AR 3681/65, Verfahren gegen Hassebroek, Beiheft, Bl. 10, Vernehmung des ehemaligen Kommandanten von Groß-Rosen Johannes Hassebroek, 16.3.1967; Staatsanwaltschaft beim Landgericht Frankfurt, Verfahren gegen Mulka u.a., 4 Ks 2/63, Bd. 42, Bl. 7462, Vernehmung des ehemaligen Kommandanten von Auschwitz Richard Baer, 30.12.1960.
39 For the fate of the *Konzentrationslager-SS* after the war and their testimony before the courts, see K. Orth, 'SS-Täter vor Gericht. Die strafrechtliche Verfolgung der Konzentrationslager-SS nach Kriegsende', in I. Wojak (ed.): *'Gerichtstag halten über uns selbst …'. Geschichte und Wirkung des ersten Frankfurter Auschwitz-Prozesses*, Frankfurt: Campus Verlag, 2001, pp. 43–60.

3 Social life in an unsocial environment

The inmates' struggle for survival

Falk Pingel

Over the last few years many of the former socialist countries have allowed researchers to work with archive material that hitherto had not been accessible, and at the same time gave them the freedom to choose topics no longer regarded as politically inappropriate or taboo. The result has been a number of studies that afford us a much deeper insight into various concentration camps.[1] Recently these individual studies have been supplemented by more comprehensive works which attempt to give an overall picture of the camps and their organization.[2] As far as the topic of this chapter is concerned, the research has certainly yielded a vast amount of new information: however, with a few exceptions, it has tended to focus on the structural and institutional aspects of the concentration camp and refrains from a more theoretical discussion concerning the social dimension that dominated inmates' daily life. Hence, it can be said that the literature has produced no fundamental changes in how we might evaluate the life-and-death struggle of the inmates and the limited opportunities they had for resistance. Nevertheless, the great merit of this recent research lies in the fact that it gives us a comprehensive history of individual camps, as well as describing in much greater detail the fate of inmates belonging to the lesser-documented categories – such as the Jehovah's Witnesses or women prisoners. Furthermore, it has revealed how the phenomenon of the concentration camp was able to expand and develop.

Outside Germany, there is a tendency to overlook the wide range of regional research projects into National Socialism, many of which have also been incorporated into the recent literature.[3] These studies have focused either on the initial period after the Nazis assumed power, at a time when the camps were expanding, or the last two years of the war, when the whole system finally collapsed. This emphasis on the beginning and the end has raised an important question. How can the historian possibly provide an overall account of the camp system from 1933 to 1945, embracing all the changes that affected the institutions themselves, the composition of camp populations and the reasons and objectives behind imprisonment, as well as detailing the horrendous living conditions and mortality rates that prevailed? In other words, can the criteria used for analysing the camp environment in Dachau in 1933 be applied equally to a study of conditions in Auschwitz-Birkenau in the year 1944? Earlier German research into the structure and development of the system had implicitly accepted that they could. But, as more and more biographical sources became available, and with the introduction of a sociological and ethnographic approach, doubts arose as to whether conditions in the death camps, with their extremely high mortality rates, could be adequately described and interpreted using the paradigms of structural and institutional historiography. Perhaps rules and regulations had already collapsed in these camps and the appalling conditions resulted rather from random factors that precluded any form of concerted counter-action. In such a case, where chaos prevails, any systematic analysis of events becomes impossible.[4] Although this point is often raised and discussed at conferences, it has never been seriously examined from a historical perspective. Instead the academic discussion has followed two other paths.

First, as far as the camp environment is concerned, the majority of more recent individual studies describe, in great detail, the adverse living conditions and the role of the SS in hastening the death of inmates. Often based on interviews and the reports of survivors, this technique of 'dense description' amassing a large amount of material is complemented by an analysis of institutional structures. However, since these studies are largely restricted to a certain region or often only examine one aspect of the camp environment, they tend to lack a comparative perspective. This makes it difficult to develop a theoretical framework for understanding camp life and finding answers to more general questions.

By contrast, the sociologist Wolfgang Sofsky adopted a different approach in which he defined the concentration camp as an autonomous unit in which the SS wielded absolute power but, at the same, delegated various responsibilities to favoured prisoners.[5] This model eschews the conventional dichotomy between the rulers and the enslaved, offering an explanation of why opposition or resistance became more difficult over time. In this system, the inmates who had been given certain responsibilities act as intermediaries. On the one hand, they can protect the mass of prisoners from excessive abuse (to what extent, however, has never been ascertained); on the other, they are a vicarious form of SS power and thus pose an ever-present threat to their fellow inmates. Sofsky's study incorporates the sociological approach adopted by early research from the post-war period, providing us with an overall theoretical framework to describe and understand the inner workings of camp life. Consequently, Sofsky constructs a static model of 'absolute power' which provides little room for an analysis of the changing social patterns and institutional structures of concentration camp society. For the most part his work is based on well-known reports from survivors who were imprisoned for their political leanings or their intellectual opposition to the regime. These accounts reflect the particular social and time perspective of educated people, who were mostly incarcerated during the war years and not only wanted to provide eye-witness accounts after liberation but also were able to write and to publish about their camp experience.

The following chapter attempts to give an interpretation of the camp environment in the light of recent research, focussing on studies conducted in German-speaking academia. It begins with an overview of the possibilities and chances for inmates to survive their incarceration. It then deals with research into specific conditions and how particular groups of prisoners reacted.

The development of the system of power (*Herrschaftssystem*) and inmate society

Life in the camps during the period when the Nazis were consolidating their power is relatively well documented as a result of eye-witness accounts from former inmates published in the 1930s – often after they had emigrated from Germany. But, with a few exceptions, no academic investigations were published until well into 1990s. Amongst others, the Sachsenhausen Memorial Site has published new material based on an exhaustive evaluation of records relating to inmates in Oranienburg.[6] This material provides evidence that the majority of prisoners came from the local area; many were acquainted with one another and shared either a common political background or had local ties that united them and transcended political differences. The inmates were relatively young, most of them belonging to the age-group 21–40. As might be expected, a classification according to occupation shows that, as a rule, they came from the working class. The statistics also reveal that the period of detention was relatively short, a matter of months rather than years. In the spring of 1933 most of the inmates were communists,[7] which probably explains why, in later years, communists were often successful in gaining positions of 'power' within the system. But in the second half of 1933, camp populations began to diversify. No longer were the inmates only political detainees; the Nazis began to incarcerate people they regarded as 'asocial' elements, for example the long-term unemployed, tramps, homosexuals and so on. From this point, we can register the influence of racism and eugenic theories on the selection process that decided who was considered 'less useful to society'. The number of Jewish detainees was still relatively small but, from the very beginning, they were individually targeted and usually segregated from the other inmates.

In 1938 and 1939, both Austria and parts of Czechoslovakia were annexed and occupied. The concentration camps became 'international', with an influx of detainees who were often not of German origin. In November 1938, the German government instigated an anti-Jewish pogrom, resulting in thousands of people being incarcerated in camps that were unable to cope with such an influx. The conditions were appalling,[8] and only improved once most of the detainees had been released after a few months. However, with the outbreak of war in 1939, tens of thousands of new prisoners were incarcerated, resulting in a camp society that fell into two groups – the 'veterans' and the 'newcomers'. This situation was to last until the final, chaotic collapse of the Nazi regime. With the advance of Germany into the Soviet Union in 1941 and the persecution of Jews in occupied Europe, the numbers in the camps rose at an alarming rate. Accommodation was totally inadequate; newcomers had no shelter, received very little food and lived in makeshift tents. The SS had devised no plan to cope with such conditions. It has become clear that, as the concentration camp system expanded, the mortality rate of the inmates increased. It was the 'newcomers' who suffered most. They were either murdered on arrival, worked to death or left to starve. In the period up to 1936, the conditions had been different; the camps had been structured and supervised more or less according to official regulations and decrees. In other words, a certain rule of order had obtained and the 'veterans' had tried to alleviate the conditions of camp life for the 'newcomers'. This form of solidarity began to crumble after 1936, as inmates began to form their own demarcated societies and affiliations. Membership of a certain group usually depended on pre-camp affiliations; those within the group could develop social bonds and so enjoyed an enhanced status in the camp and had a better chance of surviving.

During the war, the prisoners who came from occupied Europe were mostly classified by the SS as 'political' as a matter of administrative convenience, with the result that the designation was no longer clear evidence of previous political or resistance activity. Even though the absolute number of those detained on genuinely political grounds continued to increase, they formed a smaller proportion of inmates. Those who were politically involved before their detention or who could draw on experience in resistance organizations constituted a small core of communist/socialist or national/conservative inmates opposed to National Socialism. They formed themselves into opposition groups, recruiting, in particular, from German, French, Polish and Soviet prisoners, although the latter were usually classified as 'civilian workers' or 'prisoners of war'.

The prisoner functionaries – rivalry or solidarity?

The SS delegated responsibility for discipline to selected inmates who functioned as camp, block and barrack leaders. These functionaries were in charge of the day-to-day activities, implementing the orders that came from the SS. Those in charge of work details were known as 'Kapos'. Others were employed in an administrative capacity or in the camp kitchens and laundries, for example. Prior to the war, German political detainees, in particular, were eager to fill these positions, which afforded a degree of protection against the SS terror, and enabled them to improve living conditions, obtain extra rations or prevent members of their group being transferred to camps with a notoriously high mortality rate. In many camps the political detainees vied with those inmates – mostly German – who were categorized by the SS as 'common criminals' and repeat offenders whom the Nazis regarded as incurable and therefore liable for preventive detention in a concentration camp. During the war, as the policy of extermination gained ground, a bitter internal conflict between these two groups broke out.

The functionaries operated within a social network, having contact not only with the inmates (including with intimidation and violence through their superior position) but also with the SS (including dependency, bribes and resistance). Some also used their position to demand sexual favours from their fellow prisoners; a young inmate could by induced into a homosexual relationship by the offer of material rewards. They enjoyed certain privileges denied to the mass of prisoners: for example, admission to the camp brothels that were established during the war.

Within the camp the functionaries constituted a special 'elite', around 10 per cent of all the inmates.[9] As a result of the various privileges enjoyed by certain groups and categories of inmate, it becomes clear that a homogeneous society within the camps did not and could not exist, particularly since all power ultimately rested in the hands of the SS, who could impose restrictions or withdraw privileges at will. The system of functionaries led to more, rather than less, differentiation within camp society.

The inmates regarded the work of the politically organized functionaries in a positive light whenever they experienced direct benefits affecting their personal situation. For example, the functionaries often alleviated conditions in certain areas. They could, on occasion, prevent the arbitrary maltreatment and physical abuse of prisoners, or persuade the authorities to improve hygienic conditions in the sick-bays and hospital compounds – with direct results for those prisoners who had not yet succumbed totally to disease and exhaustion. In 1943, improvements of this kind were registered in many camps. However, they were also a result of a policy change in the SS Business and Administration Main Office (WVHA), the central institution then governing the camps, where a decision had been taken to organize the inmates' work force more efficiently. At the same time, this policy gave the politically organized functionaries more influence, since the SS knew quite well that the 'criminal faction', who had often been given preference over the 'politicals', were much less qualified to help in achieving the industrial output required by the WVHA.

As time wore on, the SS distanced itself from the daily running of the camps, due, in part, to a lack of personnel and also because they wished to avoid direct contact with the vast numbers of undernourished and disease-infested inmates. The functionaries were able to establish a quasi-autonomous room for manoeuvre which made them indispensable to the SS. Functionaries from the 'political' category argued that, by accepting positions of responsibility, they could ran things 'smoothly', maintain hygienic standards and reduce random and arbitrary abuse and violence on the part of the SS. They took a certain pride, grotesque as this may seem, in their abilities to run the camp and criticized other functionaries who did not live up to these 'standards'.[10] However, as a rule, they were only able to protect the members of their own group – above all to ensure their survival but also to maintain their status within the group. For most of the inmates it was not clear to what extent the functionaries were able – or even wanted – to alleviate the SS regime of terror. The inmates' contact with the SS became less frequent as the camps grew in size and it was the functionaries who were ever-present in their daily lives, at work and in their accommodation. The role of the SS was to organize and carry out the policy of extermination and they very often succeeded in making the functionaries accessories. 'It is striking how many inmates have only vague memories of the SS personnel but can vividly recall the intimidation and brutality of the individual functionaries who governed their daily routine.'[11] In court proceedings after the war, inmates were often able to give a much more detailed account of the violence they suffered at the hands of functionaries than the punishments meted out by the SS.[12]

By the winter of 1943/1944, as the end of the war approached, the supply situation worsened. Allied bombing began to have adverse effects on the industrial output of the camps and conditions became evermore chaotic, with each group concentrating increasingly on its own survival. In the autumn of 1944, Soviet advances led to the first camps in the east being closed down. Starving, emaciated prisoners were evacuated westwards by the Germans, and with their arrival the inmates were no longer able to gain any material benefits from the system of functionaries. Ruth Klüger, who was deported to Auschwitz-Birkenau aged 13, has identified a small elite in Auschwitz-Birkenau who were able to retain their position and wield some kind of influence, whilst the majority of 'normal' inmates were struggling to survive on a daily basis. Both the SS and the prisoners behaved in an arbitrary fashion, lacking any kind of coordination, as group cohesion and solidarity crumbled.[13] The historian Sylvija Kavčič, in her interviews with survivors from Ravensbrück, refers to this disintegration of collective structures when the interviewees talk about conditions in the hopelessly overcrowded camp: 'The situation resulted in everyone fighting for their own survival. Hardly anyone cared about what happened to the others.'[14]

These two extremes can be seen in Auschwitz. The brick-built barracks in the main camp, Auschwitz I, housed mostly non-Jewish, political detainees, who, as a rule, still received the official rations. Long-term Polish prisoners had organized effective resistance groups similar to those in Buchenwald, although here members ranged from right-wing nationalists to left-wing socialists and communists. The Jewish prisoners in Birkenau (Auschwitz II), by contrast, were crowded into draughty wooden huts, oppressively hot in the summer and freezing cold in the winter. They were constantly exposed to the threat of starvation, physical abuse and ultimate selection for the gas chambers. And yet, Auschwitz I and Auschwitz II were nominally under unified control; communication between both parts was possible, although for most prisoners it was impossible to move from one part of the camp to the other. This scenario epitomizes the situation that had existed in most camps since the beginning of the war. After the liberation of Buchenwald, for instance, two American soldiers, Fleck and Tenenbaum, submitted a report in which they described the so-called 'small camp' as a nightmare with intolerable and indescribable conditions. However, in the main camp they found solidly built accommodation, clean and 'OK'.[15]

Michael Wildt, commenting on Dieter Pohl and Christoph Dieckmann, who have undertaken a thorough analysis of life in camps situated in the Eastern occupied territories, concludes that the criteria used to describe death camps like Auschwitz, Majdanek and others in the East cannot be applied to those concentration camps situated on German territory which were not primarily involved in the extermination programme. Camps in the occupied East, he claims, were subjected to much more radical measures, including arbitrary killing, murder and the extermination of whole population groups, either for political or racial reasons. At the same time, various organizations and factions within the German administration were competing with each other to achieve their own objectives.[16] This analysis is undoubtedly valid for the camps in the East. However, once certain categories of prisoner had survived long enough, they began to organize themselves along the same lines as those that existed in the camps within Germany's original borders.[17] But after September 1939, older camps like Dachau, Sachsenhausen and Buchenwald also underwent changes. Some sections remained stable, while others descended into chaos, as in 'the East', with no semblance of discipline or order. The fate of the inmates was to die, through starvation, physical abuse, lack of medical attention or total apathy. They were unable to fend for themselves or react to SS commands.[18]

'Death or survival depended on whether you had shoes' ('La mort commence par les souliers') is how the French historian Robert Steegmann put it in his study of the Struthof camp in Alsace.[19] His approach is remarkable for its directness and explicitness, offering a history that covers both the inmates' daily lives and the institutional structure of the camp; at the same time he refrains from any kind of evaluation or value-judgement. His study differs from German research not only in style but also in its use of numerous statistics to underpin the text. Steegmann tries to show the background against which decisions affecting the living conditions of the inmates were taken. He relies heavily on statistical evidence when he refers to mortality rates to answer the question: 'Which prisoners died, and why?'[20] Here he introduces various factors such as category of prisoner, age, period of detention and so on. The results confirm a number of conclusions which appear in research published by myself. These, however, have not yet been corroborated owing to a lack of new evidence – but they do suggest that in the first years of the war the inmates belonging to the category of 'homosexuals' or 'asocials' whom the SS classified as 'racially inferior' had a much higher death rate than the 'political' prisoners. This situation was partly reversed from 1942 onwards. Most of the 'racially inferior' group had been decimated and there were few new arrivals in this category, which resulted in a statistical increase in mortality rates for the new 'political' detainees. Inmates with a green ('criminal') or pink ('homosexual') triangular identification mark were now a relative minority; they were the 'veterans' who were familiar with camp life and who had gained enough experience to more or less avoid any direct intimidation from the SS. However, now there was a new influx of 'political' detainees (denoted with a red triangle) – fresh, new and inexperienced inmates whose classification as political detainees was often based on rather vague criteria, since they came from different countries, varying social backgrounds and had various political leanings, often with no connection to any kind of anti-fascist activity. These developments led to a decline in social and political cohesion, with the result that the group as a whole was weakened. The statistical material contained in Steegmann's study serves to emphasize the observations and descriptions in accounts published shortly after the liberation of the camps. Inmates who lived through the first three months – and all the more so those who were still alive after the first year – had an above-average chance of surviving their incarceration, at least until the final chaotic period when the whole social structure within the camps began to disintegrate yet again.

The role of individual functionaries and how they behaved was a central aspect of many post-war trials. Lutz Niethammer and his research team have presented findings on Buchenwald that have had a great impact. Their book dealt with the Soviet trials of communist functionaries in Buchenwald, describing in detail how the various groups within the camp fought for supremacy. We learn that communist inmates used their power and influence to prevent other political groups from occupying functionary positions: for example, by manipulating the lists of names for transport to other camps and thereby endangering the lives of their fellow-prisoners. However, the trial records also reveal the limitations of functionary influence and power. A communist inmate could be concealed in the hospital compound, an area that the SS avoided as far as possible; but if the party comrade also happened to be Jewish, the risk was often deemed too great.[21] This example shows that SS racial doctrines had already affected and altered behaviour patterns within inmate society.

Cases like this show how equivocal the post-war communist interpretation of prisoner self-administration was. Initially, the Soviets put forward the theory that the functionary system constituted a core of resistance within the camp confines that benefited everybody, no matter what their background. But it soon became clear that this idealistic interpretation was subject to the whims of Stalin and the *diktat* of expediency. The Soviet military administration began to brand certain former communist functionaries as collaborators who had betrayed the Party and were responsible for the deaths of their fellow-comrades. For some communist functionaries, liberation from Buchenwald ended in imprisonment in a GULag. The German Democratic Republic adopted the same approach in subsequent trials. Camp functionaries who had been former members of the KPD were accused of making the wrong decision by accepting positions in the prisoner self-administration and thus assisting the SS in the commission of crimes. After the death of Stalin, the situation changed yet again; the accomplices were now rehabilitated as resistance fighters. The circumstances of the post-war concentration camp trials within the Soviet bloc show only too clearly how difficult and arbitrary it was, and perhaps still is, to interpret patterns of behaviour within camp society. The decisions and actions of individuals, for good or ill, mattered little. What mattered was how such actions might be interpreted within the internecine struggle of a communist doctrine and a Soviet hegemony facing the Cold War.

Today there is still no consensus on how the behaviour of politically organized inmate groups should be judged.[22] Norbert Frei and others stress the 'the inmates' strong will to survive and the resulting social cohesion within the group',[23] whereas Niethammer's research emphasizes the problems that arose for the group itself and for those who were excluded. In his concluding remarks concerning the aims of the KPD group in Buchenwald, Niethammer attempts to evaluate the different levels at which they operated. In his opinion, the KPD group was 'a team working collectively in order to survive … It actively sought to form alliances … imposed discipline within the camp and maintained standards of hygiene as far as possible.'[24] Any ethical evaluation of the work of such groups depends on the research perspective. The divergence in such evaluations is evidence of the dilemma which faced the prisoners themselves. Under the circumstances it was almost impossible to act in a way that benefited both individuals and the camp population as a whole.

Fragments of a 'closed society'

The controversies and conflicts surrounding the delegation of power reflect tactics and strategies resulting from beliefs that the inmates had adopted before their incarceration. The internal political wrangling characteristic of the various factions of the communist movement could also be found in other groups. These conflicts, frequently aggravated by differences in social status, were continued and often redefined within the camps. Prisoners with a working class background often distanced themselves from those with a professional or intellectual background, since the latter were regarded as weak, inexperienced and unable to cope with the harsh realities of camp life, often making mistakes and blunders that singled them out for maltreatment and abuse by the SS. This kind of deeply held prejudice could even be found within a particular group and was often enhanced by the brutal surroundings in which the prisoners now found themselves. The intellectual was branded as being 'no good for class warfare' – in other words, as someone who had theories but no idea how to put them into practice under camp conditions. Politically organized inmates began to shun and isolate those prisoners who wore a red triangle identification mark and yet had no party affiliations and refused to cooperate with the groups in the camp.[25] For those who were organized, the red triangle helped to preserve their pre-camp identity and to promote solidarity in the group.

The category of the 'political' detainee has always been an important feature of witness testimony as well as academic research. This group is much better documented than any other category. Many of the Nazi registration files from camps in which the 'politicals' comprised a majority have become available. In contrast, there is little material dealing with categories that were less common, for example, the 'homosexuals', who were particularly stigmatized.[26] Only recently have witnesses from this group testified to their persecution. And for the largest group of victims, the Jews who were murdered in Auschwitz, Majdanek and other death camps, there is still relatively little eye-witness documentation of their fate, due to the very low survival rate and the difficult conditions that prevailed in the immediate post-war period. On the other hand, we now have the findings of research that investigates the sufferings of 'peripheral' groups which have hitherto been more or less ignored, meaning that the fate of the 'politicals' is no longer the predominant narrative. Amongst these is the exhaustive study conducted by the Auschwitz State Museum concerning the so-called 'gypsy camp', which housed Sinti and Roma until their extermination in the gas chambers.[27] Wolfgang Ayaß is one of the very few who have investigated the persecution of another 'peripheral' group often ignored by mainstream research, namely the 'asocials' (marked by a black triangle in the camp).[28] In his comprehensive study he points out that they were more or less regarded as outcasts by the 'politicals'. The SS had branded this group as 'genetically deficient', a stigmatization that was adopted by the politically organized groups. Evidence shows that the 'politicals' regarded the 'asocials' as undisciplined, unhygienic and rowdy. Members of the 'asocial' group had often had a prison record before being detained in a concentration camp, and once inside their social and family relationships were completely destroyed. Inmates who had no contact with the outside world – even a notional contact – soon despaired of any kind of future; as a consequence the 'asocials' were adrift in camp society and, for the most part, isolated, receiving hardly any support from the other inmates.

We still need more thorough and exhaustive investigations of the plight of Jewish inmates – and their reactions.[29] From 1944 onwards, the number of Jewish prisoners incarcerated in camps situated within Germany's original borders increased. But documentation for this period is particularly scarce, since the camps expanded so rapidly, resulting in the disintegration of established structures and units. During this phase, Jews were frequently transported from one camp to another, spending little time in any one place and thus making it difficult to trace their movements. Jewish inmates occupied the lowest position in the camp hierarchy; they could rarely avoid heavy manual labour and few were able to attain a functionary position. Recent studies on satellite camps with a high Jewish population have shown that they had little chance to engage in any form of organized activity. There was a much greater variation in nationality, social background and political affiliation than in other groups – the only bond they shared was their 'Jewishness', the reason for which they had been incarcerated. It is therefore all the more remarkable, as some studies have discovered, that under these extreme conditions some semblance of religious life was possible, although examples are few and far between.[30] Whereas the fate of individual Jewish inmates belonging to socialist or communist groups is well documented, there is still not much material, at least in German research, that explains the significance of religion and membership of a religious community for the mass of Jewish prisoners.

German research focusing on the role of religion in the camps has been almost exclusively concerned with the two most important Christian denominations, namely the Protestants and the Catholics. Mention is often made of the Jehovah's Witnesses, who suffered intimidation and torture for their unshakeable beliefs – but for a long time there was no comprehensive research into their status as a separate group. The merit of recent studies of the Witnesses lies in the fact that they analyse sources relating directly to this group, rather than relying on accounts and interpretations emanating from other inmates.[31] Jehovah's Witnesses were rarely appointed as functionaries – and there is almost no record of them abusing their fellow inmates. What does become clear is their extreme group solidarity and the strength of their convictions, which manifested itself in certain forms of resistance like their refusal to do military service or use the 'Heil Hitler' greeting. Inmates from other groups often expressed admiration for this kind of obduracy. At the same time they also distanced themselves from the Jehovah's Witnesses, since such intransigence often led to brutal punishments. There was a general feeling that idealism had no place in the harsh realities of camp life, which demanded compromise in every situation. As a result, the group was virtually isolated and had little influence on the other prisoners, who lacked the inner convictions that enabled the Jehovah's Witnesses to practise their form of resistance to SS hegemony. This example shows how difficult it was to establish any kind of solidarity that might permeate the whole of camp society. Any direct initiative in this direction would invariably be registered and sabotaged by the SS. The alternative lay in clandestine, illegal cooperation, resulting in groups that relied heavily on the psychological and material interdependency of the members. These are the factors that made certain groups powerful but also, by definition, prevented them from influencing the overall population.

Nationality continued to play an important role in the camps. According to its racial ideology, the SS often treated inmates from North-Western Europe better than those who came from the East. As a rule, at least the larger national groups were housed in separate barracks. This resulted in the formation of social groups based on a common language or nationality that would enable the development of social relations. Solidarity in this form was particularly evident during the early years of the war.[32]

The fate of children in the concentration camps has sometimes been described in biographies that are often prescribed reading in schools.[33] But, surprisingly, children as a group have rarely been the subject of serious research. It is a little known fact that the number of camp children increased significantly during the last phase of the war, a phenomenon that merits much closer attention from historians.

The proportion of adolescents and children (normally defined in the literature as persons under 18 years of age) increased during the war, as the evacuation and extermination of Jewish populations gained momentum in the concentration camps situated in the East. As early as 1941/42, whole families, including the youngsters, were being transported to Auschwitz. From 1943, we find evidence that non-Jewish children in Auschwitz were integrated into the camp structure and housed in special 'children's compounds'. The numbers increased significantly when the Hungarian Jews began to arrive in Auschwitz in May 1944.[34] It is still unclear how children managed to evade selection for the gas chambers; many may have acted on their own initiative (for example, by trying to appear more healthy and robust or by claiming to be older, as Ruth Klüger did on the advice of a fellow prisoner); equally, the SS may have been more lax in the selection procedure owing to the huge influx of new arrivals and the requirement for more workers. Another possibility is that the SS had adopted a different policy with regard to children, who earlier had either been excluded from incarceration altogether or who had been consigned to the gas chambers immediately on arrival. Many pregnant women in the transports subsequently gave birth in the camp; the infants, however, were usually murdered shortly after birth. We have no evidence that the SS followed a policy of 'Germanization' of children after incarceration, although this was practised outside the camps when female forced labourers had children. Their offspring were often put into special children's homes, with survival rates that were extremely low. In Auschwitz, those under the age of 14 were not required to work.

Many children led lives 'independent' of their parents and supervisors, fending for themselves as early as 4–6 years old.[35]

In 1944, in camps with a large Jewish population, there was a significant fall in the average age of inmates. In Kaufering and Mühldorf, two satellite camps of Dachau that housed Hungarian Jews, the youngest inmates were 13 to 14 years old. In Kaufering and Mühldorf the largest group consisted of those born between 1926 and 1930 – followed by those born between 1906 and 1920, who represented the 'veteran' component. Most of these inmates had been incarcerated before 1943/44, managing to carve out a niche for survival. Those who came after had experienced only instability, being moved from one camp to another under horrific conditions, and thus had no chance to establish themselves in a camp hierarchy.[36]

Statistical analysis has shown that the mortality rate of female prisoners was frequently lower than that of males. This has led to the hypothesis that women were much better equipped to withstand the awful conditions because solidarity amongst females was greater and they were less likely to succumb to the squalor of camp life.[37] This is still a controversial subject, since the factors influencing the behaviour of inmates cannot be viewed in isolation. It is difficult to make valid comparisons, because female prisoners were separated and housed in their own camps or compounds. The lower mortality rate can often be attributed to the fact that they were given different work assignments from men. Assembly-line work in factories rather than heavy, outdoor manual-labour was the rule. It could be that both the SS and the industrial companies which benefited from slave labour were in agreement on how best to exploit the female workforce, resulting in more favourable living conditions for women. But this was not always the case. In the women's camp in Auschwitz-Birkenau, industrial companies had less influence and we have no evidence that the SS treated the female inmates differently from the male population in the rest of the camp. In the accounts of survivors from camps like these, there is no clear indication that an enhanced social cohesion existed amongst female prisoners.[38]

However, we do find exceptions; for example, when social and family ties which had existed before incarceration remained intact, as was the case in the so-called family compounds in Auschwitz or Bergen-Belsen. Inmates have reported that women recovered from the shock of imprisonment much more rapidly, very soon taking on responsibility for their family, whereas men succumbed more easily to the chaos and the lack of hygiene and food, abdicating any form of responsibility for what might befall them. We also have reports from other camps where women incarcerated with relations and family still nurtured some sort of hope for the future; by maintaining these ties they were more likely to survive than their male counterparts. It seems that the men who were in contact with their families or who still had communication with the outside world experienced much greater difficulties in adjusting to daily life within the concentration camps. They tried to subdue their feelings and emotions, in the belief that such behaviour would weaken their ability to survive the harsh conditions. This kind of interpretation seems highly plausible, conforming as it does to general, gender-specific behaviour patterns. Nevertheless, to date we have neither interviews nor reports from survivors on this subject, nor even a methodical approach that might confirm such a theory.

Studies concerning female inmates belonging to the 'asocial' category date back to the 1990s. Based on interviews with survivors, they provide a valuable contribution to our appreciation of how pre-camp experience, both social and political, affected their behaviour and social organization after incarceration. In contrast to the 'politicals', these women felt isolated and excluded from any kind of group affiliation – to much the same degree as their male counterparts in the same category. The social ostracism they had experienced in earlier life continued within the camps and frequently persisted even after liberation.[39]

Language in a society suffering from linguistic paralysis

One of the more recent fields of research into daily life in the concentration camps is concerned with the cultural and linguistic means of communication amongst inmates.[40] No documentation and interpretation of 'camp language' can ever be exhaustive, since there is simply not enough material at our disposal. Variations in camp conditions and populations also make it virtually impossible to identify a common 'dialect' or 'idiom'. Inmate accounts usually do not reflect their camp idiom, because survivors did not describe their experiences in retrospect by using the same sort of language employed in the camp, language that was characterized by short, sharp commands and responses. Any description of the horrors of camp life, any description of the valiant attempts to resist SS brutality will certainly include fragments of 'camp dialect', but will necessarily transcend the primitive form of communication that prevailed between perpetrators and victims and amongst the victims themselves. In their post-war accounts the survivors were only too ready to shake off the restrictions in communication that camp life had imposed. It is for this reason that the early reports often use highly emotional language; only later did the style become more factual and descriptive. The language actually spoken in the camps is rendered, if at all, in quoted speech.[41]

Camp language reflects the hierarchy of power and social life within the camp itself. It comprises the specialist jargon that was used by both the SS and the inmates. German was the predominant language, the language of oppression, and so here the inmates had to acquire some rudimentary knowledge in order to understand the alien environment in which they found themselves. But when various nationalities were incarcerated in the same camp, terms and expressions from other languages were often used. In Auschwitz, for instance, camp language incorporated many Polish expressions (German words, like '*organisieren*' or '*Muselmann*' were translated into Polish)[42] and Polish was also the clandestine language of resistance. In 1944, Jewish inmates from Hungary in some of the satellite camps even managed to establish their own Hungarian idiom as the dominant language in the daily struggle to survive.[43] In some Mauthausen satellite camps, the so-called 'Spanish veterans' exerted a similar influence. This phenomenon of multilingualism was not conducive to communication and resistance. The struggle about power and the dominant language among the inmates only widened the gulf between the 'rulers', all of whom spoke the ruling language, and the oppressed, who often had difficulties in understanding commands and orders of their oppressors.

As a rule, any communication was restricted to the bare necessities of life, particularly when dealing with the SS, whom inmates tried to avoid as often as possible. It tended to be one-sided; dialogue was rarely possible. The prisoners were given short, sharp commands by the SS and these were to be acknowledged in a similar fashion, verbally – or more frequently non-verbally. Any form of emotional response to the command was best avoided. The SS liked to degrade and abuse their victims, who were then expected to subject themselves to this kind of verbal torture in silence. By addressing inmates with numbers, rather than with their names, the SS tried to eradicate the individual personality of their prisoners. The grammar of camp language became nominal, in the linguistic sense. Complex sentences were shunned. One word, normally a noun or a verb, was enough to convey meaning – and a misunderstanding on the part of the inmates might have fatal consequences.

This linguistic paradigm can be observed in the way inmates communicated with each other. Their everyday life consisted in the transmission of orders, commands or advice on how to deal with an immediate problem. There was no time to think or reflect, even less to express some kind of emotional response. The behaviour associated with a civilized society, for example politeness, the shaking of hands or simple greetings, was scorned. In the concentration camps linguistic expediency ruled. Those who transgressed this rule had obviously not understood how camp life functioned – they still lived in a pre-camp world espousing codes of conduct that no longer existed in an environment where only the fittest could survive. New arrivals, in particular those from a middle-class background, found it extremely difficult to cope with these unwritten rules concerning camp communication. If they failed to adapt in a relatively short time, they inevitably succumbed to the pressure exerted by both the SS and the inmate community. In many situations it was extremely dangerous to indulge in dialogue, because the SS would invariably interpret this as a form of resistance. Most prisoners shunned any kind of linguistic solidarity with their fellow inmates.

The terminology used by the SS to cover up their criminal activities in the camps was adopted by inmates, particularly the functionaries. The research team led by Niethammer found typical SS expressions in the interrogation records of the post-war communist trials of KPD functionaries in Buchenwald.[44] As a rule, the accused did not use the word 'kill' (*töten*) but preferred to use SS terms like '*abspritzen*' when referring to the lethal injections administered to the weak and the sick in the hospital compounds. The use of such euphemisms is a clear indication that normal language was totally inadequate to describe camp life and that traditional ethical and legal criteria developed within a civilized society were inapplicable in the concentration camp environment. Accordingly, those who attempted to escape from the camp were branded – they were no longer regarded as 'comrades', a highly equivocal term amongst prisoners under any circumstances; instead they were labelled as troublemakers and miscreants, even in statements made after the liberation, since such action often resulted in collective punishments that affected all the inmates. These consequences were even cited as justification for the fact that functionaries betrayed escape plans to the SS authorities. The values and morals of the individual were replaced by a 'camp ethos', in which the term 'comrade' took on a different meaning: to succumb to the rules of a society bound together by coercion, not solidarity. This decline in any normal, civilized social cohesion and the willingness to adopt the euphemistic language employed by the SS are also evident in the way in which colloquial expressions from normal life were given new meanings and connotations. After the war began the mortality rate increased; the inmates who were left to starve were referred to as 'invalids' or '*Muselmänner*'.[45] The SS preferred to use the first term, whereas the second was the most common expression employed by inmates.

Using and understanding camp language was an important factor in the struggle for survival. At the same time, those inmates who had managed to adjust to camp life had a chance to gain access to clandestine groups in which 'normal, pre-camp' communication was possible. The communist groups, for example, continued to use 'party jargon' during their discussions. The Jehovah's Witnesses and other religious groups conversed amongst each other as before, often using an encoded form of communication. This, of course, could only happen when they were not within earshot of either the SS or unreliable functionaries. We do find examples of a secret, conspiratorial language used in the camps but these are exceptions to the rule, developed only when something 'illegal' was being planned, such as meetings, discussion groups or an attempt to requisition more food ('*organisieren*', in the camp idiom).

One of the original aims of the concentration camps was 're-education', or so the propaganda would have us believe. This necessitated the establishment of camp libraries, which for some inmates were a source of intellectual stimulation. In the older camps, situated within Germany's original borders, the political detainees, who often administered such libraries, managed to smuggle in books that the Nazis and the SS had banned. The premises were often used for illegal, clandestine meetings.[46]

Some inmates tried to cope with their incarceration and to document camp life by producing sketches and drawings portraying their daily misery. However, the SS understood how to misuse the inmates' artistic talents. They singled out musicians who were then forced to perform in the 'camp orchestra'. This is another example of the grotesque charade that the SS introduced to mask the true nature of the camps. The musicians had to play music as inmates trudged out to their slave-labour assignments and then 'welcome' them 'home' when they returned. They also provided 'background music' for speeches by camp commandants or, even more despicable, they were required to play when inmates were tortured or hanged in front of the rest of the prisoners.[47]

Face to face with death

One further group of prisoners deserves mention here: these are the members of the Special Commandos (Sonderkommandos) who were directly involved in the extermination process. Thanks to the analysis of inmate accounts which for a long time had been disregarded, it is now possible to understand, at least to some extent, the conditions under which these men operated. Their reports of their own actions enable the reader to appreciate better the desperate plight of this group of prisoners; at the same time it is almost impossible to imagine how they went about their daily task of murder in the 'death factory'.[48] They were under tremendous psychological pressure, forced to dupe new arrivals in Auschwitz by not revealing what lay in store as they led the deportees to the gas chambers and helped them to strip off their clothing. In a secretly kept record, one member of a special squad describes the almost unimaginable situation of having to ensure that the extermination process ran quietly and smoothly – when the natural reaction would be one of horror and protest. At the time of writing, he was in no doubt that the outside world would never believe what was happening within the camp: '… let me just say that you will never fully understand the facts because they are beyond belief. No one can possibly imagine these things; … only one of us can recount the horror … someone from our small group who might survive, but the chances of survival are virtually nil.'[49] Salmen Gradowski, a member of the Special Commandos, signed his report with his full name and buried it amongst the ashes of the cremated – clearly, he felt that his testimony was much more important than saving his own life.[50]

The SS distributed extra rations to members of the special squads, including alcohol. They were also commissioned to confiscate the valuables of the victims, which resulted in the common practice of barter and exchange within the group and also with the SS. And so the 'lowest of the low'[51] were also, paradoxically, 'rich'. Those inmates who worked in the special squads for a longer period also formed their own social group, usually comprising prisoners of the same nationality or linguistic background. Friedler's interviews and evaluations underline how important this group dynamic was for creating some kind of stability and solidarity, key factors in the battle to survive the daily terror of life in the special squad. Towards the end several groups in the special squads – in particular those consisting of Soviet POWs – developed an identity of their own that reinforced their will to survive despite SS oppression. According to Christian Jansen, the formation of a group dynamic often based on pre-camp affiliations stands in contrast to Sofsky's hypothesis of 'absolute power'. Jansen claims that not all inmate groups succumbed to in-fighting. Several were able to conceive a post-camp future and this enabled them, at least intellectually, to resist the ubiquitous power of the SS. The secret notes and records that have survived are sufficient testimony for such an interpretation.[52]

From 1943 onwards, the special squads in Birkenau comprised up to 400 inmates. With the deportation of Hungarian Jews in 1944, the numbers swelled to about 900 as the daily round of murder and extermination increased. The

SS administration began to falter and the special squads saw opportunities to develop their own initiatives. In theory they were isolated from the rest of the camp; in actual fact, there had always been a measure of communication with other inmates and the outside world. Some members began to make escape plans in conjunction with prisoners from the main camp, above all in order to ensure that their testimony would not be lost for future generations. Despite the high risks involved, such initiatives also produced photographic evidence of what had happened in Auschwitz.

Shortly before the liberation of Auschwitz plans for a rebellion were being put into effect. Unfortunately, the special squads and the resistance groups in the main camp could not agree on a common time line for the uprising. The SS knew that they had to obliterate any traces of the extermination programme as the Soviets advanced – and the special squads were only too aware that they would be the first to be murdered before the front would approach the camp. The resistance groups in the main camp wanted to delay any uprising in the hope that Soviet forces would provide support; understandably, the special squads were in favour of immediate action in order to ensure their own survival. The result of this breakdown in communication was an isolated act of resistance on the part of the special squads, during which most members were killed. Salmen Gradowski reflects these conflicting time perspectives in his secret diary with a mixture of wishful thinking and resignation, taking resort in a rare metaphoric language: 'If only one of us, only one person had shown enough courage to act his conscience', to overcome the split in the minds of the prisoners, it would have changed everything. The tiny spark of humanity that still existed in everyone's soul could have ignited a blaze of resistance that would have swept through the whole camp.[53]

There are similar accounts that come from special squads in Sobibór and Chełmno. They all display the same tenor. Whenever the members of a particular group or camp attempted to plan some form of resistance as a response to SS plans for their liquidation, social cohesion broke down once it became clear that individuals, rather than the whole group, would be murdered.[54]

Gideon Greif, an Israeli historian, has attempted to show why the members of the special squads acted as they did. He introduces ethical and moral criteria to explain why they followed orders and what their motivation was. His conclusion is that the special squads wanted to alleviate the fate of new arrivals. Their fate, quite simply, was death – in the gas chambers.[55] This was inevitable, no matter what might happen during the procedures of arrival. All of this may be true, but, at the same time, the members of the special squad being part of the death factory in this very moment had to distance themselves from the stripped off, naked deportees; they could show compassion neither to them nor to themselves. Reason dictated to prolong one's own life rather than to empathize with those doomed to die. Nevertheless, there is documentary evidence, albeit rare, that certain deportees or members of the special squads broke their silence and talked about what might, could and would happen. However, such 'breaches of confidence' were invariably punished by the SS.[56]

Future research perspectives

Our knowledge about the concentration camps, and particularly about the 'enforced community' (*Zwangsgemeinschaft*)[57] in which the inmates lived, is based mostly on the accounts given by the prisoners themselves. The most significant, perhaps, are the reports from eye-witnesses who not only describe their own experiences but attempt to provide a systematic analysis of the camps. Amongst these are Bruno Bettelheim, Eugen Kogon, Victor Frankl, David Rousset and Primo Levi.[58] Ruth Klüger's memoir of incarceration in her youth, is one of the most recent examples.[59] The virtue of her report lies in the conciseness of her judgements, the details contained in her observations and the almost painful lack of pathos as she describes her experiences. Almost 50 years after the events, Klüger has succeeded in conveying a degree of authenticity that is unlikely to be equalled.

In the immediate post-war years the most common model employed to interpret the phenomenon of the camps was based largely on psychoanalytical theory, as can be seen in the accounts by Bettelheim and Frankl. Less common was the sociological approach that underpins the analysis by Kogon. Research institutes and aid organizations conducted interviews with survivors in the late 1940s and early 1950s but these had no lasting influence;[60] nor did the first serious interpretations of persecution trauma and survival experiences.[61] The phase after liberation, during which so many eye-witness reports were published, was followed by a significant fall in the amount of attention paid to the concentration camps, both in the media and in academic circles. Interest was only revived when more and more Nazi perpetrators were put on trial in the early 1960s (for example, the Auschwitz trial in Germany and the Eichmann trial in Israel, both of which were widely publicized in the international media). The Munich Institute for Contemporary History, for instance, published reports on the concentration camp system that incorporated expert testimony from historians and other impartial sources that featured in the trials.[62] However, the aim of these studies was to provide further documentary confirmation of the statements made by witnesses in the trials and so they restricted themselves to official sources, ignoring other sources like inmate accounts, which were regarded as subjective. And this approach has predominated ever since. The fact that research has focused on verifiable factual and documentary evidence to describe camp life is probably the reason why there have been so few attempts to interpret the inmate society from an interdisciplinary perspective. The post-war years saw several attempts to understand the phenomenon from a psychological and psychoanalytical viewpoint; there is also a great deal of literature dealing with medical treatment and therapeutic measures for coping with the trauma of camp experience. Nevertheless, these various strands of research have yet to be coordinated in order to give us an overall picture of the defining principles that characterized incarceration and inmate society.[63]

There can be no doubt that witness statements and official documents need to be checked and verified. Immediately after the war there was frequently a strong desire to punish the perpetrators, accompanied by an urge for revenge, as well as an attempt to whitewash the complicity of certain inmates – in particular those who had been members of resistance groups.[64] But in interviews conducted many years after incarceration these factors play a minor role. Instead, the interviewees see things from a more general perspective, integrating their post-camp life into judgements and interpretations of what they experienced. Up till now we have hardly any systematic research results into how hindsight has affected and changed the emotions and feelings of survivors.

Eye-witness accounts have become indispensable sources for studies concerning specific groups within the camps; they feature to a much lesser degree in academic research, which attempts to give a systematic overview of the system as a whole. In the last two decades historians, journalists and film producers have put together a vast amount of material documenting these reports, much of which is available on video or DVD. As the last of the survivors depart, we, the historians, now have access to sources detailing daily life in the camps that have not yet been researched. This material is ideally suited for use in the educational context; however, historians must not overlook the fact that such material can and should be systematically evaluated and compared with earlier reports. To date, there has been too little analysis of the extent to which these interviews may afford perspectives on camp life that differ from those reported in the years after liberation.

The narrative structures for depicting camp life conveyed in scholarly works have already become so accepted and entrenched in our perspective that they even influence the interpretation of 'oral history', i.e. the accounts of inmates. Kavčič, for example, has structured the interviews she conducted in the 1990s on the lines of a model that has permeated the scholarly literature dealing with concentration camps (for instance: punishments, selections, group formation and functionaries).[65] There may well be other models to evaluate such interviews, applying different categories and criteria that take post-camp experience into account, thus enabling us to understand the concentration camp experience in a new light. Kavčič makes some steps in this direction in the second part of her study when she concentrates on how people remembered and interpreted the concentration camps after the Tito regime had already been established in Slovenia. She emphasizes that certain facts had been officially 'obliterated', while others were given an undeserved prominence and so changed the patterns of commemoration. What still remains open is how this might affect our present-day interpretation of the concentration camp experience.[66]

In conclusion, we can say that there is a strong case for bringing together the various strands of research that have developed over the last few decades. Future studies must try to integrate the different disciplinary approaches into a comprehensive interpretation of concentration camp society and so avoid the dichotomy between fact-oriented, 'objective' historiography on one hand, and the collection of 'subjective', personal stories of the contemporaries on the other hand. This is particularly important for comparative studies investigating the 'concentration camp phenomenon', whether in Nazi-Germany, the Soviet Union of Stalin or elsewhere in the world. If Zygmunt Bauman is right in regarding this factor as one of the defining elements that characterize the history of the twentieth century,[67] more studies are needed to examine whether Rousset's 'other

Kingdom', Adler's 'enforced community' or Kogon's 'concentration camp system' find their parallel in the camps of the GULag, just to name one other man-made inferno of the past century. So far, there have been only a few tentative steps to reveal any such interrelatedness through academic research.[68]

Translated by Michael Bacon

Notes

1 Amongst others B. Strebel, *Das KZ Ravensbrück. Geschichte eines Lagerkomplexes*, Paderborn: Schöningh 2003; W. Długoborski and F. Piper (eds), *Auschwitz 1940–1945: Central Issues in the History of the Camp*, 5 vols, Oświęcim: State Museum Auschwitz-Birkenau, 2000; vol. 1: A. Lack *et al.* (eds), *The establishment and organisation of the camp;* vol. 2: T. Iwaszko *et al.* (eds), *The prisoners – their life and work;* vol. 3: F. Piper (ed.), *Mass murder;* vol. 4: H. Świebocki (ed.): *The resistance movement;* vol. 5: D. Czech *et al.* (eds), *Epilogue;* I. Sprenger, *Groß-Rosen. Ein Konzentrationslager in Schlesien*, Vienna: Böhlau, 1996.

2 W. Benz and B. Distel (eds), *Der Ort des Terrors. Geschichte der nationalsozialistischen Konzentrationslager*, Munich: Beck; vol. 1: *Die Organisation des Terrors*, 2005; vol. 2: *Frühe Lager, Dachau, Emslandlager*, 2006; vol. 3: *Sachsenhausen, Buchenwald*, 2006; vol. 4: *Flossenbürg, Mauthausen, Ravensbrück*, 2007: vol. 5: *Hinzert, Auschwitz, Neuengamme*, 2007; vol. 6: *Natzweiler, Groß-Rosen, Stutthof*, 2008; vol. 7: *Niederhagen / Wewelsburg, Lublin-Majdanek, Arbeitsdorf, Herzogenbusch (Vught), Bergen-Belsen, Mittelbau-Dora*, 2008; vol. 8: *Riga, Warschau, Vaivara, Plaszów, Kulmhof / Chełmno, Belźec, Sobibór, Treblinka*, 2009; N. Frei, S. Steinbacher and B. C. Wagner (eds), *Ausbeutung, Vernichtung Öffentlichkeit. Neue Studien zur nationalsozialistischen Lagerpolitik*, Munich: K. G. Saur 2000; U. Herbert, K. Orth and C. Dieckmann (eds), *Die nationalsozialistischen Konzentrationslager. Entwicklung und Struktur*, 2 vols, Göttingen: Wallstein, 1998. T. Straede (ed.), *De nazistiske Koncentrationslejre. Studier og bibliografi*, Odense: Syddansk Universitetsforlag, 2009, includes case studies from the university of Odense, as well as a bibliography of Danish studies on the camps.

3 For a serial bibliography see *Gedenkstättenrundbrief*, Berlin: Stiftung Topographie des Terrors; *Informationen*, Frankfurt: Studienkreis: Deutscher Widerstand.

4 B. C. Wagner, *IG Auschwitz. Zwangsarbeit und Vernichtung von Häftlingen des Lagers Monowitz 1941–1945*, Munich: Beck 2000; M. Wildt, 'Die Lager im Osten. Kommentierende Bemerkungen', in Herbert, Orth and Dieckmann (eds), *Die nationalsozialistischen Konzentrationslager*, vol. I, pp. 508–20; Y. Gutman and M. Berenbaum (eds), *Anatomy of the Auschwitz Death Camp*, Bloomington, IN: Indiana University Press, 1994, follow a more traditional approach.

5 W. Sofsky, *The Order of Terror: the Concentration Camp*, Princeton, NJ: Princeton University Press, 1997.

6 M. Knop, H. Krause and R. Schwarz, *Die Häftlinge des Konzentrationslagers Oranienburg*, in Günter Morsch (ed.), *Konzentrationslager Oranienburg*, Oranienburg: Stiftung Brandenburgische Gedenkstätten, 1994, pp. 67–77; see also C. Baganz, *Erziehung zur 'Volksgemeinschaft'? Die frühen Konzentrationslager in Sachsen 1933–1934/37*, Berlin: Metropol, 2005; W. Benz and B. Distel (eds), *Terror ohne System. Die ersten Konzentrationslager im Nationalsozialismus 1933–1935*, Berlin: Metropol, 2001; K. Drobisch and G. Wieland, *System der Konzentrationslager 1933–1939*, Berlin: Akademie Verlag, 1993.

7 For example, two-thirds of the political detainees in the work education camp (*Arbeitserziehungslager*) Breitenau were members or supporters of the communist party; G. Richter (ed.), *Breitenau. Zur Geschichte eines nationalsozialistischen Konzentrations- und Arbeitserziehungslagers*, Kassel: Verlag Jenior & Pressler, 1993.

8 T. Hofmann, H. Loewy and H. Stein, *Pogromnacht und Holocaust: Frankfurt, Weimar, Buchenwald … Die schwierige Erinnerung an die Stationen der Verfolgung*, Vienna: Böhlau, 1994.

9 E. Raim, *Die Dachauer KZ-Außenkommandos Kaufering und Mühldorf. Rüstungsbauten und Zwangsarbeit in den letzten Kriegsjahren 1944/15*, Landsberg. Landsberger Verlagsanstalt, 1992; F. Freund, *Arbeitslager Zement. Das Konzentrationslager Ebensee und die Raketenrüstung*, Vienna: Verlag für Gesellschaftskritik, 1989.

10 B. Perz, *Projekt Quarz. Steyr-Daimler-Puch und das Konzentrationslager Melk*, Vienna: Verlag für Gesellschaftskritik, 1991, p. 265.

11 Sprenger, *Groß-Rosen,* p. 143.

12 Raim, *Die Dachauer KZ-Außenkommandos Kaufering und Mühldorf,* p. 290.

13 R. Klüger, *Still Alive: A Holocaust Girlhood Remembered*, New York: Feminist Press, 2001.

14 S. Kavčič, *Überleben und Erinnern. Slowenische Häftlinge im Frauen-Konzentrationslager Ravensbrück*, Berlin: Metropol, 2007.

15 L. Niethammer (ed.), *Der 'gesäuberte' Antifaschismus. Die SED und die roten Kapos von Buchenwald. Dokumente*, Berlin: Akademie Verlag, 1994, p. 197.

16 Wildt, 'Die Lager im Osten'.

17 F. Pingel, 'The Destruction of Human Identity in Concentration Camps: The Contribution of the Social Sciences to an Analysis of Behavior under Extreme Conditions', *Holocaust and Genocide Studies* 6, 1991, pp.167–84.

18 For an impressive description of such a special camp site in Buchenwald, see K. Kreiser, 'Sie starben allein und ruhig, ohne zu schreien oder jemanden zu rufen. 'Das "Kleine Lager" im Konzentrationslager Buchenwald', *Dachauer Hefte* 14, 1998, pp. 102–24.

19 R. Steegmann, *Struthof. Le KL-Natzweiler et ses kommandos*, Strasbourg: La Nuée Bleue, 2005, p. 365.

20 Ibid., p. 217.

21 Niethammer, *Der 'gesäuberte' Antifaschismus,* p. 470.

22 KZ-Gedenkstätte Neuengamme (ed.), *Abgeleitete Macht. Funktionshäftlinge zwischen Widerstand und Kollaboration*, Bremen: Edition Temmen, 1998.

23 Frei *et al., Ausbeutung, Vernichtung Öffentlichkeit,* p. 8.

24 Niethammer, *Der 'gesäuberte' Antifaschismus,* p.78.

25 Kavčič, *Überleben und Erinnern,* p. 132.

26 J. Müller and A. Sternweiler (eds), *Homosexuelle Männer im KZ Sachsenhausen*, Berlin: Männerschwarm, 2000; KZ-Gedenkstätte Neuengamme (ed.), *Verfolgung Homosexueller im Nationalsozialismus*, Bremen: Edition Temmen, 1999; W. Röhl, *Homosexuelle Häftlinge im Konzentrationslager Buchenwald*, Weimar: Gedenkstätte Buchenwald, 1992.

27 W. Długoborski (ed.), *Sinti und Roma im KL Auschwitz-Birkenau 1943–1944 vor dem Hintergrund ihrer Verfolgung unter der Naziherrschaft*, Oświęcim: Staatliches Museum Auschwitz, 1998.

28 W. Ayaß, *'Asoziale' im Nationalsozialismus*, Stuttgart: Klett-Cotta, 1995; see also C. Schikorra, 'Asoziale' Häftlinge in Frauen-Konzentrationslager Ravensbrück – die Spezifik einer Häftlingsgruppe', in W. Röhr and B. Berlekamp (eds), *Tod oder Überleben? Neue Forschungen zur Geschichte des Konzentrationslagers Ravensbrück*, Berlin: Edition Organon, 2001, pp. 89–122; I. Eschebach, 'Das Stigma des Asozialen. Drei Urteile der DDR-Justiz gegen ehemalige Funktionshäftlinge des Frauenkonzentrationslagers Ravensbrück', in *Abgeleitete Macht,* pp. 69–81.

29 G. Morsch and S. zur Nieden (eds), *Jüdische Häftlinge im Konzentrationslager Sachsenhausen 1936 bis 1945*, Berlin: Edition Hentrich, 2004; R.G. Saidel, *The Jewish Women of Ravensbrück Concentration Camp*, Madison, WI.: Terrace Books, 2004; L. Apel, *Jüdische Frauen im Konzentrationslager Ravensbrück 1939–1945*, Berlin: Metropol, 2003; A.-E. Wenck, *Zwischen Menschenhandel und 'Endlösung'. Das Konzentrationslager Bergen-Belsen*, Paderborn: Schöningh, 2000; H. Stein, *Juden in Buchenwald, 1937–1942*, Weimar: Gedenkstätte Buchenwald, 1992.

30 B.C. Wagner, *IG Auschwitz,* p. 134; T. Rahe, 'Jüdische Religiosität in den nationalsozialistischen Konzentrationslagern', *Geschichte in Wissenschaft und Unterricht*

44, 1993, pp. 87–101; E. Raim, *Die Dachauer KZ-Außenkommandos Kaufering und Mühldorf*, p. 255.

31 H. Hesse and J. Harder, *Und wenn ich lebenslang in einem KZ bleiben müßte … Die Zeuginnen Jehovas in den Frauenkonzentrationslagern Moringen, Lichtenburg und Ravensbrück*, Essen: Klartext, 2001; D. Garbe, *Zwischen Widerstand und Martyrium. Die Zeugen Jehovas im 'Dritten Reich'*, Munich: Oldenbourg, 1993.

32 Recent research concentrated on smaller national groups, see J. Schuyf, *Nederlanders in Neuengamme. De ervaringen van ruim 3300 Nederlanders in een Duits concentratiekamp 1940–1945*, Zaltbommel: Uitgeverij Aprilis, 2007; K. Snijders, *Nederlanders in Buchenwald 1940–1945: een verzicht over de geschiedenis van Nederlandse gevangenen die tijdens de national-socialistische bezetting van 1940–1945 in het concentratiekamp Buchenwald zaten*, Göttingen: Wallstein, 2001; G. Bergner, *Aus dem Bündnis hinter dem Stacheldraht. Italienische Häftlinge im KZ Dachau 1943–1945*, Hamburg: Verlag Dr. Kovac, 2002; 'Nationalitäten im KZ', *Dachauer Hefte* 23, 2007.

33 B. Niven, *The Buchenwald Child: Truth, Fiction and Propaganda*, New York: Camden House, 2007. Anne Frank's diary is a standard topic in the school history curriculum of many European countries; for more information about Anne Frank visit the home page of the Anne Frank House www.annefrank.org.

34 In April 1944 there were 2,846 children and adolescents in Auschwitz-Birkenau; H. Kubica, 'Children and adolescents in Auschwitz', in *Auschwitz 1940–1945*, vol. II, *The prisoners, their life and work*, p.295; *Auschwitz 1940–1945*, vol. 4: H. Świebocki, *The Resistance Movement*, p. 37. Many children and adolescents who had spent only a few weeks in Stutthof were transported to other camps, particularly to the 'Youth Camp' in Uckermark and the concentration camp in Ravensbrück. Others were sent to Auschwitz for extermination (*Stutthof. Das Konzentrationslager*, Gdańsk: Wydawnictwo 'Marpress', 1996, p. 138). To date, we have only sporadic and incidental information about children in the camps. In Nordhausen-Ellerich, children and adolescents made up 50% of the Hungarian inmates (J.-C. Wagner, *Produktion des Todes. Das KZ Mittelbau-Dora*, Göttingen, 2004, p. 33). The American soldiers Fleck and Tenenbaum state that 700 children were amongst those liberated in Buchenwald (Niethammer, *Der 'gesäuberte' Antifaschismus*, p. 197).

35 C. Callegari, ' "Non dite mai: non ce la faccio più". Giovani ebrei durante la Shoa e sviluppo della resilenza', *History of Education and Children's Literature* 1, 2006, pp. 283–310; H. Diercks, *Jugendliche Häftlinge des KZ Neuengamme aus der Sowjetunion erinnern sich*, Hamburg: Edition Temmen, 2000; Projektgruppe für die vergessenen Opfer des NS-Regimes/KZ-Gedenkstätte Neuengamme (eds), *'Und vielleicht überlebte ich nur, weil ich sehr jung war.' Verschleppt ins KZ Neuengamme. Lebensschicksale polnischer Jugendlicher*, Bremen: Edition Temmen, 1999; T. Rahe, 'Aus "rassischen" Gründen verfolgte Kinder im Konzentrationslager Bergen-Belsen', in E. Bamberger and A. Ehmann (eds), *Kinder und Jugendliche als Opfer des Holocaust. Dokumentation einer Internationalen Tagung in der Gedenkstätte Haus der Wannseekonferenz, 12. bis 14. Dezember 1994*, Heidelberg: Kultur- und Dokumentationszentrum Deutscher Sinti und Roma, 1995.

36 Raim, *Die Dachauer KZ-Außenkommandos Kaufering und Mühldorf*, p. 189; Perz, *Projekt Quarz*, p. 253. J.-C. Wagner, 'Noch einmal: Arbeit und Vernichtung. Häftlingseinsatz im KL Mittelbau-Dora 1943–1945', in Frei *et al.*, *Ausbeutung, Vernichtung Öffentlichkeit*, p. 30, has produced similar figures for Ellrich, a satellite camp of Mittelbau-Dora; 70% of the Soviet prisoners were aged between 18 and 30, whereas about half of the Belgians and French, most of whom had been incarcerated earlier, were older than 30.

37 G. Schwarz, 'Frauen in Konzentrationslager – Täterinnen und Zuschauerinnen', in Herbert, Orth and Dieckmann (eds), *Die nationalsozialistischen Konzentrationslager*, vol. II, pp. 800–21.

38 G. Pfingsten and C. Füllberg-Stolberg, 'Frauen in Konzentrationslagern – geschlechtsspezifische Bedingungen des Überlebens', in Herbert, Orth and Dieckmann (eds), *Die nationalsozialistischen Konzentrationslager*, pp. 911–38, have shown

that in the industrial satellite camp of Hannover-Limmer a group consisting mainly of French 'political' female inmates was able to achieve, at least initially, a privileged status. However, their situation and the group dynamic deteriorated as incarceration continued, until finally their situation was no different from that of the male counterparts.

39 H. Amesberger and B. Halbmayr, *Vom Leben und Überleben – Wege nach Ravensbrück*, vol. 1: *Dokumentation und Analyse*, vol. 2: *Lebensgeschichten*, Vienna: Promedia Verlag, 2001; C. Schikorra, *Kontinuitäten der Ausgrenzung. 'Asoziale' Häftlinge im Frauen-Konzentrationslager Ravensbrück*, Berlin: Metropol, 2001; Schikorra,' "Asoziale" Häftlinge in Frauen-Konzentrationslager Ravensbrück – die Spezifik einer Häftlingsgruppe'; Eschebach, 'Das Stigma des Asozialen'.

40 N. Warmbold, *Lagersprache. Zur Sprache der Opfer in den Konzentrationslagern Sachsenhausen, Dachau, Buchenwald*, diss., Universität Braunschweig, 2006; D. Wesołowska, *Wörter aus der Hölle. Die 'lagerszpracha' der Häftlinge von Auschwitz*, Kraków: Impuls, 1998.

41 R. D. Krause, 'Truth but not art? German autobiographical writings of the survivors of Nazi concentration camps, ghettos and prisons', in Y. Bauer, A. Eckhardt and F. Litell (eds), *Remembering for the Future: The impact of the Holocaust and genocide on Jews and Christians*, vol. III, Oxford: Pergamon Press, 1989, pp. 2958–72; H. Gehle, 'Atempause – Atemwende. Die Literatur der Überlebenden', in Fritz-Bauer-Institut (ed.), *Auschwitz. Geschichte, Rezeption und Wirkung*, Frankfurt: Campus, 1996; M. Körte, 'Erinnerungsliteratur', *Dachauer Hefte* 18, 2002, pp. 24–33. Based on interviews, D. Monneuse, 'Idéaltype des parcours empruntés par les rescapés des camps de concentration nazis après 1945', *Bulletin Trimestriel de la Fondation Auschwitz*, No. 96, July–September 2007, pp. 75–103, identifies three different modes of survivor stories: 1 'Le profil de la fruite' (silencing, forgetting), 2. 'Le profil de l'enfermement' (trapped in the past, unable to forget and to work through the past, traumatization), 3. 'Le profil de la résiliance' (successful coping with, accepting the concentration camp experience).

42 The term 'organizing (things)' was a common expression used in the camps to cover a multitude of activities that the SS regarded as illegal. These might include requisitioning extra food or clothes, material to heat the barracks and so on. This might be to the detriment of other inmates but often it was the only means of survival.

43 Raim, *Die Dachauer KZ-Außenkommandos Kaufering und Mühldorf*, p. 252.

44 Niethammer, *Der 'gesäuberte' Antifaschismus*, p. 147.

45 Pejorative for 'Muslim', here obviously associated with emaciated, submissive, alien.

46 T. Seela, *Lesen und Literaturbenutzung in den Konzentrationslagern. Das gedruckte Wort im antifaschistischen Widerstand der Häftlinge*, Munich: Saur, 1992; Klüger, *Still Alive*, underscores how important it was for her to have access to literature in Auschwitz.

47 M. Bruhns, *'Die Zeichnung überlebt …' Bildzeugnisse von Häftlingen des KZ-Neuengamme*. Bremen: Edition Temme, 2007; H. J. Keden, 'Musik in nationalsozialistischen Konzentrationslager', *Aus Politik und Zeitgeschichte*, 2005, no. 11, pp. 40–6; G. Fackler, *'Des Lagers Stimme' – Musik im KZ. Alltag und Häftlingskultur in den Konzentrationslagern 1933 bis 1936. Mit einer Darstellung der weiteren Entwicklung bis 1945*, Bremen: Temmen, 2000; K. Klein, *Kazett-Lyrik. Untersuchungen zu Gedichten und Liedern aus dem Konzentrationslager Sachsenhausen*, Würzburg: Königshausen & Neumann, 1995.

48 The journalists and historians Eric Friedler, Barbara Siebert and Andreas Kilian have collected and evaluated eye-witness accounts dealing with the special squad in Auschwitz, as well as conducting their own interviews in an attempt to challenge the way these inmates have been 'demonized'. Their aim is to dismantle prejudices and generate understanding for the dilemma which faced the special squads; E. Friedler, B. Siebert and A. Kilian, *Zeugen aus der Todeszone. Das jüdische Sonderkommando in Auschwitz*, Lüneburg: zu Klampen, 2002; visit also www.sonderkommando-studien.de; O. Kraus and E. Kulka, *The Death Factory: Document on Auschwitz*, Oxford: Pergamon Press, 1966.

49 Salmen Lewenthal in Staatliches Museum Auschwitz-Birkenau (ed.), *Inmitten des grauenvollen Verbrechens. Handschriften von Mitgliedern des Sonderkommandos*, Staatliches

Museum Auschwitz-Birkenau: Oświęcim, 1996, quoted in Friedler, *Zeugen aus der Todeszone*, p. 162f. These secretly kept records were buried and came to light after the liberation of Auschwitz.

50 Samen Gradowski in *Inmitten des grauenvollen Verbrechens*, p. 137.

51 S. Krakowski, *Das Todeslager Chełmno/Kulmhof*, Jerusalem and Göttingen: Yad Vashem and Wallstein, 2007.

52 C. Jansen, 'Häftlingsalltag auf dem Laagberg bei Wolfsburg', in Frei *et al.*, *Ausbeutung, Vernichtung Öffentlichkeit*, pp. 75–107; Jansen has researched a smaller labour camp with particularly harsh conditions.

53 Friedler, *Zeugen aus der Todeszone*, p. 267; see also Z. Gradowski, *Au Coeur de l'enfer. Document écrit d'un Sonderkommando d'Auschwitz – 1944*, ed. P. Mesnard, C. Saletti, Paris: Edition Kimé, 2001.

54 Shmuel Krakowski, a former member of the underground resistance in Łódź and an inmate of Auschwitz, has collected eye-witness accounts and SS reports that document the uprising in Chełmno. He reconstructs the desperate revolt undertaken by the last members of the special squad, who were due to be shot by the SS after the camp was finally closed. The resistance group killed and wounded several SS guards and personnel. Of the 40 to 50 members of the special squad, only 2 managed to escape (Krakowski, *Das Todeslager Chełmno/Kulmhof*).

55 G. Greif, 'Die moralische Problematik der 'Sonderkommando'-Häftlinge', in Herbert, Orth and Dieckmann (eds), *Die nationalsozialistischen Konzentrationslager*, pp. 1023–45.

56 D. Ambach and T. Köhler, *Lublin-Majdanek. Das Konzentrations- und Vernichtungslager im Spiegel von Zeugenaussagen*, Düsseldorf: Justizministerium des Landes Nordrhein-Westfalen, 2003.

57 This is the term used by H.-G. Adler, *Theresienstadt 1941–1945. Das Antlitz einer Zwangsgemeinschaft*, Göttingen: Wallstein, 2005.

58 B. Bettelheim, *The Informed Heart: A study of the psychological consequences of living under extreme fear and terror*, Harmondsworth: Penguin Books, 1987; E. Kogon, *The Theory and Practice of Hell: The German concentration camps and the system behind them* (with a New introduction by Nikolaus Wachsmann). New York: Farrar, Straus and Giroux, 2006; D. Rousset, *The Other Kingdom*, New York: Reynal & Hitchcock, 1947; P. Levi, *If This Is a Man*, London: Everyman's Library, 2000.

59 Klüger, *Still Alive*.

60 J. Goldstein, I.F. Lukoff, and H.A. Strauss, *Individuelles und kollektives Verhalten in Nazi-Konzentrationslagern. Soziologische und psychologische Studien zu Berichten ungarisch-jüdischer Überlebender*, Frankfurt: Campus, 1991. The interviews cited were conducted in the USA between 1949 and 1951. Only many years later, in 1991, did Herbert Strauss publish his recollections of post-war experiences.

61 W. Glicksman, 'Social differentiation in the German concentration camps', *Yivo Annual Jewish Social Sciences* 8, 1953, pp. 123–50.

62 *Anatomy of the SS State*, New York: Walker and Company, 1968.

63 H. Stoffels (ed.), *Terrorlandschaften der Seele. Beiträge zur Theorie und Therapie von Extremtraumatisierungen*, Regensburg: S. Roderer, 1994.

64 Jansen, 'Häftlingsalltag auf dem Laagberg bei Wolfsburg'.

65 Kavčič, *Überleben und Erinnern*.

66 U. Jureit and K. Orth, *Überlebensgeschichten. Gespräche mit Überlebenden des KZ-Neuengamme*, Hamburg: Dölling und Galitz, 1994; A. Wieviorka, *Déportation et génocide: entre la mémoire et l'oubli*, Paris: Hachette Littérature, 1992.

67 Z. Bauman, *Modernity and the Holocaust*, Ithaca, NY: Cornell University Press, 1989.

68 M. Buber-Neumann, *Under Two Dictators: Prisoner of Stalin and Hitler* (with an introduction by Nikolaus Wachsmann). London: Pimlico, 2008; R. Streibel and H. Schafranek (eds), *Strategie des Überlebens. Häftlingsgesellschaften in KZ und GULAG*, Vienna: Picus, 1996; G. Armanski, *Maschinen des Terrors. Das Lager (KZ und Gulag) in der Moderne*, Münster: Westfälisches Dampfboot, 1993.

4 Gender and the
concentration camps[1]

Jane Caplan

Women and gender

It is a commonplace that until recently 'gender' has been marginalized as an aspect of the history of the concentration camps.[2] One reason for this is that older organizational histories of the camps and their inmates did not leave much room for discussion of *any* kinds of collective identity or difference among inmates. Male political prisoners constituted an unspoken norm against which other groups – whether defined by gender or by other criteria – were automatically placed as marginal. It was only when inmates and guards began to be studied in more detail, in the historiography that is the subject of this volume, that different populations and experiences *within* the camps, including those shaped by gender, could come into sharper focus and receive attention in their own right.

Although the concept of gender ought not to be collapsed into the category of women (the distinction between these two terms will be discussed in a moment), in practice it is through women's history that the path to the historicization of gender has been laid. Empirical research into the specific history of women camp inmates thus depended on an impulse that was not peculiar to the history of Germany or National Socialism alone: the take-off of women's history in the 1970s and 1980s, which imported a powerful new dynamic into historical research in general. Although this movement was generally slower to spread in German historiography than in Britain and the US, the first German publications also began to appear in the 1970s. Alongside the identification of women as an independent object of study, other obviously gendered categories, notably homosexual men and lesbians, also entered the historical field of visibility. At the same time, related subjects such as sexuality and the body were disentangled from nature and studied in their status as cultural and historical artefacts; and ultimately the master-categories of men and masculinity themselves began to be dismantled and forced into historical contention, thereby questioning the power of the unmarked male to do duty for humankind in general.[3]

In the historiography of National Socialism, this development was manifested not only in new studies on the history of women, but also in gender-conscious reconceptualizations of social and political relations, now understood to be deeply marked by the sexual politics of ideology, policy, practice and everyday life in Nazi Germany. Here research has by now uncovered numerous ways in which gendered values and goals were embodied in multifarious fields stretching from the family to the battlefield. A wide and differentiated literature has now accumulated, bringing its own findings, conclusions and debates and transforming the landscape of research into Nazi Germany.[4]

After more than 30 years, research into women and gender can no longer really be called 'new'; yet it is also clear that gendered perspectives have been unable to permeate any field of historical research without a struggle to assert their relevance in each successive case and that achievements may well be partial and provisional. In our present context, this explains some historians' palpable frustration at the pace of empirical research into the camps and the depth of its impact on the rest of the historiography. The editors of a path-breaking volume of essays on women in Bergen-Belsen and Ravensbrück, published in 1994, declared that their aim was 'to insert the category of gender and to release women from the anonymity that hides behind the word "prisoner" [*Häftling*]'.[5] This claim of anonymity may seem surprising, given that memoirs by female as well as male political prisoners had begun to appear in 1945–1946, immediately after their liberation.[6] But this literature did not have much impact on the historiography or the typology of the camps that developed subsequently. Sigrid Jacobeit, a historian of the Ravensbrück camp, counted some 400 memoirs of Ravensbrück alone that had been published by the end of the 1980s, yet she also noted that only three scholarly studies of the camp had appeared by the same date.[7]

In the same 2002 volume, Jacobeit could still argue that 'the existence of the concentration camps is gendered male in public consciousness'.[8] The image of the camps as essentially male may accord with pre-war realities to some extent, given that before 1939 women composed no more than 4 to 10 per cent of all prisoners year by year. Even Himmler, reporting on the camps to SS leaders assembled in Munich in November 1938, failed to mention the women's camp in Lichtenburg.[9] But even if small numbers alone could explain historians' subsequent lack of attention, this was no longer empirically the case by the end of the war, when the huge expansion of camp inmates was accompanied by a drastic increase in the proportion of women: 202,764 out of 714,211 inmates registered in January 1945, or 28 per cent.[10] It is true that Ravensbrück was established as the only 'main camp' (*Hauptlager*) for women pre-war and has been best served by the research to date; but during the war, women's camps were constructed in several other main camps, notably Auschwitz and Majdanek, and numerous 'affiliated camps' (*Aussenlager*) for women workers were attached not only to these camps but to numerous *Hauptlager* for men.[11] Moreover, the proposition that the camps are 'gendered male' is perilously close to saying that they have no gendered identity at all: for this to be avoided, the male must be reconceptualized as more than an unproblematic norm which does not need 'gendering'.[12]

If the normative, default category of older histories of the camps remains in the unquestioned realm of the male and masculine, this has the effect of demoting other categories and identities to the role of specialized or deviant cases. So the historiographical 'marginalization' referred to at the beginning of this chapter has a dual meaning. On the one hand, marked categories like women and homosexuals are segregated into specialized studies as groups that were peculiarly the objects of gendered policies and whose members therefore had inherently gendered experiences. On the other hand, the unmarked male ostensibly escapes gender altogether – meaning that 'gender' is not treated as a universally meaningful analytic category which might help us to understand the situation of *all* inmates, male as well as female.[13]

The alternative is to write gendered groups automatically into any history, and to treat 'gender' as an analytic and historical category parallel to such accepted terms as 'class', 'religion' or 'nation'. In this company, the 'gender order' has particularly rich but complex conceptual connotations. It can be understood as a normative symbolic system of difference and power into which all of us are inserted, and indeed invested, by virtue of our sexed subjectivity: this means that none of us can escape its operations, whether or not we are conscious of them. Gender structures the identities, meanings and relationships of men and women, masculinity and femininity, heterosexuality and homosexuality, normality and deviance alike. The normative gender order typically polices (or tries to police) the actual muddlings and multiplications of those binaries. Like any symbolic system or set of practices, its terms and operations can in principle be subjected to historical investigation and analysis. But it is precisely because of the fact that 'gender' is so deeply embedded in our core human identity, in our sense of self as real women and men (not to mention our sexual identities and emotions), that the concept seems harder to historicize than those other categories, which pose fewer challenges to our core senses of identity and difference, recognition and repudiation.[14]

Even when the category of gender is accepted in principle, its scope and impact are easily neglected by historians who continue to think that it is only relevant to the realm of social history, or when women or homosexuals are the explicit subject. But this misses the point about the entanglement of gender and power. Nazi Germany was a society structured and disciplined by extreme and malevolent concepts of identity and difference: by rigid, coercive hierarchies of difference and value among human beings – racial, national, eugenic, sexual – which were imposed and enacted with exceptional and sustained violence. The concentration camps were places where the effects of that system of difference and power reached their most violent apogee (apart, that is, from the sites dedicated solely to mass physical annihilation). As a core symbolic system of difference, the gender order was bound up in the conception and exercise of power in Nazi Germany.

But how can historians code gender onto power here? Will doing this tell us things we ought to know about the concentration camps as key institutions in the Nazi system of power, which would not be obvious without it? These questions are not easy to answer. Historians of the camps, like those of the Nazi genocides, are almost defensively aware that critics may see gender as secondary or even irrelevant when compared with the primary racial and political categories of Nazi persecution – let alone that anyone might want to use the horrors of the camps merely as a means of advancing the theorization of gender difference.[15] Yet to duck this challenge may miss important insights into the performance of Nazi power, the operations of the camp system and the experiences of its inmates. It is only by recognizing the power of the gender order and incorporating its meanings into our research that we can fully understand the identities of those who were selected to people and operate the Nazi camps, the reasons why they were sent there, the character and variety of their treatment and experiences within the camps – and, not least, the limits of any single conceptual tool to explain the concentration camp universe in its entirety.

Typology and the unmarked masculine

To open up the operations of gender in the history of concentration camps, we can begin by distinguishing two long-term trajectories in the historiography of the camps: one which seeks to uncover the common or typological character of 'the camps', and another which investigates the specific empirical history of individual camps as separate institutions, albeit as part of a larger system. Typological studies such as those by Bruno Bettelheim, Terrence des Pres or the more recent study by Wolfgang Sofsky gender the camps as male virtually by default, in the sense noted by Sigrid Jacobeit above.[16] In these works, gender difference is largely ignored in favour of the 'unmarked' masculine – except where women are explicitly singled out for identification, in a gesture that only underlines their status as supplementary or exceptional to the core depiction of a masculine camp universe.

This can be demonstrated by some examples from Sofsky's book, *The Order of Terror* (1993), which was an important and influential reference point for the great expansion of empirical research into the camps in Germany from the 1990s. Sofsky's book makes successive mention of the camps for women at Moringen, Lichtenburg and Ravensbrück, and scattered references to women camp inmates: for example, a brief description of the women's section of Birkenau in 1944, of Jewish women on the forced marches in January 1945, and of the uniforms issued to women inmates.[17] But these references add to the range of evidence without being allowed to inflect the typology, and hence they are usually uncommented and unintegrated. It is equally striking that Ravensbrück is not included in a couple of tables that summarize admissions and death rates in the camps. This omission leaves the male or mixed camps to represent the deadly power of the camp system as a whole. Similarly, although the recruitment of women camp personnel gets a brief mention, the extended description of the organization and deployment of camp guards is restricted to male SS guards and the men's camps.[18] This again ignores women guards, or rather warders (*Aufseherinnen*), whose training, deployment and culture were different from those of male SS guards, as will be shown below. They cannot simply be assimilated into the male model.

Conversely, an example will suggest how a gendered perspective might alter the dynamics of Sofsky's account. His section on the 'Space and Time' of the camps is an enormously perceptive and sensitive interpretation of the camps' destruction of these two essential categories of human life. But these eloquent passages about the stripping away of any control of time from the prisoners make one aware that two of the most intimate markers of time for women, the menstrual cycle and pregnancy, are not mentioned. This is despite the fact that the cessation of menstruation was an often-remarked aspect of women's experience of the camps, while the implications of pregnancy in the camps have a poignancy that is painful to grasp. These surely deserve notice where time itself is the issue. The overall experience and meaning of 'dehumanization' must be recognized as gendered: differently inflected for men and women whose incorporation in 'the human' is organized through sexual difference.

Just as these issues are neglected or silenced, one can also detect the presence of an unacknowledged imagery of gender in Sofsky's evidence, as in his quotation from the report of a speech by Theodor Eicke, commander of the Dachau SS. Here Eicke was instructing the guards on the expected standards of behaviour, following the punishment of some of their number for excessively close relations with Dachau inmates:

> Any form of pity with 'enemies of the state' was … beneath the dignity of an SS man. There was no place for weaklings in these ranks, and they'd be better off disappearing as quickly as possible to a monastery. [Eicke] could only use men who were resolute, tough as nails. Men who obeyed every order ruthlessly.[19]

This is one instance of the pervasive imagery of manhood in Nazi and SS pronouncements, here equating weakness with chastity, and silently consigning male prisoners to a status less than that of full manhood. But this troubling relationship between power and masculinity, between absolute power and hyper-masculinity – cultivated by the SS but visible too in the military – is not remarked on here or anywhere else in this text.[20]

For Sofsky, concentration camps were sites of would-be total dehumanization, in which individual subjectivity and agency were meant to be shattered in anticipation of physical destruction. But even if we accept this model, in practice it was never fully achieved. Individual qualities and responses among camp inmates are a persistent theme in diaries and memoirs – even, perhaps, among the abject 'Muselmen' crushed into apathy by the dire effects of starvation, though here the very perception of their difference from the majority emphasized what their fellow-inmates managed to salvage of personality and humanity.[21] In this gap between the intended and the actual resided all those traits of identity, character and recognition that gender, among other factors, determined.

Marking the camp inmates

'Marking' is not just a term in the vocabulary of symbolic gender difference. In the camps, as is well known, inmates were literally marked as their numbers and grounds for detention expanded, not only with their prisoner number but with differently coloured badges (strips, circles or triangles of cloth) denoting seven categories of prisoner. The identificatory function of the badges was extended by means of a proliferating system of additional letters or other symbols denoting e.g. recidivists, escapees, later on POWs and members of different nationalities in the increasingly internationalized inmate population, while Jewish inmates were further identified with a yellow triangle. The system of triangle badges had become standardized by 1937/8. It invites us to consider the relationship between the two kinds of marking – the symbolic and badged – and to press beyond their function as labels for 'types' or categories of prisoner. Thus the listing of these badges in the historical literature has tended to follow an implicit hierarchy of honorability, almost always starting with red (political prisoners), and often placing male homosexuals (pink) at or towards the end.[22] Inmates wearing any of the other coloured triangles, including green (criminals), black ('asocials'), purple (Jehovah's Witnesses), blue (returned emigrants) and brown (gypsies), could be found in both men's and women's camps, with the exception of 'pink triangles' which were used only for men. Lesbians were not badged because female homosexual behaviour was not criminalized and they were therefore not primarily categorized by this identification.

One point should be clearly emphasized at the outset of this discussion. The National Socialist master-category of race was deeply woven through the entire pattern of detention and treatment of camp inmates from the beginning to the end. Every category of prisoner included Jewish men and women in varying proportions; they were singled out for the worst treatment, and Jewish men had the lowest survival rates even before mass extermination became an official policy. As the chapters by Dieter Pohl and Nikolaus Wachsmann show in detail, the concentration camps were threshholds of genocide for Jewish men and women alike. But before the war, there was a marked disparity between the total numbers of Jewish men and women in detention, and although Jewish women prisoners were routinely singled out for special humiliation they did not suffer the high death rates of Jewish male prisoners. This was demonstrated most strikingly in the fact that only men were detained in the mass round-ups of German Jews in June and November 1938 that brought tens of thousands of them into the camps, making them briefly the majority of all camp inmates. They were treated with the utmost brutality and at least 1,000 died in custody.[23] Conversely, detention in Ravensbrück on grounds of 'Rassenschande', or 'race defilement', was almost exclusively confined to Jewish women consigned to the camp under the *Schutzhaft* regulations.[24]

Gender obviously determined the segregation of men and women into separate camps or camp sections. However, this was not universal in the first stages of detention in 1933, when lack of facilities meant that women were sometimes held alongside men,[25] nor in the later stages of the war, when an increasing number of women's sections were added to men's camps and vice versa, and labour camps housing both sexes were established. Studying the women's camps alone will therefore not capture the full range of women's experiences, and it is here that research is only just beginning. In the early years of the regime, it appears that the authorities may have been even less prepared for the mass detention of women than of men. Thus provisional regulations issued in Saxony in August 1933 for the administration of concentration camps stated that 'Female persons are not to be admitted into concentration or labour service camps', a rule that was routinely ignored.[26] The new generation of men's camps constructed from 1936 had their counterpart in Ravensbrück, the first purpose-built camp for women, which admitted its first prisoners in early 1939. A separate men's camp was attached to Ravensbrück in April 1941, primarily to provide prison labour for the ongoing expansion of the women's camp.[27] Men's and women's camps were staffed and administered on significantly different lines initially, although with an increasing convergence after 1938 when women were moved from Moringen to Lichtenburg and then Ravensbrück. Conditions for women deteriorated sharply during the war, especially when a new women's concentration camp was opened in Auschwitz in the spring of 1942, to relieve overcrowding in Ravensbrück.[28] By the end of the war men and women alike were being shifted from site to site to meet the need for labour, in a process which blurred some of the residual distinctions between men's camps and women's camps.

On top of this, the gendered order had already significantly affected the reasons for the detention of concentration camp inmates. Thus men formed the overwhelming proportion of those held in 'protective detention' (*Schutzhaft*) as political suspects before the war. In the first wave of political repression in 1933/4, tens of thousands of men had been detained, compared with a few hundred women. In the case of communists, the proportions of detained women, at about ten per cent, reflected the proportion of women among the Communist Party (KPD) membership. For the Social Democratic Party (SPD), the other main left-wing party, the number of women prisoners was much lower than their proportionate party membership (perhaps because of their under-representation in positions of authority within the party).[29] This explains why inmate numbers were so small in the women's camp in Moringen during the first phase of the camps as sites of political repression.

This situation changed when Jehovah's Witnesses fell under increased persecution from 1935/6. Proportionally more women were active in the resistance of Jehovah's Witnesses than in any other persecuted or oppositional group. They amounted to about a third of those detained in Lichtenburg by 1938, and 40 per cent of all admissions to Ravensbrück in 1939.[30] Their social profile was distinctive: in Moringen their average age of 45 was higher than that of other inmates (for communist women, for example, it was 37), they were mostly married women with children, and often came from villages and small towns. Thereafter their relative number declined but their absolute numbers continued to rise. By contrast, among male camp inmates the proportion of Jehovah's Witnesses was far lower, nowhere more than 12 per cent (in Buchenwald in 1938).[31] A profile of political and conscientious opponents of the regime in the camps as the war began therefore looked very different for men and women. The regime was more likely to ascribe men's opposition to their political convictions, women's to their religious beliefs. This is not altered by the fact that the category of political prisoners expanded enormously during the war, because virtually all the new 'politicals' were non-German nationals (the largest groups being Russians, Ukrainians and Poles) who were automatically assigned to the 'political' category, whatever the nature of their alleged offence.[32]

Another gendered distinction can be drawn between prisoners sent into detention in the camps as criminals and as so-called 'asocials', i.e. men and women deemed unworthy to be part of the German 'people's community' (*Volksgemeinschaft*).[33] Until we have adequate comparative data on men and women held in *all* the major types of custodial institutions in Germany (i.e. jails, prisons, workhouses, camps of all kinds), it does not seem to me to be possible to give a full assessment of the ways in which offences and penalties were gendered, since similar offences might be followed by different forms and places of punishment. Moreover, although the legal authority for detention was different for criminals and asocials, in practice the distinction between the two categories was not rigid, and offenders with similar records might fall into the hands of the authorities on either count. Still, in Nazi Germany (as elsewhere) women were more likely to be labelled and prosecuted as moral delinquents, while men were treated as workshy or criminal. It must be remembered that most German criminal offenders, male and female, and many non-Germans too, were convicted in the courts and served their sentences in prisons or penitentiaries. Those who ended up in the pre-war concentration camps as 'asocials' or 'criminals' were disproportionately male and had been sent there, either directly or at the end of a prison sentence, as 'habitual' or 'hereditary' criminals under the various regulations on preventive detention.[34]

The typical male 'asocial' sent into the pre-war camps belonged to populations long regarded by the authorities as marginal, shiftless and in need of correction. Following earlier smaller-scale campaigns of detention from 1933, nationally co-ordinated police razzias in 1938 rounded up several thousand 'workshy' men and women and sent them into concentration camps under Gestapo 'protective detention' or 'police preventive detention' (*polizeiliche Vorbeugungshaft*): women to Lichtenburg, men to Sachsenhausen, Buchenwald or Dachau. The men were typically arrested as vagrants, pimps, alcoholics or simply as long-term unemployed, even if this was the result of chronic illness. By mid-August 1938, more than half of Buchenwald's 8,000 inmates were identified as 'workshy'; at the same time a new camp was established at Flossenbürg specifically for male 'asocials' and criminals. Meanwhile 'asocials' composed almost a third of the 1,165 women transferred to Ravensbrück in May 1939.[35]

The grounds for women's detention as 'asocials' were indicative of equally persistent and profoundly conventional social norms: they included unlicensed prostitutes or registered prostitutes who had missed a health inspection, abortionists and women described as 'morally weak', usually on the basis of their sexual behaviour.[36] Among the 'asocials' were 'aryan' women accused of sexual relationships with Jews, gypsies and later Poles which were forbidden on racial grounds, and rather more frequently Jewish women who had relations in the forbidden categories. Unlike men, who could be convicted under clauses 2 and 5 of the September 1935 Law for the Protection of German Blood and German Honour, women partners in these so-called offences, both Jewish and non-Jewish, were not subjected to criminal prosecution but were nevertheless persecuted through police emergency powers.[37] The total number of all these groups was not great before 1939, but in the course of the war the category of the 'asocial' became thoroughly 'feminized', as Wolfgang Ayass has put it. Since the later 1930s the problem had been transformed from that of 'male beggars' to one of 'sexually irregular' young women [38] – perhaps a promiscuous single woman, or, most opprobrious, a soldier's wife sent into a camp because of an extra-marital affair (for which there was a special term: *Kriegsehebruch*). In other words, the 'threat' presented to the social order by women was predictably sexualized or interpreted in terms of their duties as wives or mothers, by contrast to the political or criminal danger imputed to men.[39]

Criminals and 'asocials', whether male or female, were frequently held in low regard by their fellow-prisoners – a mixture of fear, hatred and disdain – although here again the research evidence is insufficient to found more than a preliminary judgment. In the case of German male criminals, this was often due to their status as prisoner functionaries. These functionaries were chosen by the SS, usually from among the German prisoner population, and they enjoyed considerable powers and privileges. German male criminals were often deliberately chosen by the SS as intermediaries to extend their regime of pitiless and capricious authority and favouritism down to the daily life of barracks, block and labour detail. Descriptions of the 'green' and 'black' functionaries in the memoir and witness literature are frequently scathing, especially in the men's camps. Primo Levi called them 'stolid and bestial', men 'to whom a career as a torturer offered an excellent alternative to detention'; the Austrian communist resister Hermann Langbein acknowledged the unfairness of a generalized condemnation of the 'greens', in a chapter titled 'The struggle between reds and greens', but went on to depict camp life in terms of this dualism, as 'a struggle between unscrupulous egoists, morally labile opportunists and the demoralized on the one side ... and the politically aware, unbroken in character, on the other'.[40] However, we should also remember that, in the older-established camps where the 'reds' were able to dominate the prisoner-functionary system, communist functionaries could be no less dreaded by those outside their circle who did not benefit from the communists' priority of sustaining their own comrades and organization, even at the expense of others.[41]

This kind of political exclusiveness was not unknown in the women's camps, notably among the German communists in Ravensbrück.[42] But even though women inmates acquired less influence over the appointment of functionaries than in the most politically organized of the men's camps, their camps lacked the men's close association of criminal with functionary. As far as the 'asocials' were concerned, more women inmates seem to have tempered their disdain with some sympathy or pity for these women, at least when they were not prisoner-functionaries. The communist detainee Margarete Buber-Neumann conceded that the prostitutes and criminals she met as *Blockälteste* (elder) of Block 2 in Ravensbrück were 'victims of society', even if she encountered 'disappointment after disappointment' in her attempt to establish basic rules of decency among them and found their tendency to denunciation 'pitiful and heartbreaking'. The same was true of another *Blockälteste* in the same block, the Catholic oppositionist Nanda Herbermann, who also struggled both to discipline and to develop sympathy for her unruly population of prostitutes.[43]

If the situation of male and female criminals and 'asocials' was comparable but differently inflected, the situation of homosexuals in the camps reflected gendered assumptions and experiences much more starkly. Homosexual acts between men, specifically sodomy, were an offence under the 1871 German Criminal Code (§175). The law was tightened up in 1935 to criminalize virtually any sexual contact between men, and to make the seduction of a younger man a specific offence. These changes accorded with the Nazi view that male homosexual activity was a criminal offence against the German race, in moral and reproductive terms. Such men were regarded as 'the antithesis of the National Socialist masculine ideal [of] physical and mental strength, heroism, and a capacity for self-sacrifice', and as useless for Nazi population-policy goals.[44] Hence the moralist propaganda surrounding the 'cleansing' of the SA in 1934, the extreme homophobic rhetoric of the surviving model *Männerbund*, the SS, and the prosecution of offenders in the Hitler Youth[45] (and hence, too, the differential application of the law in the German-occupied territories during the war, with homosexual offences being prosecuted in France, for example, but not in racially 'inferior' Poland).[46]

Male homosexuality was regarded (and not just by the Nazis) as either a learnt behaviour that could therefore be unlearned, or an inborn impulse that could be eliminated from the population chain. Hence a lot of police interest focused on the allegation of 'seduction', and the severest penalties were applied to men who 'seduced' younger men, or who had 'seduced' more than one partner, or those who were 'rent-boys' (*Stricher*). It was these men, embodying the core assumptions of Nazi homophobia, who were the most likely to be sent into preventive detention in the concentration camps, while the majority of less egregious offenders served sentences in penitentiaries and prison camps.

The estimate of how many men were held in the camps as homosexuals ranges between 10,000 and 15,000,[47] compared with something like 50,000 convictions.[48] It is usually held that homosexuals suffered particularly badly in the camps. Some were subjected to experimental surgical and medical 'treatments' intended to 'cure' their condition.[49] They were also singled out for especially savage treatment by SS guards and prisoner functionaries, faced hostility from their fellow prisoners, and had among the worst death rates (up to 60 per cent in some places or periods) compared with other groups.[50] There is certainly evidence for these conclusions, but little of it comes from testimony from 'homosexual' inmates themselves: fewer than 15 memoirs had been published by 2002.[51]

The witness material we do have is suffused by stereotypical prejudices which may affect its reliability: for example, that this group was more susceptible to ill-treatment, in other words less manly. Research on the Emsland judicial prison camp (not a concentration camp under SS supervision, but the toughest of the judicial camps) suggests that men held as homosexuals were assigned to the same work battalions as other prisoners, and that they were not singled out for worse treatment by the guards (unlike Jewish prisoners). On the other hand, they were more likely to be denounced by other prisoners to the camp authorities for allegedly making homosexual advances than were political prisoners for spreading political ideas. The Emsland camp regulations prescribed that homosexuals were to be distributed thinly throughout the barracks (again unlike Jews, who were segregated), and that they were not to be given tasks within the camp that enabled them to mix with other inmates without supervision. This may have made it difficult for them to maintain the group solidarities that assisted survival, and easier for their fellow-prisoners to act on their prejudices by reporting them for minor offences (although claims of homosexual advances without a third-party witness were often not accepted).[52] The assumption, then, that the most characteristic homosexual was the man unable to restrain his perverted urges had ongoing implications for prisoners in this category.

By contrast with this picture, female homosexuality was not criminalized in the penal code in Nazi Germany, although it was in Austria.[53] This drew on the stereotyped grounds that its implications for women's reproductive capacity were less damaging, that the offence was less clear-cut and that it had a less powerful impact on gender roles.[54] Still, under National Socialism, this form of sexual behaviour among women was unacceptable and may have been penalized when it was discovered. There is very little evidence here, but it includes perhaps a dozen prosecution cases from wartime Berlin where women were charged as 'lesbian' or with 'same-sex activity with women' or 'indecent activity with women'.[55] For women sent to the camps the evidence is even more sparse, with a handful designated as 'lesbian' either in admissions lists or camp files, and others whose designation as 'asocial' may have disguised a sexual component.[56] As far as their treatment in the camps was concerned, the Ravensbrück camp regulations prescribed penalties for what they described as 'lespische Schweinereien' (lespian [sic] vileness).[57]

Camp discipline dictated that inmates should not be able to trust one another, and hence any close friendship was liable to be broken up by the guards. From the inmates' point of view, therefore, friendships that survived official intervention were not only mutually sustaining but also gestures of solidarity and resistance. After the war, women memoirists revealed a concern to absolve their comradely friendships from any imputation of sexual intimacy, and thus to maintain the boundary between what they considered acceptable and unacceptable behaviour. In fact, they were usually reluctant to speak of sexuality at all, not least as a deliberate defence against the prurient and sensationalist public curiosity about camp conditions that greeted their return to ordinary life. When they did, we can find examples where the charge of lesbianism was added to the depiction of any hated guard or prisoner-functionary, as extra evidence of her depravity, or where it was mentioned in tones of the utmost disgust.[58] Here, as in the case of male homosexuality, the historian is limited not only by the lack of subjective evidence, but also by the assumptions or defensiveness of witnesses. On top of this the virtual invisibility of lesbianism in official records makes it hard to assess its salience as a specific target of repression.

The concentration camps were places not only where inmates' sexual identity was punished, but also where male prisoners could be the beneficiaries as well as victims of sexual exploitation and the objects of sexualized violence. This is demonstrated most blatantly in the case of the camp brothels for privileged male prisoners which were established during the war in several camps (including Mauthausen, Buchenwald, Dachau, Neuengamme and parts of the Auschwitz complex). Camp brothels were introduced in mid-1942 at Himmler's behest, with his anxiety that male-only communities, whether of prisoners or SS, were breeding-grounds for the homosexuality he detested. In practice, their rationale was more economic and political than deterrent – sexual rewards given as an incentive for labour productivity and as another way of driving wedges between privileged prisoners and the rest.[59] Male political prisoners liked to claim after the war that they never compromised themselves politically or morally by patronizing the brothels, although the evidence does not entirely bear this out.[60] But what was a 'privilege' for the male clients was not, of course, quite the same for the women who serviced them, who were also camp inmates. The often-asked question whether these women were already prostitutes or not, and whether they were volunteers or had been forced into the brothels, risks missing the central point that this was forced prostitution *tout court*. Women were lured by cynical promises of better conditions and early release, but their 'work' consumed their health and their lives, which regularly ended with untreated STDs.[61]

Camp prostitution thus correctly belongs in the catalogue of sexual exploitation and sexual violence that has been very difficult to bring to light, given the multiple inhibitions and repressions that surrounded this subject – and which after the war often echoed the sexual politics of the history itself. The very existence of the camp brothel in Buchenwald was long suppressed by the camp memorial site and the official survivors' association, as incompatible with a heroic ideal of masculine but asexual political resistance.[62] The memoir literature, which is replete with accounts of the most terrible violence and cruelty, tends only to hint at the relationship between physical and sexual violence, rather than making it explicit, especially in the case of men. The repeated references to the sadism of SS and Kapos are unmissable examples of this, so too the not infrequent ghastly association of punishment with excrement, designed to force the victim into the utmost depths of humiliation.[63] In a discussion of terror, torture and excess in the camps, Sofsky argues that 'sadism' does not capture the essential systematic character of this violence, which he likens to 'a form of military barracks harassment raised to a barbaric level, a brute and vicious hazing come unhinged'.[64] This plausibly links camp violence against men to similar contexts designed specifically to break their individuality and will; yet the element of sexualized degradation in any of these masculine sites ought not to be underplayed. Gender identity, too, was 'unhinged' by sexual or sexualized assault, in a barrage of indignity and shame that expropriated people's individuality *as* men, and *as* women.

Against a certain reticence about the sexualized victimization of men, this dimension of the suffering of women prisoners is much more likely be acknowledged. Women were the victims of physically brutal treatment at the hands of both men and women – the guards and camp personnel whose operations will be described in the next section. Even in the camps staffed by women warders, they were often in the direct power of male SS personnel, physicians as well as guards, especially at the moment of arrival in a camp when the cruel rituals of admission – being stripped, searched, shorn – were administered by or under the gaze of men. For young girls or women from sheltered backgrounds in particular, and for the other prisoners who witnessed their shame as well as their own, these systematic violations of modesty represented a degradation that might be no less grievous than the physical violence visited on men.[65] Evidence that has been painfully recovered in recent years suggests that sexual assaults by SS guards were not unknown, although this has remained exceptionally difficult to speak about and its full extent may remain concealed.[66]

The consequences of rape, and of fertility in general, were dire. It is true that many women ceased menstruation during their imprisonment, but not all (in which case they also underwent the extra indignity of having no access to sanitary protection), and some women were imprisoned when already pregnant. In Ravensbrück, racially 'acceptable' women who were pregnant on admission delivered their babies, who were then forcibly handed over to the German welfare authorities and raised elsewhere. Victims of rape, and after 1942 most pregnant women, were either forced to undergo abortion or else delivered of infants who were then left to die.[67]

It seems the case that women prisoners more often responded to the unending inhumanity and atrocity of camp existence by developing closer friendships than men did, building circles of intimacy that also offered some substitute for the agonizing absence of their families. Women's memoirs, at any rate, seem more able to conjure up the life-sustaining quality of these friendships, as well as having recourse to an unselfconscious imagery of family that came less easily to men.[68] In their own accounts, men may appear more ambivalent about the competing value of ruthless selfishness and co-operative friendship as requisites for survival in the wartime camps; more emphasized are the political networks of solidarity and resistance built up in prewar camps such as Buchenwald. It is important, however, not to gender intimacy as female and political solidarity as male survival strategies. In Ravensbrück, women prisoners built their own networks of political and national solidarity that were instrumental in preserving dignity and saving lives, while conversely men's dependence on one another does not go entirely unremarked.[69]

Before the war, men were undoubtedly exposed to far worse conditions of existence than women in the camps, in terms of both the levels of physical violence permitted and the types of labour exacted from them. As the chapter by Jens-Christian Wagner shows, prisoner labour had a series of overlapping functions during the history of the camps: as a means of breaking morale, as 'extermination through work' and as productive work for the German war economy. Before the war, work as a means to break inmates' morale took the same gruelling form in Ravensbrück and the men's camps, usually back-breaking physical labour like useless digging and carrying heavy loads. But while men were subjected to this kind of penal labour from the start, for women it began only with the move to Lichtenburg in 1937. Otherwise, a conventional ideology of the sexual division of labour meant that, while men were set to heavy labouring work in construction and quarrying, women were likely to be assigned to 'women's work' such as textile manufacture, mat-making, tailoring and the like, although some were drafted to fieldwork. This division of labour persisted to some extent during the war, with women working on the assembly side of the war industries – including in the Siemens works established at Ravensbrück. Convention did not, however, dictate any lesser level of exploitation for women in terms of exhausting hours, oppressive conditions of work and brutal supervision. And during the war women, especially Jewish women, were more likely to be drafted into heavy construction and clearance work – physically exhausting forms of labour in appalling conditions that were as lethal to them as to men.[70]

This discussion raises important questions about men's and women's survival strategies which have been reviewed in the literature cited here – notably, the extent to which both prior socialization and the conditions of camp existence gave men and women different resources and chances, whether greater or lesser; and the extent to which either sex was physically and emotionally more able to endure the exhaustion, malnutrition and inhumane treatment they suffered in the camps.[71] Here it is important not to be reductive. As Falk Pingel's chapter shows, conditions in the camps varied significantly according to time, place and the populations incarcerated, in ways that could make gender less salient than 'race' or nationality, for example. Both men's and women's camps knew the category of inmates who had sunk into starvation and despair – the 'Muselmen' of the men's camp jargon, also known as 'cripples', 'swimmers', 'donkeys' or 'cretins', whose counterparts were the 'Schmuckstücke' or 'Goldstücke' (jewels, gold coins) of the women's camps.[72] The heavy irony of the women's terms contrasts with the more literal dismissiveness of the men's. These prisoners and their epithets embodied the character of the camps as places where human identity itself was destroyed, as well as conveying inmates' desperate need to differentiate themselves from those who had already given up the battle for survival.[73]

What that identity was might be as varied as the customs, conventions and expectations of men and women from every social class and numerous nationalities, incarcerated on many different grounds; and the repertoire of defences and responses was no less varied. Our sense of differences between men's and women's responses is lop-sided in a way that continues to reflect the normative and unreflected category of the male. Recent historians have had much to say about how women's responses seem gender-specific, but not so much to say about men's reactions as such.[74] And we should be mindful that representations of men's behaviour as well as women's may themselves embody untested gender stereotypes and expectations.[75] The work of bringing these to light remains unfinished.

Camp regimes and guards

For most of the history of the camps, men and women were segregated in different camps or at least in separate sections of the same camp. This did not mean that women's camps were run exclusively by women, nor were women entirely absent from the men's camps, where they were employed in office and other supporting roles, as well as living there as wives of SS men.[76] However, the staffing of the camps and the camp regimes as a whole do show predictable and striking differences between men's and women's camps. In the first dedicated women's camp at Moringen, the internal staffing and regime resembled that of the workhouse that occupied the same site, and this at a time when men's camps were already under a punitive and often lethal disciplinary regime imposed by uniformed and armed SS troops.[77] The SS guard system in men's camps, described in detail in Karin Orth's chapter, was expanded and further militarized in the later 1930s: in fact, the concentration camp system served as the training-ground for the SS regiments that Himmler was developing as a rival to the army and as a wartime security force for Germany and its conquests. During the war these roles blurred as SS men were rotated to and from the front, and later when older armed forces personnel staffed the camps.[78] The militarization of the SS had a profound effect on the situation of male prisoners. SS troops, already trained to vicious standards of discipline, were further brutalized by their experiences at or near the eastern front, and the wartime camp regimes reflected this grim increment of terror when they returned for tours of duty there.

Not until the women's camp was moved to Lichtenburg did its regime begin to resemble that of the men's camps, although women held as political detainees in women's prisons after 1933 were often brutally treated. For the first time women inmates were under the control of an SS 'director', and SS troops were responsible for the camp's external security, with women warders supervising the women within the camp. Male guards were equipped with dogs and truncheons, corporal punishment was permitted, and the general standards of diet and discipline were measurably worse than the Moringen regime. When Ravensbrück was opened in May 1939, the system took a step further towards the men's model, although significant differences still remained. As in men's camps, external security and internal supervision were separately organized, and the administrative structure of the camp now exactly replicated that of the men's camps. The camp was under the authority of an SS commandant and SS men were responsible for security. However, prisoners were supervised by women warders both within the camp and on work details outside it, and the commandant was assisted and advised by a senior female warder, the *Oberaufseherin*, whose relations with the commandant and other male staff were far from smooth.[79] These women were attached to the Waffen-SS, but they were not members of this exclusively male and supposedly élite organization. From 1940 they wore a military-style uniform, and were equipped with pistols and dogs when escorting work squads.

Like the SS guards, these were mainly younger women, recruited when single and preferably childless (although this was by no means always the case). They were recruited locally by word of mouth, by press advertisements, and from arms factories or via the labour offices. By comparison with other jobs to which women were allocated, the conditions of work could sound attractive enough, while the moral demands of the job were played down in the advertised job descriptions. The women's preparation was usually a basic education, followed by employment in unskilled work such as the catering and service trades or in lower levels of the welfare system. In Ravensbrück they lived on-site in newly built housing, which included shared flats for single women and houses for married couples and children (who lived in a separate kindergarten during the week); these living conditions were probably superior to what they could have expected from other jobs. The evidence indicates that, although a few women left because they could not endure the camp, those who stayed quickly normalized their work, taking part in the planned leisure activities and escaping to local towns and villages for relaxation when they could.[80]

Even though Ravensbrück became the training centre for warders who were later sent to the women's camps in the east, the total numbers remained low: 3000–4000 compared with 37,600 men. This meant that some of the camps in the east were staffed by men, and women inmates probably suffered more deadly physical violence at the hands of their male than female guards. Insofar as this difficult aspect can be quantified and assessed, it is likely that women warders were no more inhibited than men in their sense of utter superiority and their physical as well as verbal violence against women prisoners, but that the direct effects of their assaults were less lethal than in the men's camps.[81] However, this did not mean that women warders were not guilty of numerous acts of brutality as well as killing; nor can they escape responsibility for staffing and operating an inhumane and murderous regime which during the war involved selections for murder by injection or gassing. The disciplinary regime in the men's camps had always involved both arbitrary violence on the part of SS guards (regulations to the contrary were meaningless) and official physical punishment, which included flogging and executions, as well as incarceration in punishment cells. The Moringen women's camp had a punishment cell, and corporal punishment was sanctioned for women with the move into Lichtenburg. Flogging then became a regular and intensified part of the Ravensbrück regime; it was carried out by women warders and also (as in the men's camps) by other prisoners. Executions began in Ravensbrück in 1941.[82] Female warders and women prisoner-functionaries alike were convicted after the war of crimes of violence against women prisoners.

The post-war depiction of men and women concentration camp guards in fact offers a final example of how the gender order operates to code male and female identities and behaviours. Numerous accounts convey a sense of horror and disgust at the women warders' betrayal of feminine characteristics and values. Thus Langbein's history of Auschwitz twice suggests, in almost identical language, that the 'demoralization' of female warders was even worse than that of men; and while he characterizes male guards in terms of their background and training, the women are described in terms of their feminine or unfeminine physical appearance.[83] For Isa Vermehren, an upper-class German prisoner in Ravensbrück, the warders presented a 'schizophrenic' appearance: 'the fullest womanly forms – along with forced masculine movements; tightly curled hair and big earrings – along with culottes and jackboots; dull, childish eyes – along with harsh, loud voices'.[84]

Recent analyses of the earliest trials and press reports of concentration camp guards have shown how gendered stereotypes were used by accusers to explain the guards' character and behaviour, and by the defendants to disclaim responsibility. On the one hand, as Ulrike Weckel and Edgar Wolfrum have argued, both male and female guards were demonized as deviant and abnormal; but because male behaviour fitted the masculine norms expected of Nazism it was less closely analysed by comparison with women, whose breach of gendered norms was rarer and thus more sensationalized and condemned. Women 'had done something that really only men do' – and furthermore had not exerted a moral restraint on men – and thus they were seen as monsters who threatened the gender order itself.[85] On the other hand, women's offences might be played down as being the result of their susceptibility to male influence or their own naivety. Women defendants could plead this in their defence, especially because they were not in a militarized command structure and therefore could not claim, like the men, to have only been following orders. In fact, when men made these claims they also subverted their demonized masculine image, albeit in a familiar military context of command and compliance. These judgments of exceptionality are perhaps understandable in the immediate aftermath of the Nazi period. It was only much later that the idea of 'ordinary men', and now 'ordinary women', has been able to make its way into the literature, and this at a time when the gender dimension of 'ordinariness' has also become more acknowledged.

How gender matters

The clearest lessons of this chapter may not be entirely surprising but they still deserve emphasis: that similar institutions and practices look different if we factor in gender; that there are gendered norms and hierarchies that serve functional and legitimizing purposes; that occupying an inferior position in the hierarchy of gender offers no automatic protection from enjoying whatever quantum of power is available;[86] and that transgressions of gender norms in such an intensively militarized and hierarchical society such as Nazi Germany were seen as unusually disturbing, and were therefore liable to be severely repressed or punished rather than being ignored or marginalized. In Nazi Germany, as in other highly activist or contested societies, the sexual and gender margins saw some of the most punitive policing of norms – even as those policing processes called the entire structure into question. For the core itself was not immune from contamination. The Nazi movement had been a 'Männerbund' (male community) since its earliest days and was saturated by military and masculine ideals and imagery, and this bore its own dangers. Thus Himmler expressed concern at the risk that homosexuality would be fostered by the 'excesssively strong masculinization' of the Nazi movement (reminding the SS to include dances in their leisure activities so that SS men could mingle with suitable young women); he insisted that the standard of behaviour of SS camp guards should be 'hard' but not 'cruel' – a distinction he was frequently at pains to assert; he notoriously claimed as one of the greatest achievements of the 'final solution of the Jewish question' that its executors had 'remained decent'

– but also 'tough' – in the face of the moral challenges of their task; and he voiced anxieties about the threat to gender difference posed by the masculinization of women.[87] These observations yield some preliminary conclusions about the 'gendering' of the concentration camp system.

First, it is arguable, as I have already indicated, that women were in fact 'supplementary' in the universe of the camps. The striking feature of the 'Dachau model' (insofar as its status as 'model' is still persuasive) is how quickly it released itself from the norms of existing custodial institutions and established new standards of brutality aimed at the total subjugation, by physical and psychological violence, of the individual will or personality. By contrast, the striking feature of the women's camps is that it took several years, until the end of 1937, before they even began to diverge from the existing institutions and norms of women's custody, and even longer before the treatment of women inmates approached the standard of brutality long applied to men. This might have been the result of official inattention, inexperience or inhibition as far as women were concerned; and had the regime lasted longer, those first few hesitant years might have seemed but a temporary first step. True to the perverse logic of the Third Reich, the moment of greatest equality was achieved when mass killing became integrated into the camps from 1942: at that point, women would be no more protected than men from elimination.

This is related to a second point, which is that the concentration camp violated or re-made men's identities in different ways from women's. As this chapter has suggested, of all the sites and operations of gender, those in which men are entangled are the most difficult to uncover, precisely because their normative status makes them self-evident and therefore inconspicuous. The tug towards gendering women as female and leaving the male norm undisturbed is hard to resist, but this chapter has tried to show how this can be done and how it might be pursued further. In the men's camps there was a virtually unbridgeable gulf between the demasculinization of the inmates, and the hyper-masculinization of their SS guards. In Sofsky's terms, the claim to absolute power created, in principle at least, a counter-position of absolute powerlessness. The SS – specious as this aspiration may have been – was supposed to be an elite of the elite, utterly demarcated from an inmate population defined as enemies of the Volk, and able to live to the full their own masculine superiority and the unmanning of their victims on a daily basis. Their position vis-à-vis the inmates was not unlike that described by Joshua Goldstein in his study *War and Gender*, where he concludes that the defining feature of war as a male pursuit is the feminization of enemies as symbolic domination.[88] The exceptions here were the prisoner functionaries whose authority was on loan from the SS, as well as other prisoners entangled in the webs of corruption and favouritism that linked guards to inmates – yet in both cases, the SS retained their one-sided power to give or withhold patronage. The power relationship in this ambiguous 'grey zone' lacked any quality of negotiation, and only underlined the moral subjugation of the inmates.[89]

In the women's camps, by contrast, there were much less well recognized or effective models of power and hierarchy to sustain the demarcation between inmate and guard, though how this played out in practice is not entirely clear. The SS retained the ultimate power over the women's camps: they provided the commandants and the external guards. To be sure, for the women inmates their female guards were just as omnipotent and vicious as were the SS men. But even though they were associated with the SS, these *Aufseherinnen* had little of the character of an élite corps. They were not recruited as such, nor, despite their ideological training, did they become an élite, but rather were invited to see themselves as employees who were doing a difficult but necessary task for Germany. Maintaining the 'femininity' of uniformed and armed women warders was potentially a harder task for women warders than for SS guards, who only had to extend to an extreme degree positive values and behaviour rooted in longstanding masculine and military codes. By contrast, women warders had to disown 'feminine' values and behaviour on the job, and were duly vilified for this perversity by inmates and postwar commentators alike. Conversely, women prisoners were demoralized by their lack of clean clothing, towels, combs and washing facilities, and young women in particular made every effort to maintain a feminine appearance, even in defiance of camp regulations.[90]

The most vicious applications of the power of life and death in Nazi Germany were indisputably racial in origin and purpose. Race, as Gisela Bock has argued, set the limits within which gender was a meaningful category,[91] and this requires us to acknowledge the ultimate priority of racial difference. But as long as gender is admitted into the picture with this caveat, the empirical evidence allows us to expose the ways in which this form of difference was played out in power structure of the concentration camp, the essential site of Nazi coercion and violence.

Notes

1 Thanks to Jan Lambertz, Robert Moeller and Nikolaus Wachsmann for advice and references for this chapter.
2 The historiography on gender and the Holocaust is much more extensive than for the concentration camps and it offers many useful insights, but it cannot be reviewed here. For starting-points see D. Ofer and L. J. Weitzman (eds) *Women in the Holocaust*, New Haven, CT: Yale University Press, 1998, and A. Grossmann, 'Women and the Holocaust: Four Recent Titles', *Holocaust and Gender Studies* 16, 1, Spring 2002, 94–107.
3 Full accounts of this research in German history can be found in K. Hagemann and J. H. Quataert (eds) *Gendering Modern German History: Rewriting Historiography*, New York/Oxford: Berghahn Books, 2007.
4 For a survey see C. Koonz, 'A Tributary and a Mainstream. Gender, Public Memory, and Historiography of Nazi Germany', in Hagemann and Quataert (eds) *Gendering Modern German History*, pp. 147–68.
5 C. Füllberg-Stolberg, M. Jung, R. Riebe and Martina Scheitenberger (eds) *Frauen in Konzentrationslagern – Bergen-Belsen, Ravensbrück*, Bremen: Temmen, 1994, p. 8.
6 The most important include *Ravensbrück*, Neuchâtel: Cahiers du Rhône, 1946; G. Tillion, *Ravensbrück*, Neuchâtel: Editions de la Baconnière, 1946; T. Bruha *et al.*, *Frauen-Konzentrationslager Ravensbrück. Geschildert von Ravensbrücker Häftlingen*, Vienna: Sternverlag, 1945; N. Herbermann, *Der gesegnete Abgrund. Schutzhäftling Nr. 6582 im Frauenkonzentrationslager Ravensbrück*, Nuremberg: Glock und Lutz, 1946; I. Vermehren, *Reise durch den letzten Akt. Ravensbrück, Buchenwald, Dachau: eine Frau berichtet*, Hamburg:

Christian Wegner, 1946. For a summary of titles available in English, see 'Suggestions for Further Reading' in the English translation of Herbermann, *The Blessed Abyss: Inmate #6582 in Ravensbrück Concentration Camp for Women*, ed. H. Baer and E. R. Baer, Detroit, MI: Wayne State University Press, 2000, pp. 253–60.

7   Sigrid Jacobeit, 'Vorwort', in I. Eschebach, S. Jacobeit and S. Wenk (eds) *Gedächtnis und Geschlecht. Deutungsmuster in der Darstellung des nationalsozialistischen Genozids*, Frankfurt/New York: Campus, 2002, p. 9.

8   Ibid., p. 10.

9   Himmler speech to SS-Gruppenführer conference, 8 November 1937, in B. Smith and A. Peterson (eds) *Heinrich Himmler. Die Geheimreden 1933 bis 1945 und andere Ansprachen*, Frankfurt: Propyläen, 1974, pp. 111–2.

10 G. Pfingsten and C. Füllberg-Stolberg, 'Frauen in Konzentrationslagern – geschlechtsspezifische Bedingungen des Überlebens', in U. Herbert, K. Orth and C. Dieckmann (eds) *Die nationalsozialistischen Konzentrationslager. Entwicklung und Struktur*, Göttingen: Wallstein, 1998, vol. 2, p. 911.

11 For recent overviews of the state of research, see B. Distel, 'Frauen in nationalsozialistischen Konzentrationslagern – Opfer und Täterinnen', in W. Benz and B. Distel (eds) *Der Ort des Terrors. Geschichte der nationalsozialistischen Konzentrationslager*, vol. 1 (Die Organisation des Terrors), Munich: C. H. Beck, 2005, pp. 195–209, and A. Leo, 'Ravensbrück – Stammlager', ibid., vol. 4 (Flossenbürg, Mauthausen, Ravensbrück), Munich: Beck, 2006, pp. 473–520; see also B. Strebel, *Das KZ Ravensbrück. Geschichte eines Lagerkomplexes*, Paderborn: Ferdinand Schöningh, 2003, pp. 22–30. For a survey of the historiography on women in the wartime *Aussenlager*, see H. Ellger, *Zwangsarbeit und weibliche Überlebensstrategien. Die Geschichte der Frauenaussenlager des Konzentrationslagers Neuengamme 1944/45*, Reihe Geschichte der Konzentrationslager, vol. 8, Berlin: Metropol, 2007, pp. 14–20.

12 For comments on this point, see U. Weckel and E. Wolfrum, 'NS-Prozesse und ihre öffentliche Resonanz aus geschlechtergeschichtlicher Perspektive', in U. Weckel and E. Wolfrum (eds), *'Bestien' und 'Befehlsempfänger'. Frauen und Männer in NS-Prozessen nach 1945*, Göttingen: Vandenhoeck und Ruprecht, 2003, pp. 9–21, and S. Wenk and I. Eschebach, 'Soziales Gedächtnis und Geschlechterdifferenz. Eine Einführung', in Eschebach, Jacobeit and Wenk (eds) *Gedächtnis und Geschlecht*, pp. 13–38.

13 A similar point is made in respect of sexuality by E. D. Heinemann, 'Sexuality and Nazism: The Doubly Unspeakable?', in D. Herzog (ed.) *Sexuality and German Fascism*, New York/Oxford: Berghahn, 2005, pp. 22–66.

14 K. Canning, *Gender History in Practice: Historical Perspectives on Bodies, Class and Citizenship*, Ithaca, NY/London: Cornell University Press, 2006, Part I, offers valuable reflections on gender theory from a German historical perspective.

15 S. Wenk and I. Eschebach, 'Soziales Gedächtnis und Geschlechterdifferenz', p. 13. For the complex relations of gender and the holocaust in historical scholarship, see e.g. G. Bock (ed.) *Genozid und Geschlecht. Jüdische Frauen im nationalsozialistischen Lagersystem*, Frankfurt/New York: Campus, 2005, also Grossmann, 'Women and the Holocaust'; on sexuality, the excellent discussion in Heinemann, 'Sexuality and Nazism'; and H. Amesberger, K. Auer and B. Halbmayr, *Sexualisierte Gewalt. Weibliche Erfahrungen in NS-Konzentrationslagern*, Vienna: Mandelbaum Verlag, 2007.

16 B. Bettelheim. *The Informed Heart: The Human Condition in Mass Society*, Harmondsworth: Penguin Books, 1987 (1st edn 1960); T. des Pres, *The Survivor: An Anatomy of Life in the Death Camps*, New York: Oxford University Press, 1976; W. Sofsky, *The Order of Terror: The Concentration Camp*, Princeton, NJ: Princeton University Press, 1997.

17 Sofsky, *Order of Terror*, pp. 23, 42,48 (camps); p. 51 (Birkenau); p. 42 (forced marches); p. 84 (uniforms).

18 Ibid., pp. 36, 43 (Tables 1 and 2); p. 109 (guards).

19 Ibid., 97, quoting from the memoirs of Rudolf Höss, the commandant of Auschwitz.

20 For this relationship, see G. Mosse, *Nationalism and Sexuality: Respectability and Abnormal Sexuality in Modern Europe*, New York: Howard Fertig, 1985, Chapter 8; S. Behrenbeck, *Der Kult um die toten Helden. Nationalsozialistische Mythen, Riten und Symbole*, Schernfeld: S-H Verlag, 1996; G. Schwarz, *Eine Frau an seine Seite. Ehefrauen in der SS-Sippengemeinschaft*, Hamburg: Hamburger Edition, 1997; J. A. Mangan (ed.) *Shaping the Superman: Fascist Body as Political Icon: Aryan Fascism*, London: Frank Cass, 1999; R. Schilling, *'Kriegshelden'. Deutungsmuster heroischer Männlichkeit in Deutschland 1813–1945*, Paderborn: Schöningh, 2004, esp. pp. 333–41; P. Diehl, *Macht – Mythos – Utopie. Die Körperbilder der SS-Männer*, Berlin: Akademie-Verlag, 2004; K. Hagemann and S. Schüler-Springorum (eds) *Home/Front: The Military, War and Gender in Twentieth-Century Germany*, Oxford/New York: Berg, 2002; T. Kühne, *Kameradschaft. Die Soldaten des nationalsozialistischen Krieges und das 20. Jahrhundert*, Göttingen: Vandenhoeck und Ruprecht, 2006; A. Timm, 'Sex with a Purpose: Prostitution, Venereal Disease, and Militarized Masculinity in the Third Reich', in Herzog (ed.) *Sexuality and German Fascism*, pp. 223–55.

21 For this view, see T. Debski, *A Battlefield of Ideas: Nazi Concentration Camps and their Polish Prisoners*, Boulder, CO: East European Monographs, 2001, pp. 88–97.

22 For examples of this, which echoed the order in which prisoner categories were listed on publicly displayed boards in the camps, see e.g. M. Broszat, 'The Concentration Camps 1933–45', in H. Krausnick, H. Buchheim, M. Broszat and H.-A. Jacobsen, *Anatomy of the SS State*, New York: Walker, 1965, p. 452; D. A. Hackett (ed.) *The Buchenwald Report*, Boulder CO: Westview, 1995, pp. 30–1; A. Pawelczynska, *Values and Violence in Auschwitz: A Sociological Analysis*, Berkeley, CA: University of California Press, 1979, pp. 85–6; and M. Buber-Neumann, *Under Two Dictators: Prisoner of Stalin and Hitler*, London: Pimlico, 2009, p. 163. The use of the categories in the camps and for postwar restitution policies is discussed in detail by A. Eberle, 'Häftlingskategorien und Kennzeichnungen', in Benz and Distel (eds) *Ort des Terrors*, vol. 1, pp. 91–109. See also the chapter by Falk Pingel in this volume.

23 See e.g. P. Longerich, *Politik der Vernichtung*, Munich: Piper, 1998, and the chapters by Dieter Pohl and Nikolaus Wachsmann in this volume.

24 The detention of Jewish women in Ravensbrück on this and other grounds is discussed in L. Apel, *Jüdische Frauen im Konzentrationslager Ravensbrück 1939–1945*, Berlin: Metropol, 2003; for a summary see Strebel, *Das KZ Ravensbrück*, pp. 126–34.

25 See e.g. C. Baganz, *Erziehung zur 'Volksgemeinschaft'? Die frühen Konzentrationslager in Sachsen 1933–34/37*, Berlin: Metropol, 2005 (Geschichte der Konzentrationslager 1933–1945, vol. 6), pp. 132–6; J. Wetzel, 'Stadelheim', in Benz and Distel (eds) *Der Ort des Terrors*, vol. 2 (Frühe Lager. Dachau. Emslandlager), Munich: C. H. Beck, 2005, pp. 169–71. The first women inmates in Moringen were admitted while the camp was still primarily a camp for male *Schutzhäftlinge*: see H. Hesse, *Das Frauen-KZ Moringen 1933–1938*, Hürth: Books on Demand GmbH, 2nd edn 2002, pp. 18–35.

26 Baganz, *Erziehung zur 'Volksgemeinschaft'?*, p. 132.

27 Strebel, *Das KZ Ravensbrück*, pp. 289–319.

28 F. Jahn, 'Auschwitz. Frauenabteilung', in Benz and Distel (eds) *Der Ort des Terrors*, vol. 4, pp. 523–8.

29 For communist women, see K.-M. Mallmann, 'Zwischen Denunziation und Roter Hilfe. Geschlechterbeziehungen und kommunistischer Widerstand', in C. Wickert (ed.) *Frauen gegen die Diktatur. Widerstand und Verfolgung im nationalsozialistischen Deutschland*, Berlin: Hentrich, 1995, pp. 82–97; for the female political detainees in the 1933/4 period, see Hesse, *Das Frauen-KZ Moringen*; and M. Kienle, *Gotteszell – das frühe Konzentrationslager für Frauen in Württemberg. Die 'Schutzhaftabteilung' im Frauengefängnis Gotteszell in Schwäbisch Gmünd März 1933 bis Januar 1934*, Ulm: Klemm & Oelschläger, 2002.

30 J. Harder and H. Hesse, 'Female Jehovah's Witnesses in Moringen Women's Concentration Camp: Women's Resistance in Nazi Germany', in H. Hesse (ed.) *Persecution and Resistance of Jehovah's Witnesses*, pp. 40–3; B. Strebel, 'Ravensbrück –

das zentrale Frauenkonzentrationslager', in Herbert, Orth and Dieckmann (eds) *Die nationalsozialistischen Konzentrationslager*, p. 221.

31 D. Garbe, *Between Resistance and Martyrdom: Jehovah's Witnesses in the Third Reich*, Madison, WI: University of Wisconsin Press/United States Holocaust Memorial Museum, 2008, p. 394.

32 See Strebel, *KZ Ravensbrück*, pp.111–68.

33 The adoption and extent of the category 'asocial' as grounds for detention is discussed in C. Schikorra, *Kontinuitäten der Ausgrenzung. 'Asoziale' Häftlinge im Frauen-konzentrationslager Ravensbrück*, Berlin: Metropol, 2001, Chapter 1; also Broszat, 'Concentration Camps', pp. 446–52. The decree on the detention of 'asocials' was enforced by the criminal police, not by the Gestapo which handled political offenders. On asocials see also R. Gellately and N. Stoltzfus (eds) *Social Outsiders in Nazi Germany*, Princeton, NJ: Princeton University Press, 2001, and W. Ayass, *'Asoziale' im Nationalsozialismus*, Stuttgart: Klett-Cotta, 1995. There is virtually no research into criminals in the camps, but see N. Wachsmann, *Hitler's Prisons: Legal Terror in Nazi Germany*, New Haven, CT/London: Yale University Press, 2004, pp. 184–8 and Chapter 8 especially.

34 During the war large numbers of convicts were purged from the prisons and sent to the camps; see Wachsmann, *Hitler's Prisons*, Chapter 8. We know very little about women convicts in this period, although as Wachsmann points out their absolute and relative numbers shot up after 1939; see pp. 231–2, 241–2, 289–90, 326–7 and Figure 5, p. 396.

35 This account taken from Ayass, *'Asoziale' im Nationalsozialismus*, pp. 138–47.

36 See principally Schikorra, *Kontinuität der Ausgrenzung*; also R. Riebe, 'Frauen im Konzentrationslager 1933–1939', *Dachauer Hefte* 1998, vol. 14: Verfolgung als Gruppenschicksal, 125–40; on prostitution and sexual promiscuity, see A. Timm, 'The Ambivalent Outsider: Prostitution, Promiscuity, and VD Control in Nazi Berlin', in Gellately and Stoltzfus (eds) *Social Outsiders in Nazi Germany*; Herzog (ed.) *Sexuality and German Fascism*; Ayass, *'Asoziale' im Nationalsozialismus*, pp. 184–96.

37 The law, one of the 'Nuremberg laws', is reprinted in J. Noakes and G. Pridham (eds) *Nazism 1919–1945: A Documentary Reader*, Exeter: Exeter University Press, 2000, vol. 2, pp. 340–7.

38 Ayass, *'Asoziale' im Nationalsozialismus*,p. 219.

39 Dagmar Herzog's contrary argument that Nazis did not repress but 'harness' prior liberal values about sex should be noted here: Herzog (ed.) *Sexuality and German Fascism*, p. 4.

40 P. Levi, *If This Is a Man*, Harmondsworth: Penguin Books, 1979, p. 97; P. Levi, *The Drowned and the Saved*, London: Abacus, 1989, p. 47; H. Langbein, *'… nicht wie die Schafe zur Schlachtbank. Widerstand in den nationalsozialistischen Konzentrationslagern*, Frankfurt: Fischer, 1980, Chapter 4: Der Kampf zwischen Roten und Grünen, pp. 45–6.

41 See K. Hartewig, 'Wolf under Wölfen? Die prekäre Macht der kommunistischen Kapos im Konzentrationslager Buchenwald', in Herbert, Orth and Dieckmann (eds) *Die nationalsozialistischen Konzentrationslager*, vol. 2, pp. 939–58.

42 See B. Strebel, 'Die "Lagergesellschaft". Aspekte der Häftlingshierarchie und Gruppenbildung in Ravensbrück', and Irmtraud Heike and Bernhard Strebel, 'Häftlingsselbstverwaltung und Funktionshäftlinge im Konzentrationslager Ravensbrück', in Füllberg-Stolberg, Jung, Riebe and Scheitenberger (eds) *Frauen in Konzentrationslager* , pp. 79–88 and 89–97; A. Grossmann, 'Zwei Erfahrungen im Kontext des Themas "Gender und Holocaust"', in S. Jacobeit and G. Philipp (eds) *Forschungsschwerpunkt Ravensbrück. Beiträge zur Geschichte des Frauen-Konzentrationslagers*, Berlin: Hentrich, 1997, pp. 136–46.

43 Buber-Neumann, *Under Two Dictators*, pp. 171–3; Herbermann, *The Blessed Abyss*, Chapters 19–21. See also Schikorra, *Kontinuität der Ausgrenzung*, pp. 206–222, for a comprehensive evaluation of the image of 'asocial' women in Ravensbrück; and Heike and Strebel, 'Häftlingsselbstverwaltung und Funktionshäftlinge'.

44 S. Micheler, 'Homophobic Propaganda and the Denunciation of Same-Sex-Desiring Men under National Socialism', in Herzog (ed.) *Sexuality and German Fascism*, p. 96.

45 G. S. Giles, 'The Denial of Homosexuality: Same-Sex Incidents in Himmler's Police and SS', in ibid.; and G. S Gilles, 'Männerbund mit Homo-Panik: Die Angst der Nazis vor der Rolle der Erotik', in B. Jellonnek and R. Lautmann (eds) *Nationalsozialistischer Terror gegen Homosexuelle. Verdrängt und ungesühnt*, Paderborn: Schöningh, 2002. Note that this led, as Giles points out, to a reluctance to investigate the true extent of homosexuality in the nation.

46 J. Müller, 'Betrifft: Haftgruppen "Homosexuelle"', in Olaf Mussmann (ed.) *Homosexuelle in Konzentrationslager*, Berlin/Bonn: Westkreuz Verlag, 2000, p. 18.

47 K. Müller, 'Totgeschlagen, totgeschwiegen? Das autobiographische Zeugnis homosexueller Überlebender', in Jellonnek and Lautmann (eds) *Nationalsozialistischer Terror gegen Homosexueller*, pp. 397 f.

48 C. von Bülow, 'Der soziale status der als homosexuell verfolgten Inhaftierten in den Emslandlagern', in Mussmann (ed.) *Homosexuelle in Konzentrationslager*, p. 44.

49 Müller 'Betrifft: Haftgruppen "Homosexuelle"', p. 16.

50 Hackett (ed.) *Buchenwald Report*, p. 173; Müller 'Betrifft: Haftgruppen "Homosexuelle"'; B. Strebel, 'Die "Rosa-Winkel-Häftlinge" im Männerlager des KZ Ravensbrück', in H. Diercks (ed.) *Verfolgung von Homosexuellen im Nationalsozialismus*, Bremen: Edition Temmen, 1999, pp. 62–9; Müller, 'Totgeschlagen, totgeschwiegen?', p. 397.

51 Ibid., p. 397.

52 See von Bülow, 'Der soziale Status der als homosexuell verfolgten Inhaftierten'.

53 In English see C. Schoppmann, *Days of Masquerade: Life Stories of Lesbians during the Third Reich*, New York: Columbia University Press, 1993.

54 C. Schoppmann, 'Zeit der Maskierung. Zur Situation lesbischer Frauen im Nationalsozialismus', in Jellonnek and Lautmann (eds) *Nationalsozialistischer Terror gegen Homosexuelle*, pp. 73–4.

55 See USHMM Archive RG-14.070M (collection from the Landesarchiv Berlin: General State Prosecutors' Office of the State Court of Berlin, 1933–1946).

56 See USHMM Archive RG-4.006M, reel 21 (list of admissions to Ravensbrück, 30 November 1940). I am grateful to Jan Lambertz for this and the above reference.

57 C. Schoppmann, '"Liebe wurde mit Prügelstrafe geahndet." Zur Situation lesbischer Frauen in den Konzentrationslagern', in Diercks (ed.) *Verfolgung von Homosexuellen*, p. 19; A. H. Mayer, '"Schwachsinn höheren Grades." Zur Verfolgung lesbischer Frauen in Österreich während der NS-Zeit', in Jellonnek and Lautmann (eds) *Nationalsozialistischer Terror gegen Homosexuelle*, pp. 83–93, is among those who argue that lesbianism was persecuted via the persecution of 'asocial' and prostitute women.

58 For these points see K. Meier, '"Es war verpönt, aber das gab's." Die Darstellung weiblicher Homosexualität in Autobiographien von weiblichen Überlebenden aus Ravensbrück und Auschwitz', in Diercks (ed.) *Verfolgung von Homosexuellen*, pp. 22–33; also W. Poltawska, *And I am Afraid of My Dreams*, London: Hodder and Stoughton, 1987, pp. 57 ff. For a similar reticence about intimate friendships among men, see Levi, *If This Is a Man*, pp. 125–6.

59 C. Paul, *Zwangsprostitution. Staatlich errichtete Bordelle im Nationalsozialismus*, Berlin: Hentrich, 1994.

60 H. Amesberger, K. Auer and B. Halbmayr, *Sexualisierte Gewalt. Weibliche Erfahrungen in NS-Konzentrationslager*, Vienna: Mandelbaum Verlag, 2007, p. 101.

61 Ibid., pp. 101–63; C. Schulz, 'Weibliche Häftlinge aus Ravensbrück in Bordellen der Männerkonzentrationslager', in Füllberg-Stolberg, Jung, Riebe and Scheitenberger (eds) *Frauen in Konzentrationslagern*, pp. 135–46; Strebel, *Das KZ Ravensbrück*, pp. 208–11; R. Sommer 'Camp Brothels: Forced Sex Labour in Nazi Concentration Camps', in D. Herzog (ed.) *Brutality and Desire: War and Sexuality in Europe*, Basingstoke: Palgrave Macmillan, 2009, pp. 168–96; also R. Sommer, *Das KZ-Bordell. Sexuelle Zwangsarbeit in nationalsozialistischen Konzentrationslagern*, Paderborn: Schöningh, 2009.

62 C. Wickert, 'Tabu Lagerbordell. Vom Umgang mit der Zwangsprostitution nach 1945', in Eschebach, Jacobeit and Wenk (eds), *Gedächtnis und Geschlecht*, pp. 41–58.
63 See for example Hackett (ed.), *Buchenwald Report*, pp. 152–3, 248–9; also p. 177 for one of the infrequent descriptions of sexualized violence, which tellingly occurs in a chapter on homosexual prisoners, even though it is not clear that the victim in this case was homosexual.
64 Sofsky, *Order of Terror*, p. 223.
65 Bruha *et al.*, *Frauen-Konzentrationslager Ravensbrück*, pp. 11–13; Amesberger, Auer and Halbmayr, *Sexualisierte Gewalt*, pp. 78–87 especially; J. Anschütz, K. Meier and S. Obajdin, '"… dieses leere Gefühl, und die Blicke der anderen." Sexuelle Gewalt gegen Frauen', in Füllberg-Stolberg, Jung, Riebe and Scheitenberger (eds) *Frauen in Konzentrationslagern*, pp. 123–33.
66 Amesberger, Auer and Halbmayr, *Sexualisierte Gewalt*, pp. 147–64; Anschütz, Meier and Obajdin, '"… dieses leere Gefühl"', pp. 130–1; Ellger, *Zwangsarbeit und weibliche Überlebensstrategien*, p. 126.
67 See T. Rahe, '"Ich wusste nicht einmal, dass ich schwanger war." Geburten im KZ Bergen-Belsen', in Füllberg-Stolberg, Jung, Riebe and Scheitenberger (eds) *Frauen in Konzentrationslagern*, pp. 147–56. There were child inmates in the camps, however – about 800 altogether in Ravensbrück, 900 liberated from Buchenwald: see B. Pawelke, 'Als Häftling geboren – Kinder in Ravensbrück', in B. Pawelke and E. Sommer-Lefkovits, *Are You Here in This Hell Too? Memoirs of Troubled Times 1944–1945*, London: Menard Press, 1995; B. Niven, *The Buchenwald Child: Truth, Fiction, and Propaganda*, Rochester NY: Camden House, 2007, pp. 18–22. See also Falk Pingel's chapter in this volume.
68 For one example, see K. Hart-Moxon, *Return to Auschwitz*, Laxton: Beth Shalom, 1997, p. 67.
69 For national solidarities among women see, for example, Tillion, *Ravensbrück*, pp. 211 f., and Bruha *et al.*, *Frauen-Konzentrationslager Ravensbrück*, p. 30; for resistance, Strebel, *Das KZ Ravensbrück*, Appendix, pp. 530–64. The classic example of a sustaining men's friendship is perhaps Primo Levi's relationship with Alberto, described in *If This Is a Man*.
70 As well as the discussion and references in Jens-Christian Wagner's chapter, see for women's work Strebel, *Das KZ Ravensbrück*, pp. 199–228; U. Brandes, C. Füllberg-Stolberg and S. Kempe, 'Arbeit im KZ-Ravensbrück', in Füllberg-Stolberg, Jung, Riebe and Scheitenberger (eds) *Frauen in Konzentrationslagern*, pp. 55–69; Ellger, *Zwangsarbeit und weibliche Überlebensstrategien*; G. Pfingsten and C. Füllberg-Stolberg, 'Frauen in Konzentrationslagern – geschlechtsspezifische Bedingungen des Überlebens', in Herbert, Orth and Dieckmann (eds) *Die nationalsozialistischen Konzentrationslager*, vol. 2, pp. 911–38.
71 See also Falk Pingel's chapter in this volume.
72 See Sofsky, *Order of Terror*, pp. 199–213 and 329; Bruha *et al.*, *Frauen-Konzentrationslager Ravensbrück*, p. 17.
73 Debski, *Battlefield of Ideas*, pp. 88–97.
74 See Falk Pingel's chapter in this volume; also for some comments on men's sexual behaviour, H. Langbein, *People in Auschwitz*, Chapel Hill, NC: University of North Carolina Press, 2004, pp. 402–13.
75 Cf. Z. Waxman, *Writing The Holocaust. Identity, Testimony, Representation*, Oxford: Oxford University Press, 2006, p. 125: 'Using a familiar, gendered conceptual framework, women's testimonies are often used to show us what we already want to see'; also S. R. Horowitz, 'Geschlechtsspezifische Erinnerungen an der Holocaust', in Jacobeit and Philipp (eds) *Forschungsschwerpunkt Ravensbrück*, pp. 131–5.
76 See G. Schwarz, 'Frauen in Konzentrationslagern – Täterinnen und Zuschauer', in Herbert, Orth and Dieckmann, eds *Die nationalsozialistischen Konzentrationslager*, pp. 800–21; and Schwarz, *Eine Frau an seine Seite*.

77 For Moringen see J. von Freyberg and U. Krause-Schmitt, *Moringen. Lichtenburg.*
Ravensbrück. Frauen im Konzentrationslager 1933–1945, Frankfurt: VAS, 1977, which covers
the history of all the main women's camps with an emphasis on inmate memories;
Hesse, *Frauen-KZ Moringen*; Hesse, 'Von der "Erziehung" zur "Ausmerzung". Das
Konzentrationslager Moringen 1933–1945', in W. Benz and B. Distel (eds), *Geschichte
der nationalsozialistischen Konzentrationslager 1933–1945*, vol. 3, Instrumentarium der
Macht. Frühe Konzentrationslager 1933–1937, Berlin: Metropol: 2003, pp. 111–46;
and J. Caplan, 'Introduction', in G. Herz, *The Women's Camp in Moringen: A Memoir
of Imprisonment in Germany 1936–1937*, New York/Oxford: Berghahn Books, 2006,
pp. 1–55. On Lichtenburg, K. Drobisch, 'Frauenkonzentrationslager im Schloss
Lichtenburg', *Dachauer Hefte* 3, 1993, pp. 101–15; and S. Endlich, 'Die Lichtenburg
1933–1939', in Benz and Distel (eds) *Herrschaft und Gewalt*, pp. 11–64. On Ravensbrück,
see above all Strebel, *Das KZ Ravensbrück*.

78 Himmler had deliberately chosen not to use older SS men as camp guards before
the war on the grounds that the aim was to militarize and harden seventeen- or
eighteen-year old youths for their future wartime duties, and that older men would be
tempted into corruption or sadism; see Smith and Peterson (eds) *Heinrich Himmler. Die
Geheimreden*, p. 32.

79 For women warders and the *Oberaufseherinnen*, see primarily S. Erpel (ed.) *Im Gefolge der
SS. Aufseherinnen des Frauen-KZ Ravensbrück*, Berlin: Metropol, 2007; also Strebel, *Das KZ
Ravensbrück*, pp. 48–102.

80 J. Toussaint, 'Nach Dienstschluss', in Erpel (ed.) *Im Gefolge der SS*, pp. 89–100.

81 See Pfingsten and Füllberg-Stolberg, 'Frauen in Konzentrationslagern'; also G.
Schwarz, 'Frauen in Konzentrationslagern – Täterinnen und Zuschauerinnen', in
Herbert, Orth and Dieckmann (eds) *Die nationalsozialistischen Konzentrationslager*, vol. 2,
pp. 800–21.

82 See Strebel, *KZ Ravensbrück*, pp. 274–88. The history of mass murder and medical
experimentation in Ravensbrück is also discussed in detail by Strebel.

83 Langbein, *People in Auschwitz*, pp. 238, 396, 399 f.

84 Vermehren, *Reise durch den letzten Akt*, p. 60.

85 Weckel and Wolfrum, 'NS-Prozesse und ihre öffentliche Resonanz'; quotation from
p. 11. See also C. Jaiser, 'Irma Grese. Zur Rezeption einer KZ-Aufseherin', in Erpel
(ed.) *Im Gefolge der SS*, pp. 338–46; C. Taake, *Angeklagt. SS-Frauen vor Gericht*, Oldenburg:
BIS, 1998; J. Duesterberg, 'Von der "Umkehr aller Weiblichkeit". Charakterbilder
einer KZ-Aufseherin', in Eschebach, Jacobeit and Wenk (eds) *Gedächtnis und Geschlecht*,
pp. 227–43. On the representation of women prisoner-functionaries, B. Durrer, 'Eine
Verfolgte als Täterin? Zur Geschichte der Blockältesten Carmen Mory', in Jacobeit
and Philipp (eds) *Forschungsschwerpunkt Ravensbrück*, pp. 86–93; and on Ilse Koch,
notorious as the wife of the commandant of Buchenwald, A. Przyrembel, 'Transfixed
by an Image: Ilse Koch, the "Kommandeuse" of Buchenwald', *German History*, 19, 3
(2001), pp. 369–99.

86 In other words, victim status does not rule out complicity. Variant views on this question
in relation to women as a group were debated in the late 1980s by US and German
historians; see e.g. G. Bock, review of C. Koonz, *Mothers in the Fatherland*, *Bulletin of
the German Historical Institute London* 9, Feb. 1989, pp. 16–24, and the summary and
references in Koonz, 'Tributary and Mainstream', p. 151. These issues are also the
subject of K. Heinsohn, B. Vogel and U. Weckel (eds) *Zwischen Karriere und Verfolgung.
Handlungsräume von Frauen im nationalsozialistischen Deutschland*, Frankfurt/New York:
Campus Verlag, 1997, and are touched on in Heinemann, 'Sexuality and Nazism'.

87 Smith and Peterson (eds) *Heinrich Himmler. Die Geheimreden*, pp. 103, 32, 99, 169–70; the
reference to decency is from Himmler's speech to SS leaders in Posen on 4 October
1943, excerpted in J. Noakes and G. Pridham (eds) *Nazism 1919–1945: A Documentary
Reader*, Exeter: Exeter University Press, 2001, vol. 3, pp. 617–8 (where the date is
misprinted as 1944). On the problem of women in uniforms in Nazi Germany, see I.

Guenther, *Nazi Chic? Fashioning Women in the Third Reich*, Oxford/New York: Berg, 2004, pp. 119–31.

88 J. Goldstein, *War and Gender. How Gender Shapes the War System and Vice Versa*, Cambridge: Cambridge University Press, 2001.

89 'Grey zone' is Primo Levi's famous term for this morally compromised arena: see Levi, *The Drowned and the Saved*, Chapter 2, and Sofsky, *Order of Terror*, Chapter 11.

90 Bruha *et al.*, *Frauen-Konzentrationslager Ravensbrück*, p. 15; Buber-Neumann, *Under Two Dictators*, p. 177.

91 G. Bock, 'Ordinary Women in Nazi Germany. Perpetrators, Victims, Followers and Bystanders', in Ofer and Weitzman (eds) *Women in the Holocaust*, pp. 96–7.

5 The public face of the camps

Karola Fings

The German Reich had not yet capitulated when the influential Cardinal Michael von Faulhaber, Archbishop of Munich and Freising since 1917, remarked in a circular to the clerics of his diocese on 2 May 1945 that:

> Blatant inhumanities, which every right-minded person abhors, have occurred in the Buchenwald and Dachau concentration camps. But I beg that not all of the SS, far less the people, are held responsible for these terrible things, of which they knew nothing and for any word of criticism of which they themselves would have been brought to Dachau.[1]

In this letter Faulhaber was reacting to the radio and press reports by the Allies since the liberation of the concentration camps, which had unsparingly laid bare to the German population the crimes perpetrated in the camps, and which had provoked international horror and abhorrence. In the same breath he drew attention to the consequences of the Allies' methods of waging war, by directly going on from the passage above:

> I urge you not to forget: if all of the terrible sufferings wrought by the air raids over our cities, all of the corpses of the people, among them women and children, buried alive or burned or torn into pieces, even from a single city, could be put together and photographed, such a picture would be no less terrible than the concentration camp pictures now being taken. The world is disgusted by these pictures from the concentration camps; but the war has also brought with it other images of horror.[2]

The position taken by the Cardinal with regard to the National Socialist concentration camps is paradigmatic for the public and private attitudes of most Germans after the war. After damning the crimes which could no longer to be denied, they utterly repudiated the suggestion that they had any role in them, or had even been aware of them. The leading clique around Adolf Hitler and individual SS perpetrators were identified as the guilty parties. At the same time Germans were presented as victims who had also suffered greatly and indeed several times over: they were presented both as victims of the National Socialist dictatorship, to which they had been obliged to submit, and as victims of the Allies, whose legitimacy as moral authorities was called into question by reference to the air raids.[3]

This claim to have known nothing about anything was for decades the preamble to the so-called 'coming to terms with the past' in both German states. It was initially left to the survivors of National Socialist persecution to develop an alternative view of the Third Reich. Particularly significant in this regard was the Buchenwald survivor Eugen Kogon, who as early as the beginning of the summer of 1945 compiled an extensive report for the Supreme Headquarters Allied Expeditionary Force (SHAEF), taking Buchenwald as a case study. When he published the revised text under the title *The SS State: The German Concentration Camp System* in 1946, his preface recommended his readers to take the last chapter in particular to heart. Entitled 'The German People and the Concentration Camps', this chapter rebutted the dictum of 'We knew nothing about this', took issue with the reactions of the Germans since the end of the war, and attempted to fathom the causes of the 'tragic complicity of the German people in the existence of the National Socialist Concentration Camps'.[4]

Kogon's approach, embedding the history of the concentration camps in a social context, was taken up by historical research only very belatedly. In the few general overviews of the concentration camps to appear in West Germany after the war, the subject was omitted, just as it has been ignored in the general surveys, compendia and encyclopaedias which have appeared in the last few years.[5] In a 1968 essay whose title echoed that of Kogon's chapter, Werner Johe was the first to discuss the contemporary knowledge and attitudes of German society towards the concentration camps.[6] Some 15 years later, Robert Gellately focused on media reports of the camps and the enormous wartime expansion of the extent to which the concentration camp system was in the public eye.[7] New knowledge has been gained in numerous case studies appearing since the 1990s which, taking main or satellite camps as examples, have microscopically examined relationships between camps and their local social milieu. Investigations of Mauthausen, Dachau, Buchenwald, Auschwitz and Mittelbau-Dora, as well as more recent studies of satellite camps, have presented in detail the various forms of cooperation and collaboration with the SS by administrative bodies, firms and populations, and thereby presented a differentiated picture of the relationship of German society to the concentration camps.[8] With its focus on the concentration camp as a result of social behaviour, this new perspective is comparable with recent research on the police and security apparatus in the Third Reich as well as that on the participation of German society in the persecution of the Jewish population.[9]

This chapter will concern itself not only with the already relatively well-researched question of the extent to which the concentration camps were a matter of public knowledge, but also with the further question of the phases and circumstances in which this knowledge emerged and the relationships that existed between the camps and German society.

Public and sinister: the concentration camp as an element of power

The omnipresent terror that accompanied the National Socialist takeover of power in 1933 was a secret in neither the cities nor the villages of the German Reich. On the basis of the so-called 'Reichstag Fire Decree' of February 1933, thousands of real or supposed enemies of the regime were arbitrarily carried off to places of internment set up for this purpose by the SA, SS or police, often in the provisional shape of cellars, pubs, factories, prisons or judicial institutions. The existence of these camps could not be overlooked, nor could there be any illusions about the nature of this imprisonment: the victims were violently hauled from their homes, humiliated or beaten on the open streets, some even shot. Those who returned from these camps bore the visible marks of physical abuse; often they were also psychologically broken. This public terror always worked in two directions, targeted both at the victim and at everybody else simultaneously. With a 'dual strategy of publicity and secrecy'[10] the regime sought in this phase to permanently eliminate its most significant opposition (the overwhelming majority of them communists, but also trade unionists and Social Democrats) and at the same time to prevent at the outset any potential resistance or even solidarity with the arrested on the part of the broader population. In part, this strategy rested upon targeted publications about so-called 'protective custody' and the sites in which it was carried out. From March 1933 onwards, there were detailed reports in local or national newspapers about the establishment of Dachau and the Emsland camps, but also on smaller internment centres such as the 'Brown House' in Cologne.[11] The aim of this information campaign was to publicize the need to isolate ostensible troublemakers. Under the headline 'A Concentration Camp for Political Prisoners', for example, an article in the *Münchner Neuesten Nachrichten* of 21 March 1933 quoted Heinrich Himmler as follows:

> On Wednesday the first concentration camp was opened in the vicinity of Dachau. Here were assembled the whole pack of communist and, where necessary, Reichsbanner and Marxist functionaries who are threatening state security, because it is not possible to burden the state in the long term by leaving individual communist officials in the ordinary prisons – and it is equally unacceptable to leave them in freedom. Our experiments in this direction only brought the result that they tried to persist with their agitation and organization. We have adopted these measures without reference to small-minded reservations, in the conviction that in this way we will be acting to reassure our nation and in its own interests.[12]

Further details about the camps were carried primarily in the local press.[13] Some of these published pictures of the buildings and their interiors and depicted an entirely negative image of the 'communists', 'leftists' and 'red hordes' who were now supposed to be being re-educated by work in the concentration camps.[14] They also offered astonishingly detailed information about conditions in the camps, individual prisoners, escape attempts and even deaths. [15] In addition, local residents were instructed in particular on how to behave: not to make contact with the prisoners, 'not to stand around unnecessarily' when columns of prisoners could be seen, and especially not to loiter near the camps or make any attempt to get entry to them. [16]

Readers might or might not pick up on the largely euphemistic descriptions of detention conditions that could be found in these articles. What the articles may have left to the canny among them to read between the lines solidified into certainties through the rapid circulation of rumours. The publicist Sebastian Haffner, who emigrated to Britain in 1938, described the lasting effect of this whispered propaganda as follows:

> Any public representation of what was taking place in the SA-cellars and the concentration camps … might potentially have provoked desperate counter-attacks in Germany itself. The dreadful stories covertly whispered around – 'Just be careful, dear neighbour! Do you know what happened to X?' – made the breaking down of all resistance much more certain. [17]

As the small camps gradually disappeared from view and the camp system was reorganized from 1934 on, there was no protest against a system of imprisonment removed from public and judicial control and reduced to just a few large camps in the hands of the SS, a process through which terroristic power was permanently anchored in the state. The reason for this lay not only in the fact that those who one might have expected to offer criticism had already been forced into emigration or into the camps themselves. It was also a consequence of propaganda which presented the camps as solely for the incarceration of 'agitators and traitors to the Fatherland', [18] who were now subjected to an imprisonment that was admittedly strict, but also aimed at re-education towards 'order, discipline and obedience' [19] – a propaganda image which found fertile soil and was therefore met with broad agreement. The pervasive climate of fear aided that process; it seemed better to accommodate oneself with the regime than to take risks which could not be calculated. The rhyme 'Dear God, keep me mum, that I don't to Dachau come' was not without reason a familiar adage in Munich and the vicinity from roughly the summer of 1933 onwards. [20] Moreover the tumultuous, revolutionary phase of the new Germany now seemed to have been channelled into calmer directions, so that the state-ordered regimentation of the camp system may have been received with a certain relief by broad sections of the population. As Sebastian Haffner explained, people had in the meantime come to terms with the existence of the camps:

> The concentration camps had now become institutions, and one was invited to get used to that and hold one's tongue. The *Gleichschaltung* (bringing into line), that is, the filling of all authorities, local administrations, large-scale businesses, and the boards of directors of all clubs and associations with Nazis continued, but now in a systematic fashion and in an almost pedantically

orderly manner with laws and decrees, and no longer so much with wild and unpredictable individual attacks. The revolution took on an official character.[21]

It should not be forgotten that the National Socialist regime did not operate by terror alone; rather, the majority of the population attached great hopes for the future to the regime – hopes which there was a willingness to sacrifice fundamental democratic rights for.

The further extension of the camp system in the second half of the 1930s took place less directly before the eyes of the general public than had been the case in the phase of the consolidation of power; but it could also rest upon two objectives which likewise enjoyed a broad popular consensus. These were, first, the harmonization of German social divisions and, second, a revision of the effects of the Versailles Treaty. The latter was initiated in a manner clearly visible to all, with the building up of the Wehrmacht, the remilitarization of the Rhineland in defiance of international law, and forced rearmament. The camps were now no longer a temporary solution, but instead were to permanently eliminate, alongside political opponents, all those who did not fit into the vision of a racially-homogeneous and productivity-oriented 'national community' (*Volksgemeinschaft*). They were also to ensure order on the 'home front' in the event of war.[22]

The ensuing period saw no more popularly directed and broadly distributed newspaper articles on the nature of the concentration camp. One can nevertheless assume that knowledge of the inhumanity of the conditions of imprisonment was more likely to have become greater, rather than smaller, over the course of time. There was, for example, carefully considered information directed at select groups, such as on the occasion of visits to the camps by members of the Association of Friends of the Reich Leader of the SS (*Freundeskreis des Reichsführers SS*), or in speeches.[23] In a speech to Wehrmacht officers on 18 January 1937, which was later printed and circulated within the Wehrmacht, Himmler made it clear that camp inmates were under strict guard by the SS-Death's Head units and 'kept in rein' by firearms, and that a further growth in prisoner numbers was to be expected:

> We must be clear that in the event of war we will have to take in [to the camps] a very considerable contingent of unreliables, if we do not want to create the conditions for nurturing extremely undesirable developments in a wartime situation.[24]

This argument was likely to have been especially attractive given the active war preparations under way at this time and the memory of the collapse of the German Reich in 1918. Just three months after the beginning of the war, these ideas were brought to the attention of a wider public through the SS magazine *Das Schwarze Korps*, whose edition of 500,000 to 700,000 copies made it the second largest political weekly in Germany:

The many thousand prisoners who are secured in the concentration camps are, partly as individuals and partly by virtue of their collective character, the same enemies of the state who wore down and destroyed Germany's domestic front during the World War ... During the World War they proved themselves to be collectively stronger than the external enemy. For while the soldier was victorious on all fronts, the internal enemy worked in the rear for Germany's defeat ... Thus the concentration camps represent island-like sites of battle on the domestic front, theatres of war in each of which a handful of men protect Germany from its internal enemies.[25]

Moreover, since the mid-1930s an increasing number of members of the Gestapo, criminal police and judiciary were occupied with camp imprisonment, while cemetery officials and employees of the register offices could draw their own conclusions on the conditions of imprisonment from reports of deaths. It would be quixotic to assume that all these people did *not* talk about their impressions within their private circle. Also, the circle of people that disappeared into the camps became ever larger: the parish priest disappeared; a colleague was missing from the workplace; a neighbour was taken away. The fear of that one might disappear behind the camp fence oneself due to diminishing loyalty to the Nazi regime increased with every abduction, yet in no way lessened the acceptance of the camp system. Rather, it reinforced anew the pressure to conform. 'Even in the dictatorship', as Eugen Kogon wrote, the Germans saw 'the arrested, not the arresters', as criminals.[26] The self-valorization which the camps facilitated may also be relevant. With threats like 'watch out, or you'll be put in a camp', certain arguments could be quickly nipped in the bud, and actual conflicts in the neighbourhood or at work could be permanently put to rest with a denunciation and the ensuing removal of the adversary.[27]

While broad informal knowledge of the concentration camps can be assumed for the pre-war years, in the war years concrete popular knowledge of the population became ever greater. Through the increase in the number of prisoners alone, ever more people became occupied with the process of admission to the camps, from the arrest up to the handover at the camp gate, whether as police officer, administrative official or railway worker. The population could not fail to see the wretched columns driven from stations to the camps. With the forced use of concentration camp prisoners as a workforce during the war, the public visibility of the concentration camp system grew once more. Although the use of prisoners was initially confined to companies run by the SS itself or a few industrial satellite camps and smaller work commandos in the direct vicinity of the camps, the number of satellite camps rose dramatically from autumn 1942. Until the end of the war, a total of more than 1,000 satellite camps were set up (alongside the 24 main concentration camps); these new camps were established in villages or towns for months or even years, and their prisoner-counts varied from a handful to several thousands.[28] Any attempt by the regime to keep this secret would have been doomed to failure from the outset; nor was it ever attempted, a few trouble spots aside. The visibility of the camp universe and, above all, the concrete visibility of the victims attained a level in the last two years of the war that went far beyond what the population had been able to see, read or hear in 1933 and 1934.

Why, then, did these insistent denials of all knowledge take place at the end of the war? The collective strategy of denial was initially a reflex against the diffuse fear that the Allies would attempt to call all Germans to account for the crimes.[29] Hidden behind this defensive strategy, however, was also something most recent research has brought ever more clearly to light. In the first place, there was a much broader complicity with the regime than the self-image of post-war society would allow. Second, individuals – who had much more room for manoeuvre in the Third Reich than they liked to admit after 1945 – had often made an active effort to turn a blind eye.

Policy on the ground and economic factors: the concentration camp as community enterprise

Until deep into the 1990s, neither local histories aimed at a popular audience nor histories of businesses in the Federal Republic were likely to include any information on the use of concentration camp prisoners in their locality or company. When there was a hint that this had been the case, the impression was given that the camp had fallen out of a clear blue sky and that the SS alone had been responsible. When one considers, however, the motives that led to the foundation of the camps – whether main or satellite camps – it is clear that although the SS ran its camps according to its own interest in actively securing and extending power, it did so in cooperation with partners. Furthermore, the practice of the camp shows that, as well as the SS, numerous other parties were necessary in order to ensure the operation of a camp in the first place. This can be shown by examples from three different phases in the development of the concentration camp system: the founding of the camps at Dachau and Buchenwald, representative for the establishment of the camp system; the main camps established from the end of the 1930s onwards, which came into existence with the attempt to make the concentration camp system profitable; and finally the booming satellite camps of the later war years, part of the crisis-management strategy of a Reich forced onto the defensive.

The choice of Dachau as the site for a large concentration camp was made by Heinrich Himmler himself. He knew of the former ammunition factory, owned by the Bavarian state, in the communities of Prittlbach and Etzenhausen and regarded it as suitable on account of its size, its isolated location and the availability of the necessary infrastructure.[30] The Dachau municipal council, which had initially set aside this site for an industrial estate as a means of combating the economic hardship of the town, welcomed the project, as did the local population, in the hope of stimulating the local economy. The desired effect was felt only briefly, however. In the long run, the added income could not offset the damage suffered to Dachau's image in becoming a 'concentration camp town'. This was not changed by the incorporation of the camp site into the municipality of Dachau in order to cream off taxes. But the overwhelmingly positive local reception of the camp facilitated the SS's implementation of their camp concept, the more so as they were dependent, especially in the initial phase, on many services provided by the local administration. The responsible authorities within the SS may in any case have learnt from the example of Dachau that it was beneficial if a camp could build upon local support. This support was likely if the community in which the camp was to be established anticipated that it would profit from the camp's presence.

Thus when in autumn 1936 the Inspection of the Concentration Camps (IKL) was seeking a new location in Thuringia for the Lichtenburg concentration camp, which had become too small, they emphasized, not without reason, the positive economic effects to be expected for the region. In the face of the Thuringian Interior Ministry's objections they pushed for the speedy selection of a suitable site with the comment that they would otherwise award the contract to another candidate: 'Several Prussian towns have already endeavoured to have the camp allocated and transferred to them and have allocated resources to this end.'[31] Eventually Ettersberg near Weimar was chosen as the site for the new camp of 'Buchenwald'. Just as in Dachau, here too the town itself did not participate in the selection of the location, but again it was just as active in its self-interested efforts to support the construction and operation of the Buchenwald concentration camp. The examples of the Dachau and Buchenwald camps demonstrate well how civilization and barbarism came to an arrangement with each other: the administrative bodies played a stabilizing role, in which they re-established order 'out of the exceptional situation', simultaneously withdrawing into their role as providers of services.[32]

Equally smoothly, if not with even more active support, the SS was able to further extend the camp system in the second half of the 1930s, not only in order to detain a greater number of prisoners, but also to expand its own numerical and financial scope. The rebuilding of the towns of Berlin, Nuremberg, Munich, Hamburg and Linz, to which Adolf Hitler wanted to give new faces as 'Führer Cities', had a significant share in this. As General Construction Inspector for the Reich Capital, Albert Speer made available initial capital to the tune of 9.5 million RM to the new SS German Earth and Stone Works Ltd (DESt), founded on 29 April 1938 to provide construction materials.[33] The funds were to be used for the construction of German Earth and Stone Works plants at Buchenwald and Sachsenhausen. In a complementary move the city of Berlin ensured itself the output of the brickworks set up adjacent to Sachsenhausen concentration camp through delivery contracts for the next ten years.

Following this example the city of Hamburg, too, cooperated with the SS, which had bought brickworks in the Neuengamme district of the town in 1938. After negotiations between Himmler and Hamburg Gauleiter Karl Kaufmann in January 1940, the extension of Neuengamme into a stand-alone concentration camp was put into effect; likewise a contract was concluded between the DESt and the city of Hamburg. Here too the city financed the extension of the works with the provision of credit and received in return the rights to the bulk of annual production. Besides the delivery of bricks, the use of prisoners, free of charge, for extensive work on dykes and canals was also agreed.[31] The establishment of the Flossenbürg, Mauthausen, Gross-Rosen and Natzweiler camps was equally closely connected with the construction of DESt granite works and quarries, which delivered building materials to the 'Führer Cities'.[35]

As far as the roles of Speer, the Gauleiter and also the representatives of the federated ministries and city administrations in the establishment of these new camps are concerned, their engagement went well beyond the limited objectives of the town administrations of Dachau or Weimar. The SS gained support in principle and financially for the extension of the camp system and its own power base. At the same time, it was clear that it was not the fate of the prisoners, but only their deployment as a workforce, that fell within public perception. This perspective eventually also underlay the foundation of the many hundreds of satellite camps which followed from 1942 onwards. The preparations for the massive deployment of concentration camp prisoners outside the camp gates had already been made in autumn 1942, and here, too, Himmler and the SS did not act, as post-war representations such as Albert Speer's would have us believe, as terroristic, power-hungry and utterly autonomous authorities.[36] Rather, several actors were involved in the decision, each serving their own interests and thereby negotiating the conditions for the deployment of prisoners. The background to the mobilization of concentration camp prisoners for the war economy was the critical situation in which the Reich found itself in 1942: the advance of German troops in Eastern Europe had faltered; the USA had entered the war; bottlenecks were evident in the armaments industry; and major attacks on German cities were now transforming the homeland into a war zone, too. Moreover, the forced recruitment of foreign workers in the occupied countries was falling far short of expectations. In mid-September 1942 Himmler and Speer – now promoted to armaments minister – agreed to deploy prisoners in the production of armaments and for the alleviation of the damage done by air-raids.

Following this key decision, local authorities and industrial and commercial concerns alike now made use of concentration camp prisoners, hiring them out from the SS according to a fixed rate. Satellite camps were set up in bombed-out schools, restaurants, barracks, factory buildings or hurriedly set-up military camps, which no longer lay on the outskirts of towns and villages, but in many cases in their centres. All these camps could not be operated by the SS on its own, but functioned instead as joint enterprises of the SS and the respective town or firm. The circle of individuals involved with the camps expanded further: construction departments or companies provided plots of land and buildings; SS guards were supplemented by local assistants; administrators organized the provision and deployment of (and the accounting for) the prisoners; civilian foremen commanded the work brigades; local doctors selected prisoners no longer capable of work; entrepreneurs did business with the SS as suppliers and providers of services to the camps.

With the deployment of prisoners in the midst of wartime society, what the early propaganda on the camps had previously claimed now became true: the prisoners would perform useful work for society. Prisoners were used in their thousands in armaments projects which would – it was hoped – help to turn the war around; they worked in the subterranean German industrial complexes, where, under murderous working conditions, heavy excavation and building work was to be carried out at top speed; they produced doors and windows for bomb-damaged buildings, constructed temporary houses, cleared streets of rubble, retrieved corpses or unexploded bombs. The utterly inhumane use of prisoners driven to the edge of their physical and psychological capabilities epitomizes the way in which National Socialist society stopped at nothing in the quest for 'final victory'.

Although the degree of public visibility of the camps was greater than in previous years and the camp boundaries were ever more permeable, the prisoners' chances of survival improved only in very few exceptional cases. The concentration camp system remained marked by dehumanization, lack of rations and extreme violence. The question of how this was possible was already being pondered at the time by prisoners who found themselves – following transfer from the relatively isolated location of a main camp to a satellite camp – among the population. In a memoir penned shortly after the war, the theologian Aimé Bonifas, deported to Buchenwald from France in 1943 as a result of his activity in the resistance, wrote of one of the sites of his persecution:

> The camp was situated directly at the village of Mackenrode. We could recognize all the houses as well as the high tower of an Protestant-Lutheran church. The view of this church was often a mystery to me in the days that followed. I have no way of judging, and I do not know, who are those who assemble there, but how can one speak of heaven so near such injustices?[37]

Looking and looking away: the concentration camp and German society

By 1944, in many towns of the German Reich a glance out of the kitchen window, a visit to the shopkeeper, a journey on the train could entail direct confrontation with the sight of concentration camp prisoners. The first encounter with the prisoners of the SS often triggered shock and surprise, as one citizen of Düsseldorf explained:

> Already soon after the first bombardments … if I travelled home by *S-Bahn* [a local train] I frequently saw a column of about 30 to 40 concentration camp prisoners on their way back to the camp. I saw them from the *S-Bahn*. … If one travelled past slowly in the *S-Bahn*, one saw, whether one wanted to or not, the faces of the wretches, their skulls shaved clean, yellowish and emaciated to the bone. The sight was so shocking, that the passengers turned away in silence and women wiped away tears.[38]

The looking and looking-away which this man, 36 years old at the time, describes here was a typical reaction on the part of the population. The physiognomy of terror was written into the prisoners. They embodied the individual's utter lack of rights and their dehumanization. Confronted with this 'true face of National Socialism' people shut their eyes.[39]

The reasons for looking away were manifold. Initially the pitiful state of the prisoners triggered a moral shock which had an extremely unsettling effect. A purely abstract notion of 'strict camp imprisonment' was something entirely different from seeing the real consequences of physical mistreatment, with the victims now standing eye to eye. The sight, as the writer Emil Barth noted in his diary on 13 December 1943 after an encounter with prisoners in Wuppertal, was one that 'damaged one's own capacity for life'.[40] Perhaps looking longer might have triggered the impulse to give succour to these people? Yet this reaction was utterly beset by fear. Hardly a single eyewitness report fails to mention the fear people had of showing sympathy towards the prisoners or even of approaching them, because of the fear that they, too, would soon find themselves on the other side of the camp fence.

This fear seemed all the more real when the menace of the concentration camp, already internalized as a threat, was renewed and strengthened by the violent actions of the SS in public. Passers-by witnessed punches and kicks, sometimes even prisoners beaten to death or shot on the street. Many residents near camps saw prisoners being humiliated and tortured, heard shots or screams, saw corpses lying in the camp. But the sight of violence did not result in any action from the general public; rather, it led to a further retreat into the private sphere. At most, people spoke among their friends about what they had witnessed; but they did not dare to offer public criticism.[41] The absence of sympathy or interest in the fate of the prisoners was also linked to the general moral deadening caused by the war, especially once Germany had declared 'total war' from 1943 onwards. The habituation to violence, the loss of close relatives, the ubiquitous destruction, as well as the everyday problems in destroyed cities, resulted in most people concentrating on what was in the interests of their own survival.

The radicalized war society, which demanded unlimited efforts from German 'national comrades' too, had in any case become accustomed to having an army of labourers working with minimal provisions and under restrictive conditions. In this context the deployment of slave labour from the concentration camps represented nothing fundamentally new, but merely another rung further down the Reich's social ladder. Those responsible in the administration of cities or businesses also generally accepted the patently bad conditions the prisoners had to suffer. They neither questioned the monopoly of power enjoyed by the SS nor took the opportunity to ask for meaningful improvements to conditions in the camps, such as better accommodation, more food or adequate medical care. In the face of bottlenecks in the war economy, only 'national comrades' were to benefit from the resources available, in accordance with the racial ordering of German society.

Habituation can also be identified on another level. From the Reich's point of view the concentration camps represented the negative centres of a racially structured society, in which the camp was a normative form of life. Arguably the overwhelming majority of the population had some experience of camps, because millions had lived for considerable periods in camps or camp-like structures: from the camps of the Hitler Youth to those of the Reich Labour Service, resettlement camps for ethnic Germans or military barracks to the various kinds of compulsory camps for Jews, Sinti and Roma, prisoners of war, foreign civilian workers or the Gestapo's so-called 're-education labour camps'. The intensive penetration of camp society and local society led – via the permanent mobilization for war and the National Socialist drive to change and transform – to a constant extension of the terrain of terror; the borders between individual types of camp were fluid. Entire districts, like the Harz where the Mittelbau-Dora concentration camp was located, but also villages like Flossenbürg, which was utterly transformed by its camp, were marked through and through by the camp regime.

Concrete interventions on behalf of the prisoners by local inhabitants were made only rarely, such as when passers-by protested against violence, individually or in small groups. Such examples prove that it was possible to limit the violence of the SS, without encountering sanctions.[42] On the whole however, the majority of the population showed no sympathy beyond a few gestures. The appearance of the uniformed, emaciated and tattered figures appeared to confirm the negative image of 'criminals' and 'asocials' in the concentration camps that had marked propaganda on the subject. The prisoners were perceived not as humans, but rather as a 'band of strange, dehumanized creatures'.[43] Only a few convinced antifascists and forced labourers offered substantial support, providing prisoners with food or helping them to escape. The prisoners experienced rejection, sometimes even an actively aggressive response, from the German population. Aimé Bonifas, quoted above, noted of his arrival in Weimar:

> Just before nightfall the transport set itself in motion. We crossed Weimar half-naked. Without shame, with malicious laughter, women gathered with their children to see us pass by. Just think, French terrorists, what a spectacle for the master-race! A Gretchen on her bicycle yelled: 'Why don't you just bump them all off?' What an unimaginably huge contrast between this cynical contempt and the sympathy of our French women.[44]

The comparison with the satellite camps in occupied Belgium and northern France shows that there was a fundamental difference between the behaviour of non-German and German societies in the vicinity of the camps. In northern France and Belgium there was open sympathy and concrete support for the prisoners, by providing food as well as by freeing prisoners or helping them to escape. This support represented a partial loss of control over the camps for the SS, but for the prisoners it brought a palpable improvement in their chances of survival. The death rates were noticeably lower than in comparable camps in the Reich; and nowhere else were so many prisoners able to escape successfully, because they were hidden from, rather than handed over to, the SS.[45]

The sociologist Wolfgang Sofsky has termed the National Socialist concentration camps 'a closed universe' within society, in which the SS exercised 'absolute power' over the prisoners.[46] The fixed barriers and posts, he suggested, turned the camp into a 'visible but secluded and silenced place of terror in the midst of society'.[47] But as the history of both the concentration camps and their satellite camps shows, this description is only partially justified. When one considers social practice, the camps were in no way hermetically sealed. Social contacts between camps and their environments are represented by the contact of residents with (in some cases hundreds of) SS guards and their families, the commercial relationships with the camps, and contact with prisoners working outside the camps. This was true not only for the many camps located within towns or villages, but even for the concentration and extermination camp of Auschwitz, a camp which – due to its enormous symbolic value – is largely not discussed in terms of its real relationships to society.[48] All camps were embedded in their environment, and their physical borders could in no way completely separate camp society from local society. Still, every SS man could, at any point, kill a prisoner. How was this possible?

The findings of recent research suggest that the fundamental reasons for this are to be sought in the consensual conduct of the majority of the population. Like the French prisoner Bonifas, the German prisoner Helmut Knöller too perceived a fundamentally different atmosphere within the German Reich than in a satellite camp in Belgium where he had to build foundations for V-weapons. When the train bringing the prisoners to Mittelbau-Dora concentration camp crossed the border into the Reich, Knöller noted: 'Here in Germany the picture was now completely the opposite: the population cheered the soldiers …'.[49]

The image of a population that cheered the guards but mocked the prisoners suggests a need to explore more closely the concept of looking and looking away. Looking away can be interpreted as a social action that signifies avoidance. It is not only lack of interest and participation that are expressed in this avoidance; it also marks a border, that between the camp and the outside world. What took place on this border is not yet fully describable, although it has begun to acquire a shape in the last few years. The difficulty of describing what happened here is primarily due to the fact that it touches on a subject which was made taboo after 1945 and which is therefore hard to get at through the sources: the social proximity of the population to the perpetrators. It was precisely those people who maintained close contacts with concentration camps, or even had access to them, who after 1945 denied most vehemently having had any knowledge of the prisoners' living conditions.[50] The same applies to those who had close social contacts with the SS guards, in the bar, in intimate relationships, or at occasional social events.[51] The boundary of a concentration camp was, however, not just a physical matter of barbed wire, watchtowers and guard-posts, but also a social boundary. It was a specifically National Socialist boundary, which divided the population into those who held on to the possibility of 'final victory' during the war and those deprived of a 'right to exist in the National Socialist state'.[52] This radical division within society was not an escalation brought about only with the advent of the war, but had already been introduced in 1933, as Sebastian Haffner very perceptively described:

> The situation of the non-Nazi Germans in summer 1933 was certainly one of the most difficult in which people could find themselves: namely, a condition of being completely and hopelessly overwhelmed, together with the after-effects of the shock of being utterly taken by surprise. ... At the same time, people faced a daily challenge – not to submit, but, rather, to defect. A small pact with the devil – and one no longer belonged to the prisoners and persecuted, but to victors and the persecutors.[53]

Through its political identification with the purpose of the camp and its social proximity to the perpetrators, German society represented an 'additional barrier around the camp', that is, a part of the camp fence.[54]

Future research

Concentration camps have written themselves deep into public consciousness – and not only among Germans – as the ultimate in inhumanity. Their symbolic charge after 1945 and the defensive strategies of the German population allowed them to become 'non-places' in public consciousness, so that the question of the camp system's relationship with society was posed only much later. Terror was in no way secret, but was present from 1933 onwards as an element in the National Socialist practice of power, through a mixture of public information, covert propaganda and knowledge founded on experience. The degree to which people were informed of the concrete realities in the camps depended not least upon how much they wanted to know. Committed opponents of the regime such as Sebastian Haffner knew early on of the inhumanity of camp imprisonment and did not give in to any illusions that this would be merely a temporary phenomenon.

To achieve a more accurate description of the German population's state of knowledge about the camps, it will be necessary to start by making an effort to systematically investigate press accounts throughout Germany, something which has so far not been undertaken. [55] However, even this would not be sufficient to provide a real grasp of 'the public face of the camps', because the most significant portion of this knowledge came from other sources and was circulated by informal discourses. It would therefore be worthwhile for future research to try to get access to this through private sources like letters and diaries. Here the value of contemporary sources would be incomparably higher than that of witness reports published only after 1945.

In general there is a consensus that it was the lack of defence of fundamental democratic rights that made the landslide victory of National Socialism possible and thereby also the establishment of a camp system outside the regular legal system. Martin Niemöller's famous words, according to which there was no longer anyone who could protest when he was taken into Sachsenhausen as a member of the 'Confessing Church' in 1937, are a powerful expression of the silence of the majority of the population in the face of the open terror against opponents of the regime.[56] Yet they do not explain how it was possible for the National Socialist concentration camp system to develop further after the regime had consolidated power. Were one to follow the popular post-war misinterpretations, German society surrendered impotently to the terroristic dictatorship of a minority. This obscures the many areas of consensus with the new rulers: the assent to a new ordering of society, acceptance of the exclusion of minorities, hopes for a new national ascendancy. Improvements in status as a consequence of the displacement of the Jewish population and economic activity brought by rearmament also benefited the majority of the population in the pre-war years. A glance at the development of the camp system shows that areas of contact between camp and locality did not expand in response to the terrorist and expansionist aspirations of the SS alone, but rather were due to functionally rational cooperation between public authorities and private companies. We therefore need further research above all into the foundation of individual camps, to shed light on who was involved and what their motivations were. In addition more case studies are needed to investigate more closely the circle of people who were involved in the camp regime, in order to achieve quantitative conclusions about the extent of involvement and a more precise description of their freedom of action and discretionary choices. Comparative studies between different camps and their various local societies could also help clarify these grey areas of complicity.

It is of central importance to an understanding of how the concentration camp functioned to see practices within the camps not in isolation, but as a process of events integrated into society. While the concentration camps of 1933 and 1934 were moulded by social upheaval and, up to the beginning of the war, by a period of internal social consolidation, in 1939 a new phase began, in which mobilization at the front and in the factories was forced through. Once again National Socialist society was radicalized, but this time it was geared towards productivity: all resources were mobilized, especially following the military defeat at Stalingrad. This was the context in which the use of concentration camps as a reservoir of labour found broad acceptance. Concentration camp prisoners were now deployed in hundreds of camps outside the relatively isolated main camps; the public visibility of the camp system as such was thus increased, but the specific components of the camps' operation – lack of food and care and extreme violence – remained the same. It is clear that the regime could rely upon a general acceptance of the camp system and an internalization of its racial model of society.

The lines of social division marked by the camp boundaries likewise continued to exist even as these boundaries pushed ever further into society. Most Germans met the prisoners – the sight of whom became ever more a part of everyday life after 1942 – with indifference. The fact that people turned their gaze away from the victims, whether out of sympathy or lack of interest, repulsion or fear, meant that the perpetrators were strengthened in what they did. The violence of the SS, which was already barely restrained by any other authority, could expand all the more uncontrollably. The terroristic potential of the regime thus gained a renewed dynamism, and – to quote Detlev Peukert – terror ate 'ever deeper … from the margins of society into its heart'.[57] And this was not the result of a radical regime of terror imposed from above, but rather a process in which many individuals participated on various levels and to varying degrees. The question of the collective responsibility of German society and the degrees of individual guilt therefore cannot yet be laid to rest.

Translated by Paul Moore

Notes

1 L. Volk (ed.), *Akten Kardinal Michael von Faulhabers 1917–1945*, Mainz: Matthias Grünewald-Verlag, 1978, vol. 2, p. 1049f.

2 Ibid.

3 Examples of similar, including private, testimonies in: K. Fings, 'Umgedeutete Vergangenheit. Erinnerungsdiskurse über Konzentrationslager', in J. E. Schulte (ed.), *Die SS, Himmler und die Wewelsburg*, Paderborn: Schöningh, 2009, pp. 417–32.

4 E. Kogon, *Der SS-Staat. Das System der deutschen Konzentrationslager*, 26th edn, Munich: Heyne, 1993, pp. 8, 405–20. This final chapter differs greatly in the English-language edition.

5 M. Broszat, 'The Concentration Camps 1933–45', in H. Krausnick *et al.* (eds), *Anatomy of the SS State*, London: Paladin, 1970, pp. 141–249; F. Pingel, *Häftlinge unter SS-Herrschaft. Widerstand, Selbstbehauptung und Vernichtung im Konzentrationslager*, Hamburg: Hoffmann und Campe, 1978; U. Herbert, K. Orth and C. Dieckmann (eds), *Die nationalsozialistischen Konzentrationslager. Entwicklung und Struktur*, 2 vols., Göttingen: Wallstein, 1998; K. Orth, *Das System der nationalsozialistischen Konzentrationslager. Eine politische Organisationsgeschichte*, Hamburg: Hamburger Edition, 1999. An article on concentration camps and local societies is also lacking in the introductory first volume of the important, nine volume encyclopaedia: W. Benz and B. Distel (eds), *Der Ort des Terrors. Geschichte der nationalsozialistischen Konzentrationslager*, Munich: C. H. Beck, 2005–2009.

6 W. Johe, 'Das deutsche Volk und das System der Konzentrationslager', in U. Büttner (ed.), *Das Unrechtsregime. Internationale Forschung über den Nationalsozialismus (Festschrift für Werner Jochmann zum 65. Geburtstag)*, Hamburg: Hans Christians Verlag, 1986, pp. 331–44.

7 R. Gellately, *Backing Hitler. Consent and Coercion in Nazi Germany*, Oxford: Oxford University Press, 2002, pp. 51–69 ('Concentration Camps and Media Reports'), pp. 204–23 ('Concentration Camps in Public Spaces').

8 G. Horwitz, *In the Shadow of Death. Living outside the Gates of Mauthausen*, New York: N.Y. Free Press, 1990; S. Steinbacher, *Dachau. Die Stadt und das Konzentrationslager in der NS-Zeit. Die Untersuchung einer Nachbarschaft* (= Münchner Studien zur neueren und neuesten Geschichte, vol. 5), 2nd edn, Frankfurt, 1994; J. Schley, *Nachbar Buchenwald. Die Stadt Weimar und ihr Konzentrationslager 1937–1945*, Cologne: Böhlau, 1999; S. Steinbacher, *"Musterstadt" Auschwitz. Germanisierung und Judenmord in Ostoberschlesien*, Munich: Saur, 2000; J.-C. Wagner, *Produktion des Todes. Das KZ Mittelbau-Dora*, Göttingen: Wallstein, 2001; T. Bütow and F. Bindernagel, *Ein KZ in der Nachbarschaft. Das Magdeburger Außenlager der Brabag und der "Freundeskreis Himmler"*, 2nd edn, Cologne: Böhlau, 2004; K. Fings, *Krieg, Gesellschaft und KZ. Himmlers SS-Baubrigaden*, Paderborn: Schöningh, 2005; C. Glauning, *Entgrenzung und KZ-System. Das Unternehmen Wüste und das Konzentrationslager in Bisingen*, Berlin: Metropol, 2006. See also the articles in *Dachauer Hefte*, 12 (1996):

124   *Karola Fings*

Konzentrationslager. Lebenswelt und Umfeld; Dachauer Hefte, 17 (2001): *Öffentlichkeit und KZ – Was wusste die Bevölkerung?*

9   To name but a few: R. Gellately, *The Gestapo and German Society: Enforcing Racial Policy 1933–1945*, Oxford: Oxford University Press, 1990; K.-M. Mallmann and G. Paul (eds), *Die Gestapo. Mythos und Realität*, Darmstadt: Primus Verlag, 1995; K.-M. Mallmann and G. Paul, *Die Gestapo im Zweiten Weltkrieg. "Heimatfront" und besetztes Europa*, Darmstadt: Primus Verlag, 2000; F. Bajohr and D. Pohl, *Der Holocaust als offenes Geheimnis. Die Deutschen, die NS-Führung und die Alliierten*, Munich: C. H. Beck, 2006, particularly pp. 15–79; P. Longerich, *"Davon haben wir nichts gewusst!" Die Deutschen und die Judenverfolgung 1933–1945*, Munich: Siedler, 2006; M. Wildt, *Volksgemeinschaft als Selbstermächtigung. Gewalt gegen Juden in der deutschen Provinz 1919 bis 1939*, Hamburg: Hamburger Edition, 2007.

10   T. Roth, 'Frühe Haft- und Folterstätten in Köln 1933/34', in J. E. Schulte (ed.), *Konzentrationslager im Rheinland und in Westfalen 1933–1945. Zentrale Steuerung und regionale Initiative*, Paderborn: Schöningh, 2005, pp. 3–24, here p. 20.

11   Examples of the extensive reporting on the camps can be found in Johe, 'Das deutsche Volk', p. 333f; S. Milton, 'Die Konzentrationslager der dreißiger Jahre im Bild der in- und ausländischen Presse', in Herbert, Orth and Dieckmann (eds), *Konzentrationslager*, pp. 135–47, here esp. 135–8; Gellately, *Backing Hitler*, pp. 77–86; Roth, 'Frühe Haftstätten', p. 7, 20.

12   *Münchner Neueste Nachrichten* Nr. 79, 21.3.1933, reprinted in Comité International de Dachau (ed.), *Konzentrationslager Dachau 1933–1945*, 9th edn, Munich: n.p., 1978, p. 44.

13   There were reports about almost all of the 'early camps' in the local press in 1933/4. See the contributions in Benz and Distel (eds), *Der Ort des Terrors*, vol. 2: Frühe Lager, Dachau, Emslandlager; Munich: C. H. Beck, 2005.

14   Cf. *Dachauer Zeitung*, 21.3.1933, quoted from Steinbacher, *Dachau*, p. 186.

15   Cf. Milton, 'Konzentrationslager', p. 137.

16   Cf. 'Schutzhaftgefangene beim Torfstechen', in *Amper-Bote*, Nr. 211, 7.9.1933; 'Warnung!', in *Amper-Bote*, Nr. 129, 2.6.1933, reprinted in: Comité International de Dachau, *Dachau*, p. 44.

17   S. Haffner, *Geschichte eines Deutschen. Die Erinnerungen 1914–1933*, 10th edn, Stuttgart: Deutsche Verlags-Anstalt, 2001, p. 124.

18   'Staatsfeinde in Obhut – Hinter den Gittern der polizeilichen Verwahre', in: *Westdeutscher Beobachter*, Nr. 213, 29.8.1933, p. 5, reprinted in Roth, 'Haft- und Folterstätten', p. 7.

19   Quote from the *Berliner Morgenpost* 7.4.1933 on Oranienburg, cited in Gellately, *Backing Hitler*, p. 83.

20   Quoted by W. Hornung (= Julius Zerfaß), *Dachau. Eine Chronik*, Zürich: Europa-Verlag, 1936, p. 34, cited by Steinbacher, *Dachau*, p. 150.

21   Haffner, *Geschichte eines Deutschen*, p. 175.

22   See U. Herbert, 'Von der Gegnerbekämpfung zur "rassischen Generalprävention". "Schutzhaft" und Konzentrationslager in der Konzeption der Gestapo-Führung 1933–1939', in Herbert, Orth and Dieckmann (eds), *Konzentrationslager*, pp. 60–86; P. Wagner, *Volksgemeinschaft ohne Verbrecher. Konzeptionen und Praxis der Kriminalpolizei in der Zeit der Weimarer Republik und des Nationalsozialismus*, Hamburg: Christians, 1996, especially pp. 254–301.

23   See Johe, 'Das deutsche Volk', pp. 335–8.

24   Speech by Himmler on 'Wesen und Aufgabe der SS und der Polizei' to a Wehrmacht 'Course in National Politics', 15–23 January 1937, reprinted in Internationales Buchenwald-Komitee/Komitee der Antifaschistischen Widerstandskämpfer der Deutschen Demokratischen Republik (ed.), *Buchenwald. Mahnung und Verpflichtung*, Berlin: Kongress-Verlag, 1960, pp. 26f.

25   'Kriegsgebiet KZ', *Das Schwarze Korps* 5 (1939), 21.12.1939, quoted in Johe, 'Das deutsche Volk', p. 338, and in Gellately, *Backing Hitler*, pp. 284f.

26 Kogon, *SS-Staat*, p. 418.

27 Threats of concentration camp imprisonment were so widespread in everyday communication that Himmler felt impelled to act, as Goebbels recorded in his diary: 'Himmler appeals in a circular against reckless threats of concentration camp. He is absolutely right. Some great mischief is done with concentration camp threats. Some district leader or mayor or other believes he can threaten concentration camp if something in public life doesn't suit him.' E. Fröhlich (ed.), *Die Tagebücher von Joseph Goebbels, Teil II, Diktate 1941–1945*, Munich: K. G. Saur, 1995, vol. 4, p. 515 (13 June 1942). On the magnitude of denunciation see G. Diewald-Kerkmann, *Politische Denunziation im NS-Regime oder Die kleine Macht der "Volksgenossen"*, Bonn: Dietz, 1995, as well as the critical overview of the literature by B. Dörner, 'NS-Herrschaft und Denunziation – Anmerkungen zu Defiziten in der Denunziationsforschung', *Historical Social Research*, vol. 26, 2001, No. 2/3, pp. 55–69.

28 See the volumes of the history of the National Socialist concentration camps edited by W. Benz and B. Distel (see note 5 above).

29 In the example of a diary kept by the Cologne doctor Wolfgang Michels in the period from 6 March to 27 May 1945, the reaction to the early Allied reports about the concentration camps is evident in exemplary manner. After an initial shock about the pictures an ever more apparent defensiveness sets in, which intensifies with the announcement of the intention of calling the German people to account for the crimes. See NS-Dokumentationszentrum der Stadt Köln, Biographische Sammlung Kriegsende, Tagebuch Wolfgang Michels. The diary is reprinted slightly abridged and with a brief biography in M. Rüther, *Köln im Zweiten Weltkrieg. Alltag und Erfahrungen 1939–1945*, Cologne: Emons, 2005, pp. 893–918.

30 The following draws upon Steinbacher, *Dachau*, especially pp. 77–84, 93–8, 118–25, 152.

31 Der Inspekteur der Konzentrationslager to Staatssekretär und Leiter des Thüringischen Ministeriums des Innern, 27.10.1936, reprinted in H. Stein (ed.), *Das Konzentrationslager Buchenwald 1937–1945. Begleitband zur Dauerausstellung*, Göttingen: Wallstein, 1999, p. 15.

32 Schley, *Nachbar Buchenwald*, p. 39.

33 E. Georg, *Die wirtschaftlichen Unternehmungen der SS*, Stuttgart: Deutsche Verlags-Anstalt, 1963, pp. 42–7; J. E. Schulte, *Zwangsarbeit und Vernichtung: Das Wirtschaftsimperium der SS. Oswald Pohl und das SS-Wirtschaftsverwaltungshauptamt 1933–1945*, Paderborn: Schöningh, 2001, pp. 103–25.

34 Contract of 6.5.1940, copy reprinted in H. Kaienburg, *Das Konzentrationslager Neuengamme 1938–1945*, Bonn: Dietz, 1997, pp. 59–63.

35 Georg, *Die wirtschaftlichen Unternehmungen der SS*, p. 44f. See also J. Skriebeleit, 'Flossenbürg-Stammlager', in Benz and Distel, *Ort des Terrors*, vol. 4, pp. 17–66, here p. 18f; F. Freund and B. Perz, 'Mauthausen', in ibid., pp. 293–346, here p. 293f; R. Steegmann, 'Natzweiler-Stammlager', in ibid., vol. 6, pp. 23–47, here pp. 23–5; I. Sprenger and W. Kumpmann, 'Groß-Rosen-Stammlager', in ibid., pp. 195–221, here pp. 195–7.

36 Speer's self-stylization as opponent of the SS proves upon closer inspection to be a construct, with which he sought – largely successfully – to exonerate himself. See A. Speer, *The Slave State: Heinrich Himmler's Masterplan for SS Supremacy*, London: Weidenfeld and Nicolson, 1981. His personal stake in the expansion of the camp system cannot be overestimated, for example in the construction of the Mittelbau-Dora concentration camp. See Wagner, *Produktion des Todes*.

37 A. Bonifas, *Häftling 20.801. Ein Zeugnis über die faschistischen Konzentrationslager*, 4th edn, Berlin: Union-Verlag, 1983, p. 126.

38 Eyewitness report by Emil Pascha, in A. Kussmann, *Ein KZ-Außenlager in Düsseldorf-Stoffeln*, Düsseldorf: n.p., 1988, p. 181.

39 See the 21.4.1945 diary entry of a teacher from the Bergedorf area of Hamburg, quoted from Johe, 'Das deutsche Volk', p. 345f.
40 E. Barth, *Lemuria. Aufzeichnungen und Meditationen*, Hamburg: Claassen & Goverts, 1947, p. 90f.
41 H. Averdunk and W. Ring, *Geschichte der Stadt Duisburg*, 2nd edn, Ratingen: Aloys Henn, 1949, p. 343.
42 Examples in Fings, *Krieg, Gesellschaft und KZ*, pp. 159–66.
43 Barth, *Lemuria*, p. 89.
44 Bonifas, *Häftling*, p. 54.
45 See the examples in Fings, *Krieg, Gesellschaft und KZ*, pp. 224–8, 242f.
46 W. Sofsky, *The Order of Terror: The Concentration Camp*, Princeton, NJ: Princeton University Press, 1997, p. 14.
47 Ibid., p. 55.
48 Steinbacher, *Auschwitz*, p. 53.
49 Archiv der Gedenkstätte Neuengamme, Nr. 1274, Letter by Helmut Knöller, 27.10.1944. By 'soldiers' the author means the prisoners' guards, who were now no longer recruited solely from the SS, but also from the army. Similar description in Kogon, *SS-Staat*, p. 418.
50 See Zentrale Stelle der Landesjustizverwaltungen Ludwigsburg, IV 406 AR 221/74, pp. 65–9, interrogations of Agnes W. and Fritz L., 3.11.1950.
51 Kussmann, *KZ-Außenlager*, p. 72.
52 The Administrative Group W (Economic Enterprises) of the SS-WVHA wrote retrospectively in July 1944 on the subject of their tasks: 'As head of the German police the Reich Leader of the SS had the task of solving problems which the Reich as such could not solve, namely securing all asocial elements which had no right to exist in the National Socialist state and making their capacity for work useful to the people as a whole. This took place in the concentration camps.' Document reprinted in W. Naasner, *SS-Wirtschaft und SS-Verwaltung. Das SS-Wirtschafts-Verwaltungshauptamt und die unter seiner Dienstaufsicht stehenden wirtschaftlichen Unternehmungen und weitere Dokumente*, Düsseldorf: Droste, 1998, p. 277.
53 Haffner, *Geschichte eines Deutschen*, p. 186.
54 Sofsky, *Ordnung des Terrors*, p. 58.
55 Milton, 'Konzentrationslager', p. 135, has already referred to this.
56 'When the Nazis came for the Communists, I did not speak out, I was not a Communist. / When they imprisoned the Social Democrats, I did not speak out, I was not a Social Democrat. / When they came for the trade unionists, I did not speak out, I was not a trade unionist. / When they came for me, there was no one left to speak out for me.' See http://www.martin-niemoeller-stiftung.de/.
57 D. Peukert, *Inside Nazi Germany: Conformity, Opposition and Racism in Everyday Life*, London: B. T. Batsford, 1987, p. 248.

6 Work and extermination in the concentration camps

Jens-Christian Wagner

Around 1.65 million people were sent to concentration camps by the SS and the Gestapo between 1933 and 1945. Almost a million of those interned in camps did not survive.[1] The overwhelming majority of the victims of the concentration camp system died during the second half of the war, from 1942 onwards, a phase in which forced labour in the armaments industry became the defining characteristic of camp imprisonment. At first sight, the high death rates in the concentration camps during the second half of the war would hardly suggest that, as far as the armaments industry was concerned, the SS was following even the most rudimentary economic rationale: to keep the urgently needed work force alive. In the specialist literature on the subject, it is therefore often claimed that the ideological goal of extermination remained paramount right up to1945, despite the demands of the war economy. In this view, no change in the function of the concentration camps can be ascertained. Rather, the unchanging exterminatory mindset of the SS was revealed programmatically in the concept 'annihilation through labour'.[2]

In fact, the concentration camp system after 1942 stood on two pillars: forced labour and genocide. Formally speaking, the concentration camps – those subordinated to Office (*Amtsgruppe*) D of the SS Business and Administration Main Office (WVHA) – were camps where the prisoners had to perform forced labour for the armaments industry, as well as two extermination camps which were primarily used for the extermination of the European Jews: Majdanek and Auschwitz.[3] This means that some prisoners in the concentration camp system were exploited as forced labourers in order to meet economic targets, while at the same time many others were murdered for ideological reasons, even though their labour was actually urgently needed. Did a contradiction exist, therefore, between economic targets and the ideological project of mass murder? Did the SS, as Adam Tooze put it, face 'an unresolvable contradiction between its genocidal racial ideology and the practical imperatives of production'?[4] This is the central question for the following discussion of the history of forced labour in the concentration camps.

The current state of research

The question of the primacy of ideology vs. economics has been a defining feature of the international debate on National Socialist rule, at least since the dispute in the left-wing theoretical periodical *Das Argument* between the British historian Tim Mason and his East German colleagues Dietrich Eichholz and Kurt Gossweiler at the end of the 1960s.[5] Going beyond apologist portrayals of the Nazi system as a 'coerced economy',[6] Mason argued for a primacy of politics, while the GDR historians, following Marxist-Leninist fascism theory, assumed the dominance of economics over politics. National Socialist extermination policy played only an ancillary role in these discussions, however, as large sections of historiography, especially in Germany, generally factored out the concentration camps and the Holocaust until the early 1980s.[7]

Encouraged by the West German *Historikerstreit*, discussion turned again to the primacy of economics vs. politics at the end of the 1980s, with publications by Götz Aly and Susanne Heim on the relationship between social policy and genocide.[8] Aly and Heim diagnosed a causal relationship between economically determined demographic planning for the occupied territories in the east, above all in Poland, and the inception of the genocide. In this interpretation, racism and antisemitism appear, at best, as epiphenomena of otherwise sober economic (and thus rational) planning. Criticism was not long in coming, and was often severe. Historians like Dan Diner, Christopher R. Browning and above all Ulrich Herbert[9] rejected the attempt to disregard the seemingly irrational ideological motivations for genocide.[10] For Herbert, racism remained the 'fixed point of reference of the system'.[11]

This discussion of the economics of the final solution encouraged academic engagement with the history of forced labour and the concentration camps. Though this began tentatively,[12] since the early 1990s the number of detailed studies of individual satellite camps established at armaments factories has become almost too large to keep track of.[13] This period has also seen the publication of histories of camp complexes[14] and individual enterprises[15] which exploited concentration camp prisoners, as well as studies posing wider-ranging questions, especially on the organizational history of forced labour in the camps.[16]

Thus we now have an extensive literature on the subject of forced labour and concentration camps. However, the relationship between ideology and economics, initially the most central question, has retreated increasingly into the background, especially in more recent studies. It seems that the ever-increasing distance in time from the coexistence of two competing political systems in East and West, which came to an end with the collapse of the socialist states in Eastern Europe, has resulted in the sidelining of structural questions which presupposed, or at least considered, the connection between capitalist rationality and the ideological will to extermination. At any event, in recent studies on the subject, interest has turned far more to questions relating to the motivations of individual perpetrators and groups of perpetrators and to the socialization of forced labour.[17]

From punishment to exploitation: forced labour in the concentration camps

Forced labour in the concentration camps was essentially determined by political and economic developments in the National Socialist regime which were external to the camps themselves. The decisive role in this was played by the war, towards which National Socialist policy was geared from the start. On 30 April 1942, Oswald Pohl, who had been appointed head of the SS-WVHA a few weeks earlier, wrote a letter to his immediate superior, Reichsführer-SS Heinrich Himmler, in which he set out programmatically the future tasks of the concentration camp administration:

> 1 The war has brought about a visible structural change in the concentration camps and fundamentally altered their function with regard to the deployment of prisoners. The custody of prisoners purely for reasons of security, re-education and prevention is no longer in the foreground. The mobilization of all prisoner manpower, first for the tasks of war (armaments escalation) and later for the construction tasks of peace, is increasingly edging into the foreground.
> 2 This recognition entails essential measures which demand a gradual transformation of the concentration camps from their earlier solely political form into an organisation commensurate with the economic tasks at hand.[18]

Already in a letter of 26 January 1942 to Richard Glücks, the inspector of the concentration camps, Himmler had announced that 'great economic tasks and duties' would 'emerge in the concentration camps in the coming weeks.'[19] Accordingly, Himmler was 'very much in agreement with everything' in the Pohl letter, as he wrote to him at the end of May 1942. But he then specified the following:

> I believe, however, that it needs to be emphasized one way or another that the issues of reviewing inmates' detention and of the aim of re-educating the re-educable in the concentration camps remain unchanged. Otherwise, the notion might arise that we are arresting people, or keeping those already arrested in custody, in order to have workers. It should thus be emphasized and made clear that the legal basis of detention remains unchanged and independent of [prisoners'] economic deployment. In any case, on top of giving 100 per cent priority to the labour we need to extract [from the prisoners], I believe that the camp commandants must take care of the re-education of the re-educable.[20]

This brings to light the tension between the original defining characteristic of prisoners' work – unproductive, humiliating hard labour – and the use of the concentration camp labour force for increasingly economic ends. Throughout the development of the camps, however, prisoners' work had been characterized by contradictions. First, productive work by 'worthless' prisoners (in the terms of National Socialist ideology) stood in opposition to the myth of the 'nobility of work'. Second, the economic interests of the SS came up against resistance from industry and from state institutions.[21] Third, terror remained a constitutive element of prisoner work until the end. However, the emergence of forced labour in the camps went through different stages which – like the development of the concentration camps as a whole – can essentially be separated into three distinct phases.

The early years of Nazi rule were still marked by mass unemployment. Initially, therefore, productive work could hardly be implemented in the camps if prisoner work was to serve as a punishment and means of 're-education'. As a result of these political-ideological considerations, the SS called on the prisoners to perform mostly meaningless and physically strenuous tasks, such as the cultivation of moorland (notably in the Esterwegen camp). Despite this, the contradiction remained between work as a punishment for prisoners deemed 'worthless' and the mystical elevation of the concept of 'work' in Nazi ideology. Even the SS attempt to resolve this contradiction, by distinguishing between prisoners who were 'capable of improvement' and those who were 'no longer re-educable', could not resolve this conflict with Nazi ideology.

The shift of economic priorities which accompanied the transition to war preparations led to changes in an increasingly militarized labour market, such as the introduction of labour conscription in 1938.[22] With this came a modification of prisoner work, which – in the face of an increasing shortage of labour – gained in economic importance. At the same time, the SS began to construct its own economic enterprises. A fundamental element in this was the extraction of building materials for Albert Speer's construction projects in the immediate pre-war years. It is no coincidence that the new concentration camps established from 1937–1938 were situated near high-value quarries and that a large part of prisoner labour consisted of work in these quarries, notably in the concentration camps Flossenbürg, Mauthausen, Gross-Rosen and Natzweiler, all founded between 1938 and 1940 (the latter two camps were established as main camps (*Hauptlager*) only in 1941).[23]

Initially, however, the growing economic significance of the concentration camps and the implementation of increasingly economically driven forced labour did not lead to any modification of working conditions. Victimization and terror continued to characterize the work of prisoners. This included physical exhaustion – as in the case of work in the quarries, carried out largely without any technical equipment – which was used as a means of 're-educating of the re-educable' (as Heinrich Himmler had put it in his letter of May 1942 to Oswald Pohl)[24] or even as a means of murder. The steady stream of new prisoners – in 1937–1938 alone, around 15,000 people defined as 'criminal' and 'asocial' were brought to the concentration camps – and the extension of prisoner work led to a dramatic deterioration in living conditions in the camps. The combination of over-crowding and the belief of the SS that the camp workforce was expendable (or even superfluous) meant that every new intake of prisoners brought with it a dramatic rise in the death rates. This reached unprecedented levels after the start of the war, with the arrival of tens of thousands of Poles and Czechs. Virtually nothing else gives us such a clear insight into the murderous working conditions in these camps as the 'stairs of death' (*Todesstiege*) at the Mauthausen concentration camp. In the course of 1940, more than a third of all prisoners of Mauthausen and its satellite camp Gusen died.[25]

During this phase, it was above all the new groups of prisoners, notably foreigners, who were confronted with working conditions which could aptly be described as 'annihilation through labour'. This term, which has been the subject of heated academic debate in relation to the third phase of the concentration camps (from 1942 onwards), can be rightly applied to the first wartime phase of the camps. In a camp like Mauthausen or in the quarry of Flossenbürg, the economic exploitation of the camp inmates and the working of prisoners to death through exhaustion were two sides of the same coin. During this phase, work in the quarries was, as Bertand Perz has rightly claimed, 'a method for the systematic killing of prisoners'.[26]

In such circumstances, it would be difficult to speak of productive work, certainly not if this means a viable economic system – to say nothing of the idea that the productive power of the worker ought to be maintained. The two brickworks in Sachsenhausen and Neuengamme, which belonged to the SS's German Earth and Stone Works (DESt) made financial losses in their first years of business, due not only to the extensive exploitation of the camp workforce but also to the economic dilettantism of the SS management.[27]

Admittedly, there were some signs of more effective concentration camp work in the SS enterprises, such as the subsidiary of the Ravensbrück camp, the Association for Textile and Leather Processing (Gesellschaft für Textil- und Lederverwertung). On the whole, however, looking at the second phase of the development of the concentration camps, the wearing down of the work force was entirely in line with the political and ideological premises of the SS and the authorities behind internment. While political prisoners were deemed 'capable of improvement', this status was not granted to prisoners detained for racial or 'preventive' reasons after 1937, and these made up the majority of prisoners in the camps from 1938 onwards. This group included those persecuted as 'criminals', 'asocials' or 'homosexuals' as well as Jews and Sinti and Roma persecuted on racial grounds. Their deployment in what Falk Pingel has called 'extermination-workplaces' (*Vernichtungsarbeitsplätzen*) was thus perfectly logical. This also applied to the numerous non-German prisoners, especially those from Eastern Europe, who were sent to the camps from 1939 onwards. If the work undertaken by these prisoners was still being conceived as a means of 're-education' by the SS leadership, this phrase could hardly disguise what was actually meant: extermination.

The high death rates during the first phase of the war were a result not only of the murderous working conditions, but also of murder itself. As well as the shooting of Soviet prisoners of war in the autumn and winter of 1941–1942,[28] this included, above all, the 'Special Treatment' action '14f13'.[29] Closely related to the 'euthanasia' killing of the mentally ill under 'Action T4', the '14f13' programme entailed the murder of sick, disabled and Jewish prisoners. At least 10,000 people, possibly even 20,000, were killed between the spring of 1941 and the spring of 1942. Alongside the ideologically motivated objective of killing Jews and the disabled, the SS also aimed to use the murders to rid itself of those inmates who were not fit for work in the overcrowded camps and who were thus viewed as useless mouths to feed. This practice of selecting prisoners who were no longer fit for work would become an organizing principle of forced labour in the concentration camps in the years which followed.

'Economic profitability': forced labour in the second half of the war.

The third phase in the development of the concentration camp system began in 1942, when, following the model of 'structural change' stipulated by Pohl, the concentration camps became increasingly integrated into the German war economy. The starting point was the failure of the German *Blitzkrieg* strategy in the invasion of the Soviet Union, which brought the prospect of a longer war of attrition and forced the National Socialist leadership to fundamentally rethink its economic war strategy.[30] The reorganization of the war economy was made necessary in particular by the shortage of labour, which became more evident each time a new cohort of German men was called up to the army. Also important was the lack of resources which, given the lack of new conquests, could no longer be offset as before. Structurally, this development was manifested in early 1942 in three factors: first, the expansion of what would later become the Ministry for Armaments into central economic control offices under Albert Speer; second, the appointment of the Gauleiter of Thüringia, Fritz Sauckel, to the position of General Plenipotentiary for Labour Deployment (GBA);[31] and third, specifically in relation to the concentration camp system, the complete integration of the office of the Inspection of the Concentration Camps (IKL) into the SS-WVHA.[32]

The WVHA's title – Business and Administration Main Office – contained its programme: at least in terms of the function assigned by Himmler and Oswald Pohl (the head of the WVHA), the concentration camp system was to be organizationally geared to the systematic exploitation of forced prisoner labour in the armaments industry. First, however, some obstacles still had to be cleared. While Himmler and Pohl saw the possible expansion of existing SS enterprises as a way to gain a foothold in the armaments industry, the armaments industry feared competition with the SS, and Speer's armaments ministry did not want to let the leadership of the arms industry slip out of its hands.[33] Initial attempts at co-operation seemed to confirm the fears of Speer's ministry. As early as 1940, an attempt made by the Heinkel Works in Oranienburg to deploy forced labourers from the nearby Sachsenhausen camp had failed because the SS had refused to make prisoners available for work beyond the confines of the camp.[34] For their part, the arms industry and the armaments ministry had reservations about the dispersal of armaments factories to the existing concentration camps; this was obvious in the case of the installation of carbine rifle production of the Wilhelm Gustloff Works in the Buchenwald camp, which began production only very slowly in the summer of 1942, and was hindered especially by the obstruction of the business management; at no point was the planned production target in Buchenwald even approximately reached.[35] A further failure was the Arbeitsdorf concentration camp in the Volkswagen factory in Fallersleben in April 1942. Here, a light metal foundry was supposed to be set up as a joint venture between the Volkswagen and the SS. But in mid-September 1942, the project collapsed because of the objections of Albert Speer, who refused to grant the necessary status of 'priority for the war economy'. In October 1942 the camp was disbanded.[36]

But three other collaborative projects between SS and industry progressed with less resistance: the use of forced concentration camp labour in a new initiative by the Heinkel Works in Oranienburg, near Sachsenhausen; by the IG Farben factory in Auschwitz-Monowitz; and by the Steyr-Daimler-Puch company in Steyr, near Mauthausen. In these three industrial plants, practices of co-operation between SS and business enterprises – detailed below – emerged which later became common during the explosion of prisoner deployment in the armaments industry in the final two years of the war.

After the failure of the first collaborative project in 1940, the Heinkel Works had used prisoners from the Sachsenhausen camp as forced labourers in its aeroplane factory at Oranienburg.[37] The state-funded Works paid either the SS or the Reich a flat rate per day for each prisoner put to work. At first, the prisoners were still accommodated at the main camp but, from September 1942 at the latest, they were housed in a barracks camp in the factory complex. The number of prisoners deployed here rose sharply after this point, from 150 in September 1942 to 4,000 (April 1943) and over 6,000 (December 1944). According to post-war statements by the SS camp commandant, the satellite camp at the Heinkel Works had been intended as a trial project for the use of forced labour from concentration camps in the armaments industry.[38] In the opinion of the SS leadership and the company management, this trial was clearly a great success and it became a model for forcing concentration camp inmates into hundreds of German armaments enterprises from 1943 onwards. In addition, representatives of other enterprises informed themselves about the experience gathered in Oranienburg – for example, the management of the Army Research Centre in Peenemünde who visited the camp in April 1943. The memorandum prepared by the Peenemünde engineers after their visit reads like a brochure advertising the use of concentration camp forced labour.[39]

The second experiment in closer SS collaboration with industry was initiated in Auschwitz-Monowitz, near the Auschwitz satellite camp, in this case in association with IG Farben.[40] As part of the chemical company's 'eastern expansion', the site may have been deliberately selected near the Auschwitz camp with a view to using forced labour. From April 1941, camp prisoners were forced to work in the construction of the IG Farben chemical works in Monowitz. At first they were still housed in the main camp at Auschwitz, which meant long journeys on foot to the partially constructed plant. From spring 1942, IG Farben had been planning the construction of a company-owned camp in Monowitz, but it was not until October 1942 that the camp was populated with 600 prisoners (deported from the Netherlands and Buchenwald to Auschwitz). In the following months, the number of prisoners increased dramatically. In the summer of 1944, the camp reached its maximum size with over 11,000 inmates. By the time the camp was closed in January 1945, the SS had brought a total of 35,000 people to Monowitz, of whom around 25,000 either fell victim to the inhuman working conditions or were selected for death in the gas chambers of Birkenau.[41]

The third project began in Austria. From spring 1941 onwards, the state armaments company Steyr-Daimler-Puch had brought forced labourers from Mauthausen, 30 kilometres away, to work in the construction of an aero-engine factory in Steyr. The prisoners were initially not housed on-site, but this changed in March 1942, when the SS assigned prisoners to the construction of a ball bearings factory in Steyr-Münichholz; the prisoners were now accommodated in a separate camp erected on site. With this, Mauthausen had set up its first satellite camp at the site of an external armaments firm.[42]

At Oranienburg, Auschwitz and Steyr, the SS and the armaments firms were able to work together closely from the start, and for the most part without conflict. This was due primarily to the good relations prevailing between the company managers and the local SS leadership. In other enterprises, however, attempts at collaboration with the SS were mostly still struggling to get off the ground in 1941–1942, since here the SS were insisting, as before, that concentration camp forced labourers could be made available only for work in armaments works sited within the existing camps. It was not until September 1942 that the SS leadership was prepared to change course. On 15 September 1942, leading representatives of the WVHA and the armaments ministry, including their respective heads Pohl and Speer, and the SS-Brigade leader for construction, Hans Kammler, held a decisive meeting. In the course of this meeting, which also saw the decision to close the Arbeitsdorf camp, Speer assured the SS of his support for construction projects at Auschwitz (in 1943 Auschwitz was expanded to become the central site for the murder of the European Jews). The WVHA, in return, distanced itself from its previous position regarding the use of forced labour, as Pohl reported to Himmler on the following day:

> Our takeover of large combined armaments projects requires, however, that we yield on one principle. We would not be able to insist narrow-mindedly that all production be transferred to the interior of our camps. We were justified in imposing this demand so long as we were only dealing with so-called 'dribs and drabs' (*Kleckerkram*), as you, Reichsführer, quite rightly referred to our work up to this point, given its limited scope. But if, tomorrow, we wanted to take over the running of a private armaments factory with 5,000, 10,000 or 15,000 prisoners, it would be quite impossible to set up such a plant *intra muros*. It must be established, as Reichsminister Prof. Speer rightly put it, on a greenfield site. Then an electric fence can be put up around it, the previously

empty factory can be manned with the requisite number of prisoners, and it can be run as an SS armaments factory … Insofar as free factories are unavailable, armaments works which have not yet reached their full capacity due to an insufficient workforce should be completely cleared, then filled 100 per cent by our prisoners. The German and foreign workers who are freed up as a result can be used to fill gaps in similar armaments factories.[43]

This did not, however, entirely meet the wishes of the armaments industry. On the one hand, the industry intended to use prisoners in the factories which already existed and not 'on a greenfield site'. On the other hand, Pohl's reference to 'SS armaments factories' shows that the legal situation, above all the question of the right of disposal over the machines and the products, had not yet been resolved. The wrangling over jurisdiction regarding the use of prisoners was finally settled in favour of the armaments industry, in a conversation a week later between Speer and Hitler.[44] Accordingly, economic production was not to be housed within concentration camps, as the SS had demanded. Instead, the intention was to make existing armaments factories available to SS prisoner commandos in exchange for a daily fee of between two and six Reichsmark, referred to as a 'prisoner fee' (*Häftlingsentgelt*). To house the prisoners, satellite camps were to be set up in armaments factories.

The 'Führer decision' (*Führerentscheid*) of September 1942 finally cleared the way for the systematic and comprehensive deployment of concentration camp prisoners in the armaments industry. Nevertheless, at first the establishment of satellite camps at armaments factories made slow progress. This was due principally to the tension between political and ideological considerations on the one hand, and pragmatic, rational, economic target setting on the other. Thus, during the same period when the loan of prisoners to industry slowly came into practice (i.e. up until the spring of 1943) almost all Jewish prisoners in concentration camps inside the Reich were transferred to the extermination camps and murdered, even though their labour was actually urgently needed.

It was only after propaganda minister Goebbels announced the onset of 'Total War' in February 1943 – in the aftermath of the defeat at Stalingrad – that real change took place, with pragmatic economic considerations gaining the upper hand (even if the ideological aims did not disappear from view). Thus, from 1943, the principle of lending prisoners to the armaments industry came into full effect, and soon a dense network of satellite camps stretched across Germany, in which inmates were set to forced labour in the armaments industry. A few figures illustrate this explosion of the concentration camp phenomenon after 1942: at the beginning of the war in September 1939, there were six main concentration camps in Germany and annexed Austria. By the end of 1943, almost 260 main and satellite camps were in existence, in July 1944 almost 600, and by January 1945 over 730.[45] This last figure was reached despite the fact that the area of German rule had been considerably reduced and numerous camps in both the east and west had been disbanded and their inmates deported back within the boundaries of the Reich. In the winter of 1944–1945, there was hardly a single town in Germany and Austria without its own satellite camp.

The SS and industry: common interests?

Even in the early cases of camp inmates being deployed in SS-owned companies, such as in the DESt or the German Armaments Works (DAW), the SS lent their prisoners to these companies in exchange for a daily fee. Until the end of 1942, this 'prisoner fee' in the SS companies was 30 pfennig per prisoner per day. For private firms, meanwhile, the fee was between three and four Reichsmarks and later between four and six Reichsmarks; the prisoners themselves did not receive a penny.[46] Already included in this sum were the costs for feeding and clothing the prisoners and the provision of guard details, but the firms had to bear the cost of other 'additional expenses', like accommodation and sometimes medical treatment of prisoners.[47] Thus, a considerable share of the responsibility for the conditions in the camps can be assigned to the enterprises themselves, as they could influence the living conditions and the survival chances of prisoners.

For the camp inmates, the fact that firms had to pay a daily fee for their forced labour – a fixed rate which did not take into account whether prisoners were forced to work eight or 12 hours, or even longer – had fatal consequences. The productivity of the weak and under-nourished prisoners was usually significantly lower than that of German civilian workers. According to statistics produced in September 1944 for the building group Gebhardt & König, which used prisoner labour from the Mittelbau-Dora concentration camp, prisoner labour only became more lucrative than the employment of free workers if the inmates, during an eight-hour shift, produced more than 50 per cent of the regular output.[48] In day-to-day practice this was very seldom the case. Only by extending working hours did the use of prisoner labour, even at much lower rates of productivity, become profitable for the firms. Many enterprises therefore did their utmost to extend prisoners' working days – often with deadly results for prisoners.

The assignment of prisoners to an armaments factory and the establishment of a satellite camp usually followed the same pattern: a firm's application for the allocation of concentration camp prisoners was first assessed by the WVHA, initially in consultation with the armaments industry, in terms of its significance for the war effort. If the decision was positive, employees of the WVHA or those responsible for 'work assignments' at the nearest main camp would visit the firm in order to check the facilities for accommodating and guarding prisoners on-site. Finally, the main camp concerned would receive instructions to send a set number of prisoners to the newly established satellite camp along with a corresponding guard detail.[49] If the firm needed particularly qualified workers, its employees could select these from the main camp.

The initiative to deploy prisoners in firms almost always came from the enterprises themselves.[50] There is therefore no question whatsoever of forced labourers being imposed upon companies by the SS. This is also illustrated by the fact that, as the war progressed, it was the Ministry of Armaments, not the

WVHA, which developed into the central directive authority for forced prisoner labour. From October 1944, businesses had to submit their applications for the allocation of concentration camp labour to the Ministry of Armaments and no longer to the SS. The ministry, after assessment, passed the requests on to the SS.[51]

Selection and segregation

About half of the satellite camps set up after 1942 were established at existing armaments companies. The other half were set up at construction projects, notably at underground production facilities of the armaments industry. This development began in the autumn of 1943 with the relocation of the missile assembly plant of Peenemünde on the island of Usedom to the underground 'Mittelwerk' near Nordhausen in the southern Harz.[52] The rapid transformation of this subterranean oil depot into a missile factory, which claimed the lives of thousands of concentration camp labourers from the Buchenwald satellite camp 'Dora' (established at the end of August 1943), developed into the benchmark project for the absurd and murderous attempt to relocate the German armaments industry to bomb-proof underground installations, in order to protect it from Allied aerial bombardment.

Coordinated by the Ministry of Armaments – whose head, Albert Speer, inspected the 'Mittelwerk' site in December 1943 – construction work started throughout Germany in the spring of 1944 on new underground installations, many of which were part of the so-called 'fighter programme' (*Jägerprogramm*): in order to break the Allied hold on German airspace, a ministerial crisis group, led by Speer's representative Karl-Otto Saur, had been established with the task of boosting the production of fighter planes and with extensive powers.[53] Part of the programme was the relocation of aircraft production underground, which was advanced with great urgency. In part, natural caves and existing tunnels were converted into underground factories, but in most cases the underground bunker complexes had to be created from scratch – an undertaking which was completely illusory from the start, not least because of the approaching end of the war. The majority of bunkers and underground complexes were thus never completed.[54]

Responsibility for the construction work fell to the SS or to the Organization Todt (OT). As for the workforce, it was mainly composed of concentration camp prisoners, alongside foreign forced workers and POWs, for whom satellite camps were set up near the building sites. At the end of 1944, according to an estimate by Oswald Pohl, over 270,000 concentration camp prisoners, including numerous Hungarian Jews, were working in murderous conditions on these SS and OT building sites, both above and below ground.[55] Around the same number of prisoners were working as forced labourers in the armaments factories at this point in time.

While the working conditions in the camps within armaments factories (which included, incidentally, the majority of the women's satellite camps) were often comparatively bearable, the satellite camps for the relocation projects were effectively death camps, like the concentration camp quarries in the early years of the war. This was due above all to the most important selection criterion used by the SS and its business partners: the notion that concentration camp labourers were expendable. The loss of prisoners working in armaments firms would have been economically detrimental – these inmates were the most highly qualified workers and had often become familiar with their tasks only after a long period of forced labour – so the SS and business administrators were careful to make sure that this workforce, or at least the prisoners categorized as specialist workers, was more or less retained. The situation was quite different for the largely unqualified 'construction prisoners' (*Bauhäftlinge*), to employ the term used in the SS sources. These prisoners were considered replaceable, since a constant supply of labour seemed readily available in great quantities in the main camps; and so the SS and business managers allowed them to be worked to death.

The practice of renting out prisoners – with firms having to pay a daily rate only for those prisoners deemed fit for work – and above all the relationship between building and production commandos set into motion a deadly mechanism of prisoner transfer, with constant selections. At the centre of this system were the overflowing main camps which developed into turntables for bringing in prisoners and shunting them on to the satellite camps. Following the SS logic of segregation, those prisoners who, in terms of their skills, were not suitable for production commandos, or who were already too weak, were sent off to the camps whose inmates had to perform the hardest construction work. In such construction commandos, the SS and business management beat the last ounce of work out of the prisoners. Anyone who was considered, even by the criteria of the SS, to be no longer capable of any work in the satellite camps was sent back to the main camp, in exchange for new prisoners. This is why the SS, after 1943, established zones for the dying in almost all the main camps; here, the prisoners who could no longer be exploited were largely abandoned (as, for instance, in the 'Small Camp' in Buchenwald, the former Uckermark 'Youth Detention Camp' at Ravensbrück or the 'Sanitary Camp' at Mauthausen).[56] For the Mittelbau camp, a satellite camp in the Boelcke barracks in Nordhausen served as a camp for the dying.

In addition, the SS also organized shipments of prisoners for extermination in other concentration camps. Until 1943, they sent prisoners who were sick or no longer able to work to Dachau; in the autumn of 1942, they were sent to Auschwitz as well. In the winter of 1943/4 it was above all Majdanek which served as a reception camp for shipments of exhausted prisoners intended for extermination. When the Majdanek camp began to be cleared, this function was taken over by Bergen-Belsen.[57]

In most cases the prisoners died in these zones for the dying as a result of deliberate neglect. In some camps they were also intentionally murdered, either by poisonous injection in the prison sick bay or in gas chambers. At Ravensbrück, in gas chambers set up at the beginning of 1945, the SS had killed (by April) 5,000–6,000 women and at least 100 men who were considered unfit for work.[58] Prisoners from Auschwitz-Monowitz, brought to the point of exhaustion by forced labour in the IG-Farben Buna Works, were also killed in gas chambers. Three kinds of selections were carried out there: first, prisoners were inspected for their ability to work during roll call and in the barracks (camp selection); second, selections were carried out in the prisoner sick bays with the intention of reducing the number of sick inmates; third, selections took place as the work columns left the camps in the morning. In each case, the selection took place through visual inspection by SS doctors. Those whom the physicians singled out as unfit to work were taken, within two days, to the gas chambers at Birkenau.[59]

Annihilation through labour?

Faced with the horrendous death rates – in some camps two-thirds of all prisoners died within a few months – some historians have referred to the living and working conditions, especially in the construction camps, as 'annihilation through labour'.[60] This concept seems to solve the apparent contradiction between the economic exploitation of the prisoner workforce, especially on the part of industry, and extermination as an ideological aim of the SS.

On closer inspection, however, the concept proves problematic. In the surviving documents this phrase is only used in two memoranda of September 1942 which recount conversations that the recently appointed Reich Minister of Justice, Otto Georg Thierack, held with Joseph Goebbels and Heinrich Himmler. According to these memoranda, the notion of annihilation through labour goes back to Goebbels, with whom Thierack conferred on 14 September 1942 regarding the transfer of prisoners from the regular penal system to the SS and their subsequent extermination. After the discussion, Thierack noted:

> With regard to the extermination of asocial life, Dr Goebbels is of the opinion that Jews and Gypsies *per se*, Poles who have served, say, three to four years in penitentiaries, and Czechs and Germans who have been sentenced to death, life imprisonment or security confinement should be exterminated. He argues that notion of annihilation through labour (*Vernichtung durch Arbeit*) would be best.[61]

Following this conversation, Thierack formally arranged with Himmler for the 'delivery of asocial elements from the penal system to the SS for annihilation through labour'.[62] According to Thierack and Himmler, those to be transferred were 'the detained Jews, Gypsies, Russians and Ukrainians, Poles with sentences of over three years, and Czechs or Germans with sentences of over eight years as decided by the Reich Justice Minister.'[63]

For the inmates transferred from regular prisons to the SS, a programme of annihilation through labour can actually be proven; accordingly the mortality rates were high among the 20,000 prisoners transferred from the penal system to the concentration camps between September 1942 and the end of the war.[64] In terms of a critical analysis of the sources, however, this does not prove that a programme of extermination existed for all groups of prisoners. On top of this, it seems doubtful that such a programme would have existed all the way until the end of the war: for the situation in 1942 is not comparable to the last year of the war, neither in the war economy nor in the concentration camp system. It is indeed striking that the arrangement between Thierack and Himmler was made at the same time as the policy decision between Speer and Himmler on the deployment of prisoners in the armaments industry. The Minister of Justice therefore ensured that the number of forced labourers in the concentration camps increased in line with the expansion of the camps' economic function, and simultaneously disposed of the groups of prisoners which he considered superfluous and who, as Hitler himself had asserted in August 1942, did not need to be 'conserved' in prisons.[65] These people were, essentially, to be annihilated through labour.

The victims of the working conditions in the concentration camps in the last two years of the Second World War, however, were clearly not confined to those groups of prisoners named in Thierack's memorandum of 1942. At Mittelbau-Dora, for instance, it was above all French and Belgian political prisoners who died: prisoners, that is, who stood relatively high in the racial hierarchy of the SS.[66] In contrast, it was among the Roma and Sinti that by far the lowest mortality rate can be found – in other words, prisoners who, together with Jews and Soviet prisoners, stood at the bottom of the Nazi racial hierarchy and whom there was substantial pressure to exterminate.[67] The reason for this was presumably that the Roma and Sinti, predominantly from Germany and Austria, were able to obtain, because they could speak German, preferential and potentially life-saving positions in the camp administration. Another reason may be the close family ties prevalent among many Roma and Sinti, since whole extended families were sent to a single camp; these ties could have contributed to the construction of networks of mutual support. The resistance fighters from France, interned for political reasons, were forced, in contrast, to be self-reliant. Since many of them were students or held academic jobs, they could not demonstrate any technical skills which would have allowed for their transfer to a production commando with relatively bearable working conditions. Instead, the SS sent them off into construction units, where they would die within a few months as a result of the debilitating forced labour.

Often it was social and job-specific reasons which determined whether a prisoner survived or not. The objective of the forced labour of French and Belgian prisoners in Mittelbau-Dora was not death, but it was certainly consciously factored in by the SS against the background of the total disposability of camp prisoners. By contrast, extermination was consciously planned for other groups of prisoners, above all Jewish prisoners. For these groups, forced labour was – at best – a means of postponing death, but it was also, especially in construction commandos, a means of causing it. In these cases the concept of annihilation through labour is appropriate, at least as a descriptive formulation.

Overall, the discussion of this concept demonstrates the narrow boundaries of a strictly intentionalist model of interpretation. As a metaphor for moral indignation, the use of the term 'annihilation through labour' by historians may be completely understandable; but it is not particularly helpful in an analytical sense, since it implies an ideological programme and, in doing so, disregards the impetus of contingent factors which emerged in the course of the war. This becomes particularly significant if the presumed programme of annihilation through labour is seen as a concept which was already being developed in the years before the war. Thus, consistent with the intentionalist tradition, Hermann Kaienburg has argued that the original decision for the concept was made as early as 1938.[68] It is beyond doubt that racism was the central ideological foundation of the Nazi regime from its beginning to its end. Racism formed the basis for the complete lack of rights and utter disposability of the concentration camp inmates. From the perspective of the SS, the life of a prisoner had no value in itself – in the final analysis not even for German political prisoners described as reformable. Ultimately, after 1942–1943 the only thing that counted was the ability to work, and this was all the more brutally exploited as the war dragged on, since the conservation of resources was no longer taken into consideration in the final months of the war. However, the use of concentration camp prisoners for forced labour in the armaments industry and in dubious construction projects – which began in 1942 and underwent massive expansion after 1943/44, resulting in prisoners dying of hunger and exhaustion – cannot be explained in terms of an extermination programme developed in the pre-war period and carried out consistently and purposefully until the end of the Nazi regime. It was, rather, self-made crisis situations, and the constraints alleged to arise from them, which combined with a foundation of racism to produce the impetus for radicalization. This radicalization allowed the camps to become death zones in which the 'turnover' of camp inmates, in a process of constant selection, continuously accelerated and expanded.

Conclusion

In the first years of the Nazi regime, forced labour in the concentration camps had no economic significance. The main aim was to use work as a means of demoralizing, terrorizing and – in Nazi ideological terms – 're-educating' the prisoners. After the start of the war, work also became a means of extermination, especially in camps with large quarries, above all for Jews and Soviet and Polish prisoners. The reaction of the Nazi leadership to the failure of *Blitzkrieg* tactics after the German invasion of the Soviet Union, and the expectation of a long war of attrition, led to the fundamental reorganization of the German war economy and, accordingly, the expansion of the economic functions of the concentration camps. The steadily increasing reservoir of forced labour in the camps was put to use in the armaments industry from 1942–1943.

The growing economic imperative in concentration camp forced labour did not, however, result in the old aims simply being abandoned. Especially when it came to those groups of prisoners whom the SS aimed put to death as soon as possible – above all Jewish prisoners – the programme of economic exploitation of the camp workforce and the aim of extermination were, at least potentially, contradictory. On closer inspection, however, this contradiction was limited solely to the question of how quickly a prisoner died. In the eyes of the SS, forced labour never meant salvation but only a deferral of the process of extermination. This affected not only those prisoners who, for ideological reasons, were the highest priority for extermination (like the predominantly Jewish workforce in the Buna Works in Auschwitz-Monowitz) but also those whose death was not necessarily intended (though it was consciously factored in, given the conditions in the camps and workplaces) – such as the thousands of French and Belgians who met an agonizing death in the construction commandos of Mittelbau-Dora. The SS considered their lives completely worthless and expendable. It was on this ideological basis that the SS, in conjunction with the armaments industry, practised the extensive exploitation of prisoner labour.

The decisive concepts for the description and analysis of forced labour in the concentration camps – and not only here, but in all other Nazi camps where inmates were forcibly put to work – are selection and segregation. Most prisoners passed through a continuous series of selections in the camps, which, step by step with their declining strength, led them to be sent to the production commandos, the construction commandos and finally the dying zones of the camps.

Through the system of spatial segregation and constant selection, the SS resolved, to a considerable extent, the contradiction between work and extermination: they attached a particular value to the respective factors of *sustaining the workforce* and *extermination*, depending on the prisoner's ability to work, offset by both the nature of their work and by racial criteria. Adam Tooze has acutely characterized this principle 'of continuous selection and replacement [as] the essence of the concentration camp labour system'.[69]

In the light of this, the older discussion about the primacy of ideology vs. economics, which gave important impetus to research into the concentration camps, seems to become superfluous in relation to forced labour in the camps. This is especially true if the concepts of work and extermination are associated rigidly with the spheres of economics and ideology respectively, since these overlap in many ways and are conditional on each other. To further complicate matters, these arguments are often founded on a positive concept of 'economics' as rational, excluding the possibility, in other words, that there might be an element of economic rationality in renouncing the reproduction of labour power. The SS and the enterprises which worked with it, actually developed – on the ideological basis of racism and antisemitism, and radicalized by the contingent factors of war – a system of forced labour which, in a perfidious way, largely overcame the contradiction between work and extermination. This has been clearly demonstrated by recent research, especially with regard to the second half of the war.

There remain, nevertheless, important issues for future research. First, it is still in many ways unclear what tangible effects forced labour had for the different groups of prisoners. Despite the fact that strict racial divisions between prisoner groups gradually diminished, there were – right up to the end of the war – still significant variations in mortality rates, often from one camp to the next. More precise micro-studies are needed here before comparative analysis and generalizing conclusions can be made. In this context, we also have to pay closer attention to the types of work which prisoners were forced to undertake. Even within the armaments commandos, there were great variations in the working conditions and, therefore, in the chances of survival.

Second, the motivations of the perpetrators need to be explored with greater precision. In the historical literature, it is often implied, without directly stating the fact, that SS and company managers had identical interests. But it is obvious that this was not the case. This raises an important question regarding the role that ideological motives – beyond economic ones – played for the companies themselves; after all, businessmen are hardly likely to be less marked by the ideological currents of their time than other sections of the population. But the numerous historical studies of businesses in the Nazi era, published over the past fifteen years, have not yet provided a convincing answer to this question. Generally speaking, we need to assess the attitude of those in businesses who planned, co-ordinated and monitored the use of concentration camp prisoners for forced labour. Frequently, the conditions for prisoners' existence and survival depended decisively on the German civilians who commanded a squad of prisoners.

Finally, the focus of research into the Nazi concentration camps, even with regard to forced labour, should also be directed more strongly to the early years of the war, which are much less well researched than the second half of the war. The history of Nazi concentration camps would then be revealed as significantly more dynamic. It is also likely that a well-informed perspective on the early years of concentration camp forced labour would allow the findings of recent studies on the second half of the war to be cast in a new light.

Translated by Tom Williams

Notes

1 Figures from M. Spoerer, *Zwangsarbeit unter dem Hakenkreuz. Ausländische Zivilarbeiter, Kriegsgefangene und Häftlinge im Deutschen Reich und im besetzten Europa 1939–1945*, Stuttgart and Munich: DVA, 2001, pp. 108 and 229, and K. Orth, *Das System der nationalsozialistischen Konzentrationslager*, Hamburg: Hamburger Edition, 1999, pp. 345–6. Not included in this figure are the almost 1.1 million Jewish concentration camp prisoners who were murdered in the gas chambers of Auschwitz and Majdanek.

2 See H. Kaienburg, *Vernichtung durch Arbeit. Der Fall Neuengamme. Die Wirtschaftsbestrebungen der SS und ihre Auswirkungen auf die Existenzbedingungen der KZ-Gefangenen*, Bonn: Dietz, 1991; H. Kaienburg, 'Funktionswandel des KZ-Kosmos? Das Konzentrationslager Neuengamme', in U. Herbert, K. Orth and C. Dieckmann (eds), *Die nationalsozialistischen Konzentrationslager. Entwicklung und Struktur*, Göttingen: Wallstein, 1998, pp. 259–84; M. Kárný, ' "Vernichtung durch Arbeit". Sterblichkeit in den NS-Konzentrationslagern', *Beiträge zur nationalsozialistischen Gesundheits- und Sozialpolitik*, vol. 5, Berlin, 1987, pp. 133–58, as well as G. Armanski, *Maschinen des Terrors. Das Lager (KZ und GULAG) in der Moderne*, Münster: Westfälisches Dampfboot, 1993, pp. 72–80.

3 See Orth, *System der nationalsozialistischen Konzentrationslager*, pp. 162–221.

4 A. Tooze, *The Wages of Destruction: The Making and Breaking of the Nazi Economy*, London: Allen Lane, 2006, p. 520. Tooze later qualifies this supposed contradiction: ibid. pp. 524–51, especially pp. 547–8.

5 See, among others, T. Mason, 'The Primacy of Politics. Politics and Economics in National Socialist Germany' in Jane Caplan (ed.), *Nazism, Fascism and the Working Class. Essays by Tim Mason*, Cambridge: Cambridge University Press, 1995, pp. 53–76;

D. Eichholtz and K. Gossweiler, 'Noch einmal: Politik und Wirtschaft 1933–1945', in *Das Argument* 10, 1968, pp. 210–27.

6 H.-E. Kannapin, *Wirtschaft unter Zwang. Anmerkungen und Analysen zur rechtlichen und politischen Verantwortung der deutschen Wirtschaft unter der Herrschaft des Nationalsozialismus im 2. Weltkrieg, besonders im Hinblick auf den Einsatz und die Behandlung von ausländischen Arbeitskräften und Konzentrationslagerhäftlingen in deutschen Industrie- und Rüstungsunternehmen*, Cologne: Deutscher Industrieverlag, 1966. Works of a similar persuasion include R. Wagenführ, *Die deutsche Industrie im Kriege 1939–1945*, Berlin: Duncker und Humblot, 1954, and H. Pfahlmann, *Fremdarbeiter und Kriegsgefangene in der deutschen Kriegswirtschaft 1939–1945*, Darmstadt: Wehr und Wissen Verlags-Gesellschaft, 1968.

7 Exceptions are E. Kolb, *Bergen-Belsen. Geschichte des "Aufenthaltslagers" 1943–1945*, Hannover: Verlag für Literatur und Zeitgeschehen, 1962, and E. Georg, *Die wirtschaftlichen Unternehmungen der SS*, Stuttgart: DVA, 1963 (Schriftenreihe der VfZ, no. 7), but above all M. Broszat, 'The Concentration Camps 1933–45', in H. Krausnick *et al.*, *Anatomy of the SS State*, London: Paladin, 1970, pp. 141–249.

8 G. Aly and S. Heim, *Sozialpolitik und Judenvernichtung. Gibt es eine Ökonomie der Endlösung?*, Berlin: Rotbuch Verlag, 1987 (Beiträge zur nationalsozialistischen Gesundheits- und Sozialpolitik, no. 5); G. Aly and S. Heim, *Architects of Annihilation: Auschwitz and the Logic of Destruction*, Princeton, NJ and Oxford: Princeton University Press, 2002.

9 See U. Herbert, *Hitler's Foreign Workers: Enforced Foreign Labour in Germany Under the Third Reich*, Cambridge: Cambridge University Press, 1997, still the standard work, and his ground-breaking essay on the relationship between work and extermination, 'Arbeit und Vernichtung. Ökonomisches Interesse und Primat der "Weltanschauung" im Nationalsozialismus', in D. Diner (ed.), *Ist der Nationalsozialismus Geschichte? Zu Historisierung und Historikerstreit*, Frankfurt: Fischer-Taschenbuch-Verlag, 1987, pp. 198–236.

10 D. Diner, 'Rassismus und rationales Kalkül. Zum Stellenwert utilitaristisch verbrämter Legitimationsstrategien in der nationalsozialistischen "Weltanschauung"', in Wolfgang Schneider (ed.), *Vernichtungspolitik. Eine Debatte über den Zusammenhang von Sozialpolitik und Genozid im nationalsozialistischen Deutschland*, Hamburg: Junius, 1991, pp. 25–35.

11 Herbert, *Arbeit und Vernichtung*, p. 236.

12 With the exception of Falk Pingel's benchmark study *Häftlinge unter SS-Herrschaft. Widerstand, Selbstbehauptung und Vernichtung im Konzentrationslager*, Hamburg: Hoffmann & Campe, 1978, however, there was, for a long time, no analytically comparative survey study available. Instead there was a preponderance of studies on individual satellite camps: see H. Vorländer (ed.), *Nationalsozialistische Konzentrationslager im Dienst der totalen Kriegführung. Sieben württembergische Außenkommandos des Konzentrationslagers Natzweiler/Elsaß*, Stuttgart: Kohlhammer, 1978; R. Fröbe *et al.*, *Konzentrationslager in Hannover. KZ-Arbeit und Rüstungsindustrie in der Spätphase des Zweiten Weltkrieges*, Hildesheim: Lax, 1985; B. Klewitz, *Die Arbeitssklaven der Dynamit Nobel. Ausgebeutet und vergessen. Sklavenarbeiter und KZ-Häftlinge in Europas größten Rüstungswerken im Zweiten Weltkrieg*, Schalksmühle: Engelbrecht, 1986; D. Vaupel, 'Einsatz von KZ-Gefangenen in der deutschen Wirtschaft und das Problem der Entschädigung überlebender Opfer nach 1945. Eine Fallstudie über jüdische Zwangsarbeiterinnen der "Verwert-Chemie" in Hessisch-Lichtenau', PhD Dissertation, Kassel, 1989; F. Freund, *'Arbeitslager Zement'. Das Konzentrationslager Ebensee und die Raketenrüstung*, Vienna: Verlag für Gesellschaftskritik, 1989; B. Perz, *Projekt Quarz. Steyr-Daimler-Puch und das Konzentrationslager Melk*, Vienna: Verlag für Gesellschaftskritik, 1991. Individual satellite camps were also represented in a volume of the *Dachauer Hefte* on the subject of 'slave labour in the concentration camps' ('Sklavenarbeit im KZ') with contributions by, among others, Ulrich Herbert, Gerd Wysocki and Zdenek Zofka: *Dachauer Hefte* 2, 1986.

13 See, for instance, E. Raim, *Die Dachauer KZ-Außenkommandos Kaufering und Mühldorf. Rüstungsbauten und Zwangsarbeit im letzten Kriegsjahr 1944/45*, Landsberg: Landsberger Verlagsanstalt, 1992; S. Romey, *Ein KZ in Wandsbek. Zwangsarbeit im Hamburger Drägerwerk*,

Hamburg: VSA, 1994; B. C. Wagner, *IG Auschwitz. Zwangsarbeit und Vernichtung von Häftlingen des Lagers Monowitz 1941–1945*, Munich: Saur, 2000 (Darstellungen und Quellen zur Geschichte von Auschwitz; no. 3); C. Glauning, *Entgrenzung und KZ-System. Das Unternehmen "Wüste" und das Konzentrationslager in Bisingen*, Berlin: Metropol, 2006. Two collections of essays also deserve mention: Hamburger Stiftung zur Förderung von Wissenschaft und Kultur (ed.), *'Deutsche Wirtschaft'. Zwangsarbeit von KZ-Häftlingen für Industrie und Behörden. Symposion 'Wirtschaft und Konzentrationslager'*, Hamburg: VSA, 1991, and H. Kaienburg (ed.), *Konzentrationslager und deutsche Wirtschaft*, Opladen: Leske and Budrich, 1996.

14 See, for instance, Kaienburg, *Vernichtung durch Arbeit*; I. Sprenger, *Groß-Rosen. Ein Konzentrationslager in Schlesien*, Cologne/Weimar/Vienna: Böhlau, 1996 (Neue Forschungen zur Schlesischen Geschichte, no. 6); M. Fabréguet, *Mauthausen. Camp de concentration national-socialiste en Autriche rattachée (1938–1945)*, Paris, Diss., 1994; J.-C. Wagner, *Produktion des Todes. Das KZ Mittelbau-Dora*, Göttingen: Wallstein, 2001; B. Strebel, *Das KZ Ravensbrück. Geschichte eines Lagerkomplexes*, Paderborn: Schöningh, 2003.

15 See, for instance, H. Mommsen and M. Grieger, *Das Volkswagenwerk und seine Arbeiter im Dritten Reich*, Düsseldorf: Econ, 1996; P. Hayes, *Industry and Ideology: IG Farben in the Nazi Era*, Cambridge: Cambridge University Press, 1987.

16 See, especially, M. Allen, *The Business of Genocide: The SS, Slave Labor, and the Concentration Camps*, Chapel Hill, NC: University of North Carolina Press, 2002; J. E. Schulte, *Zwangsarbeit und Vernichtung: Das Wirtschaftsimperium der SS. Oswald Pohl und das SS-Wirtschafts-Verwaltungshauptamt 1933–1945*, Paderborn: Schöningh, 2001; and H. Kaienburg, *Die Wirtschaft der SS*, Berlin: Metropol, 2003.

17 See, for example, T. Bütow and F. Bindernagel, *Ein KZ in der Nachbarschaft. Das Magdeburger Außenlager der Brabag und der "Freundeskreis Himmler"*, Cologne: Böhlau, 2003, as well as B. Kooger, *Rüstung unter Tage. Die Untertageverlagerung von Rüstungsbetrieben und der Einsatz von KZ-Häftlingen in Beendorf und Morsleben*, Berlin: Metropol, 2004.

18 Letter from Pohl to Himmler, 30 April 1942, Nuremberg Document (ND) R-129, printed in International Military Tribunal, *Trial of the Major War Criminals before the International Military Tribunal Nuremberg 14 November 1945–1 October 1946*, Nuremberg, 1949, vol. 38, p. 363–7 (hereafter *IMT*).

19 Letter from Himmler to Glücks, 26 January 1942, ND: NO-500, cited by U. Bauche *et al.*, *Arbeit und Vernichtung. Katalog zur ständigen Ausstellung der KZ-Gedenkstätte Neuengamme*, Hamburg: VSA, 1986, p. 93. See also the English translation reprinted in: *Trials of War Criminals before the Nuremberg Military Tribunals under Control Council Law No. 10, Nuremberg, October 1946–April 1949*, vol. V, The Pohl Case, Washington, DC: U.S. Government Printing Office, 1950, p. 365.

20 Letter of Himmler to Pohl, 29 May 1942, ND: NO-719.

21 See F. Pingel, 'Die Konzentrationslagerhäftlinge im nationalsozialistischen Arbeitseinsatz', in W. Długoborski (ed.): *Zweiter Weltkrieg und sozialer Wandel. Achsenmächte und besetzte Länder*, Göttingen: Vandenhoeck & Ruprecht, 1981 (Kritische Studien zu Geschichtswissenschaft, 47), pp. 151–63, here: p. 152.

22 See A. Kranig, *Lockung und Zwang. Zur Arbeitsverfassung im Dritten Reich*, Stuttgart: DVA, 1983 (Schriftenreihe der VfZ, no. 47), p. 79 f., and T. Mason, *Social Policy in the Third Reich: The Working Class and the 'National Community'*, Providence, RI and Oxford: Berg, 1993, pp. 247ff.

23 See the detailed study by Kaienburg, *Wirtschaft der SS*, pp. 603–770. On the working conditions in the quarry of Groß-Rosen concentration camp, see Sprenger, *Groß-Rosen*, pp. 49–51. On Flossenbürg see J. Skribeleit, 'Flossenbürg – Stammlager', in W. Benz and B. Distel (eds), *Der Ort des Terrors. Geschichte der nationalsozialistischen Konzentrationslager*, vol. 4, Munich: C. H. Beck, 2006, pp. 17–66. On Mauthausen, see F. Freund and B. Perz, 'Mauthausen – Stammlager', in: ibid. pp. 293–346.

24 Letter of Himmler to Pohl, 19 May 1942, Bundesarchiv Berlin, NS 19/3698.

25 See Freund and Perz, Mauthausen, p. 315, and M. Fabreguet, 'Entwicklung und Veränderung der Funktionen des Konzentrationslagers Mauthausen 1938–1945', in Herbert *et al.* (eds), *Konzentrationslager*, pp. 193–214, here p. 202–3. Based on other sources, Pingel, *Konzentrationslagerhäftlinge*, pp. 81–2, claims that this mortality rate reached the even higher figure of 75 per cent.

26 B. Perz, 'Der Arbeitseinsatz im KZ Mauthausen', in Herbert, Orth, Dieckmann, *Konzentrationslager*, pp. 533–57, here: p. 534. See also Pingel, *Konzentrationslagerhäftlinge*, p. 156, and Pingel., *Häftlinge*, pp. 80ff.

27 On the SS businesses, see Kaienburg, *Wirtschaft der SS*, passim.

28 The murder of Soviet prisoners of war classified as 'political commissars' claimed, in total, the lives of at least 34,000 people. This occurred across many concentration camps, but above all Sachsenhausen und Buchenwald. See Orth, *System der nationalsozialistischen Konzentrationslager*, pp. 122–31.

29 See, for a summary, ibid., pp. 114–21, as well as H. Friedlander, *The Origins of Nazi Genocide: From Euthanasia to the Final Solution*, Chapel Hill, NC: University of North Carolina Press, 1995, and the – slightly inaccurate – study by W. Grode, *Die 'Sonderbehandlung 14f13' in den Konzentrationslagern des Dritten Reichs. Ein Beitrag zur Dynamik faschistischer Vernichtungspolitik*, Frankfurt, Bern, New York: Lang, 1987.

30 See L. Herbst, *Der totale Krieg und die Ordnung der Wirtschaft. Die Kriegswirtschaft im Spannungsfeld von Politik, Ideologie und Propaganda 1939–1945*, Stuttgart: DVA, 1982 (Studien zur Zeitgeschichte, no. 21), pp. 171–218.

31 See Herbert, *Fremdarbeiter*, pp. 152ff., and D. Rebentisch, *Führerstaat und Verwaltung im Zweiten Weltkrieg. Verfassungsentwicklung und Verwaltungspolitik 1939–1945*, Stuttgart: Steiner, 1989 (*Frankfurter Historische Abhandlungen*, no. 29), pp. 356ff.; For biographical information on Sauckel, see S. Raßloff, *Fritz Sauckel – Hitlers 'Mustergauleiter' und 'Sklavenhalter'*, Erfurt: Landeszentrale für politische Bildung, 2007.

32 Himmler ordered the organizational integration of the Inspektion der Konzentrationslager with effect from the 16 March 1942: see Orth, *System der nationalsozialistischen Konzentrationslager*, pp. 163–4. According to Wagner, *IG Auschwitz*, p. 210, the integration was not achieved until 1 May 1942.

33 See also Schulte, *Zwangsarbeit und Vernichtung*, pp. 208ff., and W. Naasner, *Neue Machtzentren in der deutschen Kriegswirtschaft 1942–1945. Die Wirtschaftsorganisation der SS, das Amt des Generalbevollmächtigten für den Arbeitseinsatz und das Reichsministerium für Bewaffnung und Munition/Reichsministerium für Rüstung und Kriegsproduktion im nationalsozialistischen Herrschaftssystem*, Boppard am Rhein: Boldt, 1994 (Schriften des Bundesarchivs, no. 45), pp. 300–53.

34 See M. Grieger, '"Vernichtung durch Arbeit" in der deutschen Rüstungsindustrie', in T. Hess and T. Seidel (eds), *Vernichtung durch Fortschritt am Beispiel der Raketenproduktion im Konzentrationslager Mittelbau*, Bad Münstereifel: Westkreuz, 1995, pp. 43–60, here: p. 46.

35 See Schulte, *Zwangsarbeit und Vernichtung*, pp. 214–18.

36 See Mommsen and Grieger, *Volkswagenwerk*, pp. 502–15.

37 See also Orth, *System der nationalsozialistischen Konzentrationslager*, pp. 175ff. On the Heinkel group see L. Budraß, *Flugzeugindustrie und Luftrüstung in Deutschland 1918–1945*, Boppard am Rhein: Boldt, 1998, p. 775–93.

38 See Orth, *System der nationalsozialistischen Konzentrationslager*, p. 176.

39 See the memorandum of Arthur Rudolph (Versuchsserienwerk Heeresanstalt Peenemünde), 16 April 1943, Bundesarchiv/Militärarchiv, RH 8/v.1210, sheets 105–6, reprinted in J.-C. Wagner (ed.), *Konzentrationslager Mittelbau-Dora. Begleitband zur Ständigen Ausstellung in der KZ-Gedenkstätte Mittelbau-Dora*, Göttingen: Wallstein, 2007, p. 114–5.

40 See especially Wagner, *IG Auschwitz*; Hayes, *Industry*; for a summary, P. Hayes, 'Die IG Farben und die Zwangsarbeit von KZ-Häftlingen im Werk Auschwitz', in H. Kaienburg (ed.), *Konzentrationslager und deutsche Wirtschaft*, pp. 129–48; F. Piper, *Arbeitseinsatz der Häftlinge aus dem KL Auschwitz*, Oświęcim: Verl. Staatliches Museum, 1995; and

P. Setkiewicz, 'Häftlingsarbeit im KZ Auschwitz III-Monowitz. Die Frage nach der Wirtschaftlichkeit der Arbeit', in Herbert, Orth, Dieckmann, *Konzentrationslager*, pp. 584–605.

41 Figures according to Wagner, *IG Auschwitz*, p. 101 and p. 280–1.

42 See Perz, *Arbeitseinsatz*, pp. 535–43. The inmates of two previously existing satellite camps of the Mauthausen camp (Vöcklabruck und Bretstein) had to work for SS owned firms, especially on building sites.

43 Letter from Pohl to Himmler, 16 September 1942, ND: NI-15392.

44 See Speer's memo entitled 'Führerbesprechung' of 20–22 September 1942, ND: R-124, reproduced in *IMT*, vol. 38, pp. 359–60.

45 These figures rest on a critical assessment of the (partly erroneous and incomplete) data compiled by Gudrun Schwarz in 1990. See G. Schwarz, *Die nationalsozialistischen Lager*, Frankfurt and New York: Campus, 1990.

46 See 'Aufstellung des Amtes D II im WVHA über die Entwicklung der Häftlingsentgelte von 1942 bis 1944', 24 February 1944, ND: NO-576.

47 This is a description of the most common practice. The details of systems of hiring out prisoners varied in many respects between individual camps and firms. See also Orth, *System der nationalsozialistischen Konzentrationslager*, pp. 180–2.

48 See Wagner, *Produktion*, pp. 389–94.

49 If work commandos were made up of female prisoners, firms themselves were frequently required to recruit female surveillance staff, who then attended short training courses in the Ravensbrück concentration camp to become SS guards. See G. Schwarz, 'SS-Aufseherinnen in den nationalsozialistischen Konzentrationslagern', *Dachauer Hefte* 10, 1994, pp. 32–49.

50 See M. Spoerer, 'Profitierten Unternehmen von KZ-Arbeit? Eine kritische Analyse der Literatur', *Historische Zeitschrift*, 268, 1999, pp. 61–95.

51 See Wagner, *Produktion*, pp. 74–5.

52 On the history of the Mittelbau-Dora concentration camp see ibid., passim, and A. Sellier, *A history of the Dora Camp. The Story of the Nazi Slave Labor Camp that Manufactured V-2 Rockets*, Chicago, IL: I.R. Dee, 2003, and J. Neander, *Das Konzentrationslager 'Mittelbau' in der Endphase der nationalsozialistischen Diktatur. Zur Geschichte des letzten im 'Dritten Reich' gegründeten selbständigen Konzentrationslagers unter besonderer Berücksichtigung seiner Auflösungsphase*, Clausthal-Zellerfeld: Papierflieger, 1997.

53 See Wagner, *Produktion*, pp. 92–111.

54 The Harz ('Unternehmen Mittelbau') and the border region between Thuringia and Bavaria became centres for the relocation of war industries underground. In the *Alpenvorland*, large-scale bunker complexes were to be established, the construction of which was primarily undertaken by Hungarian Jews. See Raim, *Dachauer KZ-Kommandos*.

55 See Oswald Pohl's defence in front of the International Military Tribunal in Nuremberg on 25 August 1947, *Trials of War Criminals*, vol. 5 (The Pohl Case), pp. 445–6.

56 See Orth, *System der nationalsozialistischen Konzentrationslager*, pp. 260–9.

57 From the Mittelbau-Dora camp, for instance, the SS sent two transports to Majdanek in January and February, each containing 1,000 prisoners singled out by SS doctors as unfit for work. In April 1944 another 1,000 prisoners were sent to Bergen Belsen. Only a few prisoners survived. See Wagner, *Produktion*, p. 492–3.

58 See B. Strebel, *Das KZ Ravensbrück. Geschichte eines Lagerkomplexes*, Paderborn: Schöningh 2003, p. 468.

59 See Wagner, *IG Auschwitz*, pp. 173–92.

60 See, for instance, Kaienburg, *Vernichtung*; M. Kárný, ' "Vernichtung durch Arbeit"', pp. 133–58; M. Kárný, '"Vernichtung durch Arbeit" in Leitmeritz: Die SS-Führungsstäbe in der deutschen Kriegswirtschaft', in *1999: Zeitschrift für Sozialgeschichte des 20. Jahrhunderts* 4, 1993, pp. 37–61. In the historiography of the GDR the concept

played a prominent role from earlier on. See G. Dieckmann, 'Existenzbedingungen und Widerstand im Konzentrationslager Dora-Mittelbau unter dem Aspekt der funktionellen Einbeziehung der SS in das System der faschistischen Kriegswirtschaft', PhD Dissertation, Humboldt-Universität Berlin, East Berlin, 1968, p. 165; L. Demps, 'Zum weiteren Ausbau des staatsmonopolistischen Apparats der faschistischen Kriegswirtschaft in den Jahren 1943 bis 1945 und zur Rolle der SS und der Konzentrationslager im Rahmen der Rüstungsproduktion, dargestellt am Beispiel der unterirdischen Verlagerung von Teilen der Rüstungsproduktion', PhD Dissertation, Humboldt-Universität Berlin, East Berlin, 1970, p. 304; H. Brenner, "Vernichtung durch Arbeit", *Jahrbuch für Wirtschaftsgeschichte* 30, 1989, pp. 169–73; D. Eichholtz, *Geschichte der deutschen Kriegswirtschaft 1939–1945*, vol. II: 1941–1943, East Berlin: Akademie-Verlag, 1985, p. 233.

61 Memorandum of Otto Thierack, 14 September 1942, ND: PS-682.
62 Note by Thierack on a conversation with Himmler on 18 September 1942, ND: PS-654, reprinted in *IMT*, vol. 26, pp. 201–3, here: p. 201.
63 Ibid.
64 See N. Wachsmann, *Hitler's Prisons: Legal Terror in Nazi Germany*, New Haven, CT and London, 2004, pp. 284–302. At least two-thirds of these prisoners did not survive. While Jews, Sinti and Roma, as well as Polish prisoners were transferred to Auschwitz and Majdanek, so-called security confined prisoners ended up in concentration camps within the Reich. There they suffered the highest death rates compared with other groups of prisoners, especially in the winter of 1942–1943.
65 See ibid. pp. 208–17, 284–5.
66 See J.-C. Wagner, 'Noch einmal: Arbeit und Vernichtung. Häftlingseinsatz im KL Mittelbau-Dora', in N. Frei, S. Steinbacher and B. C. Wagner (eds), *Ausbeutung, Vernichtung, Öffentlichkeit. Neue Studien zur nationalsozialistischen Lagerpolitik*, Munich: Saur, 2000, pp. 11–41, especially pp. 29–38.
67 These are the findings of an assessment of the – incomplete – death registers, which were compiled by American investigations in 1945 on the basis of existing SS documents; National Archives Washington, DC:, Microfilm Publication M-1079, Roll 1.
68 See Kaienburg, *Vernichtung durch Arbeit*, p. 468–9, and similarly, Kaienburg, *Funktionswandel*, p. 278.
69 Tooze, *The Wages of Destruction*, p. 533.

7 The Holocaust and the concentration camps

Dieter Pohl

Prior to 1942, the Nazi concentration camps were much less important for the persecution and murder of European Jewry than had been assumed for decades after the war. Research during the last 25 years has shown that less than half of the victims of the Holocaust were killed in camps; and within this group approximately 1.2 million men, women and children were murdered in concentration camps properly speaking, i.e. those camps subsumed under the Inspection of the Concentration Camps (IKL) and later the SS Business and Administration Main Office (WVHA). The reasons for this lay both in the course of anti-Jewish policy and in the comparatively late expansion of the concentration camps into the massive system they eventually became, which did not begin until the end of 1942.[1]

For a long time the historiography on the subject developed along two separate paths, with camp history on the one side and Holocaust history on the other. Only during the 1990s did it become commonly recognized that Jews were a major element in concentration camp history from 1943 on. Recently the history of Jews in several of the major camps like Gross Rosen, Ravensbrück or Stutthof has been investigated as a separate subject.[2] Current projects for encyclopaedias of the camps enable the historian to trace the history of each satellite camp, where Jews in particular were forced to work.[3] And there is now a growing body of literature on the death marches of 1944/5, which constitute a major part of both concentration camp history and the Holocaust.[4]

Jews in concentration camps, 1933–1940

Jews were among the first victims of Nazi terror when the new regime took over at the beginning of 1933. But the initial wave of terror was not mainly directed against Jews, but predominantly against political opponents of Nazi rule, especially Communists and Social Democrats. It is estimated that in 1933 almost 100,000 persons were imprisoned for some time, almost half of them in the newly established camps, the others in improvised detention centres. Only a tiny minority among them was Jewish, as Jews were usually arrested only if they happened to be prominent political or cultural figures.

In 1934/5 the number of camps and prisoners declined significantly. Nevertheless, Jews continued to constitute part of the prisoner population. Most of them had been criminalized, for example by the new Nuremberg laws which constructed the offence of 'race defilement'. Jewish prisoners ended up in different concentration camps: between 1937 and early 1938, for example, Jewish men were almost exclusively sent to Dachau concentration camp, and a total of 2,500 to 3,000 Jewish prisoners were taken here. Jewish women were deported to the new camp in Ravensbrück when it was opened in 1939; a handful had previously been interned in the women's camps in Moringen and then Lichtenburg.

New prisoners arrived in the late 1930s. The annexations of Austria and the Sudetenland (1938) and Bohemia/Moravia (1939) were accompanied by mass arrests of suspected enemies of the Reich; among them were hundreds of Jews, mostly individuals associated with left wing parties. At the same time, Jews were also hit hard by the new socio-biological strategy of the police. Among the thousands of men arrested as 'asocials' during the wave of arrests in Germany in June 1938 ('Action Workshy Reich'), almost 20 per cent (2,500 men) were of Jewish origin, most of them unemployed or persons with a criminal record; they were sent to the new Buchenwald camp, where they were isolated and treated in an especially inhumane way. During 1938, the Star of David badge was introduced as the marker for Jewish prisoners, in most cases combined with other categories such as 'political', 'asocial' and so on. Jewish prisoners were concentrated in specific huts, which were called the 'Jew Block' (*Judenblock*) in Dachau and 'Jew Barrack' (*Judenbaracke*) in Sachsenhausen.[5]

In November 1938, Jews became concentration camp inmates on an unexpected and unprecedented scale. Almost 28,000 Jewish men were arrested and deported to the Buchenwald, Dachau and Sachsenhausen camps. The main purpose of this mass terror was to force Jews to emigrate and hand over most of their belongings to the Reich. Indeed, the great majority of those arrested had been released again by spring 1939 and emigrated. But during the weeks of their imprisonment, Jewish prisoners were treated with outrageous cruelty. They were sent to the worst labour companies and became victims of sadistic games of the SS. Also, the camps had not been prepared for the arrival of so many new prisoners: in Buchenwald 10,000 men were crammed into a special zone without proper housing or rations. An estimated 1,000 Jewish men did not survive their imprisonment in the three camps.[6]

The war years, 1939–1942

Following the German attack on Poland in September 1939, the Gestapo arrested all remaining Jewish men with (former) Polish citizenship living in the Reich. They were either deported to the newly occupied territories or to concentration camps (especially to Buchenwald). Most of them died after a few weeks; some survivors were released by mid-1940.[7] After this date, Jews played only a minor role as inmates of German concentration camps until 1942. For example, around 900 Jews were held at Buchenwald, either in protective custody or as so-called 'asocials'; around 1,600 Jews were deported to Mauthausen in 1941; and, from June 1940, some criminal and political Jewish suspects were deported to the new Auschwitz camp.[8]

Although there was no stated policy of annihilating Jews before autumn 1941, most Jewish inmates during the early war years perished. They were treated as the lowest group in the prisoner hierarchy and were often forced into the worst labour commandos. By April 1941 a new extermination programme was introduced for concentration camp inmates. During the so-called 'Action 14f13', teams of German physicians visited the camps and selected prisoners for transfer to the killing institutions of the Nazi 'euthanasia' programme. The overall aim of these crimes was to kill prisoners considered unfit for work. Jewish inmates were specifically targeted, as they were often in very bad physical shape and were considered as 'undesirable' both by the concentration camp staff and the '14f13' medical experts. Between April 1941 and April 1942 at least ten concentration camps were affected by 'Action 14f13' and at least 10,000 prisoners, probably many more, were deported to the asylum killing-centres at Bernburg, Sonnenstein and Hartheim and murdered. Especially in Buchenwald and Ravensbrück, Jewish inmates constituted a majority of the victims.[9]

New groups of Jewish prisoners entered the concentration camp system from July 1941. During the German military campaign against the Soviet Union, all Jews among captured Red Army soldiers were separated from the other POWs; they were either shot on the spot or sent to isolated zones within the POW camps. From some camps within the Reich, selected POWs – notably Red Army political functionaries, but also Jews – were taken to concentration camps. The first groups were probably transferred in July 1941, from Lamsdorf (Silesia) to Auschwitz.[10] By July/August 1941 it was decided that groups of selected 'undesirable' Soviet POWs were to be transferred to the concentration camps for immediate killing. Thus from September 1941, these men and – to a limited extent – women were killed inside the camps or at nearby execution sites like Dachau-Hebertshausen. It is currently unknown how many Jews were among the (at least) 34,000 victims. Since registration cards for all Soviet POWs in the main German prison of war camps have turned up in Moscow archives during the 1990s, it would now be possible to reconstruct their fate.[11] Overall, very few of the Soviet Jewish POWs who came into the concentration camps survived the war.

The German attack on the Soviet Union was accompanied by the beginning of the systematic murder of Jews, starting on 24 June 1941 in Lithuania. Though historians still debate the process of decision-making for the 'Final Solution', the wholesale murder of European Jewry, there is growing consensus that important steps were taken in September/October 1941. But there is no convincing evidence that the concentration camp system was affected before 1942. In fact, the military crisis of the German army near Moscow and the labour shortages within the Reich at the turn of the year shifted the focus slightly away from mass extermination towards the use of Jewish forced labourers. The main reason for this has to be seen in the utopian 'Peacetime Construction Programme' (*Friedenbauprogramm*) of the SS, a giant construction scheme for German settlements in the East. Initially, it was envisaged that Soviet POWs would be used as forced labourers for the building programme; but half of the POWs captured in 1941 were dead by early 1942 as a result of starvation, exposure and abuse. Moreover, far fewer Soviet POWs than expected were transferred from the control of the Wehrmacht to that of the SS, and the majority of those deported to the camps were considered unfit for work.

In place of Soviet POWs, the WVHA decided in January 1942 to move Jews from the first deportation wave from central Europe, which had started in October 1941, to the concentration camps. On 25 January 1942 Himmler ordered Richard Glücks, the head of the concentration camp system, to send 100,000 Jewish men and 50,000 Jewish women to the camps within the following four weeks. This would have tripled the number of concentration camp inmates and was never realized. But in April 1942, Himmler, in a general order, exempted all able-bodied Jews, predominantly men between the ages of 16 and 35, from being murdered and proposed their transfer to concentration camps.[12]

The number of Jews deported to concentration camps had been on the rise since autumn 1941. The construction of the new Majdanek camp near Lublin in particular was mostly undertaken by Jewish labourers from the region.[13] The first SS transports of Jews as part of the 'Final Solution' took place in March 1942. The Reich leadership had negotiated with the Slovak government the deportation of most Slovakian Jews to Poland. While the German negotiators offered to take over 20,000 young and able Jewish men, the Slovak authorities soon pressed for the deportation of entire Jewish families. Between late March and October 1942, around 57,000 Jews were deported, 17,000 to Auschwitz and 40,000 to the Lublin district, of whom 7,000 came to the Majdanek camp. This was by far the largest group of Jews inside the camps since 1938. In addition, the German military administration of Paris organized the deportation of 1,100 Jews from Compiègne to Auschwitz, officially as a reprisal for attacks of the French resistance. Further groups of Polish Jews, all in all about 35,000 persons, were transferred to Auschwitz between March and August 1942 from the forced labour camps of 'Organization Schmelt' (an SS organization of Jewish forced labour in the Katowice area, used for highway construction).[14] Before July 1942 (in Auschwitz) and September 1942 (in Majdanek), Jewish prisoners transported to these two camps were not normally murdered upon arrival, but were registered into the camp as prisoners. But most of them died within weeks as a result of malnourishment and extremely harsh treatment.[15]

Mass murder outside the concentration camp system

The major sites of mass murder in 1942 were the killing fields in the occupied territories of Eastern Poland and the Soviet Union and the extermination camps of 'Action Reinhardt', Bełżec, Sobibór, and Treblinka, which had been established by the regional SS and Police Leader in Lublin, Odilo Globocnik. A further extermination camp existed in Kulmhof (Chełmno) in the Warthegau (part of occupied Poland incorporated into the German Reich), where gas vans were used to murder Jews. Unlike the later practice in Auschwitz and Majdanek, there was almost no selection of Jews in any of these extermination camps. The actual separation of workers and others took place prior to the deportations, during the so-called 'ghetto clearances'.

The ghettos themselves became a major site of the Holocaust. They had been installed in several waves in Poland, especially in 1940 and early 1941, and then from autumn 1941 also in the Baltic States, eastern Poland and in several locations within the occupied Soviet territory. Though living conditions in the ghettos were generally bad, they varied significantly. In the winter of 1940/41, for example, the large ghettos in Łódź and Warsaw became the scene of mass death through starvation and epidemics. In the ghettos established from autumn 1941 onwards, the situation was different, since their establishment was already accompanied by mass murder, especially of poor and physically weak Jews. The ghettos had only minor connections to the concentration camps, since most of them were located in Eastern Europe, far away from the camps. Only the Jewish inhabitants in the cities of Oświęcim and Lublin were affected by the camps early on.

The three extermination camps of Action Reinhardt operated quite differently from the concentration camps. They were not subordinate to the IKL, but had been established by the regional SS and Police leaders in the Lublin and Warsaw districts. And the respective camp sites were comparatively small, with rather more improvised installations. Only around 25 to 30 German functionaries ran each camp, supported by 100–150 so-called 'Trawniki men' (released former Soviet POWs trained in the Trawniki forced labour camp). No more than a hundred Jews were kept alive at any one time to serve as forced labourers in the camp; this means that 99 per cent of the victims were murdered within hours after their arrival, in gas chambers using exhaust fumes. Also, Action Reinhardt extermination camps were shut down comparatively early, starting with Bełżec in December 1942; all corpses of the victims who had been killed by gas earlier on and buried thereafter were disinterred and burnt. In autumn 1943, the Treblinka and Sobibór camps were also closed down and all traces eradicated. In all, approximately 1.5 million Jews were killed in these three camps; only about 150 prisoners survived the war.[16] In the extermination camp at Kulmhof (Chełmno), more than 152,000 Jews from the Warthegau and the Łódź ghetto were killed in a similar fashion.[17]

During the liquidation of most ghettos in Poland in summer and autumn 1942, forced labour camps were established in or near these ghettos, sometimes referred to as 'work ghettos' (*Arbeitsghettos*). Only Jewish workers employed by German firms (often with their families) were allowed to stay in these labour camps, under appalling living conditions; all other Jews from the liquidated ghettos were deported to extermination camps. Germany's allies also established a system of work camps for Jews, notably in Slovakia, Hungary and Yugoslavia. During the second half of 1942, more Jews were confined in these work camps and ghettos than in concentration camps. Most of the forced labour camps in Poland were closed between the end of 1942 and July 1943, following either mass executions or deportations of inmates to extermination camps.[18]

Auschwitz as a centre of the Holocaust from mid-1942

Before July 1942, the concentration camps played no decisive role within the 'Final Solution'. Nevertheless, some mass killings of Jews already took place before then. At the end of the first deportations of the Lublin Jews to Belžec, as part of Action Reinhardt, some 2,000–3,000 Jews from the city of Lublin were brought to Majdanek on 20 April 1942; with the exception of some selected Jewish labourers, all were shot in the vicinity of the camp.[19] Despite its location in Lublin, Majdanek concentration camp was only indirectly connected to Action Reinhardt (for example, it was included in the statistics of the victims).[20]

Auschwitz and Majdanek emerged as both concentration and extermination camps in 1942. They were integrated into the deportation programme of the Reich Security Main Office (RSHA), which masterminded the 'Final Solution' in all countries, with the exception of the Soviet Union and most of Poland. The Jewish department (*Judenreferat*) in the RSHA organized the deportations, together with the German railway administration (*Reichsbahn*), while the WVHA arranged for their reception in Auschwitz and Majdanek. In contrast to other transports to the camps (predominantly of non-Jews), these deportations were known as RSHA-transports.[21] Mass deportations also changed the prisoner population inside the camps. From mid-1942 onwards, Jews already constituted half of the prisoners in Auschwitz, and at the end of the year a little less; but from 1943 they were in the majority, and ultimately in August 1944 their proportion reached 70 per cent.[22] Thus, unlike in other concentration camps, Jews were represented in all prisoner functionary positions of the Birkenau camp.

Auschwitz became *the* major extermination camp from 1943. But when, exactly, did the camp first become involved in the systematic murder of Jews? This is still an open question among historians. It is clear that mass murder in Auschwitz began on a large scale in August/September 1941, when the toxin Zyklon B was used for the first time to kill Soviet POWs and other non-Jewish inmates. There are some indications that the crematorium for the planned Birkenau sub-camp was conceived with a gas chamber already in October 1941.[23] But the construction of Birkenau was officially commissioned for the imprisonment of more Soviet POWs: no mass transports of Jews to Auschwitz were envisaged at that time.

The mass murder of Jews in Birkenau probably began during the construction of the camp in May 1942. A former farmhouse outside the actual camp area, designated as 'Bunker 1', was sealed off and used as gas chamber. Apparently the first victims came from Upper Silesia. From June/July 1942 on, a second such installation, 'Bunker 2', was also used for the killings.[24] While transports from Upper Silesia and Slovakia were already arriving at Auschwitz in early summer, the general transportation programme from western Europe did not start until 19 July 1942. Now all Jews who arrived by train at the so-called 'old ramp' near Birkenau camp had to undergo selections by the SS camp physicians. Around 20 per cent of the victims were directed to the camp as prisoners; all others were led to the bunkers and killed with Zyklon B. For a limited period, from 26 August to

9 November 1942, the deportation trains stopped before Auschwitz, in Kozle, where Jewish workers were taken away for use by Organisation Schmelt.[25]

It is not quite clear at what stage planning for the big crematoria in Auschwitz-Birkenau (nos. II–V) first included gas chambers. At the latest they were included in the detailed plans of August 1942. It finally took until March 1943 to complete the construction of Crematoria II and IV including their gas chambers, while Crematoria V and III were completed in April and June respectively.[26]

In October 1942, Himmler stepped up the murder of Jews from Germany: all Jewish inmates of concentration camps in Germany and Austria were to be deported to Auschwitz and Majdanek (in the end, all of them came to Auschwitz). Immediately afterwards, the first deportations from the cities of the Reich direct to Auschwitz began. Prior to that, German and Austrian Jews had primarily been deported to the Reichskommissariat Ostland, to Łódź or to the Lublin region with its extermination camps.[27] At first, it was mostly Jews from Berlin, the capital of the Reich, who were deported, but from spring 1943 there were also transports from other German cities.

Almost simultaneously, the deportations of Jews from the Theresienstadt ghetto to Auschwitz started. The RSHA had installed a ghetto in Theresienstadt in Bohemia for Bohemian and older German and Austrian Jews. Since this ghetto served as a camouflage operation to deceive international public opinion, the Jews deported from there to Auschwitz were not immediately killed upon arrival. In autumn 1943, a 'family camp' was installed in Birkenau camp, where all those arriving from Theresienstadt – men, women and children – had to live. They were murdered six months later, in March 1944. The same gap of six months between arrival in Auschwitz and murder apparently also applied to other inmates from Theresienstadt.[28] One of the last national groups deported to Auschwitz came from Greece, as the majority of the Greek Jews under German occupation were deported between March and May 1944, most of them to Auschwitz.[29]

Like all other concentration camps, Auschwitz developed a system of satellite camps – especially in Upper Silesia – from late 1942 onwards. But the Auschwitz satellite camps were different: in contrast to other such camps, the majority of prisoners here (from 1943) were Jewish. Among the biggest of these satellite camps were Blechhammer, Jawischowitz and Neu-Dachs (Jaworzno); some were taken over from Organisation Schmelt. But the most important was the IG Farben plant, which was built in nearby Monowice from March 1941 by predominantly Polish Auschwitz prisoners. From October 1942, a special subdivision of the main camp was established near the construction site, finally named 'Auschwitz III Monowitz' with 11,000 mainly Jewish male prisoners. The other Auschwitz satellite camps were also subordinated to the administration of Auschwitz III. Working conditions in Monowitz were extremely harsh. The camp SS periodically selected weak prisoners and sent them to Birkenau, where they were murdered in the gas chambers. According to existing evidence, more than 7,000 inmates were sent from Monowitz to Birkenau; estimates of the total number of prisoners killed reach 20,000–25,000.[30]

Majdanek was the second concentration camp which, like Auschwitz, simultaneously functioned as an extermination camp. In August 1942 a gas chamber was installed and from October that year Jews arriving in transports were systematically murdered with Zyklon B. Most of these Jews had been deported from the Białystok area in north-eastern Poland, but from early 1943 transports also arrived from the Warsaw ghetto.[31] New research has established that approximately 59,000 Jews were murdered at Majdanek, making up the majority of all inmates killed in the camp.[32]

New concentration camps for Jews: 1943

By mid-1943, Himmler considered the 'Final Solution' almost complete, as most of the European Jews under German rule had been killed. Nevertheless, due to the unfavourable course of the war since early 1943 and the growing demands on the workforce, the Germans retained a wide range of forced labour camps for Jews as well as one ghetto, in Łódź. Most of the remaining labour camps were situated in central Poland, especially in some of the more industrialized areas. These camps were quite different from concentration camps – they were much smaller, far less organized and generally subordinated to regional SS leaders – and they had almost no connections to the concentration camp system: even the forced labour camps in the Lublin area remained isolated from Majdanek until 1943.

In September/October 1943 Himmler decided to abandon those labour camps located in the more distant eastern regions and to have their inmates killed. During the so-called 'Action Harvest Festival' (*Aktion Erntefest*), 42,000 Jewish forced labourers in the Lublin area were killed within two days (3 and 4 November 1943), including some 8,000 Jewish prisoners from the city of Lublin. The latter were led to the Majdanek camp, were trenches had been prepared, and shot. Jews from the Lwow-Janowska labour camp met the same fate two weeks later.[33] Following these massacres, which killed all Jewish prisoners, most labour camps were transferred to the concentration camp system, Plaszow as an independent camp, and most of the others as sub-camps of Majdanek.

In addition to transforming some labour camps into concentration camps, Himmler also set up additional concentration camps in the nearer regions of Eastern Europe specifically for Jews. Plans to establish further concentration camps had existed since 1942, but they had initially been suspended. It was only during the dissolution of the last major ghettos in spring/summer 1943 that new camps were established in order to imprison the remaining Jewish forced labourers.

The concentration camp in Warsaw represents an exceptional case. In February 1943 Himmler had ordered the establishment of the camp to force some of the local Jews to help with the demolition of the abandoned ghetto after it was cleared. But this plan was thwarted: the Germans faced unexpected and fierce Jewish resistance during the Warsaw ghetto uprising in April 1943. The uprising was brutally put down and the survivors were deported to labour camps in the Lublin region (as planned), sent to Treblinka, or killed on the spot. When the Warsaw camp was finally opened in July 1943, two months after the crushing of the ghetto uprising, its Jewish inmates did not come from Warsaw, but from concentration camps located all over the occupied countries. In all, almost 10,000 Jews were imprisoned in the Warsaw concentration camp. In May 1944, with the Red Army moving closer and prisoner deportations to other concentration camps already underway, the camp was subordinated as a satellite camp to Majdanek. The last remaining 350 prisoners were liberated in August 1944 during the Warsaw Uprising.[34]

In the context of the dissolution of the Warsaw ghetto, Himmler also ordered the liquidation of the last ghettos in the Baltic States and in Minsk. Those inmates not murdered during the ghetto liquidations were to be transported to new concentration camps. In March 1943 the SS started to establish a new camp in the Riga suburb of Kaiserwald (Mezaparks). In August and September 1943 Jewish forced labourers from Riga and Vilnius were deported to this camp. Most of them were Jews from the Reich or the Protektorat, who had been deported to Riga in 1941/42, but they also included Latvian and Hungarian Jews. Including the numerous satellite camps, a total of 16,000 to 19,000 inmates had been held at Riga-Kaiserwald. Several thousands were killed in the camp; the majority were later evacuated to Stutthof.[35]

The camp in Kaunas had also been in planning since 1942, but was officially established only in September 1943. More than 10,000 Jews from the Kaunas ghetto, including children, were brought there. The Kaunas camp had other exceptional features: it was not subordinate to the WVHA, but to its regional branch in Riga (the SS-Wirtschafter Ostland), and it took over some structures of the internal ghetto administration. Nearly all the inmates were either killed or evacuated westwards in July 1944.[36]

Mostly out of economic necessity, the SS also set up new concentration camps in Estonia in 1943, for the purpose of extracting oil shale. The main camp at Vaivara was officially set up in September 1943; most of its inmates came from the Vilnius and Kaunas ghettos. Together with the several satellite camps, about 9,000 prisoners were registered in total. Evacuation already started in February 1944, with prisoners either taken to Stutthof or to satellite camps of Natzweiler in south-west Germany. The last prisoners were shot in September 1944, only days before the Red Army liberated the area.[37]

Among the concentration camps established exclusively for Jews was Bergen-Belsen. Its origins can be traced to the efforts of both the Allied and German governments to exchange prisoners of both sides. As the Nazi leadership was interested in liberating Germans interned in Palestine, it was willing to exchange them against Jews with relatives in Palestine and other countries. Thus, in April 1943, the SS took over a part of the POW camp in Bergen-Belsen and established a 'residence camp' (*Aufenthaltslager*) for ostensible Jewish exchange prisoners, who lived under much better circumstances than Jews in other camps. Yet most of the exchange projects ultimately failed, and from March 1944 onwards, Bergen-Belsen turned more and more into a reception camp for evacuated prisoners – both Jewish and non-Jewish – from the East. Living conditions deteriorated drastically, especially after the former Auschwitz commandant Josef Kramer took over Bergen-Belsen.[38]

Most of the new camps for Jews established in 1943 were designed to exploit the last surviving Jewish labourers east of the Reich. The SS leadership now sought to concentrate all imprisonment under its WVHA structure in order to pursue its own economic interests, reducing the influence of other agencies and regional SS leaders.

The Jews from Greater Hungary in the concentration camps

Most Jews arrived in the concentration camp system in 1944, when the majority of Jews under German rule in Europe had already been killed. The greater proportion of them came from Hungary, after the German takeover. The German occupation of Hungary had come unexpectedly. Hitler had always urged the regent Miklos Horthy to hand over the Hungarian Jews to the Germans, but Horthy refused to do so until 1944. When the Germans occupied Hungary in March 1944, in response to the Horthy government's attempt to initiate peace negotiations with the Allies, an RSHA team under Adolf Eichmann, with significant assistance from the Hungarian administration and police, organized the ghettoization and deportation of Jews within a few weeks.[39]

Between 15 May and 6 July 1944 almost 438,000 Jews were deported from Greater Hungary to Auschwitz. Most of them did not come from Trianon Hungary (i.e. Hungary in its 1919 borders) but from the territories annexed by Hungary in 1938/40 (Carpathian Ukraine and northern Transylvania). During the last phase, Jews from Trianon Hungary and even from some parts of Budapest were also deported, before Horthy put a stop to this policy on 6 July. The German occupiers aimed at both murdering and exploiting the local Jews, with Hitler suggesting that more than 100,000 Hungarian Jews should be sent to the German armament industry. In Auschwitz, around 25,000 Hungarian Jews were registered as prisoners, while more than 80,000 were kept in the camp for only one or two weeks and then sent to camps all over occupied Europe, from Belgium to Estonia. But most of the Hungarian Jews arriving in Auschwitz were immediately murdered. In a period of just seven weeks, some 320,000 Hungarian Jews were killed. The camp had to be reorganized, and the former commandant Höß returned from Berlin to supervise the killings, the biggest murder operation in his career.

Another 78,000 Hungarian Jews, predominantly women, were force-marched from Budapest to Austria, were they were either forced to build fortifications (the *Südostwall*) or to proceed to concentration camps in Austria and southern Germany (such as the Kaufering and Mühldorf branches of the Dachau camp).[40] The main purpose of these deportations was to support armaments production for the German air force within the Reich: Jewish men were supposed to build underground installations and Jewish women were supposed to work there.

The last large group of Jews deported to Auschwitz came from the only ghetto which still existed in Poland, Łódź. Here, the local Nazi administration and the Jewish Council had managed to thwart attempts to exterminate all the ghetto inmates in 1943. But after the Red Army summer offensive and advance in 1944, the ghetto was finally liquidated. Between 15 August and 2 September 1944, nearly all of the around 67,000 surviving Jews were transported from Łódź to Auschwitz; only a tiny minority of them, some 3,000 or so, were registered into the camp as prisoners. As in the case of Jews arriving from Hungary, a much larger group of deportees – around 19,000 men and women – did not stay in Auschwitz for long; instead, they were deported as 'transit Jews', kept inside the camp only for a short period, to other concentration camps.[41]

The final period: 1945

In November 1944 Himmler officially stopped the systematic murder of Jews in the concentration camps. The crematoria at Auschwitz were partly destroyed, though there are indications that parts of the installations were to be transferred to the Mauthausen camp complex.[42] Nevertheless, killings of the remaining Jews continued, and even accelerated in 1945.

With the onset of the Soviet offensive in January 1945, most concentration camps started to prepare for evacuation.[43] At this time, around 30–40 per cent of the 718,000 registered concentration camp inmates were of Jewish origin. Jews were likely to be in particularly bad physical shape and had little chances of survival. Some prisoners were further weakened by several consecutive forced marches. During the marches, the guards generally treated Jewish prisoners worse than they had already done in the camps. It is probable that more Jewish prisoners than non-Jewish ones were shot on the roads if they were unable to proceed. During these death marches there were several cases of mass murders of Jewish prisoners. One of the most infamous massacres took place in Palmnicken in the northeastern part of East Prussia, on the Baltic coast. Almost 7,000 Jews, who had been convoyed there from Stutthof camp, were shot by local Nazis on 31 January 1945.[44]

Fewer Jewish prisoners were hit by the second wave of evacuations during April 1945, from Sachsenhausen, Ravensbrück, Neuengamme, Buchenwald and Mittelbau (Dora). Only at the end of April were large numbers of Jews shifted around the system: some at the evacuation of the camps in the south of the Reich, where tens of thousands of Hungarian Jews were imprisoned, and others when the so-called Hungarian camps (*Ungarnlager*) in eastern Austria were evacuated to Mauthausen.[45] These marches were accompanied by outrageous violence against the evacuees. Meanwhile, Bergen-Belsen camp was in an infernal state by April 1945. More and more transports arrived in Bergen-Belsen, and the camp administration no longer supplied the inmates with rations. Between January and mid-April alone 35,000 inmates died from the appalling living conditions; another 14,000 were in such a bad shape that they died immediately after liberation.

The victim statistics of the evacuations are very difficult to establish, as German record-keeping broke down and the death marches during the last weeks of the Third Reich were undertaken under chaotic circumstances, with an enormous number of random killings. New estimates tend to give higher figures than previously, with at least 250,000 prisoners killed during the evacuations, probably half of them Jews.[46]

Jewish inmates and the prisoner population

Prior to the inception of the 'Final Solution' in 1942, Jews always made up a minority among the concentration camp inmates, probably between 5 and 10 per cent (the only exception was the last months of 1938 following the mass imprisonment of Jewish men after the November pogrom). Their absolute numbers even declined between 1940 and 1942, at a time when the camp system was expanding, both with the establishment of new camps and with the arrests of tens of thousands of inhabitants from the occupied countries. This situation changed gradually between 1942 and 1944, when Jews were increasingly sent to the concentration camps; most of them were killed on arrival, with only a minority exploited as forced labourers. Nevertheless, by autumn 1944 Jews probably made up one-third of all concentration camp prisoners. This meant that, at the turn of the year 1944/5, most of the Jews under German control now lived either in concentration camps or in the Budapest ghetto.

Most of the Jewish prisoners in the concentration camps were adult males. The vast majority of Jewish children murdered during the course of the 'Final Solution' had been killed by the end of 1942 because they were not considered 'fit for work'. The perpetrators applied the same reasoning to older persons. And among the Jews of working age, more men than women were selected as forced labourers, as only men were regarded as suitable for certain kinds of work. Thus, the majority of the children, the elderly and women murdered during the Nazi 'Final Solution' were already dead by the time large numbers of Jews entered the concentration camp system. Still, between 30 and 40 per cent of these Jewish prisoners were female; in Auschwitz, for example, there were 82,000 female detainees among the 204,000 registered Jewish prisoners.

Compared with other prisoner groups, Jews always had the worst chance of survival. The primary reason was the extermination of most Jews immediately after their arrival in Auschwitz and Majdanek. But even among registered prisoners, Jews were generally far more likely to die than others. The death rates among Jewish inmates were comparable only to those of Roma prisoners and inmates arrested as 'asocial' during 1942/43. In the concentration camps, a specific policy of anti-Jewish terror prevailed, which led to the deployment of Jewish inmates in the worst working facilities and their selection for the regular mass exterminations. And during the final stage of Nazi terror in 1945, Jewish prisoners had the worst chances of survival during the evacuations, whether in train transports or on death marches.

It is a matter of dispute among historians whether the SS pursued an explicit policy of 'annihilation through labour' against Jews. As far as we know, the term itself was used in the Third Reich only in reference to other murderous measures, such as the forced labour camps of *Durchgangsstrasse IV* (the German supply route for the southern armies in the Soviet Union from Lvov to Dnipropetrovsk) and the transfer of 'asocial' prisoners from the state prisons to concentration camps in 1942/43. Still, Jewish prisoners were worked to death in many camps, for example in Auschwitz-Monowitz. In most cases, the so-called *Muselmann* (the term used in the camps for an emaciated apathetic person) was in most cases a Jewish prisoner in an extreme physical condition, with a life expectancy of a few weeks within the camp. Much more than for other prisoner groups, the treatment of the Jews was primarily dominated by racism; economic expectations were only of secondary importance. From the point of view of the perpetrators, no Jewish prisoners were supposed to survive the war.[47]

Jewish prisoners not only faced the lowest chance of survival, they also had comparatively few opportunities to resist. In general, they were not deployed in the slightly better working facilities within the camp administration and they had very few contacts to the outside world, unlike some ethnic Poles in the camps. Nevertheless, already in 1942/3 individual acts of resistance occurred in the concentration camps, and even right in front of the gas chambers in the death camps. Escapes from the death camps were extremely important for the Jewish communities in Hitler's Europe. The most famous case was the escape of Rudolf Vrba and Alfred Wetzler from Auschwitz in April 1944; they immediately informed the Slovakian Jewish leadership about the extermination camp. Others succeeded in escaping in May and September 1944.[48] Organized Jewish resistance originated in the Special Commandos (*Sonderkommandos*), whose members had to work inside the crematoria. In Treblinka and Sobibór, there were uprisings by the Special Commandos in August and September 1943, and some of the prisoners were able to escape. In Auschwitz-Birkenau, too, a group of prisoners in the Special Commando planned an uprising. Though many of the conspirators were killed before it started, the rest managed to organize a revolt on 7 October 1944, destroying Crematorium IV and escaping to a nearby village, where all of them were killed.[49]

Large numbers of Jewish survivors spent the last months of the war in concentration camps, the only 'legal' way left for them to live under German rule. Probably more Jews survived in the camps than in hiding. Unlike most Jewish victims in Poland, the Baltic states and the Soviet Union, who were shot near their hometowns or murdered during Action Reinhardt, it is possible to establish most of the names of those deported to concentration camps. For most countries of origin, memorial books with lists of names have been published; in other cases, personal data is available via the Internet.[50] For some camps death registers are available.[51]

Conclusion

During the last decade our knowledge about the connection between the Holocaust and the concentration camp system has been considerably broadened. Nevertheless, lacunae remain in the historiography. The foremost task is to reconstruct in detail the role of Auschwitz within the mass murder of Jews, both in the context of the Nazi organization and regarding the Jewish camp prisoners. But the history of Jewish prisoners in other camps and their satellite camps too requires further research, especially in respect of Dachau and Mauthausen. In the long run, the new access to the archives of the International Tracing Service in Arolsen may enable historians to reconstruct most of the deportations to the concentration camps and within the camp system, making it possible to trace movements of Jewish prisoners within Europe.[52]

Overall, around 1.2 million Jewish victims – out of the total of 5.6–5.8 million Jews murdered during the 'Final Solution' – died in the concentration camp system. Most of them were not registered as prisoners, but were killed immediately upon arrival in Auschwitz or Majdanek. More than 400,000 Jews were held as prisoners of German concentration camps in the official sense. This meant that Jews constituted a minority of the prisoners but the majority of those murdered in the concentration camps.

In general, the concentration camps were not designed specifically for Jewish prisoners. From the perspective of the Nazi leadership, Jews were initially to be forced to emigrate (until 1939/41), before policy changed to deportation and ghettoization (1939–1942). From autumn 1941 on, Jews were generally meant to be murdered. But the latter policy was already modified in early 1942, when the value of the Jewish workforce was reconsidered, and a minority of Jews was to be kept alive. The two major concentration camps in Poland, Auschwitz and Majdanek, underwent a change of function. Both were originally established for Polish political prisoners, and then enlarged for Soviet POWs under SS control. In spring and summer 1942, a dual system of exploitation and mass murder was established in both camps. Those considered incapable of working – predominantly children, men and women over the age of 35 and mothers with children – were murdered upon arrival. Only about 10–20 per cent of the new arrivals were initially kept alive as forced labourers; but they, too, soon underwent selection, with all the exhausted prisoners eventually being killed.

It is very difficult to establish the number of Jewish concentration camp inmates who survived the war. Most inmates of RSHA-transports who came to Auschwitz died in the camp, the majority immediately on the arrival; only between 1 and 3 per cent of these prisoners survived the war. Overall, out of more than 200,000 registered Jewish prisoners from all over Europe in Auschwitz, 30,000 survived.[53] The situation was somewhat better for evacuees from the forced labour camps. All in all, approximately 30,000 Polish Jews survived in all concentration camps. Out of the 121,000 Jews from Hungary who were deported to the Reich and survived, a majority had been integrated into the concentration camp system for a while.[54]

The extermination system of Auschwitz developed almost in parallel to Action Reinhardt in spring 1942, and in 1943 grew into the centre of mass murder of European Jewry, culminating in 1944. Most ghetto inhabitants had been killed in 1942, with the surviving labourers kept in forced labour camps built on the former ghetto sites. In 1943, the SS leadership decided to gradually concentrate Jewish forced labour under the control of the WVHA. Thus new camps for Jews were installed in Warsaw, Riga, Kaunas and in Estonia.

During the evacuations from the East in 1944, more and more Jews from the forced labour camps were deported to concentration camps, including Hungarian Jews who either went through Auschwitz or were sent directly to the other camps. As a result, Jews constituted a large proportion of the prisoner population in the concentration camps towards the end of the Second World War; yet many of them did not live to see the liberation of the camps but died during the death marches.

Prior to the Second World War, the concentration camps had served as a testing ground for the mistreatment of Jews. But only after the turn of the year 1941/2 did forced labour and the extermination of deported Jews became an important function of the camps. The concentration camps played a specific role in the 'Final Solution'. Auschwitz more or less succeeded the Aktion Reinhardt camps and Kulmhof as the main centre of extermination. At the same time, Auschwitz gradually became the largest place for Jewish forced labour in Europe besides the Łódź ghetto. And while deportations of Jews to Majdanek stopped in summer 1944, Jewish prisoners later entered all the other concentration camps, from spring 1944 onwards. Not all the victims in the camps were murdered immediately upon their arrival, but all Jewish prisoners were destined for extermination. It was only due to their liberation by the Allies that a minority of Jewish prisoners survived the war.

Notes

1 Cf. J. Matthäus, 'Verfolgung, Ausbeutung, Vernichtung. Jüdische Häftlinge im System der Konzentrationslager', in G. Morsch and S. zur Nieden (eds), *Jüdische Häftlinge im KZ Sachsenhausen 1936–1945*, Berlin: Hentrich, 2004, pp. 64–90; W. Gruner, *Jewish Forced Labor Under the Nazis, 1938–1944: Economic Needs and Racial Aims*, New York: Berghahn, 2006.

2 See L. Apel, *Jüdische Frauen im Konzentrationslager Ravensbrück 1939–1945*, Berlin: Metropol, 2003; D. Drywa, *The Extermination of Jews in Stutthof Concentration Camp*, Gdańsk: Stutthof Muzeum in Sztutowo, 2004; B. Gutterman, *A Narrow Bridge to Life: Jewish Slave Labor and Survival in the Gross-Rosen Camp System, 1940–1945*, New York: Berghahn, 2008.

3 W. Benz and B. Distel (eds), *Der Ort des Terrors. Geschichte der nationalsozialistischen Konzentrationslager*, 8 vols., Munich: Beck 2005–2009; *The United States Holocaust Memorial Encyclopedia of Camps and Ghettos, 1933–1945*, vol. 1. Bloomington, IN: Indiana UP 2009.

4 See the contribution by Daniel Blatman in this volume.

5 Morsch and zur Nieden, *Jüdische Häftlinge im KZ Sachsenhausen*, pp. 117 ff.

6 H. Stein, *Juden in Buchenwald 1937–1942*, Weimar: Weimardruck, 1992.

7 Y. Weiss, *Deutsche und polnische Juden vor dem Holocaust: Jüdische Identität zwischen Staatsbürgerschaft und Ethnizität 1933–1940*, Munich: Oldenbourg, 2000, pp. 212–14.

8 S. Mączka (ed.), *Żydzi polscy w KL Auschwitz. Wykazy imienne*, Warsaw: Żydowski Instytut Historyczny, 2004, pp. 9 ff.

9 H. Friedlander, *The Origins of Nazi Genocide: From Euthanasia to the Final Solution*, Chapel Hill, NC: University of North Carolina Press, 1995, pp. 147–50.

10 J. Brandhuber, 'Die sowjetischen Kriegsgefangenen im Konzentrationslager Auschwitz', *Hefte von Auschwitz* 4, 1961, pp. 5–46.

11 Individual fates mentioned in P. Polian and A. Shneer, *Obrechennye pogibnut. Sudba sovetskikh voennoplennykh-evreev vo Vtoroi Mirovoi voine. Vospominaniia i dokumenty*, Moscow: Novoe Izdatelstvo 2006, pp. 43–4; registration cards are shown on the book cover.

12 J. E. Schulte, *Zwangsarbeit und Vernichtung: Das Wirtschaftsimperium der SS: Oswald Pohl und das SS-Wirtschafts-Verwaltungshauptamt 1933–1945*, Paderborn: Schöningh, 2001. See also order by Gestapo Chief Müller to Kommandeur der Sicherheitspolizei und des SD Litauen, 18.5.1942, in P. Klein (ed.), *Die Einsatzgruppen in der besetzten Sowjetunion 1941/42. Die Tätigkeits- und Lageberichte des Chefs der Sicherheitspolizei und des SD 1941/42*, Berlin: Hentrich, 1997, pp. 410f.

13 B. Schwindt, *Das Konzentrations- und Vernichtungslager Majdanek – Funktionswandel im Kontext der "Endlösung"*, Würzburg: Königshausen & Neumann, 2005.

14 S. Steinbacher, *"Musterstadt" Auschwitz. Germanisierung und Judenmord in Ostoberschlesien*, Munich: Saur, 2000, pp. 277 ff. Contrary to common assumptions in historiography, there is no evidence for a major transport from Organisation Schmelt to Auschwitz prior to March 1942.

15 *Majdanek 1942. Księga zmarłych więźniów*, Lublin: Państwowe Muzeum na Majdanku, 2004.

16 Y. Arad, *Belzec, Sobibor, Treblinka: The Operation Reinhard Death Camps*, Bloomington, IN: Indiana UP, 1987.

17 S. Krakowski, *Das Todeslager Chelmno/Kulmhof. Der Beginn der 'Endlösung'*, Göttingen: Wallstein, 2007; P. Klein, 'Vernichtungslager Kulmhof/Chelmno', in W. Benz and B. Distel (eds), *Der Ort des Terrors. Geschichte der nationalsozialistischen Konzentrationslager*, vol. 8. Munich: Beck, 2008, pp. 301–28.

18 D. Pohl, 'Die großen Zwangsarbeitslager der SS- und Polizeiführer für Juden im Generalgouvernement 1942–1945', in U. Herbert, K. Orth and C. Dieckmann (eds), *Die nationalsozialistischen Konzentrationslager*, Göttingen: Wallstein, 1998, pp. 415–38; cf. C. R. Browning, 'Jewish workers in Poland: Self-maintenance, exploitation, destruction', in his *Nazi Policy, Jewish Workers, German Killers*, Cambridge: Cambridge UP, 2000, pp. 58–88.

19 Schwindt, *Konzentrations- und Vernichtungslager Majdanek*, pp. 101–2.

20 P. Witte and S. Tyas, 'A new document on the deportation and murder of Jews during "Einsatz Reinhardt"1942', *Holocaust and Genocide Studies* 15, 2001, 468–86; T. Kranz, 'Eksterminacja Żydów na Majdanku i rola obozu w realizacji "Akcji Reinhardt"', *Zeszyty Majdanka* 22, 2003, pp. 7–55. Historians are still debating whether Auschwitz was also connected to 'Aktion Reinhardt', for example in regards to the belongings of the victims; see B. Perz and T. Sandkühler, 'Auschwitz und die "Aktion Reinhard" 1942–45', *Zeitgeschichte* 26, 2000, pp. 283–316.

21 H. Safrian, *Die Eichmann-Männer*, Vienna, Zürich: Europa 1993; Y. Lozowick, *Hitler's Bureaucrats: The Nazi Security Police and the Banality of Evil*, New York: Continuum, 2002.

22 Długoborski and Piper, *Auschwitz*, vol. 2, pp. 46–7; Y. Gutman and S. Krakowski, 'Juden im KL Auschwitz', *Sterbebücher von Auschwitz. Fragmente*, Munich: Saur 1995, vol. 1, pp. 163–94; J. E. Schulte, 'London war informiert. KZ-Expansion und Judenverfolgung. Entschlüsselte KZ-Stärkemeldungen vom Januar 1942 bis zum Januar 1943 in den britischen National Archives in Kew', *Beiträge zur Geschichte des Nationalsozialismus* 22, 2006, pp. 207–27.

23 M. T. Allen, 'The devil in the details: The gas chambers of Birkenau, October 1941', *Holocaust and Genocide Studies* 16, 2002, pp. 189–216. Cf. also the debate on the diverging statements by Auschwitz commander Rudolf Höß: K. Orth, 'Rudolf Höß und die "Endlösung der Judenfrage". Drei Argumente gegen die Datierung auf den Sommer 1941', *Werkstatt Geschichte* 6, 1997, pp. 45–57.

24 D. Czech, *Auschwitz Chronicle, 1939–1945*, New York: Holt, 1990; W. Długoborski and F. Piper (eds), *Auschwitz 1940–1945. Studien zur Geschichte des Konzentrations- und Vernichtungslagers Auschwitz*, 5 vols, Oświęcim: Państwowe Muzeum Auschwitz-Birkenau w Oświęcimiu, 1999, here vol. 2, pp. 158 ff.

25 Steinbacher, *"Musterstadt" Auschwitz*, p. 278.

26 R. J. van Pelt, *The Case for Auschwitz: Evidence from the Irving Trial*, Bloomington, IN: Indiana University Press, 2002; cf. also J. C. Pressac (ed.), *Auschwitz: Technique and Operation of the Gas Chambers*, New York: Beate Klarsfeld Foundation, 1989.

27 A. B. Gottwaldt and D. Schulle, *Die Judendeportationen aus dem deutschen Reich von 1941–1945. Eine kommentierte Chronologie*, Berlin: Marix 2005, pp. 397ff. There were smaller transports from Gliwice already in spring and a transport from Vienna on 17/18 July 1942, the fate of which cannot be determined exactly.

28 T. Brod, M. Kárný and M. Kárný, *Terezínský rodinný tábor v Osvetimi-Birkenau*, Prague: Nadace Terezínská iniciativa – Melantrich, 1994; M. Kárný, 'Das Theresienstädter Familienlager BIIb in Birkenau September 1943–Juli 1944', *Hefte von Auschwitz* 20, 1997, pp. 133–237.

29 H. Fleischer, 'Griechenland', in W. Benz (ed.), *Dimension des Völkermords*. Munich: Oldenbourg, 1991, pp. 241–74.

30 B. C. Wagner, *IG Auschwitz. Zwangsarbeit und Vernichtung von Häftlingen des Lagers Monowitz 1941–1945*, Munich: Saur, 2000; P. Setkiewicz, *Z dziejów obozów IG Farben Werk Auschwitz 1941–1945*, Oświęcim: Państwowe Muzeum Auschwitz-Birkenau w Oświęcimiu, 2006 (with lower figures).

31 T. Mencel, *Majdanek 1941–1944*, Lublin: Wydawnictwo Lubelskie, 1991; T. Mencel and T. Kranz, *Extermination of Jews at the Majdanek Concentration Camp*, Lublin: Państwowe Muzeum na Majdanku, 2007.

32 T. Kranz, 'Bookkeeping of death and prisoner mortality at Majdanek', *Yad Vashem Studies* 35, 2007, no. 1, pp. 81–109.

33 Pohl, 'Zwangsarbeitslager'.

34 B. Kopka, *Konzentrationslager Warschau. Historia i nastepstwa*, Warsaw: Instytut Pamięci Narodowej, 2007; A. Mix, 'Warschau – Stammlager', Benz and Distel (eds), *Der Ort des Terrors*. vol. 8, pp. 91–126.

35 A. Angrick and P. Klein, *Die 'Endlösung' in Riga. Ausbeutung und Vernichtung 1941–1944*, Darmstadt: WBG, 2006, pp. 391 ff.

36 C. Dieckmann, 'Das Ghetto und das Konzentrationslager in Kaunas 1941–1944', in Herbert, Dieckmann and Orth (eds), *Die nationalsozialistischen Konzentrationslager,* vol. 1, pp. 439–71.

37 R. B. Birn, 'Vaivara – Stammlager', in Benz and Distel (eds), *Der Ort des Terrors. Geschichte der nationalsozialistischen Konzentrationslager*, vol. 8, pp. 131–47; M. Dworzecki, *Histoire de camps en Estonie (1941–1944)*, Tel Aviv, 1967.

38 E. Kolb, *Bergen-Belsen 1943–1945. Vom Aufenthaltslager zum Konzentrationslager*, Göttingen: Vandenhoeck & Ruprecht, 2002; A. E. Wenck, *Zwischen Menschenhandel und 'Endlösung'. Das Konzentrationslager Bergen-Belsen*, Paderborn: Schöningh, 2000.

39 R. R. Braham, *The Politics of Genocide: The Holocaust in Hungary*, Washington, DC: Social Science Monographs, 1994; C. Gerlach and G. Aly, *Das letzte Kapitel. Realpolitik, Ideologie und der Mord an den ungarischen Juden 1944/1945*, Munich: DVA, 2002.

40 S. Szita, *Verschleppt, verhungert, vernichtet. Die Deportation von ungarischen Juden auf das Gebiet des annektierten Österreich 1944–1945*, Vienna: Eichbauer, 1999; E. Raim, *Die Dachauer KZ-Außenkommandos Kaufering und Mühldorf. Rüstungsbauten und Zwangsarbeit im letzten Kriegsjahr 1944/45*, Landsberg am Lech: Neumayer, 1992.

41 A. Strzelecki, *The Deportation of Jews from the Łódź Ghetto to KL Auschwitz and their Extermination. A Description of the Events and the Presentation of Historical Sources*, Oświęcim: Auschwitz-Birkenau State Museum, 2006

42 B. Perz and F. Freund, 'Auschwitz neu? Pläne und Maßnahmen zur Wiedererrichtung der Krematorien von Auschwitz-Birkenau in der Umgebung des KZ Mauthausen im Februar 1945', *Dachauer Hefte* 20, 2004, pp. 58–70.

43 K. Orth, *Das System der nationalsozialistischen Konzentrationslager. Eine politische Organisationsgeschichte*, Hamburg: Hamburger Edition, 1999, pp. 270–336.

44 A. Kossert, '*Endlösung* on the "Amber Shore": The massacre in January 1945 on the Baltic seashore: A repressed chapter of East Prussian history', *Leo Baeck Institute Year Book* 49, 2004, 1, pp. 3–19.

45 E. Lappin, 'The death marches of Hungarian Jews through Austria in the Spring of 1945', *Yad Vashem Studies* 28, 2000, pp. 203–42.

46 This figure given by Daniel Blatman in his forthcoming book on the Death Marches; cf. his chapter in this volume. Gerlach and Aly, *Das letzte Kapitel*, p. 413, though, suggest that the figures were lower.

47 U. Herbert, 'Labour and extermination: Economic interest and the primacy of Weltanschauung in National Socialism', *Past and Present* 138, 1993, pp. 144–95.

48 M. Gilbert, *Auschwitz and the Allies*, London: Pimlico, 2001; H. Świebocki, *London Has Been Informed ... Reports by Auschwitz Escapees*, Oświęcim: Auschwitz-Birkenau State Museum, 1997.

49 G. Greif, *We Wept Without Tears. Interviews with Jewish Survivors of the Auschwitz Sonderkommando*, New Haven, CT: Yale University Press 2005 (the author is preparing a greatly enlarged version); *Des voix sous la cendre. Manuscrits des Sonderkommandos d'Auschwitz-Birkenau*, Paris: Calmann-Lévy, 2005.

50 *Die österreichischen Opfer des Holocaust. The Austrian Victims of the Holocaust.* Vienna: Dokumentationsarchiv des österreichischen Widerstandes, 2001 (CD-ROM); S. Klarsfeld and M. Steinberg (eds), *Mémorial de la déportation des Juifs de Belgique*, Brussels, 1982; M. Kárný (ed.), *Terezínská pametní kniha. Židovské obeti nacistických deportací z Cech a Moravy 1941–1945*, Prague: Nadace Terezínská iniciativa – Melantrich, 1995; S. Klarsfeld, *Memorial to the Jews Deported From France, 1942– 1944: Documentation of the Deportation of the Victims of the Final Solution in France*, New York: Beate Klarsfeld Foundation, 1983; *In Memoriam*, The Hague: Sdu Uitgeverij Koninginnegracht, 1995; *Gedenkbuch – Opfer der Verfolgung der Juden unter der nationalsozialistischen Gewaltherrschaft in Deutschland 1933–1945*, 4 vols, Koblenz: Bundesarchiv 2006; A. Recanati, *A Memorial Book of the Deportation of the Greek Jews*, 3 vols, Jerusalem: Erez, 2006; L. P. Fargion, *Il libro della memoria: gli ebrei deportati dall'Italia (1943–1945)*, Milan: Mursia, 1991; http://www.neveklarsfeld.org/index.shtml (350,000 names of Jews from Greater Hungary).

51 Mączka, *Żydzi polscy w KL Auschwitz*; *Sterbebücher von Auschwitz. Fragmente* (fragments until December 1943; out of the 69,000 inmates contained here 30,000 were Jews. After March 1943, the deaths of Jewish prisoners were not registered any longer); *Gedenkbuch: Häftlinge des Konzentrationslagers Bergen-Belsen*, Celle: Gedenkstätte Bergen-Belsen, 2005. More databases are available at the camp memorials.

52 Yad Vashem has started a research program on deportations of Jews within Nazi Europe.

53 Y. Gutman and S. Krakowski, 'Juden im KL Auschwitz', p. 194.

54 Józef Adelson, 'W Polsce zwanej Ludowa', *Najnowsze dzieje Żydów w Polsce*, Warsaw: PWN, 1993, pp. 387–477, 398; Gerlach and Aly, *Das letzte Kapitel*, p. 409. Cf. also the Benjamin and Vladka Meed Registry of Jewish Holocaust Survivors at the US Holocaust Memorial Museum, which contains more than 185,000 names of survivors in the United States.

8 The death marches and the final phase of Nazi genocide

Daniel Blatman

The history of the violent and murderous eruption that occurred in the last period of the war, in which hundreds of thousands of camps prisoners, POWs, and forced labourers were evacuated from thousands of concentration camps or other incarceration and labour facilities along the retreat of the collapsing Reich, leaves many question marks and much confusion. In January 1945, according to Nazi records, some 714,000 prisoners were languishing in the concentration-camp network. One may confidently assume that the actual numbers were much larger, because even the administrators and operators of this camp universe could not gauge its enormous magnitude with any precision.[1] The denizens of this universe were a special microcosm of the victims of the Nazi terror. They included members of all European nationalities and some who had fallen into the snare from countries that had not been under Nazi control or that had fought against Germany. Each of these prisoners had reached his or her camp as a result of persecution, whether racial, political, religious or social. Some four months later, when the tumult of the war in Europe ceased and the Third Reich tumbled off the stage of history, at least 250,000 of them were no longer among the living. Many others perished shortly after the liberation as a result of their desperate physical condition. The final phase of the war was viciously murderous even by the horrifying standards of the Nazi genocide.

From the second half of 1944 and, especially, from the beginning of 1945, governance and administration in the German-occupied areas in Poland were badly disrupted; in the later stages of this period, the same occurred within the borders of Germany itself. The Soviets' rapid progress and the Wehrmacht's retreat touched off frantic waves of flight and evacuation as millions of civilians fled the Red Army and the fear of Soviet occupation. Accompanying the mass escape and augmenting its panic were innumerable testimonies about the brutal rape of thousands of German women and girls as well as accounts of murder, dispossession, and looting by Red Army soldiers.[2] Both German and Allied sources describe the horrific commotion that reigned in Upper Silesia during the retreat in January–February 1945. They recount the total collapse of public order and the murder of prisoners whose presence created a further pressure on roads and means of transport that were already overburdened with civilian and military traffic.[3]

The coincidence of the final evacuations of the large concentration camps in Poland (Auschwitz, Groß-Rosen, and Stutthof) and the large-scale evacuation of civilians and troops from these areas – the two events occurred within weeks of each other – strongly influenced the traditional explanation that was offered for the murder of camp prisoners, invoked in the very first post-war months. Rudolf Höß, commander of Auschwitz in 1940–1943 and subsequently a bureau chief at the WVHA (SS Business and Administration Main Office), stated in his memoirs that the tragic outcomes of the camp evacuations were due to negligently faulty preparations on the part of those tasked with implementing the evacuations, i.e., the commandants of camps in the east. According to Höß, the Auschwitz camp commandant Richard Baer left responsibility for the evacuation in the hands of junior officers whose sole interest was to clear out as quickly as possible before the Soviets came. When evacuation day arrived, they found themselves having to evacuate tens of thousands of prisoners under grim conditions of system collapse and panicky retreat, leading to the death and murder of many prisoners who could not endure the conditions of the evacuation.[4] American intelligence officials offered similar explanations immediately after the war. The mass mortality among prisoners during the evacuations, they said, were the result of sloppy preparations, severe restrictions in transport and food, harsh winter conditions and faulty logistics.[5] These structural and circumstantial explanations, however, fall short in elucidating the tragic, ghastly outcomes of the camp evacuations.

By the time the war entered its final months, the Nazi genocide was a publicly known fact. This final phase, however, hardly reverberated in either the free world's press or in Palestine. If the media mentioned the evacuation of German-held prisoners from camps in the east at all, they almost always did so in the context of Allied POWs, whose fate commanded immeasurably greater interest than that of concentration camp inmates.[6] Only in April 1945 did reportage about what had happened in the concentration camps before the liberation begin to proliferate, mainly after American armed forces reached the camps and discovered the atrocities that had preceded the evacuation.[7] This information, however, did not necessarily elicit special insights about the era of the death marches; indeed, the press did not use this term at all and ignored the genocide taking place in the concluding months of the war.

At the 1945 Nuremberg trials, too there was little reference to the evacuations. The issue arose mainly in the trial of Ernst Kaltenbrunner, Heydrich's successor as chief of the RSHA (Reich Security Main Office), and the entire legal debate focused on issues of administration and command, not on the process itself. Even in the 1946 trials of war criminals who had served in the concentration camps, the death marches were hardly treated as a unique period in the Nazi genocide. If the evacuations were mentioned at all, the prosecution again focused on determining who had been responsible for the development of the chaotic situation that led to the deaths of thousands of camp prisoners; and naturally the defendants passed the buck up the chain of command.

Although these and subsequent trials in West Germany and Austria produced a mass of immensely important documentary material which allows us to trace closely the murder of individual prisoners and, in several instances, the massacres that took place during the death marches, its ability to help us understand a broader spectrum of questions is limited. The answers to many questions – such as what happened in the evacuation convoys that evolved into lengthy death marches; who the murderers were and what their motives were; who the victims were, and how the civilian population (Polish, German, or Austrian) reacted to the hundreds of thousands of evacuation prisoners – must be sought elsewhere.

Historiography and the death marches

The paltry extent of research on the death-march period in the historiography of the Nazi genocide is puzzling given the wealth of survivors' testimonies and other available archival material. In his monumental history of the Holocaust, Raul Hilberg devotes only a few pages to the evacuations and invests most of them in the evacuation of Auschwitz, which began in the autumn of 1944 and ended with the dispersal of its prisoners to various concentration camps in Germany in January 1945. This sub-chapter, titled 'Liquidation of the Killing Centers and the End of the Destruction Process', is indicative of the then dominant approach to the murders committed in the last months of the war.[8] When the great extermination centres in the east were evacuated and destroyed, the murder apparatus typical of the 'Final Solution' was also eradicated, and the murderous marches could not be associated with the fundamentals of the Nazi genocide in its heyday. Leni Yahil relates the death-march period at greater length, noting the enormous increase in the number of camp inmates in the last year of the war due to the needs of the war economy, which resulted in a massive concentration of men and women who were considered enemies of the Reich. She ascribes the murderousness of the marches to the last effort of a crumbling regime to avenge itself on its victims for its own impending defeat.[9] Saul Friedländer, in his volume on *The Years of Extermination*, devotes only a few pages to the last months of the murders, stressing the chaos that prevailed during these months and blaming the murderous nature of the evacuations on the fact that no one was totally in charge of them.[10] Gerald Reitlinger had offered the same conclusion in his pioneering book about the destruction of European Jewry.[11]

One explanation for this lack of attention is that the death-march period has been subsumed into the overall account of the Third Reich's apocalyptic collapse. The extermination facilities had been decommissioned, the traditional murder bureaucracy had fallen apart, and the main officials in the security police, the SD (the SS security service) and the extermination camps were no longer at their posts during the months of this unorganized murder. For years, the death marches remained characteristic of the twilight era of the Third Reich as it sank toward its demise in violence, fire and blood.

It is true that some attempts to explain the matter were made, largely in the 1970s and 1980s, by Israeli scholars who tried to link this era of murder with the pre-1944 phases of the 'Final Solution'.[12] The facts that the death-march period almost directly followed the last great murder operation, aimed mainly against

Hungarian Jewry, and that Jews figured so largely and importantly among the prisoners during the evacuation months seem to have made it easier to conclude that the death marches were the last phase of the 'Final Solution'. However, the camp prisoners during these months were in fact a highly heterogeneous and complex group: Jews were only one sub-group, albeit a large one, and the framework of the 'Final Solution' cannot fully account for these deaths.

There have been only three conspicuous attempts up to now to discuss the evacuations and death marches from a comprehensive perspective. First, a year after the war, the UNRRA Central Tracing Bureau published an important documentary collection that included summaries of more than a hundred evacuations, sketches of routes taken and estimates of the number of persons murdered. This data was incomplete and not always accurate, but the very fact that an important international institution gathered them shows that the horrors of the camp evacuations had been neither entirely hidden nor forgotten. In the mid-1960s, two scholars in Czechoslovakia used this material as the basis for a pioneering book about the death marches.[13] But their study was limited to statistical summaries and description of the evacuation routes; it neither explored the interface between the death marches and the Nazi genocide policy nor did it ask where the evacuation period belongs in the overall history of the Nazi concentration camps. Second, a study published by the Polish scholar Zigmund Zonik in the mid-1980s followed in the footsteps of trials in Germany and Poland concerning the camp evacuations. Zonik, a former prisoner in Nazi concentration camps, gives us an important summary of the decision-making processes in the array of camps on the eve of the evacuations and sketches the routes that the prisoner convoys followed as they were evacuated from the west and the east.[14] His book, however, sheds little light on the murderers, the victims or the social and political infrastructure within which these prisoners were slaughtered as the war wound down.

The third study was the trail-blazing examination of the death marches within the context of the Nazi genocide policy published by Daniel Jonah Goldhagen in 1996. Goldhagen's book devotes two chapters to the death marches and treats them as one component in the totality of murder techniques that the Nazis used in the implementation of their 'Final Solution' policy.[15] The death march, Goldhagen claims, had been a conventional Nazi extermination technique against Jews from the very beginning of the occupation of Poland and was practised in three different periods. Although his interpretation of the marches was not the most criticized part of this controversial book, it can nevertheless be contested.

The first period, according to Goldhagen, encompasses the years 1939–1941, when populations were relocated and deported in pursuit of the various resettlement schemes that Himmler and sundry SS officials entertained. In one of the most murderous examples cited by Goldhagen, hundreds of Jews perished in December 1939 as they were being deported from Chełm and Hrubieszów, in eastern Poland, to the Soviet-controlled territories. This horrific case, however, actually illustrates the difference between the murders of Jews during deportation at the beginning of the war and the death-march period that occurred at its end. On 1 December 1939, some 2,000 Jewish men were assembled by the SS in Chełm and marched to Hrubieszów in the direction of the Soviet border. Between 300 and 800 Jews were murdered in the course of this march. The following day, 2,000 Jews from Hrubieszów were added to the Chełm deportees, and the death march continued for two more days. On 4 December its survivors were forced across the River Bug as Soviet soldiers on the other side fired at them in order to keep them out of Soviet-controlled territory. Those who crossed the river were forcibly returned by the Russians to the German-controlled zone.[16]

This murderous march was characteristic of the period in which the frontier between the Soviet and German occupation zones was being stabilized, and cannot be directly linked to the murders of Jews in subsequent years. Local German officials feared that a large Jewish population in German–Soviet frontier localities around Lublin would pose a menace due to its alleged support for the Red Army. The fact that only men were deported, with women left behind, further emphasizes that this was not an 'eliminationist' scheme in Goldhagen's sense of the term, but the murderous implementation of a decision flowing from political and security considerations. In the first years of the occupation of Poland, of course, tens of thousands of other Jews were deported to the Generalgouvernement from the annexed areas in the west and from other districts of Poland. But although murders took place on these cruel deportations, premeditated massacres did not. It is stretching the facts to treat this period as a deliberate preliminary to the official extermination policy.

Goldhagen's periodization moves on to 1941–1944, the years in which the extermination of the Jews proceeded with full fury. However, he offers no evidence of Jews being murdered by what he calls the 'institution' of the death march. On the contrary, this period was notable for the murder of *non*-Jews, especially Soviet POWs, by marching them hundreds of kilometres and murdering those unable to endure the hardships of the march.[17] Jews were rarely killed in death marches during these peak years of the 'Final Solution'; instead, they were murdered near their places of residence or were transported in trains that set out from stations in their towns of residence or from the ghettos in which they had been concentrated, and took them directly to murder sites that had been established for this purpose.

Goldhagen's third period coincides with the last months of the war. By now, the exigencies of the war had made it necessary to retreat from the concentration and extermination camps, and murder by evacuation became the only extermination technique available, he argues. The Germans no longer had full control over the timing of the murders: the progression of this kind of bloodshed was now dictated by the progress of the victorious Allied forces. This period is composed of three sub-periods (also recognized by historians of the concentrations camps): from the early summer of 1944, when the retreats and evacuations in eastern Poland and the Baltic countries began; from early January 1945, with the evacuation of the large camps in Poland; and from the beginning of March 1945, when evacuations on German soil began, until the surrender.[18]

Goldhagen's discussion of several of these final death marches is graphic and consistent with his general approach to the Germans' policy and practice of mass murder.[19] He summarizes his conclusions as follows:

> The German guards ... these ordinary Germans, knew that they were continuing the work that had begun and had been to a great extent already accomplished in the camp system and in other institutions of killing: to exterminate the Jewish people.[20]

However, Goldhagen does not address the more complex conclusion that a German court had already reached about the murderers' motives and the nature of the murderous spree during the Helmbrechts camp death march, which he uses extensively in order to prove his thesis:

> The goal of the evacuation was unknown to [the prisoners] as well as to the members of the guarding group, except, that is, to the accused. The accused saw in the prisoners not only enemies of the state, saboteurs, destroyers of the [German] people, anti-socials and criminals, but also creatures whose humanity was hardly to be considered. Accordingly, it was all the same to him in his mind whether a matter concerned Jewesses on non-Jewesses, whether Poles, Czechs, Russians, Hungarians, French, Dutch, or members of other nations.[21]

This judgment underscores the main weakness of Goldhagen's conclusions: the fact that the final victims of the Nazi genocide were not necessarily identified by their murderers as Jews. This point clashes with the basic premises of his work concerning the permanence of German eliminationist antisemitism. He therefore regards the death march simply as one extermination technique and not as the hallmark of a period that has its own uniqueness in the history of the Nazi genocide. Yet these are precisely the characteristics that determine the difference between the death-march murders and those that preceded them.

The death marches, then, must be seen not only as the final chapter in the history of the Nazi genocide but also as the last chapter in the history of the Nazi concentration camps. Yet just as one cannot understand them merely as outgrowths of the ideological infrastructure that led to the 'Final Solution', so too one cannot explain them solely as outgrowths of the history of the concentration camps. Although the victims of the evacuations and the death marches were camp prisoners, these actions took place outside the traditional terror domain in which the prisoners had been living and dying. What happened to the evacuation-march prisoners, how they coped with the new situation as the camps dissolved and how they struggled for survival – all this needs to be told and understood differently from their experience while living and struggling for existence as camp *inmates*.

Even the new historiography of the concentration camps discussed in this volume has given less than full attention to the death marches. For the most part, these studies treat the camp evacuations and death marches as an epilogue to the history of the camp and not as an essential element in this history. This is partially different for the monographs on the evacuation and liberation of Auschwitz, Ravensbrück, Mittelbau-Dora and Buchenwald.[22] These studies have established an important methodological fact: that the death marches and the evacuations are part of the overall history of the concentration camps. However, most of the studies on the Nazi concentration camps bid farewell to the evacuation convoys after they step past the gate of the closed and abandoned camp, in the camp to which they are evacuated or at the moment in which the Allies liberate them. They do not consider the journey itself, when the territorial location of the violence and murder changed, as did the nature and goals of the terror employed.

But the death marches should not be examined solely as part of the history of the concentration camps nor as a concluding chapter in the story of the 'Final Solution' to the Jewish problem. They were also, and primarily, as the last period of Nazi genocide, woven into the history of the concentration camps. For this purpose, we need to examine the decision-making processes related to the murders, the motivation of the perpetrators and the collective identity of the victims.

The decision-makers

The very first works about the concentration camps, dating from the mid-1960s, devoted conspicuous discussion to the question of the responsibility of Himmler and his subordinates for devising the camp evacuation process and its attendant murders. For Martin Broszat, Himmler's order to leave no living prisoners in enemy hands at the approach of enemy armies was the principal cause of the panicky and murderous evacuation that sealed the fate of hundreds of thousands of prisoners.[23] Himmler's famous order in this matter was issued on 17 June 1944, from the office of Richard Glücks, inspector-general of the concentration camps at the WVHA. According to the order, if emergency conditions came about, the HSSPF (the district SS and police commander) would be fully empowered to control the fate of the camps in his purview.[24]

The order was given in the midst of the great landing of Allied forces in France and the Red Army's massive summer offensive toward the Baltic states and Poland. These factors prompted Himmler to order the evacuation of several camps in the areas of Kovno and Riga. Furthermore, preparations for the evacuation of the enormous Majdanek concentration camp near Lublin had begun back in March 1944.[25] After Himmler decided which officials would be in charge of the process, the order was put into effect by officials in the field: the HSSPF, the Gauleiter and his officials, and the camp command. Thus, local players wielded decisive authority in timing the evacuation and arranging resources for the camp or camps under their authority.[26]

Oswald Pohl, whose purview as head of the WVHA included the camps, claimed at his trial that the directives issued in the early summer of 1944 concerning the evacuation of camps and the transfer of executive powers to the local HSSPF had been given for operational reasons – the growing difficulty of maintaining communication between the Oranienburg headquarters and the far-flung camps in the east – and did not signify a change in the attitude toward the prisoners.[27] In the summer and autumn of 1944, the evacuation of prisoners in the east to concentration camps and industrial centres in Germany accelerated but in a relatively organized fashion. The transfer of the prisoners of Auschwitz to camps in Germany was a clear example of this process. In the middle of July 1944, the three main camps of Auschwitz contained 92,208 prisoners. On 17 January 1945, when the final evacuation began, 67,000 prisoners remained.[28] Similar evacuations of prisoners from faraway camps that were in danger of falling into enemy hands occurred in the summer and early autumn of 1944 in Majdanek, labour camps in the Baltic states and the Natzweiler-Struthof concentration camp in Alsace.[29] Although these evacuations were accompanied by much hardship, suffering and abuse, they were not characterized by the rampant murderousness and atrocity of the subsequent death marches. Thus, it is difficult to assign them to the last era of the Nazi genocide.

By the spring of 1945, camp evacuations and death marches were occurring on German soil as the advance of American and British forces from the west compounded the restrictions on movement. Now the evacuees made their way through the very heart of the German population and entered a reality in which the state systems of governance and infrastructure were ceasing to function. Evidently, however, Himmler's order from June 1944 remained the basis for decisions on evacuations, although it was augmented by additional guidelines during this time. Max Pauly, commander of Neuengamme, told his interrogators after the war that in April 1945 he had met with the HSSPF of Hamburg for a last talk which included the final evacuation of the camp and the disposition of prisoners who could not be evacuated.[30] In April 1945, Pauly said, he found himself in a situation where he did not know what to do with the prisoners. The situation in almost all the other camps was similar. Confused guidelines were being forwarded by various officials: Himmler, either directly or by Richard Glücks on his behalf, or by local officials such as the HSSPF and the Gauleiter. By and large, the camp commandants were not eager to take the initiative but preferred to wait until the very last moment in order to determine the content, authority and feasibility of the orders they had received.

The question of authority remained ambiguous until the end of the war.[31] After the war, Oswald Pohl tried to hold Himmler and Hitler fully responsible for the policy that dictated brutal evacuations under all conditions and circumstances. There is no doubt that Himmler's mercurial involvement in the camp evacuations contributed to the general tangle that would have existed in any case. After the June 1944 directive, Himmler issued various guidelines on any number of occasions until the system, which had ceased to function in any case, was totally confused. In late March 1945, for example, he held working meetings in Vienna with four Gauleiters in regard to the evolving military situation in eastern Austria and repeated the well-known guideline that gave them full emergency powers. The problems discussed included the evacuation of Allied POWs and the civilian population. Baldur von Schirach, Gauleiter of Vienna, attended one of those meetings and claimed after the war that Himmler had made explicit remarks about the Jews who had been deported from Budapest and were working in labour camps in eastern Austria:

> I want the Jews now employed in industry to be taken by boat, or by bus if possible, under the most favorable food conditions and with medical care, *et cetera*, to Linz or Mauthausen. ... Please take care of these Jews and treat them well; they are my most valuable assets.[32]

The Gauleiter of Styria, Siegfried Uiberreither, in whose district thousands of Hungarian Jews of this kind had been concentrated, also remembered Himmler's guidelines. He said they were given to him orally in March 1945 and were concurrently sent on to the Gestapo. Himmler insisted that the transfer of the Jews be carried out 'in the accepted way' and demanded that the commander of Mauthausen, Franz Ziereis, treat them properly, according to his policy at that time to use the surviving Jews as 'bargaining tools' while negotiating with the Western allies.[33]

After the liberation of Buchenwald on 11 April 1945, there were reports about raids by released prisoners in nearby Weimar where they had allegedly attacked civilians. In response, Himmler, afraid of Hitler's reaction, reissued his order to the effect that under no circumstances should prisoners fall into enemy hands alive.[34] Such an order, issued amid total system collapse, severe military defeat and chaotic retreat, further amplified the dynamics of murder. The rationales behind the clashing and varying decisions had become incomprehensible: should the prisoners be liquidated in order to keep them out of enemy hands? Should they be transferred to another camp in order to continue working? Should Jewish prisoners be taken care of? The practical solutions chosen were not exceptional in the Nazi bureaucratic system. The special and serpentine path of the *Führerbefehl* was familiar throughout the Reich from other times and other complex situations. The high officials in the SS were aware of the existence of a general directive that enjoined against leaving prisoners and POWs behind, and it is altogether possible that they construed it as an instruction to execute the prisoners if the danger of their falling into enemy hands became real. The head of the RSHA, Ernst Kaltenbrunner, said at his trial that he had been unaware of an explicit order from Hitler about the murder of camp prisoners and added that in any case the person empowered to issue such orders was Himmler.[35]

It is safe to say that no single explicit, comprehensive order about the murder of camp prisoners in the event that a camp could not be evacuated is known to have been given. Instead, a combination of local instructions from various officials created an infrastructure for the murder. Joachim Neander defines these instructions as 'local murder orders' (*lokale Vernichtungsbefehle*), i.e., orders issued by low-ranking local commanders in response to specific needs or difficulties.[36] Since the junior command echelons were given such a broad mandate to resolve this issue, the decision to eliminate prisoners was handed on to those who dealt directly with the prisoners, i.e., the camp guards and staff who escorted them along the evacuation path. It was there that the prisoners' fate was sealed.

The triggermen

The evacuation turned into a mass-murder campaign as soon as the columns of prisoners began to wend their way toward the chosen destination. Once they left the camp, they were totally under the responsibility of the guards and escorts. Although the latter, of course, had not been given systematic and explicit guidelines about them, they usually understood that shooting and killing prisoners who caused trouble or attempted to escape was in no way problematic.[37] Amid the panic, the pandemonium, the unendurable stress on the congested routes of retreat, the harsh weather that often accompanied the evacuation and the reverberations of the approaching Soviet artillery, the conditions that turned the evacuations into horrific death marches took shape.

It was the convoy guards and escorts who determined the prisoners' fate. On the eve of the great evacuations of the camps in the east in January 1945, 37,674 men and 3,508 women were serving in the constellation of camps. Some 80–90 per cent of them were guards (*Wachmannschaften*). Most of them had reached the camps at the time the system was expanding, starting in 1943 with the establishment of hundreds of satellite labour camps. They were not 'careerists' in camp service and many of them had not even come from the ranks of the SS. They had reached the camp archipelago in the last years of the war, by which time the system had already become a framework of forced labour, terror and murder. They were different from the veteran camp staff. The 'newcomers', however, constituted a cadre of murderers who played a decisive role in the mass murder that took place in the last months of the war.

On 9 May 1944, Hitler issued an order empowering Himmler to mobilize superannuated soldiers (those approaching or past the age of 40) for concentration-camp duties. In the aftermath of this directive, some 10,000 Wehrmacht soldiers who had returned from the Crimea, along with servicemen from air-defence teams, non-combat technical units of the Luftwaffe and the Navy, were reassigned to service in satellite camps of the concentration camps.[38] During this last phase, ethnic Germans (*Volksdeutsche*) and groups of Ukrainians, Latvians, Lithuanians and members of other nationalities also saw duty in the camps.

The general feeling that stands out in the accounts of those camp guards who served as the convoys' escorts during the evacuation is that they had been abandoned to their fate together with the groups of exhausted prisoners, who were endangering their ability to retreat quickly from an enemy who was threatening to gain ground on them. From January 1945 until the end of the war, the escorts had to accompany tens of thousands of marching prisoners over distances that sometimes added up to tens of kilometres without appropriate overnight accommodation for them, and cope with the ravages of the weather and the prisoners' attempts to escape. Often the guards and prisoners reached a railway junction where they were supposed to board a train for the continuation of the evacuation journey, but the train came late or had been commandeered for military necessities, forcing them to continue the now-purposeless trek on foot. Thus, it is no wonder that the elimination of prisoners who found it difficult to continue marching or were suspected of wishing to escape or cause problems became a matter of routine. As the hardships of the evacuation and the danger of falling captive along with the prisoners mounted, it no longer seemed enough to dispose of those who straggled or attempted to escape. In many cases, the guards now initiated the murder of large groups of evacuees. The light trigger-finger was a manifestation of frustration and the wish to eliminate any factor that might obstruct the guards and escorts from rapidly distancing themselves from their own terror of becoming prisoners.

Another group of murderers whose professional field had little to do with the systematic liquidation of the Reich's political or racial enemies, but who engaged in large-scale murder during the death-march period, were members of the Volkssturm, the militia established in the autumn of 1944. The Volkssturm, composed of older people who were unfit for ordinary military service, was handed the hopeless task of trying to stem the advance of the Allied armies at the local level.[39] These groups of murderers operated within a specific situation. They were civilians who had been mobilized for security service near their homes. They could not contribute much to the war effort, and the real enemy, whom they regarded as a truly existential menace, was composed of concentration-camp prisoners who were circulating near their homes. The local press abounded with stories and rumours of rape and looting by camp prisoners who had managed to escape the evacuation convoys and grim warnings against giving them support.[40] During the last weeks of the war, terror-mongering rumours found attentive ears among a public that groped in the dark where reliable information was unavailable and total system collapse at hand. Social behaviour influenced by rumours can move in various circles, one of which is the eruption of violence when the familiar order is disrupted.[41] Such was the state of German society during these weeks, which created the conditions under which so many individuals joined the circle of murderers of concentration-camp prisoners during the death-march period. However, this peculiar pro-murder infrastructure could not have existed had there not been a general social consensus about the victims' identity.

The ideological consensus: image of the victim

One of the ghastliest death marches, which has been reconstructed and documented in detail before the court and afterwards in Goldhagen's book, involved a group of women prisoners from Camp Helmbrechts, a small satellite camp of Flossenbürg. Six hundred twenty-one Jewish women, the vestiges of a death march from Poland, reached this camp in early March 1945. Camp Helmbrechts had been established in late June 1944. By February 1945 the population of the camp stood at 594,[42] most of them from Poland and the USSR along with small groups of French and German prisoners. The arrival of the Jewish women boosted the prisoner population to around 1,200. On 13 April 1945, 1,171 prisoners were evacuated from the camp, including the 580 Jews who were still alive.[43] For about two weeks, they migrated on the roads, on foot and in carts. At some point, almost all the non-Jewish prisoners were released in accordance with the camp and death march commander Alois Dörr's understanding of the evacuation orders and only the few German and the Jewish prisoners continued. At least 278 women, almost all of them Jewish, perished in the death march from Helmbrechts to Volary, Czechoslovakia, where the Americans liberated the survivors. Of the fatalities, 129 met their deaths in the course of the march, the night-time stopovers, the freezing cold and starvation. Forty-nine others were murdered by the guards because they were unable to walk any further or had tried to escape. There is no exact information about the circumstances of the death of many others.[44]

When Alois Dörr was interrogated about the circumstances of this murderous evacuation, he claimed that he had not given any order to murder the prisoners and that after he found out about the murders, on the first and second days of the evacuation, he ordered prisoners to be shot only if trying to escape. Whatever the reliability of Dörr's testimony, the guards do seem to have been told something of this nature. Equally, however, Dörr did not use his authority to categorically forbid the murder of exhausted prisoners.[45]

Dörr had not given an order to commit murder (except in the case of escapees) but had not forbidden it, either. The surrender of the authority to decide on murder to those in charge in the field was not exceptional; it recurred in hundreds of death marches during those months. Dörr was aware of the extremely dire condition of the Jewish prisoners, many of whom looked like walking skeletons. One of those in charge of the prisoners during the evacuation claimed that he had warned on several occasions that the prisoners would collapse if food and water continued to be denied to them. None of this bothered Dörr in the least. The only thing that concerned him was to complete the mission, to deliver the prisoners to Dachau as quickly as possible.[46] Dörr also expected that many prisoners would collapse during the march or be murdered in cold blood by the guards. He left his guards a great deal of functional discretion: they were supposed to prevent by gunfire prisoner escapes but also not to leave ill prisoners behind under any circumstances.[47] In all these respects, Dörr was no different from others in charge of evacuation convoys and death marches.

There is no doubt whatsoever that Jewish prisoners suffered immeasurably more than others. Most of them received much smaller food rations, and when the evacuees encamped for the night the Jews were almost always left in an open field, in freezing cold, while others were led to an enclosed granary or warehouse wherever this was possible. German prisoners who continued on the death march along with Jews walked in separate groups, and were rarely beaten by the guards.[48] The main difference between Jews and non-Jews, however, was the desperate physical state of most Jews compared to other prisoners. This situation did not originate in Helmbrechts, where the Jewish women had spent only a few weeks. It was the result of the year that preceded their arrival in this camp and the death marches that they had endured en route to it. For these reasons, by the end of the death march nearly half of the Jewish prisoners were unable to march and were placed in carts, where they lay helpless and received almost no food. Dörr's inflexible instructions about denying the prisoners reasonable quantities of food even when local civilians were willing to provide it, his equanimity in the face of abuse and beating of prisoners and his refusal to provide sick prisoners with medical care when it was available indicate that to his mind the prisoners, especially the Jewish ones, were 'not human' (*nichts Menschliches hatten*).[49] The fact that nearly all the dying women were Jewish only made it easier for him to treat them this way and for the guards to pull the trigger. However, Dörr and his guards might have behaved in the same way towards other groups of prisoners in a similar physical state, as happened in innumerable other cases.

An ideology-based consensus about the dehumanization of prisoners was the salient component of the murderers' attitude toward their charges. Innumerable examples illustrate this attitude toward the death-march victims, who were described in language that reduced them to objects or to hunters' prey.[50] Without understanding the collective image of the group of victims in the murderers' eyes, one cannot explain the magnitude of the murder phenomenon. The definitive and categorical identity of the victims is the 'other' as against 'us', a dichotomy that had solid ideological underpinnings on which the motivation to murder could be built.[51] Concentration-camp prisoners had been categorically 'other' since the dawn of the Nazi era. Over the years, the prisoners increasingly acquired the imagery of a threatening, violent, law-breaking and dangerous group. By the middle of 1942, when this 'mob' from the east (Soviet POWs and many inmates of Polish origin) began to reach the camps in Germany, these facilities had become ticking time-bombs within a stone's throw of tranquil civilians' homes. From the second half of 1943, when the profusion of satellite camps became part of the landscape of German civilians' lives, the menace seemed all the more threatening.

Even though concentration-camp prisoners were the first victims of Nazi violence, no ethnic, political or social group of camp prisoners was ever singled out for total elimination. It is true that from 1944 onward camp prisoners suffered mass mortality when worked to death selectively, but even then a narrow path to salvation continued to exist – their capacity for labour. After they left the camps on the death marches and evacuations, this path became even narrower. Their collective identity as enemy, 'alien' and 'other' became much more threatening because they were no longer penned behind fences but rather fled for their lives at every opportunity. Some murderers would continue to view them as Jews; others would regard them as Communist, and elsewhere the prisoners evolved into criminals who raped women and children. Sometimes they were perceived as all of these in one.

The murderers viewed their victims through the lens of total anonymity. As almost always happens in massacres that take place in the midst of a genocidal initiative, the murderers regard the victims as a collective devoid of individual human characteristics. In this situation, a helpless group of people is murdered by another group that possesses all the power and perpetrates the massacre without being in any danger itself. One side takes action; the other, the victims, can neither escape nor resist. The event ends when the last of the victims is eradicated, when the perpetrators' murderous rage passes, or when their work is disrupted by someone more powerful than them.[52] Numerous episodes in the last chapter of the Nazi genocide ended in one of these outcomes: the final prisoners were murdered, the murderous motivation that led to the act passed, or the Allied forces came too close to the site for the slaughter to continue.

Because of the murderers' very diversity, their affiliation with varied and broad social groups, and their operation in different organizations and units, no attempt to find a personality-related common denominator among them can succeed. The population of murderers included loyal Nazis, opportunists, those who only wanted to get home safely before the Third Reich crumbled into dust, and ordinary civilians who had stumbled into a situation beyond their wildest dreams. But they adopted the pattern of Nazi racial cruelty – they 'became Nazis' – the moment they decided to undertake an action in the Nazi spirit.[53] The thousands who murdered prisoners on the death marches did not have to be antisemites or systematic ideological racists in a particular mould. Probably they had been exposed, like other segments of German society, to political indoctrination and incessant waves of antisemitic and racist slogans and propaganda. However, a large question mark hovers over the efficacy of this propaganda steamroller for so wide a range of types and individuals as those who took part in the massacres.

Most of these murderers had not served in the extermination apparatus during the years when it had operated at full strength. During the war, however, all of them, in one way or another, went through social, public or other systems in which the operating culture created space for Nazi ideology. They were products of a society that for twelve years had fostered and exposed them to a certain ethos and that transformed many of them into Nazis, even if they did not define themselves as such. They came to view the prisoners as instrumental objects to whom they often related in entirely opportunistic ways. As long as the prisoners were being led to the destination camps, met the needs of their guards and served as an insurance policy that kept them far from the front, the guards continued to lead them. But the moment they became a burden, as often happened, the guards did not hesitate to slaughter them mercilessly. An action ostensibly driven by fanatic ideological motives was often merely the manifestation of an opportunistic calculus[54] – a calculus that took account of the prospects and hazards of the evacuation, the fear of falling captive and the wish to protect families from danger and violence.

At the same time, the murders could not have taken place had the group of murderers not been closely associated with a broad social support that was given to the killing. This support had been established during the twelve years of the Nazi regime in a process that Konrad Kwiet has called 'education to murder' (*Erziehung zum Mord*).[55] What this meant was an integration of social values with the belief that these demonic enemies of the nation were doomed to total eradication. Civilians and quasi-military groups were prompted by the absence of law and order to do whatever they felt necessary to assure the welfare of their families and communities. This was a process of co-operation among randomly available forces that combined their *ad hoc* efforts in order to carry out a task whose importance was acknowledged by one and all. Each piece in this jigsaw puzzle of murderers was responsible for only one part of the actions taken: planning, forwarding of instructions, escorting, guarding, supplying auxiliary aids such as parts, fuel, or ammunition, the act of murder itself, digging the graves and the attempt at blurring the traces.[56]

Conclusion

The attempt to explain the intensity of the violence against the prisoners in relation to its timing (sometimes just a few days before the surrender) may easily boil over into ambiguous arguments. One should not forget, however, that the months of the death marches were preceded by months, if not years of violence and terror that had evolved in the concentration camp system from the day it was established. In this sense, the uninhibited murder of prisoners in death marches was a direct outgrowth of the internal development of this terror network: even if it took place outside the network's traditional territorial confines, the objects of the terror and the murders remained identical to those of the previous eras.

In addition to being a concluding chapter in the history of the concentration camps, however, the death marches are also the concluding chapter of Nazi genocide. Yet the death-march chapter is different from its precursors. In the final months of Nazi genocide, the group of victims was no longer as clearly demarcated as before. The victims of this last phase were no longer only Jews and, in many cases, no longer mainly Jews. This explains why it is so difficult to position this period within the 'Final Solution of the Jewish Question'. Placing this period within the chronology of the extermination of the Jews muddles the understanding of the uniqueness of the final phases of the Nazi genocide. The Jews were a large and special group of victims, but the fact is that the circle of victims had expanded to include members of diverse nationalities. We therefore have to examine with precision the motivation and circumstances of the murders, the different groups of murderers, the political circumstances under which the murders took place and the social infrastructure that supported them. Any attempt to explain the death-march phenomenon solely from the perspective of the 'Final Solution' leads necessarily to selectivity among the events examined, as if first the arrow is shot and then the target is drawn round it. Nevertheless, as part of the Nazi genocide, the death marches period does of course have a specific Jewish angle that must be examined within an analytical context and a broad view of the totality of underlying circumstances and factors. The presence of so many Jewish prisoners among the camp inmates at the time of the evacuations was a factor that must be treated as central in any attempt to explain the intensity of the murders that took place.

In the last months of the Nazi genocide, the extermination process became completely decentralized. The decision to pull the trigger was ultimately made by the murderer who marched alongside the group of prisoners. It was he who determined whether the timing and conditions for this act had arrived; it was he who determined the moment when the act would take place. The decision was not spontaneous or impulsive, but flowed from the use of discretion and the calculation of utility, efficiency, timing and local conditions. Never in the years of the Nazi genocide, it seems, had such extensive power been placed in the hands of so many individuals who were entitled to decide at their sole discretion whether to murder or not. This situation was quite different from the bureaucratic control, management and supervision of the act of murder, albeit often slack and eclectic, that had existed until the summer of 1944.

What began that summer as an initiative informed by an economic rationale – the wish to preserve the labour force of the camp prisoners at any cost – became in early 1945 a series of brutal evacuation marches in which guards indiscriminately murdered almost anyone who delayed their escape. As the war wound down, the uniformed murderers were joined by non-uniformed ones: civilians and quasi-military groups that were prompted by the absence of law and order to do whatever they felt necessary to assure the welfare of their families and communities. This was a co-operation among randomly available forces that combined their *ad hoc* efforts in order to carry out a task whose importance was acknowledged by one and all.

The ethnic or racial specificity of the victims as objects of the ideology that guided the act of murder also became blurred. The Nazi genocide was different in its last phases from its preceding ones and cannot be explained according to the parameters that had drawn its contours in its peak years. Although the eliminationist ideological consensus continued to exist, the image of the object of murder changed at this time. Ideologically, the target was no longer identified as the Jewish enemy (the principal racial enemy in the Nazi murder campaign), or some other racial enemy (Sinti and Roma, Poles), or a political enemy (e.g. communists, Soviet POWs). The Nazi genocide in its final phases was guided by a different ideology of murder from the one crafted in previous years. It had become nihilistic and devoid of shaping principles. Although the murders took place within a known consensus, the uniqueness and identity of the enemy that had to be annihilated had become blurred. It had turned into an imaginary and demonic threat that had lost its specific ideological component. In the last phase of the Nazi genocide, the enemy became an existential menace that appeared on Germany's own doorstep as the Third Reich was about to disappear from the face of the earth.

Notes

1 D. Rousset, *L'univers concentrationnaire*, Paris: Pavois, 1946; translated as *A World Apart*, London: Secker & Warburg, 1951.
2 Atrocities and rape of women were emphasized in the German propaganda and press, especially by Joseph Goebbels, and made a major contribution to this historical mass retreat. See N. M. Naimark, *The Russians in Germany: A History of the Soviet Zone of Occupation, 1945–1949*, Cambridge and London: Belknap Press, 1995, pp. 72–8; C. Merridale, *Ivan's War: Life and Death in the Red Army, 1939–1945*, New York: Metropolitan Books, 2006, pp. 307–11.
3 Dr. Haffner (Der Generalstaatsanwalt Kattowitz) an den Herrn Reichsminister der Justiz in Berlin, February 1, 1945, Archwium Państwowego Muzeum Auschwitz-Birkenau (APMAB), D-RF-3/RSHA/160, pp. 45–6. 'Evacuation, Refugees and Displaced Persons in Germany', 10 February 1945, Supreme Headquarters Allied Expeditions Force, RG-338, National Archives and Records Administration (NARA),

box 187, file 383.6, pp. 1–2; 'German Intel. No. 117', 26 January 1945, The National Archives (TNA), FO 371/46764.

4 S. Paskuly (ed.), *Death Dealer: The Memoirs of the SS Kommandant at Auschwitz*, Buffalo, NY: Prometheus Books, 1992, p. 234.

5 Office of Strategic Services (OSS) Report, 4 August 1945, NARA, RG–153, box 245, folder 5, p. 23.

6 Y. Bauer, 'The Death-Marches, January–May 1945', in M. R. Marrus (ed.), *The Nazi Holocaust*, vol. 9, Westport, CT: Meckler, 1989, pp. 503–4.

7 L. Leff, *Buried by the Times: The Holocaust and America's Most Important Newspaper*, New York: Cambridge University Press, 2005, pp. 294–307.

8 R. Hilberg, *The Destruction of the European Jews*, vol. 3, New Haven, CT and London: Yale University Press, 2003, pp. 1045ff.

9 L. Yahil, *The Holocaust: The Fate of European Jewry*, New York and Oxford: Oxford University Press, 1991, p. 541.

10 S. Friedländer, *Nazi Germany and the Jews 1939–1945. The Years of Extermination*, New York: HarperCollins Publishers, 2007, pp. 648–52.

11 G. Reitlinger, *The 'Final Solution': The Attempt to Exterminate the Jews of Europe 1933–1945*, New York: The Beechhurst Press, 1953, pp. 459, 461.

12 See, for example: L. Rotkirchen, 'The "Final Solution" in Its Last Stages', *Yad Vashem Studies* 8, 1970, pp. 7–29; S. Krakowski, 'The Death Marches in the Period of the Evacuation of the Camps', in Marrus, *The Nazi Holocaust*, pp. 476–90.

13 I. Malá and L. Kubátová, *Pochody Smrti*, Prague: Nakladatelství politické literatury, 1965.

14 Z. Zonik, *Anus belli. Ewakuacja i wyzwolenie hitlerowskich obozów koncentracyjnch*, Warsaw: Państwowe Wydawnictwo Naukowe, 1988.

15 D. J. Goldhagen, *Hitler's Willing Executioners. Ordinary Germans and the Holocaust*, New York: Alfred A. Knopf, 1996, Chapters 13, 14.

16 A. Horvitz, 'Mitzad HaMavet shel Yehudei Chełm VeHrubieszów leEver Nahar Bug BeDetzember 1939', *Yalkult Moreshet* 68, October 1999, pp. 52–68.

17 K. C. Berkhoff, 'The 'Russian' Prisoners of War in Nazi-Ruled Ukraine as Victims of Genocidal Massacre', *Holocaust and Genocide Studies* 15:1, 2001, pp. 1–32.

18 K. Orth, *Das System der nationalsozialistischen Konzentrationslager. Eine politische Organisationsgeschichte*, Hamburg: Hamburger Edition, 1999, pp. 270ff.

19 Goldhagen, *Hitler's Willing Executioners*, pp. 335ff.

20 Ibid, p. 371.

21 Staatsanwaltschaft beim Landesgericht Hof, Alois Dörr Case, Bundesarchiv Außenstelle Ludwigsburg, 410 AR 1750/61, the court's ruling, p. 42.

22 A. Strzelecki, *The Evacuation, Dismantling and Liberation of KL Auschwitz*, Oświęcim: Auschwitz-Birkenau State Museum, 2001; J. Neander, 'Das Konzentrationslager "Mittelbau" in der Endphase der NS-Dikatatur', D. Phil. Dissertation, University of Bremen, 1996; S. Erpel, *Zwischen Vernichtung und Befreiung. Das Frauen-Konzentrationslager Ravensbrück in der letzen Kriegsphase*, Berlin: Metropol, 2005; K. Greiser, *Die Todesmärsche von Buchenwald*, Göttingen: Wallstein, 2008.

23 M. Broszat, 'The Concentration Camps 1933–45', in H. Krausnick and M. Broszat, *Anatomy of the SS State*, Reading: Granada, 1982, pp. 248–9.

24 'Sicherung der Konnzentrationslager', *International Military Tribunal* (IMT), PS-3683.

25 J. Marszalek, *Majdanek.Obóz koncentracyjny w Lublinie*, Warsaw: Wydawnictwo Interpress, 1981, p. 177; Zonik, *Anus belli*, p. 55; Orth, *Das System*, p. 271.

26 Zonik, *Anus belli*, pp. 45–7.

27 Interrogation of Oswald Pohl, WVHA Case, Yad Vashem Archives (YVA), N4/Proc/E, box 223, p. 1341.

28 Strzelecki, *Evacuation*, p. 128.

29 E. Dziadosz and Z. Leszczyńska, 'Ewakuacja obozy i wyzwolenie', in T. Mencla (ed.), *Majdanek 1941–1944*, Lublin: Wydawnictwo Lubelskie, 1991, pp. 399–406; Christoph

Dieckmann, 'Das Ghetto und das Konzentrationslager in Kaunas 1941–1944', in U. Herbert, K. Orth and C. Dieckmann (eds), *Die nationalsozialistischen Konzentrationslager. Entwicklung und Struktur*, vol.1, Göttingen: Wallstein Verlag, 1998, p. 458; A. Streim, 'Konzentrationslager auf dem Gebiet der Sowjetunion', *Dachauer Hefte* 5, November 1989, pp. 174–6; R. Steegmann, *Struthof. Le KL-Natzweiler et ses kommandos: une rébuleuse concentrationnaire des deux côtés du Rhin 1941–1945*, Strasbourg: Nuée Bleue, 2005, pp. 159–72.

30 Interrogation of Bassewitz-Behr, Feb. 12, 1946, and deposition of Max Pauly, 30 March 1946, TNA, WO 309/408; H. Kaienburg, *Das Konzentrationslager Neuengamme 1938–1945*, Bonn: J. H. W. Dietz Nachfolger, 1997, pp. 268–83.

31 Hermann Pister, commander of Buchenwald, made several clashing decisions between 2 April and 7 April 1945: to leave the camp intact and turn it over to the Americans or to evacuate all of the prisoners, some of them, or the Jewish prisoners only. Buchenwald Case, NARA, RG–153, box 243, folder 1, p.50; Interrogation of Hermann Pister, NARA, RG–153, box 256, p. 6; D. Blatman, 'The Death Marches, January–May 1945: Who Was Responsible for What?', *Yad Vashem Studies* 28, 2000, pp. 149–51. The commander of Ravensbrück, Fritz Suhren, also received vague orders in early 1945 from Richard Glücks or the HSSPF about the evacuation of prisoners from the satellite camps for which he was responsible, but the question of what to do with them and where to send them was totally unclear to him. Orth, *Das System*, pp. 288–9.

32 Testimony of Baldur von Schirach, 24 May 1946, IMT vol. XIV, p. 440.

33 Interrogation of Siegfried Uiberreither, 5 March 1946, Dokumentationsarchiv des österreichischen Widerstandes, 12.6Z7, pp. 6–7, 9, 11, 17–18.

34 Testimony of Rudolf Höß, IMT vol. XI, pp. 352–4. In the matter of Himmler's April 1945 directive and its effect on the fate of the prisoners in the last weeks of the war, see S. Záméčník, '"Kein Häftling darf lebend in die Hände des Feindes fallen". Zur Existentz des Himmler-Befehls vom 14–18 April 1945', *Dachauer Hefte* 1, 1985, pp. 219–31; E. Kupfer-Koberwitz, *Die Mächtigen und die Hilflosen. Als Häftling in Dachau*, Stuttgart: Friedrich Vorwerk, 1960, p. 260.

35 Testimony of Ernst Kaltenbrunner, IMT, NO-2366.

36 Neander, *Das Konzentrationslager Mittelbau*, p. 98.

37 Deposition of Hans Schurtz, former chief of Auschwitz *Politische Abteilung*, Prozess Höss, APMAB, Hd/16a, p. 115; Orth, *Das System*, pp. 277–8.

38 H. Boberach, 'Die Überführung von Soldaten des Heeres und der Luftwaffe in die SS-Totenkopfverbände zur Bewachung von Konzentrationslagern 1944', *Militärgeschichtliche Mitteilungen* 2, 1983, pp. 185–90; W. Sofsky, *The Order of Terror: The Concentration Camp*, Princeton, NJ: Princeton University Press, 1997, p. 102.

39 On the Volkssturm, see D. K. Yelton, *Hitler's Volkssturm: The Nazi Militia and the Fall of Germany 1944–1945*, Lawrence, KS: University Press of Kansas, 2002; K. Mammach, *Der Volkssturm. Das letzte Aufgebot 1944/45*, Cologne: Pahl-Rugenstein, 1981.

40 For example, 'Männer und Frauen in Hannover-Stadt und Land!', *Hannoversche Zeitung*, 30 March 1945; 'Achtet auf entwichene KZ-Häftlinge!', *Lüneburger Zeitung*, 11 April 1945.

41 In this matter, see G. W. Allport and L. Postman, *The Psychology of Rumor*, New York: Henry Holt and Company, 1947.

42 Dörr Case (see footnote 21), exhibits I, p. 169; Goldhagen, *Hitler's Willing Executioners*, pp. 335–54.

43 Dörr Case (see footnote 21), the court's ruling, p. 30.

44 Ibid., exhibits I, p. 180; the court's ruling ibid., pp. 77–9.

45 Testimony by Charlotte Sturmmer, May 13, 1945, ibid., exhibits I, pp. 71–2; Testimony of Herta Hasse-Breitmann, 13 May 1945, ibid., p. 77.

46 Testimony of Max Reimann, 16 November 1962, ibid, exhibits II, pp. 387–8.

47 Ibid., exhibits I, p. 161; the court's ruling ibid., pp. 40–1.

48 Testimony of Margarete Rycerz, 27 January 1965, ibid, exhibits II, p. 404.

49 Ibid., the court's ruling, p. 84.
50 In many cases the search and shutting down of escaped inmates was described by the manhunters who participated in that action as 'hunting zebras' or 'catching rabbits'. See *DDR-Justiz und NS-Verbrechen*, Amsterdam and Munich: Amsterdam University Press, K.G. Sauer Verlag, 2004, vol. 4, p. 260, vol. 5, pp. 730–1.
51 See J. Sémelin, *Purify and Destroy: The Political Uses of Massacre and Genocide*, New York: Columbia University Press, 2005, pp. 293–4.
52 M. Levene, 'Introduction', in M. Levene and P. Roberts (eds), *The Massacre in History*, New York, Oxford: Berghahn Books, 1999, pp. 5–6.
53 In this matter, see Z. Bauman, *Modernity and the Holocaust*, Cambridge: Polity Press, 1989, pp. 152–3.
54 D. L. Bergen, 'Death Throes and Killing Frenzies: A Response to Hans Mommsen's "The Dissolution of the Third Reich: Crisis Management and Collapse, 1943–1945"', *Bulletin of the German Historical Institute* 27, 2000, pp. 25–37.
55 K. Kwiet, 'Erziehung zum Mord – Zwei Beispiele zur Kontinuität der deutschen "Endlösung der Judenfrage"', in M. Grüner, R. Hachtmann and H. G. Haupt (eds), *Geschichte und Emanzipation. Festschrift für Reinhard Rürup*, Frankfurt, New York: Campus Verlag, 1999, pp. 436–8.
56 D. Gring, 'Das Massaker von Gardelegen', *Dachauer Hefte* 20, Oktober 2004, pp. 118–19.

9 The afterlife of the camps

Harold Marcuse

While the histories of most Nazi concentration camps are now fairly well known, what happened with them after liberation until their reincarnation as museums or memorial sites is generally not. Surveying the former Nazi camps that dotted Europe at the end of the war, we can say there are five basic uses to which they have been put since 1945. Chronologically the first use was to educate the local populace about the conditions in the camps as they were found at liberation. The very first camps to be liberated had been emptied of prisoners before the arrival of the Allied armies, but even there sufficient evidence of horrific atrocities remained that the liberators were moved to force local civilians to view the premises and participate in clean-up work. In addition to this punitive pedagogy, in those camps whose inmates had not been murdered or completely evacuated prior to liberation, such forced tours overlapped with the second use: nursing the hundreds, thousands, and even tens of thousands of survivors back to health. This use as a medical and recuperation facility usually lasted from several weeks to a few months, in some cases up to a year or more, until political conditions became suitable for the survivors to return to their home countries or emigrate to find new homes.

The third use was most common in occupied Germany, where the victorious Allies used larger camps, especially those close to urban centres, to imprison large numbers of Germans who fell into the 'automatic arrest' categories, until their trials or denazification hearings could be held. In some cases those judicial proceedings were held in the former camps as well, most notably in Dachau, where from November 1945 until August 1947 personnel from Dachau, Mauthausen, Flossenbürg, Buchenwald and Dora-Nordhausen were tried.[1] Although there were strong practical reasons for reusing the concentration camps as penal facilities, punitive education was undoubtedly a consideration, now directed at giving suspected perpetrators a taste of their own medicine, as opposed to enlightening the putative bystanders.

The fourth use harks back to the first, education, but with two differences: commemoration of the heroism or suffering of the victims became an important component, and this next phase of education was also what one might term retrospectively prospective – looking back to select and preserve certain aspects of a camp's history for the future. Explicit measures to preserve parts of former camps for educational use first occurred in countries that had been conquered and occupied by Nazi Germany, especially in those camps that had served as instruments of political repression, such as Auschwitz in Poland. Even there, however, the preservation and conversion to memorial sites took some time to implement, and often did not begin until the use as an internment camp was over.

The fifth fate tended to befall the more remote concentration camps and extermination centres, as well as the vast majority of the satellite camps, some of which were huge facilities for tens of thousands of inmates. They were simply abandoned and ignored for decades, often until the 1980s or 1990s, many of them until today.[2] Natzweiler in France and Gross Rosen in Poland are examples of more remote large camps, Gusen in Austria and Kaufering in Bavaria of huge satellite camps. This was also the fate of Belžec, Chełmno, Sobibór and Treblinka, the relatively remote 'Action Reinhardt' extermination centres in Poland that the Nazis dismantled and effaced in 1943–1944, before their retreat. The memorialization of those sites did not begin until the 1960s, as we will see below.

Although some country-based illustrated overviews about memorials at sites of Nazi persecution were published as early as the 1960s,[3] the scholarly literature about the postwar histories of the concentration camp sites did not begin until the 1980s, with Konnilyn Feig's *Hitler's Death Camps: The Sanity of Madness*, published in 1981.[4] Feig's book includes descriptions of and uses documents from many of the main camp memorial sites since she began visiting them in the early 1960s. Works by Detlef Garbe (1983) and Bernd Eichmann (1986) offer somewhat more detailed and up-to-date summaries of the histories of the main memorial sites, while the sites in West Germany were comprehensively cataloged by Ulrike Puvogel in a project sponsored by the Federal Centre for Political Education, which was published in 1987 (based on much shorter preliminary versions) and later updated for western Germany (1996) and the new eastern German states (1997).[5] The 1987 version contains references to the scant previously published literature, which was mostly in pamphlet and article form. Gisela Lehrke's 1987 dissertation on 'historical-political education at sites of resistance' was supported by a grant in parallel with Puvogel's documentation, while offering a more analytical approach.[6]

The 1990s saw the publication of geographically more extensive works such as Sybil Milton and Ira Nowinski's *In Fitting Memory* (1991), which includes an annotated bibliography;[7] James Young's *Texture of Memory* (1993), which offers some primary research on a few selected sites;[8] and the more journalistic overview by Judith Miller in *One by One by One* (1990).[9] Since the mid-1990s detailed scholarly anthologies or monographs have begun appearing about the postwar histories of some camps,[10] while the camp-based essays in the multi-volume reference work *Der Ort des Terrors* (2005–) include fairly detailed sections on the postwar histories of the main concentration camps that often draw on hitherto unpublished primary material.[11]

Liberation and punitive pedagogy: the media blitz

Most of the concentration camps liberated before April 1945 had been almost completely evacuated prior to the arrival of Allied troops.[12] These included Majdanek near Lublin in eastern Poland (24 July 1944),[13] Natzweiler-Struthof in France (November 1944),[14] and Gross Rosen near Wrocław (Breslau) in south-central Poland (13 February 1945).[15] The largest camp that was not fully evacuated during this early phase was Auschwitz, where about 7,600 inmates were still alive in its three main camps when Soviet troops entered the complex on 27 January 1945.[16] With an end to the war still at least months away, these liberated prisoners were given initial aid and then released to find their own ways home, often taking circuitous routes, as the odyssey recounted by Auschwitz survivor Primo Levi attests.[17] Levi also describes how, on the morning after liberation, 20 Polish civilians summoned by the Soviets began to clear away corpses and clean the camp, with additional local residents arriving in the following days.[18] The use of local labour for clean-up and burial details had already been practised at Majdanek, as surviving film footage attests.[19] Such civilian labour details are documented for numerous camps liberated later as well, such as Belsen in April 1945[20] and Sachsenhausen in early May.[21]

The Allied response changed dramatically in early April, when Allied army units overran, captured or received in surrender the first unevacuated camps. Ohrdruf, a Buchenwald satellite camp liberated on 4 April 1945, tipped the balance from clean-up to forced tours. US soldiers found up to 100 charred and machine-gunned bodies lying about, over 3,200 corpses in mass graves, and more corpses stacked in various sheds.[22] On 11 April, US troops entered Dora-Nordhausen, finding 3,000 corpses and 700 surviving inmates.[23] The next day, Allied Supreme Commander Eisenhower, along with Generals Bradley and Patton, toured Ohrdruf. Afterward they ordered 2,000 townspeople to bury the dead. That same day, US forces liberated Buchenwald, with about 19,000 unevacuated survivors,[24] and Belsen's commandant Kramer surrendered his camp to British forces, which entered it on 15 April to find about 10,000 corpses and 55,000 survivors, who were dying at a rate of approximately 500 per day.[25]

Also on 12 April, General Patton, after visiting Buchenwald, ordered the mayor of Weimar to send at least 1,000 Weimar citizens to tour the main camp the next day.[26] On 19 April, after more reports of horrific scenes from liberated branch camps had come in, Eisenhower telegraphed Washington and London, requesting that delegations of US congressmen, British members of parliament and journalists be sent to Germany to tour the camps. Thus began what I call the 'media blitz': the blanketing in the first weeks of May 1945 of the US, British and German public spheres with newspaper, magazine and radio reports, posters, brochures and films about concentration camp atrocities.[27] Whereas Allied governments had previously refrained from corroborating reports about atrocities in the camps for fear of increasing anxieties among family members about the treatment of captured soldiers, a full-scale official public relations campaign was now launched.[28] This media blitz peaked in May 1945 and continued during the summer, when it served to justify a relatively harsh occupation regime. This informational campaign experienced a brief revival during the main Nuremberg Trial beginning in November 1945 through early 1946.[29] Then, as the conflict between the capitalist and communist blocs re-emerged in 1947, occupation policy softened and the camps faded from public attention, with, for example, decreasing media coverage of the trials of concentration camp personnel.[30]

Displaced persons' camps

Parallel to the punitive pedagogical use of the camps at liberation was the urgent need to care for the survivors, who also needed to be housed until they could return to their home countries. When the war in Europe ended on 8 May 1945, on German soil there were approximately 6 million foreign slave labourers, 2 million prisoners of war, and 750,000 concentration camp inmates, most of them foreigners.[31] While the vast majority of these people were eager to return home as soon as their health permitted, several groups posed particular problems, including Jews wishing to emigrate to Palestine, Soviets who had fought on the side of the Germans, and non-communist Poles wary of their new Soviet-friendly government. For these groups, the United Nations Relief and Rehabilitation Administration (UNRRA) set up displaced persons (DP) camps, at first in the prisoner compounds of some former concentration camps, but soon moving them to adjacent SS or German army installations that had better infrastructure and fewer trappings of prisons.

The shift away from this use of the former camps accelerated when a July 1945 report by Earl Harrison, the US representative on the Intergovernmental Committee on Refugees, to US president Truman, alerted a broader public to the need for longer-term DP camps. The crucial passage from that report, which US president Truman relayed to Allied Supreme Commander Eisenhower in an August letter published shortly thereafter in the *New York Times*, stated: 'we appear to be treating the Jews as the Nazis treated them except that we do not exterminate them'.[32] In the wake of that pronouncement most DPs were moved out of the former concentration camps.

After liberation, Belsen and Dachau had the largest DP populations. In Belsen the concentration camp barracks were burnt down in mid-May, after many thousands of survivors had been moved to Belsen camps II, III, IV and V.[33] In May, liberated Soviet POWs and slave labourers were moved to the nearby Fallingbostel camp, and most western Europeans returned home. This left 10,000–12,000 mostly Polish Jews, who were housed in the German army barracks of camp II, which became known as Belsen-Höhne. While the number of Jewish DPs in camps throughout the British zone fell dramatically after the founding of the state of Israel in May 1948, the Belsen-Höhne DP camp did not close until March 1950. During that period, in spite of the Belsen DPs' focus on emigration, a centre of Jewish culture in Germany developed there.[34]

In Dachau, by early June 1945 most of the nearly 40 national groups had returned home, leaving about 2,000 Catholic Poles, over a thousand Hungarians and Romanians and a few hundred Russians who did not want to return to their communist-controlled homelands, as well as an unknown but large number of Jews.[35] US military rabbi Abraham Klausner was instrumental in improving the lives of Jewish DPs in Dachau and other camps in Bavaria in May and early June 1945, by ensuring that all Jewish survivors were moved out of former concentration camps to a hospital in the St Ottilien convent about 35 miles away, or to predominantly Jewish DP camps such as the one set up in the former German army barracks at Landsberg.[36] Some of the Catholic Polish survivors remaining in Dachau were employed by the US army as guards for German 'automatic arrest' suspects who were being rounded up over the summer. We know almost nothing about what happened to those DPs who remained in or at the Dachau camp after early July 1945, when it formally became War Crimes Enclosure no. 1 of the US counterintelligence corps.[37]

As for other former camps, Neuengamme housed DPs for about four weeks after the end of the war,[38] and Flossenbürg had 1,500–2,500 mostly Polish residents until the end of 1947.[39] Some former Nazi camps, *after* their subsequent use for interning Nazi suspects, were converted to long-term settlements for refugees uprooted after the end of the war. In addition to Dachau, which we will examine in greater detail below, Westerbork in Holland served that purpose. Members of the National-Socialist Movement of the Netherlands NSB were interned there until 1948, after which it was used first by the Dutch military, then from 1950 to 1971 to house refugees from Dutch colonies.[40]

Internment camps

Allied proposals for interning German suspects as the country was conquered date back in various forms to 1944.[41] The plans were consolidated in paragraph II.A.5 of the Potsdam Agreement of 2 August 1945.[42] Well before that pronouncement, however, of necessity some former concentration camps were already being used to hold captured camp personnel. Occupation policymakers, in an attempt to prevent sabotage or even insurgent movements, had already ordered mass internments. For example, in 'Operation Tally-Ho', a two-day raid beginning in the night of 21–22 July 1945, 80,000 German suspects in the US zone were rounded up and interned.[43]

The following list illustrates the extent to which the former main concentration camps were used for internment:[44]

- Buchenwald: NKVD (Soviet People's Commissariat for Internal Affairs) Special Camp No. 2, 20 August 1945–February 1950; up to 16,371 inmates (usually 10,000–12,000; 28,455 total over time);[45]
- Dachau, US Counterintelligence Corps War Crimes Enclosure no. 1, early July 1945–31 August 1948; capacity 30,000 inmates;[46]
- Esterwegen, British No. 9 Civil Internment Camp, then from 1 July 1946 to July 1947 No. 101 Prison Camp with up to 2,612 suspected war criminals, mainly former camp guards;[47]

- Flossenbürg, US Military Government internment camp, July 1945–April 1946; up to 4,000 inmates;[48]
- Neuengamme, British No. 6 Civil Internment Camp, June 1945–13 August 1948; up to 8,000 inmates;[49]
- Sachsenhausen, NKVD Special Camp No. 7, 7 August 1945–January 1950; capacity 14,000, c. 60,000 total over time.[50]

Conditions in these internment camps were harsh, especially during the 'hunger winters' of 1945–1946 and 1946–1947 when food and heating fuel was scarce throughout occupied Germany. However, the internees of these camps did not suffer from mistreatment, overwork and intentional physical abuse like their concentration camp predecessors, but rather from inactivity and neglect. The conditions in camps in the US and British occupation zones were harsh, especially in terms of low rations, but acceptable, without unusual mortality rates.[51] However, in the Soviet camps the death rate due to malnutrition and disease at times rose to staggering proportions. Over the five years of the Sachsenhausen internment camp's existence, for example, approximately 12,000 of the 60,000 prisoners died.[52] This 1:5 death rate compares to the 1:4.7 death rate of officially registered inmates in the Sachsenhausen concentration camp.[53]

The use of former concentration camps as internment camps was never intended to be more than a temporary solution until denazification reviews and trials could be conducted.[54] As the number of internees dwindled and conditions in postwar Germany stabilized, efforts to memorialize the camps and those who had died in them began to gain traction. The scope of these initiatives varied widely, however, from *ad hoc* suggestions by groups of liberated prisoners, to state-sponsored projects. The first camps to be preserved as memorials were not the first camps that had been erected, but the first ones to be liberated. Formerly Nazi-occupied countries such as Poland, Czechoslovakia and Belgium soon passed laws stipulating that former concentration camps be preserved.[55]

Poland: from the martyrdom of Poles to the extermination of Jews

Eight major German camps were set up on Polish soil: the four concentration camps Auschwitz, Majdanek, Gross Rosen and Stutthof, and the four Action Reinhardt extermination centres Bełżec, Chełmno, Sobibór and Treblinka. By the 1960s, the Polish government had included three of them among the five state museums overseen by its Advisory Board of the Museums of Martyrology.[56] Reflecting postwar Poland's emphasis on Polish resistance and victimization, those official museums included Auschwitz, Majdanek and Stutthof. The extermination centres, which were not only much more remote but had also been dismantled and planted over by the Nazis in 1943–1944, were not memorialized until the 1960s, and then only with more or less elaborate sculptures and small exhibitions. Since the 1990s, with private and institutional help from the United States, the

Sobibór and Bełżec memorial sites have been expanded and now include explicit documentation of the extermination of Jewish Poles that was carried out there.

On 1 May 1945, even before Germany's surrender, Poland's provisional government placed 'those parts of the concentration camp in Oświęcim that were connected to the immediate destruction of millions of people' under the administration of its Ministry of Culture and Art, which was also charged with developing a concept for a museum.[57] The Ministry approved a formal proposal in February 1946, and by April camp survivors were working to create a museum, which was officially opened on 14 June 1947, the seventh anniversary of the arrival of the first prisoners.[58] In July 1947 the Polish parliament passed a law stipulating that all remains in the camp must be preserved. Around 1950 a small gravestone-like memorial was erected by private initiative near Birkenau crematorium II. Its simple inscription in Polish, Yiddish and Hebrew focused on the Jewish victims of Birkenau: 'In memory of the millions of Jewish martyrs and fighters, exterminated in the camp Auschwitz-Birkenau by the National Socialist race murderers, 1940–1945'.[59] The original exhibition in Auschwitz I was expanded first in 1950, and again in 1955 after Stalin's death. At that time it filled five of the two-storey stone barracks of the Auschwitz main camp.

The tenth anniversary of the liberation of Auschwitz in 1955 provided the impetus to replace that first private Jewish memorial with a more official one at the far end of the 'ramp' in view of the entrance gate. The new memorial was a 3 metres high, nearly cubical 'urn' on a plinth.[60] We know little about it, except that it was conceived as a temporary solution to be replaced by a memorial that better reflected the magnitude of the events in Birkenau.[61]

Guidelines for an international design competition, published by the Auschwitz survivors' organization in 1957, underscored the legal requirement that the remains of the camp not be altered. The selection committee met in April 1958 to judge 426 designs submitted by artists from 31 countries. After two additional limited competitions, a hybrid design was chosen and finally completed in May 1967. From 1960 to 1968 a number of exhibitions designed by national organizations were opened in various barracks. A number of modifications to the Birkenau and Auschwitz I sites were made in 1994–1995, after the fall of the communist government in 1989, including new signage, new inscriptions on the 1967 Birkenau memorial, and the revamping of several national exhibitions.[62]

The early realization of the Auschwitz memorial site and museum was paralleled at Majdanek, the second largest Nazi concentration camp in Poland, which was located only three miles from the major city of Lublin.[63] In July 1944, Majdanek became the first Nazi concentration camp to be liberated. Evacuations had reduced the number of inmates to about 700 before the Germans abandoned the camp as the Red Army approached. The Germans left behind mountains of evidence of the horrific crimes they had perpetrated there, for example more than 750,000 shoes, hundreds of cubic metres of human ash, and intact gas chambers whose walls were still stained by prussic acid gas. Already in November 1944, the provisionally governing Polish Committee of National Liberation declared the former camp to be a 'memorial site of the martyrdom of the peoples of Poland and other nations', a decision confirmed by the Polish parliament in 1947.

A first historical exhibition displaying the remains found in the camp opened in 1945, and in 1949 the site was planted over with trees. In 1954 a new exhibition with a manifestly pro-communist orientation was opened. It lasted until 1961, when a major overhaul of the site was conducted. The trees from 1949 were felled, preservation work was carried out on all of the buildings in the prisoners' part of the camp (including the barracks, gas chambers, crematorium, guard towers and fencing), while the buildings in the SS garrison were torn down. A redesigned main exhibition opened in 1962; ten years later it was moved into a group of new buildings located closer to the road accessing the camp. A fourth, post-communist exhibition replaced it in 1999.

Gross Rosen, liberated in February 1945, remained in the possession of the Soviet army until its extensive intact remains were turned over to Polish authorities in March 1947.[64] That September, a competition for a mausoleum design was conducted, for which a cornerstone was already laid in November, although the memorial itself was not dedicated until 1953. The winning design was a bronze statue of a powerful standing man looking upward, set on an inscribed pedestal in front of a squat, pyramidally-topped tower mausoleum made of granite from the camp's quarry and containing the ashes of victims of the camp. During a 1963 renovation the heroic statue was replaced by a large bowl. The former camp grounds were placed under the administration of the Auschwitz museum in 1950, and a small exhibition was opened in the left wing of the gatehouse building in 1958. In 1963, when the ensemble was placed on the national registry of historic sites, extensive repairs were carried out on the camp buildings. Trees and bushes were removed from along the camp fence and the SS casino was torn down, except for some offices where the site watchman lived. In 1970, responsibility for the site was transferred to the Historical Museum in Wrocław, which began to collect documents and artefacts about the camp's history. The Wrocław museum rebuilt the SS casino in 1978–1982 to house a new exhibition and film screening room. In 1983, at the urging of camp survivors and local authorities, the Gross Rosen site was given the status of a state museum, which, however, it only held until 1999, when responsibility returned to the provincial level.

Stutthof, about 30 miles east of Gdańsk and two miles from the Baltic coast, is less remote than Gross Rosen, and it attained the status of a state museum earlier and permanently, in 1961, with a first exhibition opening in 1962.[65] The museum, installed in the crematorium building by artist Wiktor Tolkin, tells the history of the camp. Artefacts from the daily life of the camp are displayed in the remaining barracks. Also designed by Tolkin and dedicated in May 1968, the central memorial is located near the gas chamber and crematorium. It is comprised of a wall 48 metres long and 3.5 metres high, bearing bas reliefs and containing a reliquary with incompletely burnt human bones. It culminates in an 11 metre high sculpted block with figures symbolizing resistance. In 1967 the Ministry of Culture and Art took responsibility for the site, and opened an archive and research library. In the first dozen years of the museum's existence, the number of visitors, including many Polish school classes, increased more than tenfold, from 62,000 in 1962 to 257,000 in 1968, to 650,000 in 1974.

Austria: from eradication to reluctant preservation

The early memorialization of Mauthausen in Austria followed a similar but in revealing ways slightly different path from Auschwitz. Austrian support for Nazi Germany's annexation of their country in 1938 had been enthusiastic and widespread, and after 1945 a substantial proportion of the populace still identified with the perpetrators. Thus many Austrians preferred to eradicate, not preserve reminders of the system of repression and murder.[66]

When US tanks rolled up to Mauthausen and its nearby branch camps on 5 May 1945, they found approximately 20,000 survivors, many of whom were so sick that thousands died in the followings days.[67] Hundreds of local residents were brought in to bury the dead in mass graves. No detailed history of the camp over the next months has been written, but we do know that already on 16 May 1945 a ceremony was held to honour 2,500 Soviet survivors who were returning home. According to a 9 July agreement about the borders of zones of occupation, on 24 July US troops began to withdraw from the area, and the Soviet troops who replaced them used the barracks of the presumably empty camp as housing from autumn 1945 until May 1946. At a ceremony commemorating the first anniversary of liberation, which was held outside the Soviet-occupied camp, ground was broken for a planned memorial. However, that external location soon became obsolete, since the Soviets approved a March 1947 request from the Austrian national government to return the camp in order to erect a memorial site 'for the wantonly murdered fighters for the freedom of nations'. An April 1947 inspection tour of the site, which had been abandoned for almost a year, revealed that it had been used for grazing cows, growing potatoes and dumping rubbish, and that many of the buildings had been scavenged by the local populace. At that time there was extensive debate about whether the camp should be restored or 'beautified'; ultimately, economic considerations were paramount in the decision that the camp would be cleaned up and preserved, but neither restored nor prettified with planting.

When the camp was transferred to Austrian control on 20 June 1947, a first memorial plaque was mounted on one of the entrance towers.[68] In February 1948 the Soviets erected a slender stele monument between the headquarters building and the camp gate for Soviet General Karbyschew, who had been executed in the camp in February 1945. In May 1949 a central memorial was dedicated on the former roll-call square in the camp itself: a plain stone sarcophagus with the Latin inscription, 'From the fate of the dead the living shall learn'. The founding in 1953 of the International Mauthausen Committee created an organization that could press for expanding the memorial site. One of its first proposals, initiated in 1951 before the official creation of the organization (and never realized), was the construction of a huge 34 by 38 metre ossuary building, whose 8 metre square and 18 metre high tower would contain the bones of all of the camp victims buried in cemeteries and mass graves in the area. For the tenth anniversary of liberation in 1955 a large monument was completed for the 'Russian camp', and trilingual German, French and Russian signage was installed. Beginning with France in 1949 and Poland in 1956, and ending with West Germany in 1983, about a dozen countries – usually organizations of camp survivors took responsibility – erected memorials on the terrain where the barracks of the SS camp had stood, between the camp wall and the granite quarry where prisoners had been worked to death.[69] In 1970 the first plaque for a non-national group, namely for the female victims of the camp, was mounted, followed by a memorial for the camp's murdered Jews in 1975, a plaque for homosexuals in 1984, and one for Sinti and Roma in 1998.[70]

Since the 1980s, increasing numbers of secondary-school students visit the memorial site as part of a recommended curriculum, their numbers climbing from some 6,000 in 1970 to 16,000 in 1975 and 65,000 in 1985, which is roughly equivalent to the number of pupils visiting other Austrian national museums each year.[71] From the 1970s the museum was increasingly visited by Austrian army officers as part of their education. The suggestion of the survivors' organization that new recruits be sworn in at the memorial site was approved by the defence minister in 1983, and since then the induction of soldiers into the Austrian army takes place in the Mauthausen memorial site. After a number of high-publicity events, such as a visit by the Pope in 1988 and a concert in the quarry by the Vienna Philharmonic in 2000, a reform study was initiated by the government. It resulted in the construction of a large new visitors' centre, completed in 2003, innovations such as expanded but less intrusive signage throughout the site, and a project to interview the remaining 800 Mauthausen survivors.

West Germany: survivor mobilization against state hindrance

The development of memorial sites at the four main concentration camps on the territory that later became West Germany followed a haphazard trajectory with some similarities to that of Mauthausen. However, since cultural matters in the West German federal system are administered at the state level, each of the states of Lower Saxony, Bavaria and Hamburg left its own stamp on its memorial sites. Not until 1995, when a national foundation for concentration camp memorial sites was created to deal with the funding of the formerly national-level East German concentration camp memorial sites after unification, was there institutionalized support at the national level. As in Austria, lobbying efforts by camp survivors were crucial at every stage of the creation and expansion of the educational memorial sites.

In Bergen-Belsen the camp barracks had been burnt down shortly after liberation in an attempt to curb rampant epidemics. Although little was left of the camp buildings, the British army quickly decided to preserve some remains of the camp, as demonstrated by contemporary signs in English and German that indicated the punitive pedagogical impulse behind the measure:

> This is the site of the infamous Belsen concentration camp, liberated by the British on 15th April 1945. 10,000 unburied dead were found here, another 13,000 have since died. All of them victims of the German New Order in Europe and an example of Nazi Kultur.[72]

In April 1946, the Central Jewish Committee British Zone (i.e. Jewish survivors still living in the adjacent former army barracks) dedicated a traditional memorial, a square column crowned by a small stone sphere, in the field between the mass graves. Later that year or in 1947, the British occupiers had German POWs erect a larger memorial, an obelisk with a long wall, which was completed by the Lower Saxony government in the following years. That memorial was dedicated by West German president Heuss in April 1952.[73] The 25 metre high obelisk was accompanied by a 50 metre long stone wall bearing inscriptions from 14 of the 40 countries whose citizens had died in the Belsen camp.[74] In the second half of the 1950s, when Anne Frank's diary was meeting with great acclaim as a book and on stage and screen, many thousands of German and foreign young people made 'pilgrimages' to the site of her death.[75] In the wake of this attention, the Lower Saxony state government commissioned a history of the camp and a modest 'document house', which opened in 1966.[76] It was replaced by a larger new exhibition building including pedagogical facilities in 1990, and expanded once again in 2007.[77]

In Dachau, as in Belsen, the occupying military authorities ordered the local government to erect a memorial, which also experienced a number of protracted delays. In June 1945 the Associated Press reported that German civilians would erect two 15 metre high columns topped by a cross and a star of David at a mass grave near the camp, where thousands of victims of the camp were buried.[78] The columns were to be made of stone from the Nazi party rally grounds in Nuremberg. This plan was abandoned shortly thereafter, when the German designer's affiliation with the Nazi party became known. Shortly before the inception of the first trial of concentration camp personnel in Dachau in November 1945, survivors set up a small exhibition in some of the rooms of the crematorium/gas chamber building, and another proposal for a memorial was presented to the public: a model of a gigantic 35 metres wide and 26 metres high 'monument of liberation' was displayed in Dachau Town Hall during a 9 November 1945 commemorative ceremony. That proposal was subsequently criticized on symbolic, aesthetic and practical grounds, and was soon scrapped as well. After a memorial competition conducted in 1946 yielded no satisfactory results, the project was quietly forgotten.

At the same time the drive behind rigorous denazification was waning, and in a series of amnesties the Dachau internment camp gradually emptied. Echoing the Nazi propaganda image of the concentration camps, in January 1948 the Bavarian parliament unanimously passed a resolution petitioning the US Military government to transfer the camp to Bavaria to use as a 'work camp ... for the re-education of work-shy elements to productive citizens'.[79] By the time that the transfer took place that summer, the Cold War was heating up and the flow of ethnic German refugees crossing the border from Czechoslovakia into Bavaria increased to a flood. The Bavarian government decided instead to convert most of the partially modified concentration camp barracks into apartments for refugee families, with some serving as stores, health and dental clinics, workshops, a school, offices, a communal bathing facility, and a cinema. Before winter set in, about 600 families moved into the newly renovated former concentration camp barracks, where most of them would remain for the next 15 years, until camp survivors succeeded in pressuring the Bavarian government to relocate them and convert the entire site into a memorial.

In the meantime, the memorial mandated by the US army had been forgotten until September 1949, when a mining operation uncovered several human skeletons not far from a mass grave of Dachau inmates.[80] To quell the ensuing scandal, in 1950 the small exhibition in the crematorium was revamped, and a bronze statue of an 'unknown concentration camp inmate' was placed near the entrance. After another competition a more modest memorial at the mass grave was erected between 1950 and 1952: a 10.5 metre high octagonal stone hall. However, by the time of its completion international attention had waned. The Bavarian Ministry of Finance, in response to petitions from city and county officials, had the crematorium exhibition removed in 1953, and in 1955 the Dachau county governor introduced a bill into parliament to have the crematorium itself torn down. These initiatives prompted the camp survivors to form an international organization in 1955 to push for the preservation of the camp as a memorial site. Their tenacity gradually met with success, with a temporary exhibition reinstalled in the crematorium in 1960 and the relocation of the ethnic German refugee families to nearby housing projects after 1963. Although the survivors' desire to preserve some of the extensively modified barracks was not fulfilled, and the US army did not relinquish its control of the former camp prison, the west wing of the camp administration building and the entry gatehouse (which were all part of the US Eastman Barracks sited in the former SS camp), in 1965 the memorial site was opened. It had a museum in the central wing of the large administration building near the camp entrance, and two barracks were reconstructed for demonstration purposes, one with interior furnishings representing three phases of the camp's history. In 1968 a large, central international memorial was dedicated on the roll-call square, based on a design selected during an international competition in 1958–1959.

As in Mauthausen, throughout the 1970s and 1980s the number of visitors to the Dachau museum, especially school classes, increased sharply, in Dachau from about 350,000 visitors per year in the early 1970s to 900,000 in the late 1980s.[81] The opposition of Dachau city officials to expanding the camp's pedagogical infrastructure was more tenacious than that of the state of Bavaria. The city managed to delay the creation of a youth hostel from its first proposal in 1970 for almost three decades until 1998. By that time the 1965 exhibition was somewhat out-of-date, and the Bavarian state police, which had taken over the former SS camp from the US army in 1971, had relinquished the gatehouse and the west wing of the museum building to the memorial site. This prompted a complete redesign of the museum, which reopened in 2003. The relocation of the memorial site entrance to the original camp gatehouse, planned by the survivors since 1959, was completed in 2005, and a new visitors' centre outside the former camp opened in 2008.

As in Dachau, when the internment camp in Neuengamme emptied in 1947, the military government prepared to transfer it back to local authorities, who were eager to use it as a prison.[82] Unlike Dachau, their plan was not overtaken by a massive influx of refugees, and a prison was opened in the brick buildings on the site in 1948. By 1950 the concentration camp barracks had been torn down to enable construction of the new prison, while concentration camp workshops were reused as work sites for prison inmates, and SS residences as housing for prison personnel. A massive youth penal complex on the adjacent site of the brick factory was completed in 1970. After years of protest by camp survivors and local support groups, in 1989 the Hamburg Senate decreed that both prisons would be closed and relocated.[83] The 1950 prison was ultimately closed in June 2003, and the 1970 facility in February 2006.

In the intervening decades, all memorial activity had to take place outside the former Neuengamme *Schutzhaftlager*. In 1953 pressure from French survivors supported by British occupation officials led the city of Hamburg to dedicate a first memorial, a 7 metre high tapered cylinder bearing the simple inscription 'To the Victims 1938–1945', on the site of the former camp garden.[84] The survivors formed an international association in 1958, and, when they learnt in 1960 of plans to expand the prison even further, proposed a much more elaborate memorial with national inscriptions. In 1965 local officials again pre-empted the survivors' plan with a much simpler alternative, a 27 metre high rectangular stele with a stone inscription wall near the access road. The engravers chiselling the inscription made a mistake that reveals the level of misconception in the 1960s about how bad conditions in the Nazi camps had been: they dropped a zero from the number of victims, so that 55,000 became 5,500.[85] The survivors, who were disappointed by this simple design, were allowed to add an abstract bronze sculpture of a fallen, emaciated 'deportee'. After much more lobbying and unfavourable publicity, the Hamburg government added a small 'document house' nearby in 1981.[86] In 1995, when a new exhibition was opened in the former camp workshops, the document house was turned into a 'house of commemoration', hung with banners listing the names of Neuengamme's victims.[87]

After the liberation of Flossenbürg on 23 April 1945 medical facilities were set up for the 1,500–1,600 inmates who had been left behind from the 16,000 inmates left in the camp on 20 April.[88] While some of the corpses that had accumulated in the final days of the camp were being burnt in the crematorium, the local populace was put to work burying inmates who had lived until liberation, but who were still dying at a rate of 30 per day during the first week thereafter. Contemporaneous with the use of parts of the camp for interning Nazi suspects from July 1945 to April 1946, other parts served until 1948 as a United Nations Relief and Rehabilitation Administration (UNRRA) displaced persons camp, primarily for Catholic Poles who did not want to return to Soviet-dominated Poland. This group of camp survivors initiated the first memorials in the Flossenbürg camp.

In June 1946 a Committee for Erecting the Monument and Chappel (this was the spelling in the group's printed letterhead) in Concentration Camp Flossenbürg was constituted. It included representatives of the refugees in the UNRRA camp, local mayors and town administrators, and businessmen. Although the committee was never able to attain official recognition by the military government or the United Nations (it unsuccessfully tried to place the site under UN protection), it did succeed in creating a number of memorials. Several watchtowers were dismantled and their bricks used to build a chapel to 'Jesus in Prison' attached to a remaining watchtower. In the 'valley of death' leading away from the chapel, human ash from the camp was piled into a large pyramid and covered with turf. An adjacent 'square of nations' was marked by stone plaques bearing the insignia of the nations whose citizens had died in Flossenbürg.[89] On the rectangular brick chimney of the crematorium, an inscription in Polish and English – '1938–1945 were buried in the concentration camp Flossenbürg' – headed a list of 18 nations (including 'Jewish'), followed by the number of deaths as determined by the memorial committee. Listed in decreasing order from 26,430 Russians to two Americans (soldiers who died during liberation), they totalled 73,296 (the correct total is now estimated to be 30,000[90]). This sign did not last long, however, and later incarnations of the camp as a memorial site never again presented this level of detail about the death toll or horrific conditions that had prevailed in the Nazi camp.

The state of Bavaria took over the UNRRA camp in 1947, and used it to house refugee families from former Silesia, East Prussia and the Sudetenland.[91] In 1958 the village of Flossenbürg took over ownership of some parts of the former camp and began to sell off the barracks. In 1963 the town council decided to tear down most of the camp prison building, while other stone buildings were rented to local businesses. The former SS mess hall was turned into a restaurant, the camp laundry into offices, and both the massive camp *Kommandantur* and the administration building of the DESt (German Earth and Stone Works), an SS company that had run the camp quarry, were converted into apartments for low-income residents. In 1979 a shabby exhibition was installed in the unheated remaining cells of the former camp prison; it was improved in 1984, when a local school teacher was commissioned to offer tours upon request. An initiative by foreign and German youth groups, begun in 1995, finally prompted the Bavarian government to purchase more of the remaining camp buildings, remove some of the postwar construction from the site, and install a much expanded exhibition in the former kitchen and laundry buildings. That work was completed in July 2007.[92]

East Germany: state heroization vs. survivor preservation

In contrast to West Germany, where the development of educational memorial sites was characterized by survivors' grass-roots lobbying efforts gradually overcoming resistance in the local populace and bureaucracy, in East Germany the construction of memorial sites in former concentration camps was directed centrally by the national government. 'Anti-fascist resistance', embodied by communists who had suffered and died in the camps, was a cornerstone of the new socialist state's legitimacy.[93] Buchenwald, where some of the most prominent communist prisoners, including party leader and former presidential candidate Ernst Thälmann, had been imprisoned and murdered, played a leading role.

In July 1949, before the closure of the Soviet internment camp in February 1950, and even before the establishment of the state of East Germany in October 1949, Soviet military government told the German association of former persecutees VVN (Vereinigung der Verfolgten des Naziregimes) 'to install a national museum in Buchenwald', modelled after those in Auschwitz and Theresienstadt.[94] Efforts thereafter concentrated on two areas: a large site encompassing several mass graves overlooking Weimar on the opposite side of the hill, and the former camp itself. After a national competition in 1952, top-level SED (Socialist Unity Party) politicians increasingly took the initiative away from the VVN.[95] State officials worked with various artists and architects to design and build a 55 metre high bell tower with a paved trapezoidal procession route connecting three funnel-shaped mass graves, ending at a larger-than-life sized group of eleven bronze figures at the base of the tower. This monumental memorial was dedicated in September 1958. During that period the barracks of the former camp were torn down, a network of interpretative signs erected, and a large museum of 'anti-fascist resistance' installed in the two-storey former camp laundry. As an official National Site of Commemoration and Warning (Nationale Mahn- und Gedenkstätte), mandatory visits by school classes and swearing-in ceremonies for army conscripts were held there. In contrast to the rising numbers of visitors during the 1970s and 1980s in Dachau and Mauthausen, the Buchenwald figures remained relatively constant at around 400,000 per year from 1960 until the unification of Germany in 1989–1990.[96] After East Germany became part of the Federal Republic of Germany in 1990 the museum and memorial site were reoriented away from a focus on resistance to a more victim-centred paradigm. In spite of strong opposition from communist camp survivors, in 1995 a redesigned exhibition about the concentration camp was opened, again in the former camp laundry, as was a newly constructed museum about the history of the postwar Soviet internment camp, located outside the camp perimeter near previously unmarked internment camp graves.[97]

Soon after the Buchenwald memorial site was completed, the national memorial sites in Ravensbrück and Sachsenhausen followed suit. As in Buchenwald, various memorialization attempts in those two former camps in the late 1940s and early 1950s led only to provisional solutions. Not until 1955, when the East German national government decided that there were to be three national memorial sites and created a central committee to oversee nationwide fund-raising efforts, did concerted efforts to create permanent memorial sites begin.

The next memorial site to be completed, in September 1959, was at the Ravensbrück concentration camp for women inmates about 35 miles northwest of Berlin, with a first exhibition in the former camp prison ('bunker') opening the following year.[98] The main artistic memorial, 'Carrier', a 4 metre high bronze sculpture of a female prisoner holding the drooping body of a dead comrade, is set atop a 7 metre tall pylon on a stone platform extending into an adjacent lake, above the spot where ashes from the crematorium had been dumped. In 1984 the museum in the 'bunker' was replaced by the Antifascist Resistance Fighters' Museum in the former SS administration building, which had been used by the Soviet army until 1977. From 1982 to 1984 the former camp prison was converted to house 17 'exhibitions of the nations' designed by countries whose citizens had been imprisoned in Ravensbrück. After German unification in 1990, three additional non-national rooms were added: for the participants of the 20 July 1944 assassination attempt on Hitler who had been imprisoned in Ravensbrück (1991), for Jews (1992) and for Sinti and Roma (1994).

Sachsenhausen, on the eastern outskirts of Berlin, which was much larger and more central both as a camp and as a memorial site, was not opened as a memorial site until 1961. After the Soviets turned their internment camp on the site over to the East German authorities in 1950, East German army units were stationed in the SS section of the camp, while the unused prisoners' compound fell into disrepair.[99] In 1953 the crematorium was blown up, and prior to a commemorative ceremony in the camp in May 1954 most of the former prisoners barracks were demolished. At that time, while survivors were planning to create a memorial site, police trainees used bricks from the former camp prison to construct a provisional memorial on the roll-call square.[100]

Since most of the barracks had been razed without their knowledge or approval, the Sachsenhausen survivors were forced to revise their memorial plan for the entire site.[101] As in Buchenwald, their wish to preserve and rebuild parts of the site so as to represent the daily life of the inmates came into conflict with the vision of state planners who wanted a more heroic memorialization.[102] A collective of East German architects who had submitted designs for Buchenwald recommended that 'In the camps on German soil it will be good to express the victory (*Überwindung*) over SS rule by dismantling and demolishing the remains and replacing them with a planned design.'

Thus the architects legitimized the continued demolition of structures on the site, much to the chagrin of the survivors.[103] The final result, dedicated in April 1961, turned the entire triangular prisoners' compound into an aesthetic ensemble. A wide opening in the central axis of the main camp street allows entering visitors to see the 40 metre tall reinforced concrete tower near the apex of the triangle at the opposite side of the camp. At its base is a 4–5 metre high heroic sculpture 'Liberation', depicting a Soviet soldier with his arms around the shoulders of two strong inmates standing slightly in front of him. A second memorial sculpture in bronze is set among the ruins of the Sachsenhausen crematorium and execution site nearby, outside the triangle's perimeter. Only moderately larger than life size, it depicts a standing and a bent-over inmate holding a cloth supporting the corpse of a comrade.

Three museums were opened in Sachsenhausen in 1961. The first, devoted to everyday life in the camp, resistance, and liberation, was installed in the former prisoners' kitchen, while a Museum of the European Peoples' Antifascist Struggle for Freedom, with 19 individual exhibitions, each devoted to a different country, was installed in a new building outside the camp gate. Finally, after protests from Jewish survivors in Israel since the late 1950s, a Museum of Resistance Fighters and the Suffering of Jewish Citizens was installed in two barracks reconstructed from original parts near the front edge of the camp.[104] The Jewish museum was damaged in an arson attack in 1992, after which a charred portion of the barrack was put behind glass and left in damaged condition, so that when the museum reopened in 1997 it also documented the continued virulence of antisemitism in Germany. Otherwise, post-1990 changes to this East German memorial site have been gradual. A part of the camp used by Soviet troops until 1990 was made publicly accessible, and the national exhibits in the international museum outside the gate were removed, with the building now being used for temporary exhibitions.[105] A number of smaller documentary exhibitions have been installed around the site, and in 2004 a new visitors' centre was opened in a building outside the prisoners' compound that had once been the camp armoury.

Conclusion

What can we learn from this overview of the histories of the physical sites of former concentration camps? The first postwar uses as hospitals, showcases of Nazi brutality, and internment camps were dictated by pragmatic concerns that were uppermost during the exceptional situation at the end of the war. Thereafter, however, the former camps followed very different trajectories. A few were preserved as museums almost immediately, while others were converted to prisons or refugee housing. In the latter cases the impulse to create an educational memorial site emerged only gradually, and in some cases not at all. What determined that trajectory?

First, we see that the situation at and shortly after liberation played an important role in determining especially the early uses of a camp, but also its medium-term fate. The camps that had been evacuated or destroyed before the arrival of the Allies did not become part of the 'media blitz' at the end of the war, and usually waited many years, often until the 1960s, until they became well enough known that a constituency emerged for their memorialization. This was the case with the effaced Action Reinhardt camps in Poland, as well as at camps like Flossenbürg, Gross Rosen, Natzweiler, Neuengamme and Stutthof. In some of those cases geographical remoteness also played a role.

Second, we note that the size of a camp, whether measured by number of inmates, number of victims or territorial extent, did not determine the timing or magnitude of later memorialization. Camps that had had roughly equivalent numbers of inmates and victims often had very different postwar trajectories that resulted in widely varying memorial sites. This effect is most noticeable in the often large camps not discussed here that never became popular memorial sites, such as Płaszów in Poland and Natzweiler in France, or large satellite camps such as Allach and Kaufering (attached to Dachau), Ebensee (Mauthausen), Bremen-

Farge (Neuengamme) or Amersfoort in Holland, some of which had tens of thousands of inmates.

Rather, third, the timing and extent of memorialization depended on the human agency primarily of the survivors (to a small extent also of the victorious occupying powers), and their relationship with the postwar state authorities controlling the sites. In general, evacuated camps such as Neuengamme were not memorialized until the survivors returned to lobby for their preservation. If the survivors were uninterested in memorialization, as at Belsen, where legions of Jewish victims had arrived from elsewhere at the end of the war and only wanted to emigrate, the site inched toward oblivion once the survivors left, until a younger generation of Germans took note and directed international attention back to it. In cases where the commemorative interests of the survivors overlapped with those of the state, as in East Germany, elaborate aesthetic and educational memorials were constructed in short order, albeit not necessarily according to the wishes of the survivors. When survivor and state interests were directly at odds, as in Dachau or Neuengamme, the survivors' push for educational memorialization took longer and was more halting. Over time, as the anti-commemorative impulses of the cohorts of the perpetrators and bystanders were overcome by the more open or curious attitudes of later generations, commemorative, educational and preservation efforts resulted in increasingly elaborate memorial sites.[106]

In recent decades, as marginalized groups of victims such as Sinti (gypsies) or homosexuals have gained public recognition, several concentration camp memorial sites have added memorials and exhibitions about their histories as well. The first memorial to recognize a marginalized group was the addition of an inscription for the Sinti to the memorial wall at Bergen-Belsen in 1982;[107] Ravensbrück followed suit with an exhibit in 1994, Buchenwald with a memorial in one of the outlined barracks in 1995, and Mauthausen with a plaque in 1998. The first memorial for homosexuals in a former camp was the 1984 plaque in Mauthausen mentioned above; similar plaques were unveiled in Neuengamme in 1985 and in Sachsenhausen in 1991, while one in Dachau was first displayed in a private space (the Lutheran chapel) in 1985 and finally brought to the main museum for public display in 1995.[108] Jehovah's Witnesses were first memorialized in Neuengamme in 2006.

As the above overview shows, detailed, source-based studies of the postwar history have been written for only a handful of major camps, and studies of even the largest satellite camps are rare. The most reliable information on the development of the major camp memorial sites is to be found in reference works such as the Benz and Distel collection *Der Ort des Terrors* (8 vols., 2005–).[109] Especially for camps in eastern Europe, where linguistic barriers and until recently government taboos have hindered historical research, very little is known about their postwar uses. Jasenovać camp south of Zagreb in Croatia, for example, was memorialized in 1963, but was again in use for internment in the 1990s.[110] Similarly, to date there are no works that look specifically at uses such as displaced person and internment camps, although a few books and articles based on primary sources examine internment camps in individual allied zones of occupation.[111]

Scholarly work on the human and material – as opposed to the physical – legacies of the Nazi camps is also still in an early phase, with only a few pockets of in-depth research based on primary sources. An overview of the trials of the perpetrators, a number of which were conducted in the former camps, has recently been attempted in anthology form by P. Heberer and J. Matthäus in their *Atrocities on Trial: Historical Perspectives on the Politics of Prosecuting War Crimes* (2008).[112] The trials held in Germany are by far the best documented, with (up to 2008) a 38-volume primary source collection of the judgments and summaries of the existing literature.[113] The financial aftermath of the National Socialist camp systems can be subsumed under the German term *Wiedergutmachung*, literally 'making good again'. H. G. Hockerts has written a historical overview with a conceptual clarification of the differences between restitution (of assets stolen or expropriated from individuals, *Rückerstattung* in German) and compensation (for injury or loss or unpaid labour, or *Entschädigung*), as well as references to the specialized literature, while M. Henry offers a comprehensive discussion of specifically Jewish claims.[114]

Future research would not only need to create monographic, primary source-based portrayals of the postwar histories of other major camps similar to those we now have for Buchenwald, Dachau, Mauthausen, Ravensbrück and Sachsenhausen, but would need to investigate the legions of lesser-known large camps and branch camps. The histories of the camp survivor organizations that were to a great extent responsible for the preservation of remains and the creation of educational memorial sites have yet to be written. Except for East and West Germany and Austria, we know almost nothing about the often intense wrangling first between survivors and governmental authorities, then among and between successor generations and reluctant bureaucrats, out of which specific memorial conceptions emerged in other countries. Finally, the study of memorial site didactics and the effects of those memorial conceptions on the millions of visitors to former concentration camps each year is still in its infancy.[115]

Notes

1 See L. Eiber and R. Sigel (eds.), *Dachauer Prozesse. NS-Verbrechen vor amerikanischen Militärgerichten in Dachau 1945–48, Verfahren, Ergebnisse, Nachwirkungen*, Göttingen: Wallstein, 2007. Most trials of camp personnel were held in cities, however: the first Auschwitz trial was in Cracow, the first Belsen, Neuengamme and Ravensbrück trials in Hamburg, the Natzweiler trial in Wuppertal, and the Sachsenhausen trial in Berlin-Pankow. There were often several trials for personnel from the same camp. For example, there were Natzweiler trials in Rastatt and Metz as well.

2 I do not discuss these cases in detail in this chapter, but this argument is made in several 1980s books: D. Garbe (ed.), *Die vergessenen KZs? Gedenkstätten für die Opfer des NS-Terrors in der Bundesrepublik*, Bornheim-Merten: Lamuv, 1983; 'Die vergessenen Lager', *Dachauer Hefte* 5(1985); B. Eichmann, *Versteinert, verharmlost, vergessen. KZ-Gedenkstätten in der Bundesrepublik Deutschland*, Frankfurt: Fischer Taschenbuch, 1986.

3 For example: Council for the Preservation of Monuments to Resistance and Martyrdom (ed.), *Scenes of Fighting and Martyrdom Guide: War Years in Poland, 1939–1945*, Warsaw: Sport i Turystyka Publications, 1966; A. Rieth, *Monuments to the*

Victims of Tyranny, New York: Praeger, 1969; E. Fein, *Die Steine Reden. Gedenkstätten des österreichischen Freiheitskampfes, Mahnmale für die Opfer des Faschismus. Eine Dokumentation*, Vienna: Europaverlag, 1975; W. Ramaker, *Sta een ogenblik stil ... Monumentenboek 1940– 1945*, Kampen: Kok, 1980. G. Schafft, *Die KZ-Mahn- und Gedenkstätten in Deutschland*, Berlin: Dietz, 1996, should also be named in this context.

4 K. Feig, *Hitler's Death Camps: The Sanity of Madness*, New York: Holmes & Meier, 1981.

5 Garbe (ed.), *Die vergessenen KZs?*; Eichmann, *Versteinert*; U. Puvogel, *Gedenkstätten für die Opfer des Nationalsozialismus auf dem Gebiet der Bundesrepublik Deutschland*, Bonn: Bundeszentrale für politische Bildung, 1980, 2nd edn 1981; U. Puvogel, *Gedenkstätten für die Opfer des Nationalsozialismus: Eine Dokumentation*, Bonn: Bundeszentrale, 1987; U. Puvogel, *Gedenkstätten für die Opfer des Nationalsozialismus*, Bonn: Bundeszentrale, 2003, available at: http://www.bpb.de/publikationen/.

6 G. Lehrke, *Gedenkstätten für Opfer des Nationalsozialismus. Historisch-politische Bildung an Orten des Widerstands und der Verfolgung*, Frankfurt: Campus, 1988. Chapter 4 especially offers historical information about West German sites.

7 S. Milton and I. Nowinski, *In Fitting Memory: The Art and Politics of Holocaust Memorials*, Detroit, MI: Wayne State University Press, 1991.

8 J. E. Young, *The Texture of Memory: Holocaust Memorials and Meaning*, New Haven, CT: Yale University Press, 1993.

9 J. Miller, *One, by One, by One: Facing the Holocaust*, New York: Simon and Schuster, 1990.

10 G. Morsch (ed.), *Von der Erinnerung zum Monument. Die Entstehungsgeschichte der Nationalen Mahn- und Gedenkstätte Sachsenhausen*, Berlin: Ed. Hentrich, 1996; I. Eschebach, S. Jacobeit, and S. Lanwerd, *Die Sprache des Gedenkens. Zur Geschichte der Gedenkstätte Ravensbrück 1945–1995*, Berlin: Edition Hentrich, 1999; H. Marcuse, *Legacies of Dachau: The Uses and Abuses of a Concentration Camp, 1933–2001*, Cambridge: Cambridge University Press, 2001, and B. Perz, *Die KZ-Gedenkstätte Mauthausen. 1945 bis zur Gegenwart*, Innsbruck: StudienVerlag, 2006. Additional, mostly shorter monographs about other camps are cited in the various sections below.

11 W. Benz and B. Distel (eds.), *Der Ort des Terrors. Geschichte der Nationalsozialistischen Konzentrationslager*, 8 vols., Munich: C. H. Beck, 2005–2008.

12 For an additional overview of the liberation of the Nazi camps, see R. Abzug and J. Wetzel, 'Die Befreiung', in Benz and Distel (eds.), ibid., vol. 1, pp. 313–28.

13 In Majdanek, *c.* 480 prisoners, mainly disabled Soviet POWs, were liberated in the camp; see J. Marszałek, *Majdanek: Konzentrationslager Lublin*, Warsaw: Interpress, 1984, pp. 188ff.

14 The discovery of Natzweiler is described in: R. H. Abzug, *Inside the Vicious Heart: Americans and the Liberation of Nazi Concentration Camps*, New York: Oxford University Press, 1985, pp. 3–10.

15 United States Holocaust Memorial Museum, *Holocaust Encyclopedia*. 'Gross-Rosen', http://www.ushmm.org/wlc/en/index.php?ModuleId=10005454 (accessed 20 January 2008).

16 R. J. van Pelt, *The Case for Auschwitz: Evidence from the Irving Trial*, Bloomington, IN: Indiana University Press, 2002, p. 158. The Stammlager had *c.* 1,200 survivors, Birkenau 5,800, and Monowitz about 600. Some 60,000 inmates had been evacuated in the preceding weeks.

17 P. Levi, *The Reawakening (La Tregua): A Liberated Prisoner's Long March Home through East Europe*, 1st American edn, Boston, MA: Little Brown, 1965.

18 Levi, *Reawakening* (1995 ed.), pp. 19f.

19 A clip of Soviet film footage showing Lubliners burying the dead is available at: http://www.ushmm.org/wlc/media_fi.php?lang=en&ModuleId=10005131&MediaId=210.

20 For literature on Belsen and more than a dozen other cases, see Marcuse, *Legacies of Dachau*, p. 421f, note 48.

21 See S. zur Nieden, 'Vom Interregnum zum Speziallager', in Morsch (ed.), *Von der Erinnerung zum Monument*, pp. 68–76· p 73f.

22 See Abzug, *Inside the Vicious Heart*, pp. 21–30. After touring the camp with 25 Ohrdruf residents on 7 April, the mayor of Ohrdruf and his wife committed suicide. See M. Overesch, *Buchenwald und die DDR: Oder die Suche nach Selbstlegitimation*, Göttingen: Vandenhoeck & Ruprecht, 1995, p. 99.

23 Abzug, *Inside the Vicious Heart*, pp. 30–44.

24 Overesch, *Buchenwald*, p. 36f.

25 J. Reilly, *Belsen. The Liberation of a Concentration Camp*, London: Routledge, 1998, p. 22, pp. 25f.

26 Documents about the tour are reprinted in Overesch, *Buchenwald*, p. 99, pp. 106–8.

27 Marcuse, *Legacies of Dachau*, pp. 52–5. See also C. Brink, *Ikonen der Vernichtung. Öffentlicher Gebrauch von Fotografien aus nationalsozialistischen Konzentrationslagern nach 1945*, Berlin: Akademie Verlag, 1998.

28 In addition to my own account in the previous note, see the older narratives by Abzug, *Inside the Vicious Heart*, and J. Bridgman, *The End of the Holocaust: The Liberation of the Camps*, Portland, OR: Areopagitica Press, 1990, and most recently van Pelt, *The Case for Auschwitz*, pp. 156–68.

29 J. Shandler, *While America Watches: Televising the Holocaust*, New York: Oxford University Press, 1999, pp. 8–24.

30 See Marcuse, *Legacies of Dachau*, pp. 85–108. For a case study of the German reception of the Dachau trials, see R. Sigel, 'Die Dachauer Prozesse und die deutsche Öffentlichkeit', in Eiber and Sigel (eds.), *Dachauer Prozesse*, pp. 67–85.

31 M. Weinmann and International Tracing Service, *Das nationalsozialistische Lagersystem*, Frankfurt: Zweitausendeins, 1990, CXXXIII.

32 B. D. Hulen, 'President Orders Eisenhower To End New Abuse of Jews', *New York Times*, 30 Sept. 1945, pp. 1 and 39. The report is reprinted in L. Dinnerstein, *America and the Survivors of the Holocaust*, New York: Columbia University Press, 1982, pp. 291ff. Truman's letter and Harrison's report are also available online at: http://www.jewishvirtuallibrary.org/jsource/Holocaust/truman_on_harrison.html.

33 Reilly, *Belsen*, pp. 17–117 offers an excellent overview for Belsen. On DPs in postwar Germany more generally, see A. Königseder, *Lebensmut im Wartesaal. Die jüdischen DPs (displaced persons) im Nachkriegsdeutschland,*, Frankfurt: Fischer, 1994.

34 See S. E. Bloch and World Federation of Bergen-Belsen Associations, *Umkum un Oyfkum. Holocaust and Rebirth, Bergen-Belsen, 1945–1965*, New York: Bergen-Belsen Memorial Press of the World Federation of Bergen-Belsen Associations, 1965.

35 See Marcuse, *Legacies*, 64ff., 263f.

36 On Klausner see A. Grobman and J. L. Magnes Museum, *Rekindling the Flame: American Jewish Chaplains and the Survivors of European Jewry, 1944–1948*, Detroit, MI: Wayne State University Press, 1993.

37 F. McCourt, in *'Tis. A Memoir*, New York: Simon & Shuster, 1999, p. 94, quotes a GI saying that the helpers employed by the US army were 'Hungarians, Yugoslavians, Czechs, Romanians', but from interviews with local residents I presume that Poles predominated.

38 H. Wember, *Umerziehung im Lager. Internierung und Bestrafung von Nationalsozialisten in der Britischen Besatzungszone Deutschlands*, Essen: Klartext, 1991, p. 70.

39 P. Heigl, *Konzentrationslager Flossenbürg in Geschichte und Gegenwart*, Regensburg: Mittelbayerische Druckerei- und Verlags-Gesellschaft, 1989.

40 This information is available on flyers available at the Westerbork memorial site; see also 'Marked for Life.' http://www.kampwesterbork.nl/site1.2/English/KAMP/k09.html (accessed 16 February 2008).

41 Wember, *Umerziehung Im Lager*, 13–16.

42 The full text of the Potsdam agreement is available at the Yale Avalon project: http://www.yale.edu/lawweb/avalon/decade/decade17.htm.

43 See J. Gimbel, *A German Community under American Occupation. Marburg, 1945–52*, Stanford, CA: Stanford University Press, 1961, p. 49, citing OMGUS Monthly Report no. 1, 20 August 1945, pp. 2, 13. The US national archives has a file of information on this operation, which still awaits a detailed examination; see http://www.archives.gov/iwg/declassified-records/rg-338-us-army-command.

44 Very little has been written about the Allied internment camps as a whole. One of the few exceptions is C. Schick, 'Die Internierungslager', in M. Broszat *et al.* (eds.), *Von Stalingrad zur Währungsreform. Zur Sozialgeschichte des Umbruchs in Deutschland*, Munich: Oldenbourg, 1988, pp. 301–25. See also L. Niethammer, 'Internierungslager in Deutschland nach 1945. Vergleich und offene Fragen', in C. Jansen *et al.* (eds.), *Von der Aufgabe der Freiheit. Politische Verantwortung und bürgerliche Gesellschaft im 19. und 20. Jahrhundert*, Berlin: Akademie Verlag, 1995, 474ff.

45 B. Ritscher, *Spezlager Nr. 2 Buchenwald. Zur Geschichte des Lagers Buchenwald, 1945 bis 1950*, 2nd, revised edition, Weimar-Buchenwald: Gedenkstätte Buchenwald, 1995, pp. 131–5. See also 'Geschichte des sowjetischen Speziallagers (2)', http://www.buchenwald.de/media_de/ct_ges_hist1.html.

46 Marcuse, *Legacies of Dachau*, pp. 68–70 and p. 161.

47 Wember, *Umerziehung Im Lager*, p. 81f.

48 Heigl, *Konzentrationslager Flossenbürg in Geschichte und Gegenwart*, p. 80.

49 Wember, *Umerziehung Im Lager*, pp. 70–3. See also http://www.kz-gedenkstaette-neuengamme.de/index.php?id=399 (accessed 11 April 2008), which lists 7,987 as the maximum number of inmates, and says they were guarded by Belgian troops from July to November 1945.

50 B. Kühle, S*peziallager Nr. 7. Sachsenhausen, 1945–1950*, Berlin: Brandenburgisches Verlagshaus, 1990, p. 17; also G. Morsch and Gedenkstätte und Museum Sachsenhausen, *Sowjetisches Speziallager Nr. 7/Nr. 1 in Sachsenhausen (1945–1950). Katalog der Ausstellung in der Gedenkstätte und Museum Sachsenhausen*, Berlin: Metropol, 2005.

51 See Wember, *Umerziehung im Lager*, 91ff., 109ff., 244ff.; G. Hammermann, 'Das Internierungs- und Kriegsgefangenenlager Dachau 1945–1948', in W. Benz and A. Königseder (eds.), *Das Konzentrationslager Dachau. Geschichte und Wirkung nationalsozialistischer Repression*, Berlin: Metropol, 2008, pp. 125–46, esp.142ff.

52 See http://www.stiftung-bg.de/gums/en/geschichte/speziallager/spezial01.htm (accessed 23 January 2009).

53 According to the Holocaust encyclopedia of the United States Holocaust Memorial Museum (USHMM), at least 30,000 of the 140,000 officially registered inmates died; that figure does not include 18,000 Soviet POWs who were executed but never registered. If those figures are included, the camp-era mortality rate becomes 1:3.3. See http://www.ushmm.org/wlc/article.php?ModuleId=10005538 (accessed 23 January 2009).

54 For an excellent overview of denazification, see A. Biddiscombe, *The Denazification of Germany: A History 1945–1950*, Stroud: Tempus, 2007.

55 On Czechoslovakia, see http://de.wikipedia.org/wiki/Theresienstadt_1945–1948, accessed 19 October 2007, based on articles in Czech in the *Theresienstädter Blätter* in 1990 and 1996. See also V. Blodig, 'Die Gedenkstätte Theresienstadt gestern und heute', *Dachauer Hefte* 11 (1995), pp. 102–8. On Belgium, see 'Breendonk II', at the bottom of: http://www.breendonk.be/EN/fort.html (accessed 19 October 2007). On the reception of the memorial, see also: http://www.breendonk.be/EN/memorial.html.

56 Feig, *Hitler's Death Camps*, p. 315.

57 J. Huener, *Auschwitz, Poland, and the Politics of Commemoration, 1945-1979*, Athens, OH: Ohio University Press, 2003, p. 60; for the following see pp. 62, 69, 112ff.

58 On the origins of the Auschwitz museum see I. Engelhardt, *A Topography of Memory: Representations of the Holocaust at Dachau and Buchenwald in Comparison with Auschwitz, Yad Vashem and Washington, DC*, Brussels: Peter Lang, 2002, pp. 161–5. The dates are

conveniently summarized on the Auschwitz museum website: 'Dates in the History of the Memorial and Museum,' http://www.auschwitz.org.pl/new/index.php?language=EN&tryb=stale&id=425 (accessed 3 November 2007); see also the narrative at http://www.auschwitz.org.pl/new/index.php?language=EN&tryb=stale&id=426. The July 1947 opening is described in Huener, *Auschwitz*, 32ff.

59 See U. Wrocklage, 'Auschwitz-Birkenau – Die Rampe', in D. Hoffmann (ed.), *Das Gedächtnis der Dinge. KZ-Relikte und KZ-Denkmäler, 1945–1995*, Frankfurt: Campus, 1997, pp. 278–309: p. 289.

60 On the 'urn' from 1955, see Wrocklage, 'Auschwitz-Birkenau', p. 291 with note 46, and Hoffmann's introduction, p. 25.

61 On the history of this Auschwitz memorial, see H. Marcuse, 'Memorializing the Holocaust: History and Theory', *American Historical Review*, forthcoming February 2010.

62 The Birkenau inscription, repeated in 20 languages, was changed from 'Four million people suffered and died here at the hands of the Nazi murderers between the years 1940 and 1945', to 'For ever let this place be a cry of despair and a warning to humanity, where the Nazis murdered about one and a half million men, women, and children, mainly Jews from various countries of Europe. Auschwitz-Birkenau, 1940–1945.'

63 The following portrayal is based on the timeline on the Majdanek museum's website: 'The State Museum at Majdanek: The Most Important Events' (2006), http://www.majdanek.pl/articles.php?acid=22&lng=1 (accessed 9 May 2008). For photographs and additional information about Majdanek, see Young, *Texture of Memory*, 124ff., and Milton/Nowinski, *In Fitting Memory*, pp. 148–52.

64 The Gross Rosen memorial is barely documented in English-language publications. For two scant references, see: Council for the Preservation of Monuments to Resistance and Martyrdom (ed.), *Scenes of Fighting and Martyrdom Guide*, p. 324f with ill. 276, and Milton and Nowinski, *In Fitting Memory*, p. 326. The following information is taken primarily from the museum's website: 'Muzeum Gross Rosen', http://www.gross-rosen.pl/eng/showpage.php?pageID=5 (accessed 9 May 2008).

65 The English-language literature on Stutthof is as sparse as that on Gross Rosen. See Feig, *Hitler's Death Camps*, 193f, citing T. Matusiak, *Stutthof*, Gdańsk: Zakłady Graficzne, 1969, pp. 48–54. See also: http://www.inyourpocket.com/poland/gdansk/sightseeing/category/58897-Stutthof.html (accessed 8 Feb. 2008). The Stutthof state museum's website offers little information about its postwar history; see http://www.stutthof.pl/en/museummap/upamietnienie.htm (accessed 8 February 2008). Drywa's contribution to Benz and Distel (eds.), *Ort des Terrors*, vol. 6, 521f, neither cites sources nor offers additional information.

66 G. Horwitz, *In the Shadow of Death: Living outside the Gates of Mauthausen*, New York: Free Press, 1990, pp. 168–72.

67 For this and the following, see: Perz, *Die KZ-Gedenkstätte Mauthausen*.

68 See Perz, *Die KZ-Gedenkstätte*, 66f (plaque), 170f (Karbyschew), 135–9 (international committee and ossuary), 130 and 145 (signage).

69 Information about these memorials can be found in H. Schmid and N. Dobrowolskij, *Kunst, die einem Kollektiv entspricht. Der internationale Denkmalhain in der KZ-Gedenkstätte Mauthausen*, Vienna: Bundesministerium für Inneres, 2007. The Mauthausen memorial site maintains a page linking to photographs of each of the 22 memorials and plaques at: http://www.mauthausen-memorial.at/db/admin/de/index_main.php?cbereich=1&cthema=355 (accessed 4 April 2008).

70 See Perz, *Die KZ-Gedenkstätte*, 187f (women), p. 186 (Jews), and 190f (homosexuals and Roma).

71 See Perz, *Die KZ-Gedenkstätte*, p. 237 (pupil visits), pp. 244ff. (Austrian army), p. 246 (papal visit), p. 257 (memorial concert), and pp. 259ff. (reform study).

72 A photograph of the sign can be found at: http://isurvived.org/Bergen-Belsen_liberation.html (accessed 19 October 2007). The German version of the sign is depicted at http://www.bbc.co.uk/ww2peopleswar/stories/50/a8378850.shtml. A *terminus ante quem* is given by the publication of the photograph in D. Sington, *Belsen Uncovered*, London: Duckworth, 1946.

73 A translation of Heuss's dedication speech is printed in R. Stackelberg and S. A. Winkle, *The Nazi Germany Sourcebook: An Anthology of Texts*, New York: Routledge, 2002, 401f.

74 F. Bischoff, *Das Lager Bergen-Belsen. Dokumente und Bilder mit erläuternden Texten. Im Auftrage des Niedersächsischen Ministers des Innern*, Hannover: Verlag für Literatur und Zeitgeschehen, 1966, p. 32. An inscription for the Sinti (Gypsies) was added in 1982.

75 For details and further references on this 'Anne Frank wave', see Marcuse, *Legacies of Dachau*, pp. 200–3.

76 The commissioned history was: E. Kolb, *Bergen Belsen. Geschichte des 'Aufenthaltslagers' 1943–1945*, Hannover: Verlag für Literatur und Zeitgeschehen, 1962. This was the first monographic history of a concentration camp written by a non-Jewish German scholar.

77 See http://www.bergenbelsen.de/en/chronik/, and http://www.bergenbelsen.de/en/neugestaltung/ (accessed 21 March 2008).

78 For this and the following memorials, see Marcuse, *Legacies of Dachau*, pp. 189–94. On the Koelle sculptures see also Hoffmann, 'Dachau', pp. 58–62.

79 On the prison and refugee settlement projects, see Marcuse, *Legacies of Dachau*, pp. 158–70.

80 For this and the following see Marcuse, *Legacies of Dachau*, pp. 142–51 (mass grave), pp. 170–86 (exhibitions and demolition attempt), and pp. 242–61 (establishment of the memorial site). The skeletons turned out to have nothing to do with the concentration camp.

81 Again, see Marcuse, *Legacies of Dachau*, p. 333 and ill. 73 (visitor statistics), p. 388 (teachers), and pp. 382–8 (youth hostel). As research by Rudi Hartmann has shown, many more visitors tour the site than enter the museum, where the count is taken.

82 The following portrayal follows U. Wrocklage, 'Neuengamme', in Hoffmann (ed.), *Gedächtnis der Dinge*, pp. 178–205: 186ff.

83 See D. Garbe and KZ-Gedenkstätte Neuengamme, *Die Arbeit der KZ-Gedenkstätte Neuengamme 1981 bis 2001. Rückblicke-Ausblicke. Eine Dokumentation der Aktivitäten 20 Jahre nach der Eröffnung des Dokumentenhauses in Hamburg-Neuengamme*, Hamburg: KZ-Gedenkstätte Neuengamme, 2001; also 'Justizvollzugsanstalt', http://www.kz-gedenkstaette-neuengamme.de/index.php?id=400 (accessed 18 April 2008), and B. Niven, *Facing the Nazi Past: United Germany and the Legacy of the Third Reich*, New York: Routledge, 2002, p. 30.

84 In addition to Wrocklage, see F. Bringmann, *Neuengamme – verdrängt, vergessen, bewältigt? Die 'zweite' Geschichte des Konzentrationslagers Neuengamme 1945 bis 1985*, Hamburg: VSA-Verlag, 1987, pp. 62–4.

85 See Bringmann, *Neuengamme*, p. 91.

86 See D. Garbe, 'Neuengamme', in: Garbe (ed.), *Die vergessenen KZs?*, pp. 37–68.

87 See http://www.kz-gedenkstaette-neuengamme.de/index.php?id=404 (accessed 11 April 2008).

88 See Heigl, *Konzentrationslager Flossenbürg in Geschichte und Gegenwart*, p. 37, pp. 79–96.

89 An excellent collection of historical and present-day photographs of Flossenbürg can be found at http://www.thirdreichruins.com/flossenburg.htm. The ash may have been that of corpses found in the camp at liberation and cremated before May 1, when that programme was stopped. See Heigl, *Flossenbürg*, p. 63, p. 67. Prisoners who died after liberation were buried in the centre of Flossenbürg village.

90 See http://www.gedenkstaette-flossenbuerg.de/opfer.html (accessed 24 April 2008).

91 On the dissolution of the UNRRA camp see http://www.gedenkstaette-flossenbuerg. de/1945.html (accessed 24 April 2008); the other information is after Heigl, *Konzentrationslager Flossenbürg*, pp. 97–109.

92 On the 1995 initiative, see H. Simon-Pelanda, 'Vergessenes Konzentrationslager: Flossenbürg', *Dachauer Hefte* 11(1995), pp. 50–5. For an overview of the construction beginning in 2004 and the 2007 exhibition, see http://www.gedenkstaette-flossenbuerg.de/ausstellung/index.php (accessed 24 April 2008).

93 Overesch, *Buchenwald*, Chapter 4 discusses many of the former Buchenwald inmates who led local and regional government in the first years after 1945.

94 See Overesch, *Buchenwald*, pp. 261–4; also 'Geschichte der Gedenkstätte', http://www.buchenwald.de/media_de/ct_ges_gedenk.html (accessed 24 April 2008).

95 In addition to Overesch, *Buchenwald*, Chapters 4 and 5, see V. Knigge, 'Buchenwald', in Hoffmann (ed.), *Gedächtnis der Dinge* , pp. 95f.

96 See Marcuse, *Legacies of Dachau*, ill. 74, based on statistics in Gitta Günther, *Buchenwald*, Weimar: Ständige Kommissionen Kultur der Stadtverordnetenversammlung Weimar und des Kreistages Weimar-Land in Zusammenarbeit mit dem Stadtmuseum Weimar, 1983, p. 59, and from the Buchenwald memorial site.

97 See U. Härtl, *Die Neukonzeption der Gedenkstätte Buchenwald. Die Gedenkstätte Buchenwald seit 1989/90*, Weimar: Stiftung Gedenkstätten Buchenwald und Mittelbau-Dora, 2001.

98 See Eschebach, Jacobeit, and Lanwerd, *Die Sprache des Gedenken* and the memorial site's page http://www.ravensbrueck.de/mgr/english/memorial/1959bis1992. htm (accessed 2 November 2007). See also U. Puvogel, *Gedenkstätten für die Opfer des Nationalsozialismus: Eine Dokumentation*, 2nd revised edn, Bonn: Bundeszentrale für Politische Bildung, 1995, vol. 2, p. 272.

99 In addition to Morsch (ed.), *Von der Erinnerung zum Monument* see 'Sachsenhausen National Memorial' and the subsequent links, at http://www.stiftung-bg.de/gums/ en/geschichte/natmahn/natmahn01.htm (accessed 25 April 2008).

100 See S. zur Nieden, 'Erste Initiativen für Mahnmale in Oranienburg und Sachsenhausen', in ibid., pp. 125–32: 128ff., with photographs.

101 My portrayal follows U. Köpp, 'Die Studien des Buchenwald-Kollektivs für die Gestaltung der Gedenkstätte Sachsenhausen 1956', in Morsch (ed.), *Von der Erinnerung zum Monument*, pp. 158–63.

102 The plan favoured by the survivors was sketched by Reinhold Linger, a landscape architect who had already submitted a design in the Buchenwald competition with Bertolt Brecht and Fritz Cremer. See U. Köpp, 'Der Entwurf Reinhold Lingers für die Gedenkstätte Sachsenhausen', in Morsch (ed.), *Von der Erinnerung zum Monument*, pp. 148–57.

103 See U. Köpp, 'Die Projektierung der Gedenkstätte Sachsenhausen und die Diskussionen im Wissenschaft-Künstlerischen Beirat beim Ministerium für Kultur', in Morsch (ed.), *Von der Erinnerung zum Monument*, pp. 217–31.

104 The three museums are described in three essays by Susanne zur Nieden in Morsch (ed.), *Von der Erinnerung zum Monument*, pp. 255–78. On the politics at the dedication, see J. Herf, *Divided Memory: The Nazi Past in the Two Germanys*, Cambridge, MA: Harvard University Press, 1997, pp. 175–80.

105 Although there were plans to do an extensive revision of the site, including an international design competition, none of them have been realized. See 'New Design' and the subsequent links, at: http://www.stiftung-bg.de/gums/en/ausstellungen/ neugestaltung/neugestaltung_re.htm (accessed 2 May 2008).

106 I develop the effect of changing generational attitudes in shaping the afterlives of the camps more fully in Marcuse, *Legacies of Dachau*, Chapter 12.

107 See H. Marcuse, F. Schimmelfennig and J. Spielmann, *Steine des Anstosses. Nationalsozialismus und Zweiter Weltkrieg in Denkmalen, 1945–1985*, Hamburg: Museum für Hamburgische Geschichte, 1985, p. 7.

108 See Marcuse, *Legacies of Dachau*, pp. 354f and ill. 82.

109 See note 11.

110 See Rieth, *Monuments to the Victims*, p. 61; USHMM Holocaust Encyclopedia 'Jasenovać', http://www.ushmm.org/wlc/article.php?ModuleId=10005449 and http://www.ushmm.org/museum/exhibit/online/jasenovac/frameset.html; on the postwar history http://en.wikipedia.org/wiki/Jasenovac_concentration_camp#Later_events (all accessed 30 January 2009).

111 See Wember, *Umerziehung im Lager*, and Hammermann, 'Das Internierungs- und Kriegsgefangenenlager Dachau 1945–1948', pp. 125–46.

112 P. Heberer and J. Matthäus (eds.), *Atrocities on Trial: Historical Perspectives on the Politics of Prosecuting War Crimes*, Lincoln, NE: University of Nebraska Press, 2008.

113 K. Bracher *et al.* (eds.), *Justiz und NS-Verbrechen. Sammlung deutscher Strafurteile wegen nationalsozialistischer Tötungsverbrechen 1945–1966 [1945–1999]*, Amsterdam: University Press Amsterdam, 1968–2008. For a summary, see J. Zarusky, 'Die juristische Aufarbeitung der KZ-Verbrechen', in Benz and Distel (eds.), *Ort des Terrors*, vol. 1, pp. 345–62.

114 H. G. Hockerts, '*Wiedergutmachung* in Germany: Balancing Historical Accounts, 1945–2000', in D. Diner and G. Wunberg (eds.), *Restitution and Memory: Material Restoration in Europe*, New York: Berghahn Books, 2007, pp. 323–81; M. Henry, *Confronting the Perpetrators: A History of the Claims Conference*, London: Valentine Mitchell, 2007.

115 See A. Eberle, *Pädagogik und Gedenkkultur. Bildungsarbeit an NS-Gedenkorten zwischen Wissensvermittlung, Opfergedenken und Menschenrechtserziehung*, Würzburg: Ergon, 2008; A. Ehmann *et al.* (eds.), *Praxis der Gedenkstättenpädagogik. Erfahrungen und Perspektiven*, Opladen: Leske and Budrich, 1995.

Composite bibliography of works cited

Abzug, R., *Inside the Vicious Heart: Americans and the Liberation of Nazi Concentration Camps*, New York: Oxford University Press, 1985.
—— and J. Wetzel, 'Die Befreiung', in W. Benz and B. Distel (eds) *Der Ort des Terrors. Geschichte der nationalsozialistischen Konzentrationslager*, Munich: Beck; vol. 1: *Die Organisation des Terrors*, 2005, pp. 313–28.
Adelson, J., '*W Polsce zwanej Ludowa'. Najnowsze dzieje Żydów w Polsce*, Warsaw: PWN, 1993.
Adler, H.-G., *Theresienstadt 1941–1945. Das Antlitz einer Zwangsgemeinschaft*, Göttingen: Wallstein, 2005.
Allen, M., *The Business of Genocide: The SS, Slave Labor, and the Concentration Camps*, Chapel Hill, NC: University of North Carolina Press, 2002.
——, 'The Devil in the Details: The Gas Chambers of Birkenau, October 1941', *Holocaust and Genocide Studies* 16, 2002, pp. 189–216.
Allport, G. W. and Postman, L., *The Psychology of Rumor*, New York: Henry Holt and Company, 1947.
Aly, G., *et al.* (eds) *Sozialpolitik und Judenvernichtung*, Berlin: Rotbuch, 1987.
——, 'Die Wohlfühl-Diktatur', *Der Spiegel* 10, 2005, pp. 56–62.
—— and S. Helm, *Architects of Annihilation: Auschwitz and the Logic of Destruction*, Princeton, NJ and Oxford: Princeton University Press, 2002.
Ambach, D. and Köhler, T., *Lublin-Majdanek. Das Konzentrations- und Vernichtungslager im Spiegel von Zeugenaussagen*, Düsseldorf: Justizministerium des Landes Nordrhein-Westfalen, 2003.
Amesberger, H. and Halbmayr, B., *Vom Leben und Überleben – Wege nach Ravensbrück*, vol. 1: *Dokumentation und Analyse*, vol. 2: *Lebensgeschichten*, Vienna: Promedia Verlag, 2001.
——, Auer, K. and Halbmayr, B., *Sexualisierte Gewalt. Weibliche Erfahrungen in NS-Konzentrationslagern*, Vienna: Mandelbaum Verlag, 2007.
Angrick, A. and Klein, P., *Die 'Endlösung' in Riga. Ausbeutung und Vernichtung 1941–1944*, Darmstadt: WBG, 2006.
Anschütz, J., Meier, K. and Obajdin, S., '"… dieses leere Gefühl, und die Blicke der anderen." Sexuelle Gewalt gegen Frauen', in C. Füllberg-Stolberg, M. Jung, R. Riebe and M. Scheitenberger (eds) *Frauen in Konzentrationslagern – Bergen-Belsen, Ravensbrück*, Bremen: Temmen, 1994, pp. 123–33.
Apel, L., *Jüdische Frauen im Konzentrationslager Ravensbrück 1939–1945*, Berlin: Metropol, 2003.
Arad, Y., *Belzec, Sobibor, Treblinka: The Operation Reinhard Death Camps*, Bloomington, IN: Indiana University Press, 1987.
Arendt, H., *The Origins of Totalitarianism*, San Diego, CA: Harcourt, 1968.
Armanski, G., *Maschinen des Terrors. Das Lager (KZ und Gulag) in der Moderne*, Münster: Westfälisches Dampfboot, 1993.

Averdunk, H. and Ring, W., *Geschichte der Stadt Duisburg*, 2nd edn, Ratingen: Aloys Henn, 1949.

Ayaß, W., *'Asoziale' im Nationalsozialismus*, Stuttgart: Klett-Cotta, 1995.

——, (ed.) *'Gemeinschaftsfremde'. Quellen zur Verfolgung von 'Asozialen'*, Koblenz: Bundesarchiv, 1998.

Bader, U. and Welter, W., 'Das SS-Sonderlager/KZ-Hinzert', in W. Benz and B. Distel (eds) *Der Ort des Terrors. Geschichte der nationalsozialistischen Konzentrationslager*, Munich: Beck; vol. 5: *Hinzert, Auschwitz, Neuengamme*, 2007, pp. 17–42.

Baganz, C., *Erziehung zur 'Volksgemeinschaft'? Die frühen Konzentrationslager in Sachsen 1933–1934/37*, Berlin: Metropol 2005.

Bajohr, F. and Pohl, D., *Der Holocaust als offenes Geheimnis. Die Deutschen, die NS-Führung und die Alliierten*, Munich: C. H. Beck, 2006.

Barkai, A.,'"Schicksalsjahr 1938": Kontinuität und Verschärfung der wirtschaftlichen Ausplünderung der deutschen Juden', in U. Büttner (ed.) *Das Unrechtsregime*, Hamburg: Christians, 1986, pp. 45–67.

Barth, E., *Lemuria. Aufzeichnungen und Meditationen*, Hamburg: Claassen & Goverts, 1947.

Bauche, U. *et al.*, *Arbeit und Vernichtung. Katalog zur ständigen Ausstellung der KZ-Gedenkstätte Neuengamme*, Hamburg: VSA, 1986.

Bauer, Y., 'The Death-Marches, January–May 1945', in M. R. Marrus (ed.) *The Nazi Holocaust*, vol. 9 , Westport, CT: Meckler, 1989, pp. 491–511.

Bauman, Z., *Modernity and the Holocaust*, Ithaca, NY: Cornell University Press, 1989.

Behrenbeck, S., *Der Kult um die toten Helden. Nationalsozialistische Mythen, Riten und Symbole*, Schernfeld: S-H Verlag, 1996.

Beimler, H., *Four Weeks in the Hands of Hitler's Hell-Hounds: The Nazi Murder Camp of Dachau*, London: Modern Books, 1933.

Benz, W. and Distel, B., (eds) *Terror ohne System. Die ersten Konzentrationslager im Nationalsozialismus 1933–1935*, Berlin: Metropol, 2001.

——, (eds) *Herrschaft und Gewalt. Frühe Konzentrationslager 1933–1939*, Berlin: Metropol, 2002.

——, (eds) *Instrumentarium der Macht. Frühe Konzentrationslager 1933–1937*, Berlin: Metropol, 2003.

——, (eds) *Der Ort des Terrors. Geschichte der nationalsozialistischen Konzentrationslager*, Munich: Beck; vol. 1: *Die Organisation des Terrors*, 2005; vol. 2: *Frühe Lager, Dachau, Emslandlager*, 2006; vol. 3: *Sachsenhausen, Buchenwald*, 2006; vol. 4: *Flossenbürg, Mauthausen, Ravensbrück*, 2007; vol. 5: *Hinzert, Auschwitz, Neuengamme*, 2007; vol. 6: *Natzweiler, Groß-Rosen, Stutthof*, 2008; vol. 7: *Niederhagen/Wewelsburg, Lublin-Majdanek, Arbeitsdorf, Herzogenbusch (Vught), Bergen-Belsen, Mittelbau-Dora*, 2008; vol. 8: *Riga, Warschau, Vaivara, Plaszów, Kulmhof/Chelmno, Belžec, Sobibór, Treblinka*, 2009.

Bergen, D. L.,'Death Throes and Killing Frenzies: A Response to Hans Mommsen's "The Dissolution of the Third Reich: Crisis Management and Collapse, 1943–1945"', *Bulletin of the German Historical Institute* 27, 2000, pp. 25–37.

Bergner, O., *Aus dem Bündnis hinter dem Stacheldraht. Italienische Häftlinge im KZ Dachau 1943–1945*, Hamburg: Verlag Dr. Kovac, 2002.

Berkhoff, K. C., The 'Russian Prisoners of War in Nazi-Ruled Ukraine as Victims of Genocidal Massacre', *Holocaust and Genocide Studies* 15, 2001, pp. 1–32.

Bettelheim, B., 'Behaviour in Extreme Situations', *Journal of Abnormal and Social Psychology* 38, 1943, pp. 417–52.

——, *The Informed Heart*, Harmondsworth: Penguin Books, 1987.

Biddiscombe, P., *The Denazification of Germany: A History 1945–1950*, Stroud: Tempus, 2007.

Billig, J., *L'Hitlérisme et le système concentrationnaire*, Paris: Presses Universitaires de France, 1967.

——, *Les camps de concentration dans l'économie du Reich hitlérien*, Paris: Presses Universitaires de France, 1973.

Birn, R. B., 'Vaivara – Stammlager', in W. Benz and B. Distel (eds) *Der Ort des Terrors. Geschichte der nationalsozialistischen Konzentrationslager*, Munich: Beck, vol. 8: *Riga, Warschau, Vaivara, Plaszów, Kulmhof/Chełmno, Bełżec, Sobibór, Treblinka*, 2009, pp. 131–47.

Bischoff, F., *Das Lager Bergen-Belsen: Dokumente und Bilder mit erläuternden Texten*, Hannover: Verlag für Literatur und Zeitgeschehen, 1966.

Blatman, D., 'The Death Marches, January–May 1945: Who Was Responsible for What?', *Yad Vashem Studies* 28, 2000, pp. 155–201.

——, 'Die Todesmärsche – Entscheidungsträger, Mörder und Opfer', in U. Herbert, K. Orth and C. Dieckmann (eds) *Die nationalsozialistischen Konzentrationslager. Entwicklung und Struktur*, vol. 2, Göttingen: Wallstein, 1998, pp. 1063–92.

Bloch, S. E. and World Federation of Bergen-Belsen Associations, *Umkum un Oyfkum. Holocaust and Rebirth, Bergen-Belsen, 1945–1965*, New York: Bergen-Belsen Memorial Press of the World Federation of Bergen-Belsen Associations, 1965.

Blodig, V., 'Die Gedenkstätte Theresienstadt gestern und heute', *Dachauer Hefte* 11, 1995, pp. 102–8.

Boberach, H., 'Die Überführung von Soldaten des Heeres und der Luftwaffe in die SS-Totenkopfverbände zur Bewachung von Konzentrationslagern 1944', *Militärgeschichtliche Mitteilungen* 2, 1983, pp. 185–90.

Bock, G., Review of Claudia Koonz, *Mothers in the Fatherland*, *Bulletin of the German Historical Institute London* 9, Feb. 1989, pp. 16–24.

——, 'Ordinary Women in Nazi Germany: Perpetrators, Victims, Followers and Bystanders', in D. Ofer and L. J. Weitzman (eds) *Women in the Holocaust*, New Haven, CT: Yale University Press, 1998.

——, (ed.) *Genozid und Geschlecht. Jüdische Frauen im nationalsozialistischen Lagersystem*, Frankfurt/New York: Campus, 2005.

Bonifas, A., *Häftling 20.801. Ein Zeugnis über die faschistischen Konzentrationslager*, 4th edn, Berlin: Union-Verlag, 1983.

Borowski, T., *This Way for the Gas, Ladies and Gentlemen*, London: Cape, 1967.

Bracher, K. *et al.* (eds) *Justiz und NS-Verbrechen. Sammlung deutscher Strafurteile wegen nationalsozialistischer Tötungsverbrechen 1945–1966 [1945–1999]*, Amsterdam: University Press Amsterdam, 1968–2008.

Braham, R. R., *The Politics of Genocide: The Holocaust in Hungary*, Washington, DC: Social Science Monographs, 1994.

Brandes, U., Füllberg-Stolberg, C. and Kempe, S., 'Arbeit im KZ-Ravensbrück', in C. Füllberg-Stolberg, M. Jung, R. Riebe and M. Scheitenberger (eds) *Frauen in Konzentrationslagern – Bergen-Belsen, Ravensbrück*, Bremen: Edition Temmen, 1994, pp. 55–69.

Brandhuber, J., 'Die sowjetischen Kriegsgefangenen im Konzentrationslager Auschwitz', *Hefte von Auschwitz* 4, 1961, pp. 5–46.

Brenner, H., '"Vernichtung durch Arbeit"', *Jahrbuch für Wirtschaftsgeschichte* 30, 1989, pp. 169–73.

Bridgman, J., *The End of the Holocaust: The Liberation of the Camps*, Portland, OR: Areopagitica Press, 1990.

Bringmann, F., *Neuengamme – verdrängt, vergessen, bewältigt? Die zweite Geschichte des Konzentrationslagers Neuengamme 1945 bis 1985*, Hamburg: VSA-Verlag, 1987.

Brink, C., *Ikonen der Vernichtung: Öffentlicher Gebrauch von Fotografien aus nationalsozialistischen Konzentrationslagern nach 1945*, Berlin: Akademie Verlag, 1998.

Brod, T., Kárný, M. and Kárný, M., *Terezínský rodinný tábor v Osvetimi-Birkenau*, Prague: Nadace Terezínská iniciativa – Melantrich, 1994.

Broszat, M., 'The Concentration Camps 1933–45', in H. Krausnick, H. Buchheim, M. Broszat and H.-A. Jacobsen, *Anatomy of the SS State*, New York: Walker, 1965, pp. 141–249.

——, Einleitung', in M. Broszat (ed.), *Studien zur Geschichte der Konzentrationslager*, Stuttgart: DVA, 1970.

——, (ed.) *Kommandant in Auschwitz*, Munich: dtv, 1994.

Browning, C. R., *Ordinary Men: Reserve Police Battalion 101 and the Final Solution in Poland*, New York: Harper Collins, 1992.

——, 'Jewish Workers in Poland. Self-maintenance, Exploitation, Destruction', in C. R. Browning (ed.) *Nazi Policy, Jewish Workers, German Killers*, Cambridge: Cambridge University Press, 2000.

——, *The Origins of the Final Solution*, London: Heinemann, 2004.

Bruha, T. *et al.*, *Frauen-Konzentrationslager Ravensbrück. Geschildert von Ravensbrücker Häftlingen*, Vienna: Sternverlag, 1945.

Bruhns, M., '*Die Zeichnung überlebt ...*' Bildzeugnisse von Häftlingen des KZ-Neuengamme*. Bremen: Edition Temmen, 2007.

Buber-Neumann, M., *Under Two Dictators: Prisoner of Stalin and Hitler* (with an Introduction by Nikolaus Wachsmann), London: Pimlico, 2008.

Budraß, L., *Flugzeugindustrie und Luftrüstung in Deutschland 1918–1945*, Boppard am Rhein: Boldt, 1998.

Buggeln, M., 'Building to Death: Prisoner Forced Labour in the German War Economy – The Neuengamme Subcamps, 1942–1945', in *European History Quarterly* (forthcoming).

Bülow, C. von, 'Der soziale Status der als homosexuell verfolgten Inhaftierten in den Emslandlagern', in O. Mussmann (ed.) *Homosexuelle in Konzentrationslager*, Berlin/Bonn: Westkreuz Verlag, 2000, pp. 44–58.

Bütow, T. and Bindernagel, F., *Ein KZ in der Nachbarschaft. Das Magdeburger Außenlager der Brabag und der 'Freundeskreis Himmler'*, 2nd edn, Cologne: Böhlau, 2004.

Büttner, U., (ed.) *Das Unrechtsregime*, Hamburg: Christians, 1986.

Callegari, C., '"Non dite mai: non ce la faccio più". Giovani ebrei durante la Shoa e sviluppo della resilenza', *History of Education & Children's Literature* 1, 2006, pp. 283–310.

Canning, K., *Gender History in Practice: Historical Perspectives on Bodies, Class and Citizenship*, Ithaca, NY/London: Cornell University Press, 2006.

Caplan, J., (ed.) *Nazism, Fascism and the Working Class: Essays by Tim Mason*, Cambridge: Cambridge University Press, 1995.

——, 'Political Detention and the Origin of the Concentration Camps in Nazi Germany, 1933–1935/6', in N. Gregor (ed.) *Nazism, War and Genocide*, Exeter: University of Exeter Press, 2005, pp. 22–41.

——, 'Introduction', in Gabriele Herz, *The Women's Camp in Moringen: A Memoir of Imprisonment in Germany 1936–1937*, New York/Oxford: Berghahn Books, 2006, pp. 1–55.

——, (ed.) *Short Oxford History of Germany: The Third Reich*, Oxford: Oxford University Press, 2008

Cohen, E. A., *Human Behaviour in the Concentration Camp*, London: Free Associaton Books, 1954.

Comité International de Dachau (ed.) *Konzentrationslager Dachau 1933–1945*, 9th edn, Munich: n.p., 1978.

Council for the Preservation of Monuments to Resistance and Martyrdom (ed.) *Scenes of Fighting and Martyrdom Guide: War Years in Poland, 1939–1945*, Warsaw: Sport i Turystyka Publications, 1966.

Czech, D., *Auschwitz Chronicle, 1939–1945*, New York: Holt, 1990.

Dachauer Hefte, 2 (1986): *Sklavenarbeit im KZ*; 3 (1987): *Frauen. Verfolgung und Widerstand*; 11 (1995): *Orte der Erinnerung*; 12 (1996) *Konzentrationslager. Lebenswelt und Umfeld*; 14 (1998): *Verfolgung als Gruppenschicksal*; 15 (1999): *KZ-Aussenlager*; 17 (2001): *Öffentlichkeit und KZ – Was wusste die Bevölkerung?*; 23 (2007): *Nationalitäten im KZ*.

DDR-Justiz und NS-Verbrechen, Amsterdam and Munich: Amsterdam University Press, Sauer, 2004, vol. 4.

Debski, T., *A Battlefield of Ideas: Nazi Concentration Camps and their Polish Prisoners*, Boulder, CO: East European Monographs, 2001.

Demps, L., 'Zum weiteren Ausbau des staatsmonopolistischen Apparats der faschistischen Kriegswirtschaft in den Jahren 1943 bis 1945 und zur Rolle der SS und der Konzentrationslager im Rahmen der Rüstungsproduktion, dargestellt am Beispiel der unterirdischen Verlagerung von Teilen der Rüstungsproduktion', PhD Dissertation, Humboldt University, Berlin, 1970.

des Pres, T., *The Survivor: An Anatomy of Life in the Death Camps*, New York: Oxford University Press, 1976.

Des voix sous la cendre. Manuscrits des Sonderkommandos d'Auschwitz-Birkenau, Paris: Calmann-Lévy, 2005.

Dicks, H. V., *Licensed Mass Murder: A Sociopsychological Study of some SS Killers*, New York: Basic Books, 1972.

Die österreichischen Opfer des Holocaust. The Austrian Victims of the Holocaust, Vienna: Dokumentationsarchiv des österreichischen Widerstandes, 2001 (CD-ROM).

Dieckmann, C., 'Das Ghetto und das Konzentrationslager in Kaunas 1941–1944', in U. Herbert, K. Orth and C. Dieckmann (eds), *Die nationalsozialistischen Konzentrationslager. Entwicklung und Struktur*, vol. 1, Göttingen: Wallstein, 1998, pp. 439–71.

Dieckmann, G., 'Existenzbedingungen und Widerstand im Konzentrationslager Dora-Mittelbau unter dem Aspekt der funktionellen Einbeziehung der SS in das System der faschistischen Kriegswirtschaft', PhD Dissertation, Humboldt University, Berlin, 1968.

Diehl, P., *Macht – Mythos – Utopie. Die Körperbilder der SS-Männer*, Berlin: Akademie-Verlag, 2004.

Diehl-Thiele, P., *Partei und Staat im Dritten Reich: Untersuchungen zum Verhältnis von NSDAP und allgemeiner innerer Staatsverwaltung 1933–1945*, Munich: Beck, 1971.

Diercks, H., *Jugendliche Häftlinge des KZ Neuengamme aus der Sowjetunion erinnern sich*, Hamburg: Edition Temmen, 2000.

——, (ed) *Verfolgung von Homosexuellen im Nationalsozialismus*, Bremen: Edition Temmen, 1999.

Diewald-Kerkmann, G., *Politische Denunziation im NS-Regime oder Die kleine Macht der 'Volksgenossen'*, Bonn: Dietz, 1995.

Diner, D., 'Rassismus und rationales Kalkül. Zum Stellenwert utilitaristisch verbrämter Legitimationsstrategien in der nationalsozialistischen "Weltanschauung"', in Wolfgang Schneider (ed.) *Vernichtungspolitik. Eine Debatte über den Zusammenhang von Sozialpolitik und Genozid im nationalsozialistischen Deutschland*, Hamburg: Junius, 1991, pp. 25–35.

—— and Wunberg G., (eds) *Restitution and Memory: Material Restoration in Europe*, New York: Berghahn Books, 2007.

Dinnerstein, L., *America and the Survivors of the Holocaust*, New York: Columbia University Press, 1982.

Distel, B., '"Die letzte Warnung vor der Vernichtung". Zur Verschleppung der "Aktionsjuden" in die Konzentrationslager nach dem 9. November 1938', *Zeitschrift für Geschichtswissenschaft* 46, 1998, pp. 985–90.

——, 'Frauen in nationalsozialistischen Konzentrationslagern – Opfer und Täterinnen', in W. Benz and B. Distel (eds) *Der Ort des Terrors. Geschichte der nationalsozialistischen Konzentrationslager*, Munich: Beck, vol. 1: *Die Organisation des Terrors*, 2005, pp. 195–209.

Długoborski, W., (ed.) *Sinti und Roma im KL Auschwitz-Birkenau 1943–1944 vor dem Hintergrund ihrer Verfolgung unter der Naziherrschaft*, Oświęcim: Staatliches Museum, 1998.

—— and Piper, F. (eds) *Auschwitz 1940–1945. Central Issues in the History of the Camp*, 5 vols, Oświęcim: State Museum, 2000; vol. 1: A. Lack *et al.* (eds), *The establishment and organisation of the camp;* vol. 2: T. Iwaszko *et al.* (eds), *The prisoners – Their life and work;* vol. 3: F. Piper (ed.), *Mass murder;* vol. 4: H. Świebocki (ed.): *The resistance movement;* vol. 5: D. Czech *et al.* (eds), *Epilogue.*

Dörner, B., 'NS-Herrschaft und Denunziation – Anmerkungen zu Defiziten in der Denunziationsforschung', *Historical Social Research* 26, 2001, pp. 55–69.

Drobisch, K., 'Frauenkonzentrationslager im Schloss Lichtenburg', *Dachauer Hefte* 3, 1993, pp. 101–15.

—— and Wieland, G., *System der Konzentrationslager 1933–1939*, Berlin: Akademie Verlag, 1993.

Drywa, D., *The Extermination of Jews in Stutthof Concentration Camp*, Gdańsk: Muzeum Sztutowo, 2004.

——, 'Stutthof – Stammlager', in W. Benz and B. Distel (eds) *Der Ort des Terrors. Geschichte der nationalsozialistischen Konzentrationslager*, Munich: Beck, vol. 6: *Natzweiler, Groß-Rosen, Stutthof*, 2008, pp. 477–529.

Duesterberg, J., 'Von der "Umkehr aller Weiblichkeit". Charakterbilder einer KZ-Aufseherin', in I. Eschebach, S. Jacobeit and S. Wenk (eds) *Gedächtnis und Geschlecht. Deutungsmuster in der Darstellung des nationalsozialistischen Genozids*, Frankfurt/New York: Campus, 2002, pp. 227–43.

Durrer, B., 'Eine Verfolgte als Täterin? Zur Geschichte der Blockältesten Carmen Mory', in S. Jacobeit and G. Philipp (eds) *Forschungsschwerpunkt Ravensbrück. Beiträge zur Geschichte des Frauen-Konzentrationslagers*, Berlin: Edition Hentrich, 1997, pp. 86–93.

Dworzecki, M., *Histoire de camps en Estonie (1941–1944)*, Tel Aviv: n.p., 1967.

Dziadosz, E. and Leszczyńska, Z., 'Ewakuacja obozy i wyzwolenie', in T. Mencla (ed.) *Majdanek 1941–1944*, Lublin: Wydawnictwo Lubelskie, 1991, pp. 399–406.

Eberle, A., 'Häftlingskategorien und Kennzeichnungen', in W. Benz and B. Distel (eds) *Der Ort des Terrors. Geschichte der nationalsozialistischen Konzentrationslager*, Munich: Beck, vol. 1: *Die Organisation des Terrors*, 2005, pp. 91–109.

——, *Pädagogik und Gedenkkultur. Bildungsarbeit an NS-Gedenkorten zwischen Wissensvermittlung, Opfergedenken und Menschenrechtserziehung*, Würzburg: Ergon, 2008.

Ehmann, A. *et al.*, (eds) *Praxis der Gedenkstättenpädagogik: Erfahrungen und Perspektiven*, Opladen: Leske und Budrich, 1995.

Eiber, L. and Sigel, R., (eds) *Dachauer Prozesse: NS-Verbrechen vor amerikanischen Militärgerichten in Dachau 1945–48. Verfahren, Ergebnisse, Nachwirkungen*, Göttingen: Wallstein, 2007.

Eichholtz, D., *Geschichte der deutschen Kriegswirtschaft 1939–1945*, vol. II: 1941–1943, East Berlin: Akademie-Verlag, 1985.

—— and K. Gossweiler, 'Noch einmal: Politik und Wirtschaft 1933–1945', *Das Argument* 10, 1968, pp. 210–27.

Eichmann, B., *Versteinert, verharmlost, vergessen. KZ-Gedenkstätten in der Bundesrepublik Deutschland*, Frankfurt: Fischer, 1986.

Ellger, H., *Zwangsarbeit und weibliche Überlebensstrategien. Die Geschichte der Frauenaussenlager des Konzentrationslagers Neuengamme 1944/45*, Berlin: Metropol, 2007.

Endlich, S., 'Die Lichtenburg 1933–1939. Haftort politischer Prominenz und Frauen-KZ', in W. Benz and B. Distel (eds) *Herrschaft und Gewalt. Frühe Konzentrationslager 1933–1939*, Berlin: Metropol, 2002, pp. 11–64.

Engelhardt, I., *A Topography of Memory: Representations of the Holocaust at Dachau and Buchenwald in Comparison with Auschwitz, Yad Vashem and Washington, DC*, Brussels: Peter Lang, 2002.

Erpel, S., *Zwischen Vernichtung und Befreiung. Das Frauen-Konzentrationslager Ravensbrück in der letzen Kriegsphase*, Berlin: Metropol, 2005.

—— (ed.) *Im Gefolge der SS. Aufseherinnen des Frauen-KZ Ravensbrück*, Berlin: Metropol, 2007.

Eschebach, I., 'Das Stigma des Asozialen. Drei Urteile der DDR-Justiz gegen ehemalige Funktionshäftlinge des Frauenkonzentrationslagers Ravensbrück', in KZ-Gedenkstätte Neuengamme (ed.) *Abgeleitete Macht. Funktionshäftlinge zwischen Widerstand und Kollaboration*, Bremen: Edition Temmen, 1998, pp. 69–81.

——, Jacobeit, S. and Lanwerd, S., *Die Sprache des Gedenkens: Zur Geschichte der Gedenkstätte Ravensbrück 1945–1995*, Berlin: Edition Hentrich, 1999.

——, Jacobeit, S. and Wenk, S., (eds) *Gedächtnis und Geschlecht. Deutungsmuster in der Darstellung des nationalsozialistischen Genozids*, Frankfurt/New York: Campus, 2002.

Evans, R. J., 'Coercion and Consent in Nazi Germany', *Proceedings of the British Academy* 151, 2007, pp. 53–81.

Fabréguet, M., 'Entwicklung und Veränderung der Funktionen des Konzentrationslagers Mauthausen 1938–1945', in U. Herbert, K. Orth and C. Dieckmann (eds) *Die Nationalsozialistischen Konzentrationslager. Entwicklung und Struktur*, 2 vols, Göttingen: Wallstein, 1998, vol. 1, pp. 193–214.

——, *Mauthausen. Camp de concentration national-socialiste en Autriche rattachée*, Paris: Honoré Champion Éditeur, 1999.

Fackler, G., *'Des Lagers Stimme' – Musik im KZ. Alltag und Häftlingskultur in den Konzentrationslagern 1933 bis 1936* Bremen: Edition Temmen, 2000.

Fargion, J. P., *Il libro della memoria: gli ebrei deportati dall'Italia (1943–1945)*, Milan: Mursia, 1991.

Favre, M., '"Wir können vielleicht die Schlafräume besichtigen": Originalton einer Reportage aus dem KZ Oranienburg (1933)', *Rundfunk und Geschichte* 24, 1998, pp. 164–70.

Feig, K., *Hitler's Death Camps: The Sanity of Madness*, New York: Holmes & Meier, 1981.

Fein, E., *Die Steine Reden: Gedenkstätten des österreichischen Freiheitskampfes, Mahnmale für die Opfer des Faschismus. Eine Dokumentation*, Vienna: Europaverlag, 1975.

Fings, K., *Krieg, Gesellschaft und KZ. Himmlers SS-Baubrigaden*, Paderborn: Ferdinand Schöningh, 2005.

——, 'Umgedeutete Vergangenheit. Erinnerungsdiskurse über Konzentrationslager', in J. E. Schulte (ed.) *Die SS, Himmler und die Wewelsburg*, Paderborn: Schöningh, 2009.

Fleischer, H., 'Griechenland', in W. Benz (ed.) *Dimension des Völkermords*. Munich: Oldenbourg, 1991, pp. 241–74.

Frankl, V., *Man's Search for Meaning*, New York: Washington Square Press, 1984.

Frei, N., Steinbacher, S. and Wagner, B. C. (eds) *Ausbeutung, Vernichtung, Öffentlichkeit. Neue Studien zur nationalsozialistischen Lagerpolitik*, Munich: Saur, 2000.

Freund, F., *Arbeitslager Zement. Das Konzentrationslager Ebensee und die Raketenrüstung*, Vienna: Verlag für Gesellschaftskritik, 1989.

——, 'Mauthausen: Zu Strukturen von Haupt- und Außenlagern', *Dachauer Hefte* 15, 1999, 254–72.

—— and B. Perz, 'Mauthausen – Stammlager', in W. Benz and B. Distel (eds) *Der Ort des Terrors. Geschichte der nationalsozialistischen Konzentrationslager*, Munich: Beck, vol. 4: *Flossenbürg, Mauthausen, Ravensbrück*, 2007, pp. 293–346.

Freyberg, J. von and Krause-Schmitt, U., *Moringen. Lichtenburg. Ravensbrück. Frauen im Konzentrationslager 1933–1945*, Frankfurt: VAS, 1977.

Friedlander, H., *The Origins of Nazi Genocide: From Euthanasia to the Final Solution*, Chapel Hill, NC: University of North Carolina Press, 1995.

Friedländer, S., *Nazi Germany and the Jews 1939–1945: The Years of Extermination*, New York: Harper Collins Publishers, 2007.

Friedler, E., Siebert, B. and Kilian, A., *Zeugen aus der Todeszone. Das jüdische Sonderkommando in Auschwitz*, Lüneburg: zu Klampen, 2002.

Fröbe, R., 'Hans Kammler: Technokrat der Vernichtung', in R. Smelser and E. Syring (eds) *Die SS: Elite unter dem Totenkopf*, Paderborn: Schöningh, 2000, pp. 305–19.

—— et al., *Konzentrationslager in Hannover. KZ-Arbeit und Rüstungsindustrie in der Spätphase des Zweiten Weltkrieges*, Hildesheim: Lax, 1985.

Fröhlich, E., (ed.) *Die Tagebücher von Joseph Goebbels, Teil II: Diktate 1941–1945*, vol. 4, Munich: Saur, 1995.

Füllberg-Stolberg, C., Jung, M., Riebe, R. and Scheitenberger, M., (eds) *Frauen in Konzentrationslagern – Bergen-Belsen, Ravensbrück*, Bremen: Edition Temmen, 1994.

Garbe, D., (ed.) *Die vergessenen KZs? Gedenkstätten für die Opfer des NS-Terrors in der Bundesrepublik*, Bornheim-Merten: Lamuv, 1983.

——, *Zwischen Widerstand und Martyrium. Die Zeugen Jehovas im 'Dritten Reich'*, Munich: Oldenbourg, 1993.

——, *Between Resistance and Martyrdom: Jehovah's Witnesses in the Third Reich*, Madison, WI: University of Wisconsin Press/United States Holocaust Memorial Museum, 2008.

——, and KZ-Gedenkstätte Neuengamme, *Die Arbeit der KZ-Gedenkstätte Neuengamme 1981 bis 2001: Rückblicke-Ausblicke. Eine Dokumentation der Aktivitäten 20 Jahre nach der Eröffnung des Dokumentenhauses in Hamburg-Neuengamme*, Hamburg: KZ-Gedenkstätte Neuengamme, 2001.

Gedenkbuch. Häftlinge des Konzentrationslagers Bergen-Belsen, Celle: Gedenkstätte Bergen-Belsen, 2005.

Gedenkbuch – Opfer der Verfolgung der Juden unter der nationalsozialistischen Gewaltherrschaft in Deutschland 1933–1945, Koblenz: Bundesarchiv, 4 vols, 2006.

Gehle, H., 'Atempause – Atemwende. Die Literatur der Überlebenden', in Fritz-Bauer-Institut (ed.) *Auschwitz: Geschichte, Rezeption und Wirkung*, Frankfurt: Campus, 1996, pp.161–88.

Gellately, R., *The Gestapo and German Society: Enforcing Racial Policy 1933–1945*, Oxford: Oxford University Press, 1990.

——, *Backing Hitler: Consent and Coercion in Nazi Germany*, Oxford: Oxford University Press, 2002.

—— and Stoltzfus, N., (eds) *Social Outsiders in Nazi Germany*, Princeton, NJ: Princeton University Press, 2001.

Georg, E., *Die wirtschaftlichen Unternehmungen der SS*, Stuttgart: Deutsche Verlags-Anstalt, 1963.

Gerlach, C. and Aly, G., *Das letzte Kapitel. Realpolitik, Ideologie und der Mord an den ungarischen Juden 1944/1945*, Munich: DVA, 2002.

Gilbert, G. M., *The Psychology of Dictatorship: Based on an Examination of the Leaders of Nazi Germany*, New York: Ronald, 1950.

Gilbert, M., *Auschwitz and the Allies*, London: Pimlico, 2001.

Giles, G. S., 'Männerbund mit Homo-Panik: Die Angst der Nazis vor der Rolle der Erotik', in B. Jellonnek and R. Lautmann (eds) *Nationalsozialistischer Terror gegen Homosexuelle. Verdrängt und ungesühnt*, Paderborn: Schöningh, 2002, pp. 105–18.

——, 'The Denial of Homosexuality: Same-Sex Incidents in Himmler's Police and SS', in D. Herzog (ed.) *Sexuality and German Fascism*, New York/Oxford: Berghahn, 2005, pp. 256–90.

Gimbel, J., *A German Community under American Occupation: Marburg, 1945–52*, Stanford, CA: Stanford University Press, 1961.

Glauning, C., *Entgrenzung und KZ-System. Das Unternehmen 'Wüste' und das Konzentrationslager in Bisingen*, Berlin: Metropol, 2006.

Glicksman, W., 'Social differentiation in the German concentration camps', *Yivo Annual Jewish Social Sciences* 8, 1953, pp. 123–50.

Goldhagen, D. J., *Hitler's Willing Executioners.: Ordinary Germans and the Holocaust*, New York: Knopf, 1996.

Goldstein, J., *War and Gender: How Gender Shapes the War System and Vice Versa*, Cambridge: Cambridge University Press, 2001.

——, Lukoff, I. K. and Strauss, H. A., *Individuelles und kollektives Verhalten in Nazi-Konzentrationslagern: soziologische und psychologische Studien zu Berichten ungarisch-jüdischer Überlebender*, Frankfurt: Campus, 1991.

Gottwaldt, A. B. and Schulle, D., *Die Judendeportationen aus dem deutschen Reich von 1941–1945. Eine kommentierte Chronologie*, Berlin: Marix, 2005.

Gradowski, Z., *Au Coeur de l'enfer. Document écrit d'un Sonderkommando d'Auschwitz – 1944*, ed. P. Mesnard and C. Saletti, Paris: Edition Kimé, 2001.

Gregor, N., (ed.) *Nazism, War and Genocide*, Exeter: University of Exeter Press, 2005.

Greif, G., 'Die moralische Problematik der "Sonderkommando"–Häftlinge', in U. Herbert, K. Orth and C. Dieckmann (eds) *Die nationalsozialistischen Konzentrationslager. Entwicklung und Struktur*, vol. 1, Göttingen: Wallstein, 1998, pp. 1023–45.

——, *We Wept Without Tears: Interviews with Jewish Survivors of the Auschwitz Sonderkommando*, New Haven, CT: Yale University Press, 2005.

Greiser, K., *Die Todesmärsche von Buchenwald. Räumung, Befreiung und Spuren der Erinnerung*, Göttingen: Wallstein, 2008.

Grieger, M., '"Vernichtung durch Arbeit" in der deutschen Rüstungsindustrie', in T. Hess and T. Seidel (eds) *Vernichtung durch Fortschritt am Beispiel der Raketenproduktion im Konzentrationslager Mittelbau*, Bad Münstereifel: Westkreuz, 1995, pp. 43–60.

Gring, D., 'Das Massaker von Gardelegen', *Dachauer Hefte* 20, 2004, pp. 112–26.

Grobman, A., *Rekindling the Flame: American Jewish Chaplains and the Survivors of European Jewry, 1944–1948*, Detroit, MI: Wayne State University Press, 1993.

Grode, W., *Die 'Sonderbehandlung 14f13' in den Konzentrationslagern des Dritten Reichs. Ein Beitrag zur Dynamik faschistischer Vernichtungspolitik*, Frankfurt: Lang, 1987.

Grossmann, A., 'Zwei Erfahrungen im Kontext des Themas "Gender und Holocaust"', in S. Jacobeit and G. Philipp (eds) *Forschungsschwerpunkt Ravensbrück. Beiträge zur Geschichte des Frauen-Konzentrationslagers*, Berlin: Edition Hentrich, 1997, pp. 136–46.

——, 'Women and the Holocaust: Four Recent Titles', *Holocaust and Gender Studies* 16, 2002, 94–107.

Gruchmann, L., *Justiz im Dritten Reich*, Munich: Oldenbourg, 1990.

Grüner, M., Hachtmann, R. and Haupt, H. G. (eds), *Geschichte und Emanzipation. Festschrift für Reinhard Rürup*, Frankfurt, New York: Campus, 1999,

Gruner, W., *Jewish Forced Labor Under the Nazis, 1938–1944: Economic Needs and Racial Aims*, New York: Berghahn, 2006.

Guenther, I., *Nazi Chic? Fashioning Women in the Third Reich*, Oxford/New York: Berg, 2004.

Günther, G., *Buchenwald*, Weimar: Ständige Kommissionen Kultur der Stadtverordneten-versammlung Weimar und des Kreistages Weimar-Land in Zusammenarbeit mit dem Stadtmuseum Weimar, 1983.

Gutman, Y. and Berenbaum, M., (eds) *Anatomy of the Auschwitz Death Camp*, Bloomington, IN: Indiana University Press, 1994.

——— and S. Krakowski, 'Juden im KL Auschwitz', in *Sterbebücher von Auschwitz. Fragmente*, Munich: Saur 1995, vol. 1, pp. 163–94.

Gutterman, B., *A Narrow Bridge to Life: Jewish Slave Labor and Survival in the Gross-Rosen Camp System, 1940–1945*, New York: Berghahn, 2008.

Hackett, D. A., (ed.) *The Buchenwald Report*, Boulder, CO: Westview, 1995.

Haffner, S., *Geschichte eines Deutschen. Die Erinnerungen 1914–1933*, 10th edn, Stuttgart and Munich: DVA, 2001.

Hagemann, K. and Quataert, J. H., (eds) *Gendering Modern German History: Rewriting Historiography*, New York/Oxford: Berghahn, 2007.

——— and Schüler-Springorum, S. (eds) *Home/Front: The Military, War and Gender in Twentieth-Century Germany*, Oxford/New York: Berg, 2002.

Hamburger Stiftung zur Förderung von Wissenschaft und Kultur, (ed.) *'Deutsche Wirtschaft'. Zwangsarbeit von KZ-Häftlingen für Industrie und Behörden. Symposion 'Wirtschaft und Konzentrationslager'*, Hamburg: VSA, 1991.

Hammermann, G., 'Das Internierungs- und Kriegsgefangenenlager Dachau 1945–1948', in W. Benz and A. Königseder (eds) *Das Konzentrationslager Dachau: Geschichte und Wirkung nationalsozialistischer Repression*, Berlin: Metropol, 2008, pp. 125–146.

Harder, J. and Hesse, H., 'Female Jehovah's Witnesses in Moringen Women's Concentration Camp: Women's Resistance in Nazi Germany', in H. Hesse (ed.) *Persecution and Resistance of Jehovah's Witnesses during the Nazi Regime 1933–1945*, Bremen: Edition Temmen, 2001, pp. 36–59.

Hartewig, K., 'Wolf under Wölfen? Die prekäre Macht der kommunistischen Kapos im Konzentrationslager Buchenwald', in U. Herbert, K. Orth and C. Dieckmann (eds) *Die nationalsozialistischen Konzentrationslager. Entwicklung und Struktur*, Göttingen: Wallstein, 1998, vol. 2, pp. 939–58.

Härtl, U., *Die Neukonzeption der Gedenkstätte Buchenwald. Die Gedenkstätte Buchenwald seit 1989/90*, Weimar: Stiftung Gedenkstätten Buchenwald und Mittelbau-Dora, 2001.

Hart-Moxon, K., *Return to Auschwitz*, Newark, UK: Beth Shalom, 1997.

Hayes, P., *Industry and Ideology: IG Farben in the Nazi Era*, Cambridge: Cambridge University Press, 1987.

———, 'Die IG Farben und die Zwangsarbeit von KZ-Häftlingen im Werk Auschwitz', in H. Kaienburg (ed.) *Konzentrationslager und deutsche Wirtschaft 1939–1945*, Opladen: Leske und Budrich, 1996, pp. 129–48.

Heberer, P. and Matthäus, J., (eds) *Atrocities on Trial: Historical Perspectives on the Politics of Prosecuting War Crimes*, Lincoln, NE: University of Nebraska Press, 2008.

Heigl, P., *Konzentrationslager Flossenbürg in Geschichte und Gegenwart*, Regensburg: Mittelbayerische Druckerei- und Verlags-Gesellschaft, 1989.

Heike, I. and Strebel, B., 'Häftlingsselbstverwaltung und Funktionshäftlinge im Konzentrationslager Ravensbrück', in C. Füllberg-Stolberg, M. Jung, R. Riebe and M. Scheitenberger (eds) *Frauen in Konzentrationslagern – Bergen–Belsen, Ravensbrück*, Bremen Edition: Temmen, 1994, pp. 89–97.

Heinemann, E. D., 'Sexuality and Nazism: The Doubly Unspeakable?', in D. Herzog (ed.) *Sexuality and German Fascism*, New York/Oxford: Berghahn, 2005, pp. 22–66.

Heinsohn, K., Vogel, B. and Weckel, U., (eds) *Zwischen Karriere und Verfolgung. Handlungsräume von Frauen im nationalsozialistischen Deutschland*, Frankfurt/New York: Campus, 1997.

Henry, M., *Confronting the Perpetrators: A History of the Claims Conference*, London: Vallentine Mitchell, 2007.

Herbermann, N., *Der gesegnete Abgrund. Schutzhäftling Nr. 6582 im Frauenkonzentrationslager Ravensbrück*, Nuremberg: Glock und Lutz, 1946 (English edn *The Blessed Abyss: Inmate #6582 in Ravensbrück Concentration Camp for Women*, ed. H. Baer and E. R. Baer, Detroit, MI: Wayne State University Press, 2000).

Herbert, U., 'Arbeit und Vernichtung. Ökonomisches Interesse und Primat der "Weltanschauung" im Nationalsozialismus', in D. Diner (ed.) *Ist der Nationalsozialismus Geschichte? Zu Historisierung und Historikerstreit*, Frankfurt: Fischer, 1987, pp. 198–236.

——, 'Labour and Extermination: Economic Interest and the Primacy of Weltanschauung in National Socialism', *Past and Present* 138, 1993, pp. 144–95.

——, *Best. Biographische Studien über Radikalismus, Weltanschauung und Vernunft 1903–1989*, Bonn: Dietz, 1996.

——, *Hitler's Foreign Workers: Enforced Foreign Labour in Germany Under the Third Reich*, Cambridge: Cambridge University Press, 1997.

——, 'Von der Gegnerbekämpfung zur "rassischen Generalprävention". "Schutzhaft" und Konzentrationslager in der Konzeption der Gestapo-Führung 1933–1939', in U. Herbert, K. Orth and C. Dieckmann (eds) *Die nationalsozialistischen Konzentrationslager. Entwicklung und Struktur*, vol. 1, Göttingen: Wallstein, 1998, pp. 60–86

——, Orth, K. and Dieckmann C., (eds) *Die nationalsozialistischen Konzentrationslager. Entwicklung und Struktur*, 2 vols, Göttingen: Wallstein, 1998.

——, Orth, K. and Dieckmann C., 'Die nationalsozialistischen Konzentrationslager. Geschichte, Erinnerung, Forschung', in U. Herbert, K. Orth and C. Dieckmann (eds) *Die nationalsozialistischen Konzentrationslager. Entwicklung und Struktur*, vol. 1, Göttingen: Wallstein, 1998, pp. 17–40.

Herbst, L., *Der totale Krieg und die Ordnung der Wirtschaft. Die Kriegswirtschaft im Spannungsfeld von Politik, Ideologie und Propaganda 1939–1945*, Stuttgart: DVA, 1982.

Herf, J., *Divided Memory: The Nazi Past in the Two Germanys*, Cambridge, MA: Harvard University Press, 1997.

Herz, G., *The Women's Camp in Moringen: A Memoir of Imprisonment in Germany 1936-1937*, ed. and introduced by J. Caplan, New York/Oxford: Berghahn, 2006.

Herzog, D. (ed.) *Sexuality and German Fascism*, New York/Oxford: Berghahn, 2005.

Hesse, H. (ed.) *Persecution and Resistance of Jehovah's Witnesses during the Nazi Regime 1933–1945*, Bremen: Edition Temmen, 2001.

——, *Das Frauen-KZ Moringen 1933–1938*, Hürth: Books on Demand GmbH, 2nd edn, 2002.

——, 'Von der "Erziehung" zur "Ausmerzung". Das Konzentrationslager Moringen 1933–1945', in W. Benz and B. Distel (eds) *Instrumentarium der Macht. Frühe Konzentrationslager 1933–1937*, Berlin: Metropol, 2003, pp. 111–46.

—— and Harder, H., '*Und wenn ich lebenslang in einem KZ bleiben müßte …*' *Die Zeuginnen Jehovas in den Frauenkonzentrationslagern Moringen, Lichtenburg und Ravensbrück*, Essen: Klartext, 2001.

Hilberg, R., *The Destruction of the European Jews*, New Haven, CT and London: Yale University Press, 2003.

Hockerts, H. G., '*Wiedergutmachung* in Germany: Balancing Historical Accounts, 1945–2000', in D. Diner and G. Wunberg (eds) *Restitution and Memory: Material Restoration in Europe*, New York: Berghahn, 2007, pp. 323–81.

Hoffman, D., (ed) *Das Gedächtnis der Dinge. KZ-Relikte und KZ-Denkmäler 1945–1995*, Frankfurt: Campus, 1998.

Hofmann, T., Loewy, H. and Stein, H., *Pogromnacht und Holocaust. Frankfurt, Weimar, Buchenwald … Die schwierige Erinnerung an die Stationen der Verfolgung*, Vienna: Böhlau 1994.

Horowitz, S. R., 'Geschlechtsspezifische Erinnerungen an der Holocaust', in S. Jacobeit and G. Philipp (eds) *Forschungsschwerpunkt Ravensbrück. Beiträge zur Geschichte des Frauen-Konzentrationslagers*, Berlin: Edition Hentrich, 1997, pp. 131-5

Horvits, A., 'Mitzad HaMavet shel Yehudei Chełm VeHrubieszów leEver Nahar Bug BeDetzember 1939', *Yalkult Moreshet* 68, October 1999, pp. 52–68.

Horwitz, G., *In the Shadow of Death: Living outside the Gates of Mauthausen*, New York: Free Press, 1990.

Huener, J., *Auschwitz, Poland, and the Politics of Commemoration, 1945–1979*, Athens, OH: Ohio University Press, 2003.

In Memoriam, The Hague: Sdu Uitgeverij Koninginnegracht, 1995.

International Military Tribunal, *Trial of the Major War Criminals before the International Military Tribunal Nuremberg 14 November 1945–1 October 1946*, Nuremberg, 1947–49, 42 vols.

Internationales Buchenwald-Komitee/Komitee der Antifaschistischen Widerstandskämpfer der Deutschen Demokratischen Republik, (ed.) *Buchenwald. Mahnung und Verpflichtung*, Berlin: Kongress-Verlag, 1960.

Iwaszko, T., 'Reasons for Confinement in the Camp and Categories of Prisoners', in W. Długoborski and F. Piper (eds), *Auschwitz 1940–1945*, 5 vols, Oświęcim, 2000, vol. 2, pp. 11–44.

Jahn, F., 'Auschwitz. Frauenabteilung', in W. Benz and B. Distel (eds) *Der Ort des Terrors. Geschichte der nationalsozialistischen Konzentrationslager*, Munich: Beck, vol. 4: *Flossenbürg, Mauthausen, Ravensbrück*, 2006, pp. 523–8.

Jaiser, C., 'Irma Grese. Zur Rezeption einer KZ-Aufseherin', in S. Erpel (ed.) *Im Gefolge der SS. Aufseherinnen des Frauen-KZ Ravensbrück*, Berlin: Metropol, 2007, pp. 338–46.

Jansen, C., 'Häftlingsalltag auf dem Laagberg bei Wolfsburg', in N. Frei, S. Steinbacher and B. C. Wagner (eds) *Ausbeutung, Vernichtung, Öffentlichkeit. Neue Studien zur nationalsozialistischen Lagerpolitik*, Munich: Saur, 2000, pp. 75–107.

Johe, W., 'Das deutsche Volk und das System der Konzentrationslager', in U. Büttner (ed.) *Das Unrechtsregime*. Hamburg: Christians, 1986, pp. 331–44.

John-Stucke, K., 'Konzentrationslager Niederhagen/Wewelsburg', in J. E. Schulte (ed.) *Konzentrationslager im Rheinland und in Westfalen, 1933–1945*, Paderborn: Schöningh, 2005, pp. 97–111.

Jureit, U. and Orth, K., *Überlebensgeschichten. Gespräche mit Überlebenden des KZ-Neuengamme*, Hamburg: Dölling und Galitz, 1994.

Kaienburg, H., *'Vernichtung durch Arbeit'. Der Fall Neuengamme. Die Wirtschaftsbestrebungen der SS und ihre Auswirkungen auf die Existenzbedingungen der KZ-Gefangenen*, Bonn: Dietz, 1991.

——, (ed.) *Konzentrationslager und deutsche Wirtschaft 1939–1945*, Opladen: Leske und Budrich, 1996.

——, *Das Konzentrationslager Neuengamme 1938–1945*, Bonn: Dietz, 1997.

——, 'Funktionswandel des KZ-Kosmos? Das Konzentrationslager Neuengamme', in U. Herbert, K. Orth, C. Dieckmann (eds) *Die nationalsozialistischen Konzentrationslager. Entwicklung und Struktur*, vol. 1, Göttingen: Wallstein, 1998, pp. 259–84.

——, *Die Wirtschaft der SS*, Berlin: Metropol, 2003.

——, *Der Militär- und Wirtschaftskomplex der SS im KZ-Standort Sachsenhausen-Oranienburg*, Berlin: Metropol, 2006.

——, 'Sachsenhausen – Stammlager', in W. Benz and B. Distel (eds) *Der Ort des Terrors. Geschichte der nationalsozialistischen Konzentrationslager*, Munich: Beck, vol. 3: *Sachsenhausen, Buchenwald*, 2006, pp. 17–72.

Kannapin, H.-E., *Wirtschaft unter Zwang. Anmerkungen und Analysen zur rechtlichen und politischen Verantwortung der deutschen Wirtschaft unter der Herrschaft des Nationalsozialismus im 2. Weltkrieg, besonders im Hinblick auf den Einsatz und die Behandlung von ausländischen Arbeitskräften und Konzentrationslagerhäftlingen in deutschen Industrie- und Rüstungsunternehmen*, Cologne: Deutscher Industrieverlag, 1966.

Kárný, M.,'Waffen-SS und Konzentrationslager', *Jahrbuch für Geschichte* 33, 1986, pp. 231–61.

——, '"Vernichtung durch Arbeit". Sterblichkeit in den NS-Konzentrationslagern', in G. Aly *et al.* (eds) *Sozialpolitik und Judenvernichtung*, Berlin: Rotbuch, 1987, pp. 133–58.

——, '"Vernichtung durch Arbeit"' in Leitmeritz: Die SS-Führungsstäbe in der deutschen Kriegswirtschaft', in *1999: Zeitschrift für Sozialgeschichte des 20. Jahrhunderts* 4, 1993, pp. 37–61.

——, (ed.) *Terezínská pametní kniha. Zidovské obeti nacistických deportací z Cech a Moravy 1941–1945*, Prague: Nadace Terezínská iniciativa – Melantrich, 1995.

——, 'Das Theresienstädter Familienlager BIIb in Birkenau September 1943–Juli 1944', *Hefte von Auschwitz* 20, 1997, pp. 133–237.

Kautsky, B., *Teufel und Verdammte*, Zürich: Gutenberg, 1946.

Kavčič, S., *Überleben und Erinnern. Slowenische Häftlinge im Frauen-Konzentrationslager Ravensbrück*, Berlin: Metropol 2007.

Keden, H. J., 'Musik in nationalsozialistischen Konzentrationslager', *Aus Politik und Zeitgeschichte* 11 2005, pp. 40–6.

Keller, R. and Otto R., 'Sowjetische Kriegsgefangene in Konzentrationslagern der SS', in J. Ibel (ed.) *Einvernehmliche Zusammenarbeit? Wehrmacht, Gestapo, SS und sowjetische Kriegsgefangene*, Berlin: Metropol, 2008.

Kershaw, I., *The Nazi Dictatorship: Problems and Perspectives of Interpretation*, London: Arnold, 4th edn. 2000.

Kienle, M., *Gottteszell – das frühe Konzentrationslager für Frauen in Württemberg. Die 'Schutzhaftabteilung' im Frauengefängnis Gottteszell in Schwäbisch Gmünd März 1933 bis Januar 1934*, Ulm: Klemm & Oelschläger, 2002.

Klarsfeld, S., *Memorial to the Jews Deported From France, 1942–1944: Documentation of the Deportation of the Victims of the Final Solution in France*, New York: Beate Klarsfeld Foundation, 1983.

—— and M. Steinberg (eds) *Mémorial de la déportation des Juifs de Belgique*, Brussels, 1982.

Klein, K., *Kazett-Lyrik. Untersuchungen zu Gedichten und Liedern aus dem Konzentrationslager Sachsenhausen*, Würzburg: Königshausen & Neumann, 1995.

Klein P., (ed.) *Die Einsatzgruppen in der besetzten Sowjetunion 1941/42. Die Tätigkeits- und Lageberichte des Chefs der Sicherheitspolizei und des SD 1941/42*, Berlin: Edition Hentrich, 1997.

——, 'Vernichtungslager Kulmhof/Chełmno', in W. Benz and B. Distel (eds) *Der Ort des Terrors. Geschichte der nationalsozialistischen Konzentrationslager*, Munich: Beck, vol. 8: *Riga, Warschau, Vaivara, Plaszów, Kulmhof/Chełmno, Belzec, Sobibór, Treblinka*, 2008, pp. 301–28.

Klewitz, B., *Die Arbeitssklaven der Dynamit Nobel. Ausgebeutet und vergessen. Sklavenarbeiter und KZ-Häftlinge in Europas größten Rüstungswerken im Zweiten Weltkrieg*, Schalksmühle: Engelbrecht, 1986.

Kłodziński, S., 'Die ersten Vergasungen von Häftlingen und Kriegsgefangenen im Konzentrationslager Auschwitz', in Hamburger Institut für Sozialforschung (ed.) *Die Auschwitz-Hefte*, 2 vols, Hamburg: Rogner & Bernhard, 1994, vol. 1, pp. 261–75.

Klüger, R., *Still Alive: A Holocaust Girlhood Remembered*, New York: Feminist Press, 2001.

Knigge, V., 'Buchenwald', in D. Hoffmann (ed.) *Das Gedächtnis der Dinge. KZ-Relikte und KZ-Denkmäler, 1945–1995*, Frankfurt: Campus, 1997, pp. 94–173.

Knop, M., Krause, H. and Schwarz, R., 'Die Häftlinge des Konzentrationslagers Oranienburg', in G. Morsch (ed.) *Konzentrationslager Oranienburg*, Oranienburg: Stiftung Brandenburgische Gedenkstätten, 1994, pp. 67–77.

Koening, E., 'Auschwitz III – Blechhammer', *Dachauer Hefte* 15, 1999, pp. 134–52.

Kogon, E., *Der SS-Staat. Das System der deutschen Konzentrationslager*, 26th edn, Munich: Heyne, 1993.

——, *The Theory and Practice of Hell: The German Concentration Camps and the System Behind Them* (with a new introduction by Nikolaus Wachsmann), New York: Farrar, Straus and Giroux, 2006.

——, Langbein, H. and Rückerl A. (eds) *Nationalsozialistische Massentötungen durch Giftgas*, Frankfurt: Fischer, 1983.

Kolb, E., *Bergen-Belsen. Geschichte des 'Aufenthaltslagers' 1943–1945*, Hannover: Verlag für Literatur und Zeitgeschehen, 1962.

——, *Bergen-Belsen, 1943–1945. Vom Aufenthaltslager zum Konzentrationslager*, Göttingen: Vandenhoeck & Ruprecht, 2002.

Königseder, A., *Lebensmut im Wartesaal: Die jüdischen DPs (displaced persons) im Nachkriegsdeutschland*, Frankfurt: Fischer, 1994.

Kooger, B., *Rüstung unter Tage. Die Untertageverlagerung von Rüstungsbetrieben und der Einsatz von KZ-Häftlingen in Beendorf und Morsleben*, Berlin: Metropol, 2004.

Koonz, C., 'A Tributary and a Mainstream: Gender, Public Memory, and Historiography of Nazi Germany', in K. Hagemann and J. Quataert (eds) *Gendering Modern German History: Rewriting Historiography*, New York/Oxford: Berghahn, 2007, pp. 147–68.

Kopka, B., *Konzentrationslager Warschau. Historia i nastepstwa*, Warsaw: Instytut Pamięci Narodowej, 2007.

Köpp, U., 'Der Entwurf Reinhold Lingers für die Gedenkstätte Sachsenhausen', in G. Morsch (ed.) *Von der Erinnerung zum Monument. Die Entstehungsgeschichte der Nationalen Mahn- und Gedenkstätte Sachsenhausen*, Berlin: Edition Hentrich, 1996, pp. 148–57.

——, 'Die Studien des Buchenwald-Kollektivs für die Gestaltung der Gedenkstätte Sachsenhausen 1956', in G. Morsch (ed.) *Von der Erinnerung zum Monument. Die Entstehungsgeschichte der Nationalen Mahn- und Gedenkstätte Sachsenhausen*, Berlin: Edition Hentrich, 1996, pp. 158–63.

——, 'Die Projektierung der Gedenkstätte Sachsenhausen und die Diskussionen im Wissenschaft-Künstlerischen Beirat beim Ministerium für Kultur', in G. Morsch (ed.) *Von der Erinnerung zum Monument. Die Entstehungsgeschichte der Nationalen Mahn- und Gedenkstätte Sachsenhausen*, Berlin: Edition Hentrich, 1996, pp. 217–31.

Körte, M., 'Erinnerungsliteratur', *Dachauer Hefte* 18, 2002, pp. 24–33.

Kosmala, B., 'Polnische Häftlinge im Konzentrationslager Dachau 1939–1945', *Dachauer Hefte* 21, 2005, pp. 94–113.

Kossert, A., '*Endlösung* on the "Amber Shore": The Massacre in January 1945 on the Baltic Seashore: A Repressed Chapter of East Prussian History', *Leo Baeck Institute Year Book* 49, 2004, pp. 3–19.

Krakowski, S., 'The Death Marches in the Period of the Evacuation of the Camps', in M. R. Marrus (ed.) *The Nazi Holocaust*, vol. 9, Westport, CT: Meckler, 1989, pp. 476–90.

——, *Das Todeslager Chełmno/Kulmhof. Der Beginn der 'Endlösung'*, Jerusalem and Göttingen: Yad Vashem and Wallstein, 2007.

Kranig, A., *Lockung und Zwang. Zur Arbeitsverfassung im Dritten Reich*, Stuttgart: DVA, 1983.

Kranz, T., 'Eksterminacja Żydów na Majdanku i rola obozu w realizacji "Akcji Reinhardt"' *Zeszyty Majdanka* 22, 2003, pp. 7–55.

——, *Extermination of Jews at the Majdanek Concentration Camp*, Lublin: State Museum, 2007.

——, 'Bookkeeping of Death and Prisoner Mortality at Majdanek', *Yad Vashem Studies* 35, 2007, pp. 81–109.

Kraus, O. and Kulka, E., *The Death Factory. Documents on Auschwitz*, Oxford: Pergamon Press, 1966.

Krause, R. D., 'Truth but not art? German autobiographical writings of the survivors of Nazi Concentration camps, Ghettos and Prisons' in Y. Bauer, A. Eckhardt and F. Litell (eds) *Remembering for the Future. The Impact of the Holocaust and Genocide on Jews and Christians*, vol. 3, Oxford: Pergamon Press, 1989, pp. 2958–72.

Krausnick, H., Buchheim, H., Broszat, M. and Jacobsen, H.-A., *Anatomy of the SS State*, New York: Walker, 1965.

Kreiser, K.,'"Sie starben allein und ruhig, ohne zu schreien oder jemanden zu rufen." Das "Kleine Lager" im Konzentrationslager Buchenwald', *Dachauer Hefte* 14, 1998, pp. 102–24.

Kubica, H., 'Children and Adolescents in Auschwitz', in W. Długoborski and F. Piper (eds) *Auschwitz 1940–1945*, Oświęcim: State Museum, vol. 2, *The Prisoners – Their Life and Work*, pp. 285–318.

Kühle, B., *Speziallager Nr. 7. Sachsenhausen, 1945–1950*, Berlin: Brandenburgisches Verlagshaus, 1990.

Kühne, T., *Kameradschaft. Die Soldaten des nationalsozialistischen Krieges und das 20. Jahrhundert*, Göttingen: Vandenhoeck und Ruprecht, 2006.

Kühnrich, H., *Der KZ-Staat 1933–1945*, Berlin: Dietz, 1960.

Külow, K., 'Jüdische Häftlinge im KZ Sachsenhausen 1939 bis 1942', in G. Morsch and S. zur Nieden (eds) *Jüdische Häftlinge im Konzentrationslager Sachsenhausen 1936 bis 1945*, Berlin: Edition Hentrich, 2004, pp. 180–99.

Kupfer-Koberwitz, E., *Die Mächtigen und die Hilflosen. Als Häftling in Dachau*, Stuttgart: Friedrich Vorwerk, 1960.

Kussmann, A., *Ein KZ-Außenlager in Düsseldorf-Stoffeln*, Düsseldorf: n.p., 1988.

Kwiet, K., 'Erziehung zum Mord – Zwei Beispiele zur Kontinuität der deutschen "Endlösung der Judenfrage"', in M. Grüner, R. Hachtmann and H. G. Haupt (eds) *Geschichte und Emanzipation. Festschrift für Reinhard Rürup*, Frankfurt, New York: Campus, 1999, pp. 435–57.

KZ-Gedenkstätte Neuengamme, (ed.) *Abgeleitete Macht. Funktionshäftlinge zwischen Widerstand und Kollaboration*, Bremen: Edition Temmen, 1998.

Langbein, H., '… nicht wie die Schafe zur Schlachtbank. Widerstand in den nationalsozialistischen Konzentrationslagern*, Frankfurt: Fischer, 1980.

——, *People in Auschwitz*, Chapel Hill, NC: University of North Carolina Press, 2004.

Langhammer, S., 'Die reichsweite Verhaftungsaktion vom 9. März 1937', *Hallische Beiträge zur Zeitgeschichte* 1, 2007, pp. 55–77.

Langhoff, W., *Rubber Truncheon: Being an Account of Thirteen Months Spent in a Concentration Camp*, London: Constable, 1935.

Lappin, E., 'The Death Marches of Hungarian Jews through Austria in the Spring of 1945', *Yad Vashem Studies* 28, 2000, pp. 203–42.

Lasik, A., 'Historical-Social Profile of the Auschwitz SS', in Y. Gutmann and M. Berenbaum (eds) *Anatomy of the Auschwitz Death Camp*, Bloomington, IN: Indiana University Press, 1994, pp. 271–87.

Leff, L., *Buried by the Times: The Holocaust and America's Most Important Newspaper*, New York: Cambridge University Press, 2005.

Lehrke, G., *Gedenkstätten für Opfer des Nationalsozialismus: Historisch-politische Bildung an Orten des Widerstands und der Verfolgung*, Frankfurt: Campus, 1988.

Leo, A., 'Ravensbrück – Stammlager', in W. Benz and B. Distel (eds) *Der Ort des Terrors. Geschichte der nationalsozialistischen Konzentrationslager*. Munich: Beck, vol. 4: *Flossenbürg, Mauthausen, Ravensbrück*, 2006, pp. 473–520.

Levene, M., 'Introduction', in M. Levene and P. Roberts (eds) *The Massacre in History*, New York and Oxford: Berghahn, 1999, pp. 1–38.

Levi, P., *The Reawakening (La Tregua). A Liberated Prisoner's Long March Home through East Europe*, 1st American edn, Boston, MA: Little Brown, 1965.

——, *The Drowned and the Saved*, London: Abacus, 1989.

——, *If This Is a Man*, London: Everyman's Library, 2000.

Lifton, R. J., *The Nazi Doctors*, New York: Basic Books, 1986.

Litten, I., *A Mother Fights Hitler*, London: Allen & Unwin, 1940.

Longerich, P., *Politik der Vernichtung*, Munich: Piper, 1998.

——, *'Davon haben wir nichts gewusst!' Die Deutschen und die Judenverfolgung 1933–1945*, Munich: Siedler, 2006.

——, *Heinrich Himmler*, Munich: Siedler, 2008.

Lozowick, Y., *Hitler's Bureaucrats: The Nazi Security Police and the Banality of Evil*, New York: Continuum, 2002.

Mączka S. M., (ed.) *Żydzi polscy w KL Auschwitz. Wykazy imienne*, Warsaw: Żydowski Instytut Historyczny, 2004.

Mahn- und Gedenkstätte Buchenwald (ed.) *Buchenwald. Mahnung und Verpflichtung*, Berlin: VEB, 1983.

Majdanek 1942. Księga zmarłych więźniów, Lublin: Państwowe Muzeum, 2004.

Malá, I. and Kubátová, L., *Pochody Smrti*, Prague: Nakladatelství politické literatury, 1965.

Mallmann, K.-M., 'Zwischen Denunziation und Roter Hilfe. Geschlechterbeziehungen und kommunistischer Widerstand', in C. Wickert (ed.) *Frauen gegen die Diktatur. Widerstand und Verfolgung im nationalsozialistischen Deutschland*, Berlin: Edition Hentrich, 1995, pp. 82–97.

—— and G. Paul, (eds) *Die Gestapo im Zweiten Weltkrieg. 'Heimatfront' und besetztes Europa*, Darmstadt: Primus Verlag, 2000.

—— and G. Paul (eds) *Die Gestapo. Mythos und Realität*, Darmstadt: Primus Verlag, 1995.

Mammach, K., *Der Volkssturm. Das letzte Aufgebot 1944/45*, Cologne: Pahl-Rugenstein, 1981.

Mangan, J. A. (ed.) *Shaping the Superman: Fascist Body as Political Icon: Aryan Fascism*, London: Frank Cass, 1999.

Mann, M., *The Dark Side of Democracy*, Cambridge: Cambridge University Press, 2005.

Marcuse, H., *Legacies of Dachau: The Uses and Abuses of a Concentration Camp, 1933–2001*, Cambridge: Cambridge University Press, 2001.

——, 'Memorializing the Holocaust: History and Theory', *American Historical Review*, forthcoming 2010.

——, F. Schimmelfennig and J. Spielmann, *Steine des Anstosses: Nationalsozialismus und Zweiter Weltkrieg in Denkmalen, 1945–1985*, Hamburg: Museum für Hamburgische Geschichte, 1985.

Maršálek, H., *Die Geschichte des Konzentrationslagers Mauthausen*, 3rd edn, Vienna: Lagergemeinschaft Mauthausen, 1995.

Marszalek, J., *Majdanek. Obóz koncentracyjny w Lublinie*, Warsaw: Wydawnictwo Interpress, 1981.

——, *Majdanek. Konzentrationslager Lublin*, Warsaw: Interpress, 1984.

Mason, T., *Social Policy in the Third Reich: The Working Class and the 'National Community'*, Providence, RI and Oxford: Berg, 1993.

——, 'The Primacy of Politics: Politics and Economics in National Socialist Germany' in J. Caplan (ed.) *Nazism, Fascism and the Working Class: Essays by Tim Mason*, Cambridge: Cambridge University Press, 1995, pp. 53–76.

Matthäus, J., 'Verfolgung, Ausbeutung, Vernichtung. Jüdische Häftlinge im System der Konzentrationslager', in G. Morsch and S. zur Nieden (eds) *Jüdische Häftlinge im KZ Sachsenhausen 1936–1945*, Berlin: Edition Hentrich, 2004, pp. 64–90.

Matusiak, T., *Stutthof*, Gdańsk: Zakłady Graficzne, 1969.

Mayer, A. H., '"Schwachsinn höheren Grades." Zur Verfolgung lesbischer Frauen in Österreich während der NS-Zeit', in B. Jellonnek and R. Lautmann (eds) *Nationalsozialistischer Terror gegen Homosexuelle. Verdrängt und ungesühnt*, Paderborn: Schöningh, 2002, pp. 83–93.

Mayer-von Götz, I., *Terror im Zentrum der Macht. Die frühen Konzentrationslager in Berlin 1933/34–1936*, Berlin: Metropol, 2008.

McCourt, F., *'Tis: A Memoir*, New York: Simon & Schuster, 1999.

Megargee, G. P., (ed.) *The United States Holocaust Memorial Museum Encyclopedia of Camps and Ghettos*, vol. 1: *Early Camps, Youth Camps, and Concentration Camps and Sub-Camps under the SS-Business Administration Main Office (WVHA)*, Bloomington, IN/Washington, DC: Indiana University Press and USHMM, 2009.

Meier, K., '"Es war verpönt, aber das gab's." Die Darstellung weiblicher Homosexualität in Autobiographien von weiblichen Überlebenden aus Ravensbrück und Auschwitz', in H. Diercks (ed.) *Verfolgung von Homosexuellen im Nationalsozialismus*, Bremen: Edition Temmen, 1999, pp. 22–33.

Mencel, T., *Majdanek 1941–1944*, Lublin: Wydawnictwo Lubelskie, 1991

—— and T. Kranz, *Extermination of Jews at the Majdanek Concentration Camp*, Lublin: State Museum, 2007.

Merridale, C., *Ivan's War: Life and Death in the Red Army, 1939–1945*, New York: Metropolitan Books, 2006.

Micheler, S., 'Homophobic Propaganda and the Denunciation of Same-Sex-Desiring Men under National Socialism', in D. Herzog (ed.) *Sexuality and German Fascism*, New York/Oxford: Berghahn, 2005, pp. 95–130.

Miller, J., *One, by One, by One: Facing the Holocaust*, New York: Simon and Schuster, 1990.

Milton, S., 'Die Konzentrationslager der dreißiger Jahre im Bild der in- und ausländischen Presse', in U. Herbert, K. Orth and C. Dieckmann (eds) *Die nationalsozialistischen Konzentrationslager. Entwicklung und Struktur*, vol. 1, Göttingen: Wallstein, 1998, pp. 135–47.

—— and Nowinski, I., *In Fitting Memory: The Art and Politics of Holocaust Memorials*, Detroit, MI: Wayne State University Press, 1991.

Milward, A., Review of Billig, *Les Camps*, in *The Journal of Modern History* 48, 1976, pp. 567–8.

Mix, A., 'Warschau – Stammlager', in W. Benz and B. Distel (eds) *Der Ort des Terrors. Geschichte der nationalsozialistischen Konzentrationslager*, Munich: Beck, vol. 8: *Riga, Warschau, Vaivara, Plaszów, Kulmhof/Chełmno, Belżec, Sobibór, Treblinka*, 2008, pp. 91–126.

Mommsen, H. and Grieger, G., *Das Volkswagenwerk und seine Arbeiter im Dritten Reich*, Düsseldorf: Econ, 1996.

Monneuse, D., 'Idéaltype des parcours empruntés par les rescapés des camps de concentration nazis après 1945', *Bulletin Trimestriel de la Fondation Auschwitz* 96, July–September 2007, pp. 75–103.

Morsch, G. (ed.) *Von der Erinnerung zum Monument. Die Entstehungsgeschichte der Nationalen Mahn- und Gedenkstätte Sachsenhausen*, Berlin: Edition Hentrich, 1996.

——, 'Organisations- und Verwaltungsstruktur der Konzentrationslager' in W. Benz and B. Distel (eds) *Der Ort des Terrors. Geschichte der nationalsozialistischen Konzentrationslager*, Munich: Beck, vol. 1: *Die Organisation des Terrors*, 2005, pp. 58–75.

——, (ed.) *From Sachsenburg to Sachsenhausen*, Berlin: Metropol, 2007.

——, 'Formation and Construction of the Sachsenhausen Concentration Camp', in G. Morsch (ed.) *From Sachsenburg to Sachsenhausen*, Berlin: Metropol, 2007, pp. 87–194.

—— and Gedenkstätte und Museum Sachsenhausen, *Sowjetisches Speziallager Nr. 7/Nr. 1 in Sachsenhausen (1945–1950)*, Berlin: Metropol, 2005.

——, and zur Nieden, S., (eds) *Jüdische Häftlinge im Konzentrationslager Sachsenhausen 1936 bis 1945*, Berlin: Edition Hentrich, 2004.

Mosse, G., *Nationalism and Sexuality: Respectability and Abnormal Sexuality in Modern Europe*, New York: Howard Fertig, 1985.

Mühsam, K., *Der Leidensweg Erich Mühsams*, Zurich: Mopr, 1935.

Müller, J., 'Betrifft: Haftgruppen "Homosexuelle"', in O. Mussmann (ed.) *Homosexuelle in Konzentrationslager*, Berlin/Bonn: Westkreuz Verlag, 2000, pp. 10–30.

—— and Sternweiler, A., (eds) *Homosexuelle Männer im KZ Sachsenhausen*, Berlin: Männerschwarm, 2000.

Müller, K., 'Totgeschlagen, totgeschwiegen? Das autobiographische Zeugnis homosexueller Überlebender', in B. Jellonnek and R. Lautmann (eds) *Nationalsozialistischer Terror gegen Homosexuelle. Verdrängt und ungesühnt*, Paderborn: Schöningh, 2002, pp. 397–418.

Naasner, W., *Neue Machtzentren in der deutschen Kriegswirtschaft 1942–1945. Die Wirtschaftsorganisation der SS, das Amt des Generalbevollmächtigten für den Arbeitseinsatz und das Reichsministerium für Bewaffnung und Munition/Reichsministerium für Rüstung und Kriegsproduktion im nationalsozialistischen Herrschaftssystem*, Boppard am Rhein: Boldt, 1994.

——, *SS-Wirtschaft und SS-Verwaltung. Das SS-Wirtschafts-Verwaltungshauptamt und die unter seiner Dienstaufsicht stehenden wirtschaftlichen Unternehmungen und weitere Dokumente*, Düsseldorf: Droste, 1998.

Naimark, N. M., *The Russians in Germany: A History of the Soviet Zone of Occupation, 1945–1949*, Cambridge and London: Belknap Press, 1995.

Naujocks, H., *Mein Leben in Sachsenhausen 1936–1942*, Berlin: Dietz, 1989.

Neander, J., 'Das Konzentrationslager "Mittelbau" in der Endphase der NS-Dikatatur', PhD Dissertation, University of Bremen, 1996.

——, *Das Konzentrationslager 'Mittelbau' in der Endphase der nationalsozialistischen Diktatur. Zur Geschichte des letzten im 'Dritten Reich' gegründeten selbständigen Konzentrationslagers unter besonderer Berücksichtigung seiner Auflösungsphase*, Clausthal-Zellerfeld: Papierflieger, 1997.

Neufeld, J., *The Rocket and the Reich*, Cambridge, MA: Harvard University Press, 1996.

zur Nieden, S., 'Vom Interregnum zum Speziallager', in G. Morsch (ed.) *Von der Erinnerung zum Monument. Die Entstehungsgeschichte der Nationalen Mahn- und Gedenkstätte Sachsenhausen*, Berlin: Edition Hentrich, 1996, pp. 68–76.

——, 'Erste Initiativen für Mahnmale in Oranienburg und Sachsenhausen', in G. Morsch (ed.) *Von der Erinnerung zum Monument. Die Entstehungsgeschichte der Nationalen Mahn- und Gedenkstätte Sachsenhausen*, Berlin: Edition Hentrich, 1996, pp. 125–32.

Niethammer, L. (ed.) *Der 'gesäuberte' Antifaschismus. Die SED und die roten Kapos von Buchenwald. Dokumente*, Berlin: Akademie Verlag, 1994.

——, 'Internierungslager in Deutschland nach 1945: Vergleich und offene Fragen', in C. Jansen *et al.* (eds) *Von der Aufgabe der Freiheit: Politische Verantwortung und bürgerliche Gesellschaft im 19. und 20. Jahrhundert*, Berlin: Akademie Verlag, 1995, pp. 469–92.

Niven, B., *Facing the Nazi Past: United Germany and the Legacy of the Third Reich*, New York: Routledge, 2002.

——, *The Buchenwald Child: Truth, Fiction and Propaganda*, Rochester, NY: Camden House, 2007.

Noakes, J. and Pridham, G., (eds) *Nazism. 1919–1945*, 4 vols., Exeter: Exeter University Press, 1998–2001.

Ofer, D. and Weitzman, L. J., (eds) *Women in the Holocaust*, New Haven, CT: Yale University Press, 1998.

Orth, K., 'Rudolf Höß und die "Endlösung der Judenfrage". Drei Argumente gegen die Datierung auf den Sommer 1941', *Werkstatt Geschichte* 6, 1997, pp. 45–57.

——, *Das System der nationalsozialistischen Konzentrationslager. Eine politische Organisationsgeschichte*, Hamburg: Hamburger Edition, 1999.

——, 'SS-Täter vor Gericht. Die strafrechtliche Verfolgung der Konzentrationslager-SS nach Kriegsende', in I. Wojak (ed.) *'Gerichtstag halten über uns selbst ...' Geschichte und Wirkung des ersten Frankfurter Auschwitz-Prozesses*, Frankfurt: Campus Verlag, 2001, pp. 43–60.

——, *Die Konzentrationslager-SS*, Munich: dtv, 2004.

Otto, R., *Wehrmacht, Gestapo und sowjetische Kriegsgefangene im deutschen Reichsgebiet 1941/42*, Munich: Oldenbourg, 1998.

——, 'Rache an politischen Gegnern und Privatinteressen: Das Konzentrationslager Leschwitz bei Görlitz', in W. Benz and B. Distel (eds) *Herrschaft und Gewalt. Frühe Konzentrationslager 1933–1939*, Berlin: Metropol, 2002, pp. 237–44.

Overesch, M., *Buchenwald und die DDR: Oder die Suche nach Selbstlegitimation*, Göttingen: Vandenhoeck & Ruprecht, 1995.

Paskuly, S. (ed.) *Rudolph Höß, Death Dealer: The Memoirs of the SS Kommandant at Auschwitz*, Buffalo, NY: Prometheus Books, 1992.

Patel, K. K., '"Auslese" und "Ausmerze". Das Janusgesicht der nationalsozialistischen Lager', *Zeitschrift für Geschichtswissenschaft* 54, 2006, pp. 339–65.

Paul, C., *Zwangsprostitution. Staatlich errichtete Bordelle im Nationalsozialismus*, Berlin: Edition Hentrich, 1994.

Pawelczynska, A., *Values and Violence in Auschwitz: A Sociological Analysis*, Berkeley, CA: University of California Press, 1979.

Pawelke, B., 'Als Häftling geboren – Kinder in Ravensbrück', in C. Füllberg-Stolberg, M. Jung, R. Riebe and M. Scheitenberger (eds) *Frauen in Konzentrationslagern – Bergen-Belsen, Ravensbrück*, Bremen: Edition Temmen, 1994, pp. 157–66.

Pelt, R. J. van, *The Case for Auschwitz: Evidence from the Irving Trial*, Bloomington, IN: Indiana University Press, 2002.

Perz, B., *Projekt Quarz. Steyr-Daimler-Puch und das Konzentrationslager Melk*, Vienna: Verlag für Gesellschaftskritik, 1991.

——, 'Wehrmacht und KZ-Bewachung', *Mittelweg* 36, 1995, pp. 69–82.

——, '"... müssen zu reißenden Bestien erzogen werden". Der Einsatz von Hunden zur Bewachung in den Konzentrationslagern', *Dachauer Hefte* 12, 1996, 39–58.

——, 'Der Arbeitseinsatz im KZ Mauthausen', in U. Herbert, K. Orth and C. Dieckmann (eds) *Die nationalsozialistischen Konzentrationslager. Entwicklung und Struktur*, vol. 2, Göttingen: Wallstein, 1998, pp. 533–57.

——, *Die KZ-Gedenkstätte Mauthausen: 1945 bis zur Gegenwart*, Innsbruck: Studien Verlag, 2006.

—— and Freund, F., 'Auschwitz neu? Pläne und Maßnahmen zur Wiedererrichtung der Krematorien von Auschwitz-Birkenau in der Umgebung des KZ Mauthausen im Februar 1945', *Dachauer Hefte* 20, 2004, pp. 58–70.

—— and Sandkühler, T., 'Auschwitz und die "Aktion Reinhard" 1942–45', *Zeitgeschichte* 26, 2000, pp. 283–316.

Peukert, D., *Inside Nazi Germany: Conformity, Opposition and Racism in Everyday Life*, London: Batsford, 1987.

Pfahlmann, H., *Fremdarbeiter und Kriegsgefangene in der deutschen Kriegswirtschaft 1939–1945*, Darmstadt: Wehr und Wissen Verlags-Gesellschaft, 1968.

Pfingsten, G. and Füllberg-Stolberg, C., 'Frauen in Konzentrationslagern – geschlechtsspezifische Bedingungen des Überlebens', in U. Herbert, K. Orth and C. Dieckmann (eds) *Die nationalsozialistischen Konzentrationslager. Entwicklung und Struktur*, vol. 2, Göttingen: Wallstein, 1998, pp. 911–38.

Pingel, F., *Häftlinge unter SS-Herrschaft. Widerstand, Selbstbehauptung und Vernichtung im Konzentrationslager*, Hamburg: Hoffmann und Campe, 1978.

——, 'Die Konzentrationslagerhäftlinge im nationalsozialistischen Arbeitseinsatz', in W. Długoborski (ed.) *Zweiter Weltkrieg und sozialer Wandel. Achsenmächte und besetzte Länder*, Göttingen: Vandenhoeck & Ruprecht, 1981, pp. 151–63.

——, 'The Destruction of Human Identity in Concentration Camps: The Contribution of the Social Sciences to an Analysis of Behavior under Extreme Conditions', *Holocaust and Genocide Studies* 6, 1991, pp.167–84.

Piper, F., *Die Zahl der Opfer von Auschwitz*, Oświęcim: Staatliches Museum, 1993.

——, *Arbeitseinsatz der Häftlinge aus dem KL Auschwitz*, Oświęcim. Staatliches Museum, 1995.

Pohl, D., 'Die großen Zwangsarbeitslager der SS- und Polizeiführer für Juden im Generalgouvernement 1942–1945', in U. Herbert, K. Orth and C. Dieckmann (eds) *Die nationalsozialistischen Konzentrationslager. Entwicklung und Struktur*, vol. 1, Göttingen: Wallstein, 1998, pp. 415–38.

Polian, P. and Shneer, A., *Obrechennye pogibnut. Sudba sovetskikh voennoplennykh-evreev vo Vtoroi Mirovoi voine. Vospominaniia i dokumenty*, Moscow: Novoe Izdatelstvo, 2006.

Poltawska, W., *And I am Afraid of My Dreams*, London: Hodder and Stoughton, 1987.

Pressac, J. C., (ed.) *Auschwitz: Technique and Operation of the Gas Chambers*, New York: Beate Klarsfeld Foundation, 1989.

Projektgruppe für die vergessenen Opfer des NS-Regimes/KZ-Gedenkstätte Neuengamme, (eds) *'Und vielleicht überlebte ich nur, weil ich sehr jung war.' Verschleppt ins KZ Neuengamme: Lebensschicksale polnischer Jugendlicher*, Bremen: Edition Temmen, 1999.

Puvogel, U., *Gedenkstätten für die Opfer des Nationalsozialismus auf dem Gebiet der Bundesrepublik Deutschland*, Bonn: Bundeszentrale für politische Bildung, 1980, 2nd edn 1981.

——, *Gedenkstätten für die Opfer des Nationalsozialismus: Eine Dokumentation*, 2nd revised edn, Bonn: Bundeszentrale für politische Bildung, 1995.

——, *Gedenkstätten für die Opfer des Nationalsozialismus*, Bonn: Bundeszentrale für politische Bildung, 2003.

Przyrembel, A., 'Transfixed by an Image: Ilse Koch, the "Kommandeuse" of Buchenwald', *German History* 19, 2001, pp. 369–99.

Rahe, T., 'Jüdische Religiosität in den nationalsozialistischen Konzentrationslagern', *Geschichte in Wissenschaft und Unterricht* 44, 1993, pp. 87–101.

——, '"Ich wusste nicht einmal, dass ich schwanger war." Geburten im KZ Bergen-Belsen', in C. Füllberg-Stolberg, M. Jung, R. Riebe and M. Scheitenberger (eds) *Frauen in Konzentrationslagern – Bergen-Belsen, Ravensbrück*, Bremen: Edition Temmen, 1994, pp. 147–56.

——, 'Aus "rassischen" Gründen verfolgte Kinder im Konzentrationslager Bergen-Belsen', in E. Bamberger and A. Ehmann (eds) *Kinder und Jugendliche als Opfer des Holocaust. Dokumentation einer Internationalen Tagung in der Gedenkstätte Haus der Wannseekonferenz, 12. bis*

14. Dezember 1994, Heidelberg: Kultur- und Dokumentationszentrum Deutscher Sinti und Roma, 1995.

Raim, E., *Die Dachauer KZ-Außenkommandos Kaufering und Mühldorf. Rüstungsbauten und Zwangsarbeit in den letzten Kriegsjahren 1944/45*, Landsberg: Landsberger Verlagsanstalt, 1992.

Ramaker, W., *Sta een ogenblik stil … Monumentenboek 1940–1945*, Kampen: Kok, 1980.

Raßloff, S., *Fritz Sauckel – Hitlers 'Mustergauleiter' und 'Sklavenhalter'*, Erfurt: Landeszentrale für politische Bildung, 2007.

Rebentisch, D., *Führerstaat und Verwaltung im Zweiten Weltkrieg. Verfassungsentwicklung und Verwaltungspolitik 1939–1945*, Stuttgart: Steiner, 1989.

Recanati, A., *A Memorial Book of the Deportation of the Greek Jews*, 3 vols, Jerusalem: Erez, 2006.

Reichsjustizministerium, (ed.) *Das Gefängniswesen in Deutschland*, Berlin: 1935.

Reilly, J., *Belsen: The Liberation of a Concentration Camp*, London: Routledge, 1998.

Reitlinger, G., *The Final Solution: The Attempt to Exterminate the Jews of Europe 1933–1945*, New York: The Beechhurst Press, 1953.

Richardi, H. G., *Schule der Gewalt. Das Konzentrationslager Dachau*, Munich: Piper, 1995.

Richter, G. (ed.) *Breitenau. Zur Geschichte eines nationalsozialistischen Konzentrations- und Arbeitserziehungslagers*, Kassel: Verlag Jenior & Pressler, 1993.

Riebe, R., 'Frauen im Konzentrationslager 1933–1939', *Dachauer Hefte* 14, 1998, pp. 125–40.

Rieth, A., *Monuments to the Victims of Tyranny*, New York: Praeger, 1969.

Ritscher, B., *Spezlager Nr. 2 Buchenwald. Zur Geschichte des Lagers Buchenwald, 1945 bis 1950*, 2nd revised edn, Weimar: Gedenkstätte Buchenwald, 1995.

Röhl, W., *Homosexuelle Häftlinge im Konzentrationslager Buchenwald*, Weimar: Gedenkstätte Buchenwald 1992.

Romey, S., *Ein KZ in Wandsbek. Zwangsarbeit im Hamburger Drägerwerk*, Hamburg: VSA, 1994.

Roth, T., 'Frühe Haft- und Folterstätten in Köln 1933/34', in J. E. Schulte (ed.) *Konzentrationslager im Rheinland und in Westfalen 1933–1945. Zentrale Steuerung und regionale Initiative*, Paderborn: Schöningh, 2005, pp. 3–24.

Rotkirchen, L., 'The 'Final Solution' in its Last Stages', *Yad Vashem Studies* 8, 1970, pp. 7–29.

Rousset, D., *L'univers concentrationnaire*, Paris: Pavois, 1946.

——, *The Other Kingdom*, New York: Reynal & Hitchcock, 1947.

Rüter, C. F. and Mildt, D. W., (eds) *Justiz und NS Verbrechen*, vol. 34, Amsterdam, 2005.

Rüther, M., *Köln im Zweiten Weltkrieg. Alltag und Erfahrungen 1939–1945*, Cologne: Emons, 2005.

Safrian, H., *Die Eichmann-Männer*, Vienna and Zürich: Europa, 1993.

Saidel, R. G., *The Jewish Women of Ravensbrück Concentration Camp*, Madison, WI: Terrace Books, 2004.

Schafft, G., *Die KZ-Mahn- und Gedenkstätten in Deutschland*, Berlin: Dietz, 1996.

Schick, C., 'Die Internierungslager', in M. Broszat, K.-D. Henke and H. Woller (eds) *Von Stalingrad zur Währungsreform. Zur Sozialgeschichte des Umbruchs in Deutschland*, Munich: Oldenbourg, 1988, pp. 301–25.

Schikorra, C., *Kontinuitäten der Ausgrenzung. 'Asoziale' Häftlinge im Frauen-Konzentrationslager Ravensbrück*, Berlin: Metropol, 2001.

——, '"Asoziale" Häftlinge in Frauen-Konzentrationslager Ravensbrück – die Spezifik einer Häftlingsgruppe', in W. Röhr and B. Berlekamp (eds) *Tod oder Überleben? Neue Forschungen zur Geschichte des Konzentrationslagers Ravensbrück*, Berlin: Edition Organon, 2001, pp. 89–122.

Schilde, K., 'Vom Tempelhofer Feld-Gefängnis zum Schutzhaftlager: Das "Columbia-Haus" in Berlin', in W. Benz and B. Distel (eds) *Herrschaft und Gewalt. Frühe Konzentrationslager 1933–1939*, Berlin: Metropol, 2002, pp. 65–82.

Schilling, R., *'Kriegshelden'. Deutungsmuster heroischer Männlichkeit in Deutschland 1813–1945*, Paderborn: Schöningh, 2004.

Schley, J., *Nachbar Buchenwald. Die Stadt Weimar und ihr Konzentrationslager 1937–1945*, Cologne: Böhlau, 1999.

Schmid, H. and Dobrowolskij, N., *Kunst, die einem Kollektiv entspricht. Der internationale Denkmalhain in der KZ-Gedenkstätte Mauthausen*, Vienna: Bundesministerium für Inneres, 2007.

Schneider, M., *Unterm Hakenkreuz. Arbeiter und Arbeiterbewegung 1933 bis 1939*, Bonn: Dietz, 1999.

Schoppmann, C., *Days of Masquerade. Life Stories of Lesbians during the Third Reich*, New York: Columbia University Press, 1993.

——, '"Liebe wurde mit Prügelstrafe geahndet." Zur Situation lesbischer Frauen in den Konzentrationslagern', in H. Diercks (ed.) *Verfolgung von Homosexuellen im Nationalsozialismus*, Bremen: Edition Temmen, 1999, pp. 14–21.

——, 'Zeit der Maskierung. Zur Situation lesbischer Frauen im Nationalsozialismus', in B. Jellonnek and R. Lautmann (eds) *Nationalsozialistischer Terror gegen Homosexuelle. Verdrängt und ungesühnt*, Paderborn: Schöningh, 2002, pp. 71–81.

Schulte, J. E., *Zwangsarbeit und Vernichtung. Das Wirtschaftsimperium der SS. Oswald Pohl und das SS-Wirtschaftsverwaltungshauptamt 1933–1945*, Paderborn: Schöningh, 2001.

——, 'London war informiert. KZ Expansion und Judenverfolgung', in R. Hachtmann and W. Süß (eds) *Hitlers Kommissare. Sondergewalten in der nationalsozialistischen Diktatur*, Göttingen: Wallstein, 2006, pp. 207–27.

Schulz, C., 'Weibliche Häftlinge aus Ravensbrück in Bordellen der Männerkonzentrationslager', in C. Füllberg-Stolberg, M. Jung, R. Riebe and M. Scheitenberger (eds) *Frauen in Konzentrationslagern – Bergen-Belsen, Ravensbrück*, Bremen: Edition Temmen, 1994, pp. 135–46.

Schuyf, J., *Nederlanders in Neuengamme. De ervaringen van ruim 3300 Nederlanders in een Duits concentratiekamp 1940–1945*, Zaltbommel: Uitgeverij Aprilis, 2007.

Schwarz, G., *Die nationalsozialistischen Lager*, Frankfurt and New York: Campus, 1990.

——, 'SS-Aufseherinnen in den nationalsozialistischen Konzentrationslagern', *Dachauer Hefte* 10, 1994, pp. 32–49.

——, *Eine Frau an seiner Seite. Ehefrauen in der 'SS-Sippengemeinschaft'*, Hamburg: Hamburger Edition, 1997.

——, 'Frauen in Konzentrationslager – Täterinnen und Zuschauerinnen', in U. Herbert, K. Orth and C. Dieckmann (eds) *Die Nationalsozialistischen Konzentrationslager. Entwicklung und Struktur*, vol. 2, Göttingen: Wallstein, 1998, pp. 800–21.

Schwindt, B., *Das Konzentrations- und Vernichtungslager Majdanek – Funktionswandel im Kontext der 'Endlösung'*, Würzburg: Königshausen & Neumann, 2005.

Seela, T., 'Lesen und Literaturbenutzung in den Konzentrationslagern. Das gedruckte Wort im antifaschistischen Widerstand der Häftlinge', PhD Dissertation, Humboldt University, Berlin, 1990.

Seger, G., *Oranienburg. Erster authentischer Bericht eines aus dem Konzentrationslager Geflüchteten*, Karlsbad: Graphia, 1934.

Segev, T., *Soldiers of Evil: The Commandants of the Nazi Concentration Camps*, New York: McGraw Hill, 1988.

Sellier, A., *A History of the Dora Camp: The Story of the Nazi Slave Labor Camp that Manufactured V-2 Rockets*, Chicago, IL: I. R. Dee, 2003.

Sémelin, J. *Purify and Destroy: The Political Uses of Massacre and Genocide*, New York: Columbia University Press, 2005.

Setkiewicz, P., 'Häftlingsarbeit im KZ Auschwitz III–Monowitz. Die Frage nach der Wirtschaftlichkeit der Arbeit', in U. Herbert, K. Orth and C. Dieckmann (eds) *Die nationalsozialistischen Konzentrationslager. Entwicklung und Struktur*, vol. 2, Göttingen: Wallstein, 1998, pp. 584–605.

——, *Z dziejów obozów IG Farben Werk Auschwitz 1941–1945*, Oświęcim: Państwowe Muzeum, 2006.

Shandler, J., *While America Watches: Televising the Holocaust*, New York: Oxford University Press, 1999.

Sigel, R., 'Die Dachauer Prozesse und die deutsche Öffentlichkeit', in L. Eiber and R. Sigel (eds) *Dachauer Prozesse: NS-Verbrechen vor amerikanischen Militärgerichten in Dachau 1945–48 Verfahren, Ergebnisse, Nachwirkungen*, Göttingen: Wallstein, 2007, pp. 67–85.

Simon-Pelanda, H., 'Vergessenes Konzentrationslager: Flossenbürg', *Dachauer Hefte* 11, 1995, p. 50.

Sington, D., *Belsen Uncovered*, London: Duckworth, 1946.

Skribeleit, J., 'Flossenbürg – Stammlager', in W. Benz and B. Distel (eds) *Der Ort des Terrors. Geschichte der nationalsozialistischen Konzentrationslager*, Munich: Beck, vol. 4: *Flossenbürg, Mauthausen, Ravensbrück*, 2007, pp. 17–66.

Smith, B. and Peterson, A., (eds) *Heinrich Himmler. Die Geheimreden 1933 bis 1945 und andere Ansprachen*, Frankfurt: Propyläen, 1974.

Snijders, K., *Nederlanders in Buchenwald 1940–1945: een verzicht over de geschiedenis van Nederlandse gevangenen die tijdens de national-socialistische bezetting van 1940–1945 in het concentratiekamp Buchenwald zaten*, Göttingen: Wallstein, 2001.

Sofsky, W., *The Order of Terror: The Concentration Camp*, Princeton, NJ: Princeton University Press, 1997.

Sommer, R., *Daz KZ-Bordell. Sexuelle Zwangsarbeit in natioalsozialistischen Konzentrationslagern*, Paderborn: Schöningh, 2009.

——, 'Camp Brothels: Forced Sex Labour in Nazi Concentration Camps', in D. Herzog (ed.) *Brutality and Desire. War and Sexuality in Europe*, Basingstoke: Palgrave Macmillan, 2009, pp. 168–96.

Sommer-Lefkovits, E., *Are You Here in This Hell Too? Memoirs of Troubled Times 1944–1945*, London: Menard Press, 1995.

Speer, A., *The Slave State: Heinrich Himmler's Masterplan for SS Supremacy*, London: Weidenfeld and Nicolson, 1981.

Spoerer, M., 'Profitierten Unternehmen von KZ-Arbeit? Eine kritische Analyse der Literatur', *Historische Zeitschrift* 268, 1999, pp. 61–95.

——, *Zwangsarbeit unter dem Hakenkreuz. Ausländische Zivilarbeiter, Kriegsgefangene und Häftlinge im Deutschen Reich und im besetzten Europa 1939–1945*, Stuttgart and Munich: DVA, 2001.

Sprenger, I., *Groß-Rosen. Ein Konzentrationslager in Schlesien*, Vienna: Böhlau 1996.

—— and W. Kumpmann, 'Groß-Rosen – Stammlager', in W. Benz and B. Distel (eds) *Der Ort des Terrors. Geschichte der nationalsozialistischen Konzentrationslager*, Munich: Beck; vol. 6: *Natzweiler, Groß-Rosen, Stutthof*, 2008, pp. 195–221.

Staatliches Museum Auschwitz-Birkenau, *Inmitten des grauenvollen Verbrechens. Handschriften von Mitgliedern des Sonderkommandos*, Oświęcim: Staatliches Museum, 1996.

Stackelberg, R. and Winkle, S. A., *The Nazi Germany Sourcebook: An Anthology of Texts*, New York: Routledge, 2002.

Steegmann, R., *Struthof. Le KL-Natzweiler et ses kommandos*, Strasbourg: La Nuée Bleue, 2005.

——, 'Natzweiler – Stammlager', in W. Benz and B. Distel (eds) *Der Ort des Terrors. Geschichte der nationalsozialistischen Konzentrationslager*, Munich: Beck, vol. 6: *Natzweiler, Groß-Rosen, Stutthof*, 2008, pp. 23–47.

Stein, H., *Juden in Buchenwald, 1937–1942*, Weimar: Gedenkstätte Buchenwald, 1992.

——, 'Funktionswandel des Konzentrationslagers Buchenwald im Spiegel der Lagerstatistiken', in U. Herbert, K. Orth and C. Dieckmann (eds) *Die nationalsozialistischen Konzentrationslager. Entwicklung und Struktur*, vol. 1, Göttingen: Wallstein, 1998, pp. 167–92.

——, (ed.) *Das Konzentrationslager Buchenwald 1937–1945. Begleitband zur Dauerausstellung*, Göttingen: Wallstein, 1999.

Steinbacher, S., *Dachau. Die Stadt und das Konzentrationslager in der NS-Zeit. Die Untersuchung einer Nachbarschaft*, 2nd edn, Frankfurt: Lang, 1994.

——, *'Musterstadt' Auschwitz. Germanisierung und Judenmord in Ostoberschlesien*, Munich: Saur, 2000.

——, *Auschwitz. Geschichte und Nachgeschichte*, Munich: Beck, 2004.

Stoffels, H. (ed.) *Terrorlandschaften der Seele. Beiträge zur Theorie und Therapie von Extremtraumatisierungen*, Regensburg: S. Roderer, 1994.

Straede, T. (ed.), *De nazistiske Koncentrationslejre. Studier og bibliografi*, Odense: Syddansk Universitetsforlag, 2009.

Strebel, B., *Das KZ Ravensbrück. Geschichte eines Lagerkomplexes*, Paderborn: Schöningh, 2003.

——, 'Die "Lagergesellschaft". Aspekte der Häftlingshierarchie und Gruppenbildung in Ravensbrück', in C. Füllberg-Stolberg, M. Jung, R. Riebe and M. Scheitenberger (eds) *Frauen in Konzentrationslagern – Bergen-Belsen, Ravensbrück*, Bremen: Edition Temmen, 1994, pp. 79–88.

——, 'Ravensbrück – das zentrale Frauenkonzentrationslager', in U. Herbert, K. Orth and C. Dieckmann (eds) *Die nationalsozialistischen Konzentrationslager. Entwicklung und Struktur*, Göttingen: Wallstein, 1998, vol. 1, pp. 215–58.

——, 'Die "Rosa-Winkel-Häftlinge" im Männerlager des KZ Ravensbrück', in H. Diercks (ed.) *Verfolgung von Homosexuellen im Nationalsozialismus*, Bremen: Edition Temmen, 1999, pp. 62–9.

Streibel, R. and Schafranek, H., (eds) *Strategie des Überlebens. Häftlingsgesellschaften in KZ und GULAG*, Vienna: Picus, 1996.

Streim, A., 'Konzentrationslager auf dem Gebiet der Sowjetunion', *Dachauer Hefte* 5, 1989, pp. 174–87.

Strzelecki, A., *Endphase des KL Auschwitz. Evakuierung, Liquidierung und Befreiung des Lagers*, Oświęcim: Staatliches Museum, 1995.

——, *The Evacuation, Dismantling and Liberation of KL Auschwitz*, Oświęcim: State Museum, 2001.

——, *The Deportation of Jews from the Łódź Ghetto to KL Auschwitz and their Extermination. A Description of the Events and the Presentation of Historical Sources*, Oświęcim: State Museum, 2006.

Stutthof. Das Konzentrationslager, Gdańsk: Wydawnictwo 'Marpress', 1996.

Suhr, E., *Die Emslandlager*, Bremen: Donant und Temmen, 1985.

Świebocki, H., *London Has Been Informed … : Reports by Auschwitz Escapees*, Oświęcim: State Museum, 1997.

Sydnor, C., *Soldiers of Destruction: The SS Death's Head Division, 1933–1945*, London: Guild, 1989.

Szita, S., *Verschleppt, verhungert, vernichtet. Die Deportation von ungarischen Juden auf das Gebiet des annektierten Österreich 1944–1945*, Vienna: Eichbauer, 1999.

Taake, C., *Angeklagt. SS-Frauen vor Gericht*, Oldenburg: BIS, 1998.

Terhorst, K. L., *Polizeiliche planmäßige Überwachung und polizeiliche Vorbeugungshaft im Dritten Reich*, Heidelberg: Müller, 1985.

Tillion, G., *Ravensbrück*, Neuchâtel: Editions de la Baconnière, 1946.

——, *Ravensbrück*, Paris: Seuil, 1988.

Timm, A., 'The Ambivalent Outsider: Prostitution, Promiscuity, and VD Control in Nazi Berlin', in R. Gellately and N. Stoltzfus (eds) *Social Outsiders in Nazi Germany*, Princeton, NJ: Princeton University Press, 2001, pp. 192–211.

——, 'Sex with a Purpose: Prostitution, Venereal Disease, and Militarized Masculinity in the Third Reich', in D. Herzog (ed.) *Sexuality and German Fascism*, New York/Oxford: Berghahn, 2005, pp. 223–55.

Todorov, T., *Facing the Extreme. Moral Life in the Concentration Camps*, London: Phoenix, 1999.

Tooze, A., *The Wages of Destruction: The Making and Breaking of the Nazi Economy*, London: Allen Lane, 2006.

Toussaint, J., 'Nach Dienstschluss', in S. Erpel (ed.) *Im Gefolge der SS. Aufseherinnen des Frauen-KZ Ravensbrück*, Berlin: Metropol, 2007, pp. 89–100.

Trials of War Criminals before the Nuremberg Military Tribunals under Control Council Law No. 10, Nuremberg, October 1946–April 1949, vol. V, The Pohl Case, Washington, DC: U.S. Government Printing Office, 1950.

Tuchel, J., *Konzentrationslager. Organisationsgeschichte und Funktion der 'Inspektion der Konzentrationslager' 1934–1938*, Boppard am Rhein: Boldt, 1991.

——, *Die Inspektion der Konzentrationslager, 1938–1945*, Berlin: Edition Hentrich, 1994.

——, 'Die Wachmannschaften der Konzentrationslager 1939 bis 1945 – Ergebnisse und offene Fragen der Forschung', in A. Gottwaldt *et al* (eds) *NS-Gewaltherrschaft. Beiträge zur historischen Forschung und juristischen Aufarbeitung*, Berlin: Edition Hentrich, 2005.

—— and R. Schattenfroh, *Zentrale des Terrors*, Frankfurt: Büchergilde, 1987.

Union für Recht und Freiheit, (ed.) *Der Strafvollzug im III. Reich: Denkschrift und Materialsammlung*, Prague: Melantrich, 1936.

Vaupel, V., 'Einsatz von KZ-Gefangenen in der deutschen Wirtschaft und das Problem der Entschädigung überlebender Opfer nach 1945. Eine Fallstudie über jüdische Zwangsarbeiterinnen der "Verwert-Chemie" in Hessisch-Lichtenau', PhD Dissertation, Kassel, 1989.

Vermehren, I., *Reise durch den letzten Akt. Ravensbrück, Buchenwald, Dachau: eine Frau berichtet*, Hamburg: Christian Wegner, 1946.

Volk, L. (ed.) *Akten Kardinal Michael von Faulhabers 1917–1945*, vol. 2, Mainz: Matthias Grünewald-Verlag, 1978.

Vorländer, H. (ed.) *Nationalsozialistische Konzentrationslager im Dienst der totalen Kriegführung. Sieben württembergische Außenkommandos des Konzentrationslagers Natzweiler/Elsaß*, Stuttgart: Kohlhammer, 1978.

Wachsmann, N., '"Annihilation through Labour": The Killing of State Prisoners in the Third Reich', *Journal of Modern History* 71, 1999, pp. 624–59.

——, *Hitler's Prisons: Legal Terror in Nazi Germany*, New Haven, CT and London: Yale University Press, 2004.

——, 'Introduction', in E. Kogon, *The Theory and Practice of Hell*, New York: Farrar, Straus and Giroux, 2006, pp. xi–xxi.

——, 'Looking into the Abyss: Historians and the Nazi Concentration Camps', *European History Quarterly*, 36, 2006, pp. 247–78.

——, 'The Policy of Exclusion: Repression in the Nazi State, 1933–1939', in J. Caplan (ed.) *Short Oxford History of Germany: The Third Reich*, Oxford: Oxford University Press, 2008, pp. 122–45.

Wagenführ, R., *Die deutsche Industrie im Kriege 1939–1945*, Berlin: Duncker und Humblot, 1954.

Wagner, B. C., *IG Auschwitz. Zwangsarbeit und Vernichtung von Häftlingen des Lagers Monowitz 1941–1945*, Munich: Saur, 2000.

Wagner, J.-C., 'Noch einmal: Arbeit und Vernichtung. Häftlingseinsatz im KL Mittelbau-Dora 1943–1945', in N. Frei, S. Steinbacher and B. C. Wagner (eds) *Ausbeutung, Vernichtung, Öffentlichkeit. Neue Studien zur nationalsozialistischen Lagerpolitik*, Munich: Saur, 2000, pp. 11–41.

——, *Produktion des Todes. Das KZ Mittelbau-Dora*, Göttingen: Wallstein, 2001.

——, (ed.) *Konzentrationslager Mittelbau-Dora. Begleitband zur ständigen Ausstellung in der KZ-Gedenkstätte Mittelbau-Dora*, Göttingen: Wallstein, 2007.

Wagner, P., *Volksgemeinschaft ohne Verbrecher. Konzeptionen und Praxis der Kriminalpolizei in der Zeit der Weimarer Republik und des Nationalsozialismus*, Hamburg: Christians, 1996.

Warmbold, N., 'Lagersprache. Zur Sprache der Opfer in den Konzentrationslagern Sachsenhausen, Dachau, Buchenwald', PhD Dissertation, Universität Braunschweig, 2006.

Waxman, Z., *Writing The Holocaust: Identity, Testimony, Representation*, Oxford: Oxford University Press, 2006.

Wegner, B., *The Waffen SS: Organization, Ideology and Function*, Oxford: Basil Blackwell, 1990.

Weckel, U., 'NS-Prozesse und ihre öffentliche Resonanz aus geschlechtergeschichtlicher Perspektive', in U. Weckel and E. Wolfrum (eds), *'Bestien' und 'Befehlsempfänger'. Frauen und Männer in NS-Prozessen nach 1945*, Göttingen: Vandenhoeck und Ruprecht 2003, pp. 9–21.

—— and Wolfrum, E., (eds) *'Bestien' und 'Befehlsempfänger'. Frauen und Männer in NS-Prozessen nach 1945*, Göttingen: Vandenhoeck und Ruprecht, 2003.

Weinmann, M. and International Tracing Service, *Das nationalsozialistische Lagersystem*, Frankfurt: Zweitausendeins, 1990.

Weiss, Y., *Deutsche und polnische Juden vor dem Holocaust. Jüdische Identität zwischen Staatsbürgerschaft und Ethnizität 1933–1940*, Munich: Oldenbourg, 2000.

Wember, H., *Umerziehung im Lager. Internierung und Bestrafung von Nationalsozialisten in der britischen Besatzungszone Deutschlands*, Essen: Klartext , 1991.

Wenck, A.-E., *Zwischen Menschenhandel und 'Endlösung'. Das Konzentrationslager Bergen-Belsen*, Paderborn: Schöningh 2000.

Wenk, S. and Eschebach, I., 'Soziales Gedächtnis und Geschlechterdifferenz. Eine Einführung', in I. Eschebach, S. Jacobeit and S. Wenk (eds) *Gedächtnis und Geschlecht. Deutungsmuster in der Darstellung des nationalsozialistischen Genozids*, Frankfurt/New York: Campus, 2002, pp. 13–38.

Wesołowska, D., *Wörter aus der Hölle. Die 'lagerszpracha' der Häftlinge von Auschwitz*, Cracow: Impuls, 1998.

Wetzel, J., 'Stadelheim', in W. Benz and B. Distel (eds) *Der Ort des Terrors. Geschichte der nationalsozialistischen Konzentrationslager*, Munich: Beck, vol. 2 *Frühe Lager, Dachau. Emslandlager*, 2005, pp. 169–71.

White, E., 'Majdanek: Cornerstone of Himmler's SS Empire in the East', *Simon Wiesenthal Centre Annual* 7, 1990, pp. 3–21.

Wickert, C., 'Tabu Lagerbordell. Vom Umgang mit der Zwangsprostitution nach 1945', in I. Eschebach, S. Jacobeit and S. Wenk (eds) *Gedächtnis und Geschlecht. Deutungsmuster in der Darstellung des nationalsozialistischen Genozids*, Frankfurt/New York: Campus, 2002, pp. 41–58.

Wieviorka, A., *Déportation et génocide: entre la mémoire et l'oubli*, Paris: Hachette Littérature, 1992.

Wildt, M., 'Die Lager im Osten. Kommentierende Bemerkungen', in U. Herbert, K. Orth and C. Dieckmann (eds) *Die nationalsozialistischen Konzentrationslager. Entwicklung und Struktur*, vol. 1, Göttingen: Wallstein, 1998, pp. 508–20.

——, *Generation des Unbedingten. Das Führungskorps des Reichssicherheitshauptamtes*, Hamburg: Hamburger Edition, 2003.

——, *Volksgemeinschaft als Selbstermächtigung. Gewalt gegen Juden in der deutschen Provinz 1919 bis 1939*, Hamburg: Hamburger Edition, 2007.

Wippermann, W., *Konzentrationslager. Geschichte, Nachgeschichte, Gedenken*, Berlin: Elefanten Press, 1999.

Wisskirchen, J., 'Schutzhaft in der Rheinprovinz', in W. Benz and B. Distel (eds) *Herrschaft und Gewalt. Frühe Konzentrationslager 1933–1939*, Berlin: Metropol, 2002, pp. 129–56.

Witte, P. and Tyas, S., 'A New Document on the Deportation and Murder of Jews during "Einsatz Reinhardt" 1942', *Holocaust and Genocide Studies* 15, 2001, pp. 468–86.

Wohlfeld, U., 'Im Hotel "Zum Großherzog". Das Konzentrationslager Bad Sulza, 1933–1937', in W. Benz and B. Distel (eds) *Instrumentarium der Macht. Frühe Konzentrationslager 1933–1937*, Berlin: Metropol, 2003, pp. 263–75.

Wormser-Migot, O., *Le systéme concentrationnaire (1933–45)*, Paris: Presses Universitaires de France, 1968.

——, *L'ère des camps*, Paris: Union Générale d'Éditions, 1973.

Wrocklage, U., 'Neuengamme', in D. Hoffmann (ed.) *Das Gedächtnis der Dinge. KZ-Relikte und KZ-Denkmäler, 1945–1995*, Frankfurt: Campus, 1997, pp. 178–205.

——, 'Auschwitz-Birkenau – Die Rampe', in D. Hoffmann (ed.) *Das Gedächtnis der Dinge. KZ-Relikte und KZ-Denkmäler, 1945–1995*, Frankfurt: Campus, 1997, pp. 278–309.

Wünschmann, K., 'Jüdische Häftlinge im KZ Osthofen', in Landeszentrale für politische Bildung Rheinland-Pfalz (ed.) *Vor 75 Jahren: 'Am Anfang stand die Gewalt …'*, Mainz: LPB, 2008, pp. 18–33.

Yahil, L., *The Holocaust:The Fate of European Jewry*, New York and Oxford: Oxford University Press, 1991.

Yelton, D. K., *Hitler's Volkssturm: The Nazi Militia and the Fall of Germany 1944–1945*, Lawrence, KS: University Press of Kansas, 2002.

Young, J. E., *The Texture of Memory: Holocaust Memorials and Meaning*, New Haven, CT: Yale University Press, 1993.

Záméčník, S., '"Kein Häftling darf lebend in die Hände des Feindes fallen". Zur Existenz des Himmler-Befehls vom 14–18 April 1945', *Dachauer Hefte* 1, 1985, pp. 219–31.

——, *Das war Dachau*, Luxembourg: Comité International de Dachau, 2002.

——, 'Dachau – Stammlager', in W. Benz and B. Distel (eds) *Der Ort des Terrors. Geschichte der nationalsozialistischen Konzentrationslager*, Munich: Beck, vol. 2: *Frühe Lager, Dachau, Emsland*, 2006, pp. 233–74.

Zarusky, J., 'Die juristische Aufarbeitung der KZ-Verbrechen', in W. Benz and B. Distel (eds) *Der Ort des Terrors. Geschichte der nationalsozialistischen Konzentrationslager*, Munich: Beck; vol. 1: *Die Organisation des Terrors*, 2005, pp. 345–62.

Zonik, Z., *Anus belli. Ewakuacja i wyzwolenie hitlerowskich obozów koncentracyjnch*, Warsaw: Państwowe Wydawnictwo Naukowe, 1988.

Index

Made in the USA
Columbia, SC
17 December 2022

74274523R00141